Readers Theatre Handbook

Readers Theatre Handbook

A DRAMATIC APPROACH TO LITERATURE

REVISED EDITION

LESLIE IRENE COGER
Southwest Missouri State University

MELVIN R. WHITE
California State University, Hayward

SCOTT, FORESMAN AND COMPANY
Glenview, Illinois   Brighton, England

Library of Congress Catalog Card Number: 73-81110
ISBN: 0-673-07859-0

Regional offices of Scott, Foresman and Company are located in Dallas,
Texas; Glenview, Illinois; Oakland, New Jersey; Palo Alto, California;
Tucker, Georgia; and Brighton, England.

Permission to reprint the following pictures is gratefully acknowledged: *To Kill a
Mockingbird,* courtesy of Robert Wilhoit, Drury College; high school literature class,
courtesy of Eleanor Baird, Canyon High School; *The Mikado,* courtesy of Preston
Magruder, University of Arkansas; *Mary Poppins,* University of Missouri production,
directed by Charles Closser, Jr.; *Skin of Our Teeth,* courtesy of Brooklyn College of
the City University of New York; *God Bless You, Mr. Rosewater* and *A Singular
Man,* directed by Elbert R. Bowen, courtesy of Elbert R. Bowen, Central Michigan
University; *America: Love It or Leave It,* courtesy of James W. Carlsen, United
States International University; *The Waking,* courtesy of Karen Connell Hold,
Onondaga Community College; *Moby Dick: Rehearsed,* University of Missouri pro-
duction, directed by John Rude, courtesy of Frances L. McCurdy; *Lost in the Stars,*
courtesy of Lucille Breneman, University of Hawaii (photo by Bren Breneman);
Nobody Loves a Drunken Indian, courtesy of Pearl H. Galloway, University of
Arkansas; *The Odyssey: A Modern Sequel,* courtesy of Claribel Baird, University of
Michigan; *I Never Promised You a Rose Garden* and *Lord of the Rings,* courtesy of
Marion L. Kleinau, Southern Illinois University; *What Color Is Black?* courtesy of
Bernard Goldman, Los Angeles Trade-Technological College; *Shakespeare vs. Shaw*
and *The Unknown Soldier and His Wife,* courtesy of Jeanne Hall, California State
University, Hayward; *A Casual Approach to Violence,* courtesy of Ted D. Colson,
North Texas State University; *Ladies' Lib,* courtesy of Fran Tanner, College of
Southern Idaho; *The Hollow Crown,* courtesy of Noreen LaBarge Mitchell, director
(Designed by J. Wendell Johnson. Photo by James Lioi. San Jose State College pro-
duction.); *Dandelion Wine, The Boarding House,* and *Brecht on Brecht,* courtesy of
William E. McDonnell, University of Wisconsin, Eau Claire; *The Last Summer,*
California State University, Hayward, production; *Henry and Ribsy, Clever Gretel,
Up the Down Staircase, Nothing Gold Can Stay, Troilus and Cressida, Adam and
Eve, Education Is a Riot, The Sound of the Sixties, Mother to Son, James and the
Giant Peach, Maria, Chitty-Chitty-Bang-Bang, The Children's Story, Passionella,* and
The Murder of Lidice, courtesy of Southwest Missouri State University. The photo-
graph on p. 204 is by Wayne Schiska.

PREFACE
TO THE REVISED EDITION

ECHO FOR THREE VOICES.	Readers Theatre . . .
	Readers Theatre . . .
	Readers Theatre . . .
VOICE ONE.	What is it?
VOICES ONE AND TWO.	It is theatre:
VOICE THREE.	Theatre with a script.
VOICE ONE.	Theatre of the Mind,
VOICE TWO.	Creating with words
VOICE THREE.	People who are alive,
VOICE ONE.	Who think and feel,
VOICE TWO.	Who know the enjoyment of life.
VOICE THREE.	Fun!
VOICE ONE.	Excitement!
VOICE TWO.	Entertainment!
VOICE THREE.	Magic!
ALL VOICES.	(*After a pause.*) Presenting with our voices . . .
VOICE ONE.	A realistic impression,
VOICE TWO.	A mental picture,
ALL VOICES.	To occur in your minds.
ECHO FOR THREE VOICES.	Readers Theatre . . .
	Readers Theatre . . .
	Readers Theatre . . .
VOICE ONE.	A vocal message,
VOICE TWO.	A mental vision,
VOICE THREE.	People living events of sadness,
VOICE ONE.	Happiness,
VOICE TWO.	And love.
VOICE THREE.	Authors . . .
VOICE ONE.	Telling the human story,
VOICE TWO.	Satirizing man's frailties,
VOICE ONE.	Relating his bias,
VOICE THREE.	Creating worlds of fantasy,

VOICE TWO.	And telling the humor of being human.
ALL VOICES.	Birth . . . Life . . . Death . . . Readers Theatre!
VOICE TWO.	An intimate sharing of literature
VOICE THREE.	Between an audience and the readers.

In this way a group of readers might introduce to an audience the purposes and techniques of Readers Theatre.

Readers Theatre is in a period of expansion, of greatly increased experimentation. This Revised Edition of the first Readers Theatre textbook is designed to meet the changing needs of both the beginner and the experienced practitioner. We emphasize this because we have learned that the First Edition has been used not only in beginning oral interpretation and Readers Theatre classes in colleges and universities, but also in graduate classes and in many secondary schools as well. We have rewritten and expanded much of the textual material, but our key premise remains the same: There is no *one* way of presenting literature in Readers Theatre.

Many features which have proved especially useful remain intact. In Part One, Origins, Concepts, and Precepts, current trends are emphasized. The discussion of the "theatre" element in Readers Theatre has been clarified, and the section on staging—settings, costuming, and lighting—has been expanded, as has the discussion of directing. Problems of multimedia in Readers Theatre are considered, and further assistance is given on adapting scripts. Chapter Six, Readers Theatre Is for Children, Too, has been expanded greatly, reflecting the increased interest and activity in this area.

In Part Two, we present an almost entirely new series of summary-descriptions of "how it was done," including diagrams and/or photos of many productions.

Part Three, Sample Scripts for Readers Theatre, offers a broad range of literary-dramatic materials, including eight new scripts, as well as three from the First Edition which have been retained for their usefulness in demonstrating techniques of adapting material as well as for their continuing popularity. We emphasize that the production notes are included (and the extent to which they are provided varies) only to suggest how a working manuscript *might* be prepared, not how it *must* be developed, and to demonstrate that there are no fixed rules to be followed.

Part Four, Selected Articles for Further Study, has been omitted from the Revised Edition, as too many have said, "I can find those in the library. Give us more sample scripts instead." This we have done. But since we value the writings of others active in Readers Theatre, an extensive Selected and Annotated Bibliography follows Part Three for those who wish to pursue their study of Readers Theatre further.

We express our appreciation once again to the many who have provided opinions, essays, and photographs for this Revised Edition. As a result of their cooperative spirit, this Edition reflects not only our own continuing interest, experimentation, and study, but the activities of countless others, as well. We are deeply indebted and most grateful to Verne Powers of Scott, Foresman and Company for his tremendous contribution. To him we owe our profound thanks, as we owe appreciative gratitude to Diane Culhane for her considerate editing. We also wish to give thanks to Jerry Darnall for his help in preparing the drawings to illustrate the concept of focus in relation to Readers Theatre and to Richard Hieronymus for his assistance in writing the brief introductory script for this Preface.

Leslie Irene Coger
Melvin R. White

TABLE OF CONTENTS

PART TWO / THIS IS THE WAY IT WAS DONE

PART THREE / SAMPLE SCRIPTS FOR READERS THEATRE

PART ONE

Origins, Concepts, and Precepts

CHAPTER ONE

Readers Theatre: An Introduction

Alfred North Whitehead, discussing the aims of education, said, "Above all, the art of reading aloud should be cultivated."[1] In this cultivation, the oral art of Readers Theatre can play a unique and useful role. In Readers Theatre, the director's goal is to present a literary script with oral interpreters using their voices and bodies to suggest the intellectual, emotional, and sensory experiences inherent in the literature. Through their vivid reading the interpreters cause the audience members to see in their minds' eyes the characters in action in the world of the literature. The readers may or may not be aided in their interpretive function by lighting, music, sound effects, simple costuming, and nonillusory staging. Primarily, this is theatre of the imagination, theatre of the mind. Readers Theatre is an effective stimulant for understanding literature, for developing skills in reading aloud, and for adding to enjoyment and to the aesthetic, cultural enrichment of the readers and their audiences.

DEFINITIONS OF READERS THEATRE

This art form has a varied nature and a dual origin; thus, many labels have been used to identify this way of presenting literature to an audience. Readers Theatre is also called Interpreters Theatre, Platform Theatre, Concert Theatre, Chamber Theatre, Group Reading, Multiple Reading, Staged Reading, Story Theatre, or Play Reading. The most widely used terms are Readers Theatre and Interpreters Theatre.

---

[1] *The Aims of Education and Other Essays* (New York: The Macmillan Company, 1929), p. 78.

Basically, Readers Theatre is a medium in which two or more oral interpreters through vivid vocal and physical clues cause an audience to see and hear characters expressing their attitudes toward an action so vitally that the literature becomes a living experience—both for the readers and for their audience. In other words, the readers share the attitudes, viewpoints, and actions of a literary piece with an audience, causing that audience to experience the literature. Definitions of Readers Theatre vary somewhat, but they agree on basic principles. Johnnye Akin of Denver University has called it "a form of oral interpretation in which all types of literature may be projected by means of characterized readings enhanced by theatrical effects."[2] Keith Brooks, Eugene Bahn, and L. LaMont Okey define it as "a group activity in which a piece of literature is communicated from manuscript to an audience through the oral interpretation approach of vocal and physical suggestion."[3]

Wallace Bacon, of Northwestern University, makes a distinction between the terms Readers Theatre and Chamber Theatre. He states:

> The term *Readers Theatre* is sometimes reserved for group performances of dramatic texts. It sometimes includes also the group reading of such narrative-dramatic poems as Browning's *The Ring and the Book* or a style of reading a short story or novel with several readers participating. It is possible to call the rendition of any kind of material by a group of readers by the name Readers Theatre; in this case our further classification, *Chamber Theatre,* would no longer be useful.
>
> Hence we shall choose here to limit the term, to emphasize the word *theatre,* and to distinguish between Readers Theatre and Chamber Theatre. Readers Theatre, in our discussion, embraces the group reading of material involving delineated characters, with or without the presence of a narrator, in such a manner as to establish the usual locus of the piece not onstage with the readers but in the imagination of the audience. The reading of expository prose by a group of readers would not, therefore, be included in our definition. The reading of biblical psalms by a group would not be included. But the reading of Browning's "Pied Piper of Hamlin," with readers taking the parts of the Mayor, the Piper, and the Little Lame Boy, would be included, provided that the usual locus was offstage. And clearly a reading of *King Lear* by a group of readers would be included—again provided that the locus was not onstage.[4]

Joanna Hawkins Maclay defines Readers Theatre as a technique for staging literary texts in such a way that the text is featured, by which she means the production clarifies, illuminates, extends, or provides insights

---

[2] A Denver University brochure announcing a contest for Readers Theatre scripts (1962).
[3] *The Communicative Act of Oral Interpretation* (Boston: Allyn and Bacon, Inc., 1967), p. 387.
[4] *The Art of Interpretation,* 2nd ed. (New York: Holt, Rinehart & Winston, Inc., 1972), p. 407. Reprinted by permission. See p. 76 for a discussion of the term "locus," and p. 50 for a discussion of the term "Chamber Theatre."

into the text. In the light of this definition she maintains that all of literature may be chosen for Readers Theatre presentation, not only plays, but also prose fiction and other literary genre. She makes no distinction between the terms Chamber Theatre and Readers Theatre as she defines it. To her Chamber Theatre is Readers Theatre in which the literature is narrative in form.[5]

Elton Abernathy defines Readers Theatre as "group reading which invites extensive imaginative participation of the audience," the communication to be primarily "through the ear to the mind's eye," the emphasis upon "suggestion rather than identification, upon vivid reading rather than on acting."[6]

In his definition of oral interpretation, which lies at the heart of Readers Theatre, Don Geiger of the University of California at Berkeley has singled out certain considerations which are particularly pertinent: " . . . oral interpretation, then, is an unformulable amalgam of acting, public speaking, critical reaction, and sympathetic sharing. . . . It presumes to be, like other kinds of literary interpretation, a critical illumination publicly offered in behalf of literature."[7] These writers, as well as most of the others who have expressed their ideas on the subject, all seem to agree that its purpose is to illuminate the literature and that the essence of Readers Theatre is creative oral reading which calls forth mental images of characters performing an action that exists primarily in the minds of the participants— both the readers' and the audience's.

THE THEATRE IN READERS THEATRE

Both "readers" and "theatre" are crucial elements in this medium. The readers are interpreters, who must bring life and meaning to the symbols on the page by vocal and physical means. Just as a pianist must bring out the music from the written score by means of the piano, so the reader by means of his voice and body interprets the written score. The reader is the artist-agent. The literature must contain the theatre—and it must be animated for an audience in performance. Where, then, is the *theatre* in Readers Theatre?

Lope de Vega in the fourteenth century said that all that was needed for theatre were two boards and a passion. To him, the essentials were a passion, implying an actor presenting this passion, and a place to present it,

---

5 *Readers Theatre: Toward a Grammar of Practice* (New York: Random House, 1971), pp. 7–10.
6 *Directing Speech Activities* (Wolfe City, Texas: The University Press, 1970), p. 51.
7 *The Sound, Sense, and Performance of Literature* (Glenview, Illinois: Scott, Foresman and Company, 1963), p. 86 and Preface.

which suggests an audience to be stirred. De Vega felt that theatre was a social experience in which an audience was moved by the emotions expressed by the actors. In Readers Theatre the "actors" are readers or interpreters. We shall consider theatre an aesthetic experience resulting from a combination of three ingredients—literature, the source of the passion; effective performances by actor/readers; and a participating audience—each possessing interacting properties.

Special elements are needed in literature for Readers Theatre. It is obvious that dramatic literature, plays written for the theatre, are suitable materials. Dramatic poems and much narrative prose fiction also have the ingredients necessary for theatre: *delineated characters in a plotted dramatic action.* The term "dramatic" makes promises to an audience. The audience can expect characters capable of stirring a response and of compelling its interest in their interactions as they seek their goals. The more sensitive the characters, the more subtle the action, and the more magnified the picture of human conduct with its social implications, the stronger will be their power to bring the audience to a state of awareness, of insight. For literature, then, to contain the dramatic element expected in theatre, it needs provocative, compelling characters engaged in an action capable of stirring the imagination and/or emotions of an audience, bringing it to a state of awareness.

This does not exclude the use of other types of literature in Readers Theatre, but it implies that other forms must be given special treatment to make them fulfill the expectations of an audience that came to see *theatre.* Many programs labeled Readers Theatre should be called reading hours, recitals, group readings, or choral speaking rather than any name involving the term "theatre." True, there is a vital place for such programs. Just as, in music, individual singers give recitals and groups provide chamber singing and opera, so different types of reading programs may be presented. Each has its place. But reading-hour type programs which do not offer those necessary ingredients, action and interaction, should not be called Readers Theatre. For example, a compiled script of war poems read by a group of interpreters in solo or choral form is not necessarily theatre. As long as it remains a collection of individual poems, each expressing a point of view but having *no interaction of personae or characters,* it is not theatre. The key word for theatre in Readers Theatre is "interaction." A collection of materials can be made to function as a gestalt, as a dramatic whole; the segments, if they have focus, point of view, and interaction of characters, may be placed contextually to coalesce into a whole that is greater than its parts.[8] This interaction of characters and actions that results in theatre works something like the formula for expressing emotion in T. S. Eliot's "objective correlative." Eliot says, "The only way of express-

---

[8] See "Every Face Tells a Story," pp. 152–154.

ing emotion in the form of art is by finding an 'objective correlative'; in other words, a set of objects, a situation, a chain of events which shall be the formula of that *particular* emotion; such that when the external facts, which must terminate in sensory experience, are given, the emotion is immediately evoked."[9] These interacting segments have an effect something like that of the play *Marat/Sade,* with its "segments lacking logical connections but arranged in contextual patterns in order to penetrate the subcognitive level of audience awareness."[10]

A second factor is equally important. No theatre will be present until the literature is embodied, is brought stirringly alive through the medium of the vocal intonations and bodily tensions of the actor/readers who must evoke the characters, speak their language (the paralinguistic and kinesic elements as well as the verbal), and manifest the intricate nuances of tensions and attitudes expressed in the literature. Insight into literature is of no avail, and no *evocative* theatre results, if the reader is incapable of expressing the insight in understandable and moving form. *Effective performance,* then, is the second essential element in Readers Theatre. In Readers Theatre the presentation uses the techniques unique to the oral interpreter who creates the world of the literature on a mental screen in the collective minds of readers and of audience members. Those directors who are tending toward complete staging, complete costuming, and literal action on stage are nullifying the uniqueness of Readers Theatre as a theatre of the mind, a theatre of the imagination, and are merging it with conventional theatre.

The third ingredient, the *audience,* has a very special, participational, imaginative role in Readers Theatre. The members of the audience supply a portion of the performance in that their imaginations must complete all the suggestions of characterizations, action, and setting. Stimulated by the descriptions in the text as read by the interpreters, the audience member evokes in his mind's eye the characters in action, and empathically becomes one with them. He thus uses double vision. He sees the actor/readers on stage before him, but superimposed over them he views the characters interacting in the world of the literature. To fulfill his role in Readers Theatre, he must give himself over to the performance. Not only must there be a "willing suspension of disbelief," but there must also be a definite focus and concentration on the happenings in the world of the literature.

Appraisal, criticism, or thoughts of the techniques used must not intrude on the performance in which the audience member is participating. *Theatre does not equate with literary analysis or literary criticism.* These appraisals

---

9 "Hamlet and His Problems," *Athenaeum,* September 26, 1919, as reprinted in *Critiques and Essays,* ed. Robert Stallman (New York: The Ronald Press Co., 1949), p. 387.
10 Bernard Beckerman, *Dynamics of Drama* (New York: Alfred A. Knopf, Inc., 1970), p. 156.

may come later, but if they occupy the mind of the audience member during the performance they interfere with his contribution to the work, and lacking his participation, the performance will be incomplete and the illusion and the import of the literature will elude him. It is like reading a book. To fully enjoy it, a person must, at least for the moment, accept the author's ideas. As Wayne C. Booth wrote in *The Rhetoric of Fiction,* "Regardless of my real beliefs and practices, I must subordinate my mind and heart to the book if I am to enjoy it to the full."[11] Readers Theatre is not, as has been said, a critical analysis of a text—it is an aesthetic experience. Although in preparation it demands careful study and analysis of the literature, it does not become "theatre" until it is realized in performance. The audience which is a part of that performance must function with the bright eyes of a creative participant, not with the wrinkled forehead of a critic.

Where, then, is the *theatre* in Readers Theatre? It lies in literature encompassing interaction of characters in an action vividly performed —embodied, if you will—by skilled readers using the techniques of interpretation and by participating, double-visioned audience members. In an interview, Earl Keffer of Eastern Montana College expressed it for us all when he said, "We get such ovations that it's downright embarrassing, and all we're really doing is letting people use their own imaginations in a world made slightly numb by having everything canned and pre-digested. . . . Books are for sharing, good writing was meant to be listened to, and imagination is for everyone."[12]

Clearly, this oral-interpretation art performs a threefold service: for the reader, for the audience, and for the literature itself. In addition, it is a way of vitalizing the study of literature, of achieving personal growth in students, and of enriching the cultural life of the community.

GROWTH OF READERS THEATRE AS AN ACADEMIC ACTIVITY

Increasingly, teachers are recognizing the exciting possibilities of this approach in developing an appreciation of the best that mankind has written. Many colleges and universities offer courses in Readers Theatre, undergraduate as well as graduate, and special workshops, while others make Readers Theatre a part of their classes in oral interpretation. Growing out of these academic studies are a great many extracurricular and cocurricular performances. Readers Theatre presentations are commonly found listed as part of the regular theatre season at many colleges and universities,

---

11 Chicago: The University of Chicago Press, 1961, p. 138.
12 Francis I. Kafka, "What's All This About Readers' Theatre?" *Encore,* March–April, 1965, p. 5.

something unheard of a few years ago. The widespread use of this popular form of theatre is clearly evident in the annual listing of productions prepared by the Bibliography Committee of the Interpretation Division of the Speech Communications Association, in the reports of performances enumerated in the *Educational Theatre Journal,* and in the Speech Communication Association listings of doctoral dissertations. Programs about Readers Theatre are being included more frequently in the events at regional and national speech and drama conferences. Interpretation festivals and workshops that devote themselves mainly, if not entirely, to group reading activities include the East Stroudsburg Interpretation Festival, Temple University Reading Festival, Kutztown Reading Festival, Interpreters Theatre Alliance, and Towson State College's *New Horizons.* Others, such as the Annual Desert Interpretation Festival at the University of Arizona, the Ozarks Spring Interpretation Festival at Southwest Missouri State University, the Invitational Interpretative Reading Festival at Central Michigan University, the Southern California Invitational Oral Interpretation Festival at Saddleback Community College, the Flint Hills Oral Interpretation Festival at Kansas State Teachers College, and the Annual Snowbird Festival at Florida Technological University, allot one third to one half of the conference hours to group reading activities, primarily Readers Theatre.

Public-speaking students, Canyon High School, Castro Valley, Calif., perform before an English literature class, bringing vitality to an excerpt from a novel the class is studying.

Not only is Readers Theatre employed extensively on college and university campuses, but it is also used meaningfully on the secondary school level. It is recommended strongly in the course of study for high school theatre arts teachers which was prepared by a curriculum committee of the American Theatre Association.[13] Readers Theatre is used to animate history, science, sociology, art, and other subjects. History classes, for example, find *The Crucible* makes the study of the Salem witch trials far more meaningful, *Inherit the Wind* illuminates the Scopes trial, *Galileo* turns scientific investigation into a personal experience, and biographies of Van Gogh and other artists animate the art movements of which they were a part. Readers Theatre not only allows the student to study about the great characters in history, science, and art, but enables him to become one with them.[14] Classes prepare Readers Theatre performances for assemblies, educable mentally retarded students do work in Readers Theatre to assist them with their reading skills, and foreign language departments stage Readers Theatre productions in French, Spanish, and other languages to increase the oral skills of their students. In 1969 Robert Crain, of Ione High School, Ione, California, founded the Annual Mother Lode Readers Theatre Festival, probably the first such secondary school event focusing entirely on group reading activities. These are but a few examples of how Readers Theatre is being used increasingly to create an appreciation of literature and for other purposes, both in colleges and universities and in secondary schools.

VITALIZED LITERARY STUDY

When literature becomes an enjoyable, personalized experience, it takes on a significance, a new excitement. The study of the written page becomes fun when it prepares the reader for sharing literary material with an audience. And reading literature aloud deepens the reader's understanding of the text, for in giving it voice he experiences the writing more completely, more comprehensibly, than he does in silent reading. Not only must he discern and understand the attitude of the author, but he must express that attitude with his voice and his body. In this sense, the oral reader reembodies

---

13 *Course of Study in Theatre Arts at the Secondary School Level,* rev. ed. (Washington, D.C.: American Theatre Association, 1968), pp. 103–10.
14 Radford B. Kuykendall in "Oral Interpretation and Readers' Theatre," *The Bulletin of the National Association of Secondary School Principals,* 54, no. 350 (December 1970), 90, 92, wrote of its use in other classes: "Its value in speech classes is obvious, but it can do much to vitalize the literature class, the history or social science class, or to supplement the drama class. . . . Core or pontoon-scheduled courses may make use of the readers' theatre format to relate concepts of common denominators from different subject areas. . . . Handicapped students, disadvantaged students, students who do not 'look the part' for a play, those who have grown so rapidly in body that they feel miserable in their awkwardness and lack of poise—many of these can find genuine opportunity in readers' theatre."

In an exciting Chamber Theatre production of James Joyce's short story The Boarding House, *a music stand becomes a card table on which Mrs. Mooney and the Narrator play cards, with Mr. Doran framed in the background.*

the original speaker or the creator of the text. Not only must he *recognize* the tone[15] of the poem, but he is stimulated to *reproduce* the tone.

Oral reading, as used in Readers Theatre, is one of the best ways to know and to feel the full meaning of literature because, audibly expressed, it appeals not only to the mind but to the whole range of the senses. If a student is to understand and enjoy a literary text, he will first, as Henri Bergson said, "have to reinvent it, or in other words appropriate to a certain extent the inspiration of the author. To do so he must fall into step with him by adopting his gesture, his attitudes, his gait, by which I mean learning to read the text aloud with the proper intonation and inflection."[16] Working from such a highly personalized viewpoint, the student comes to realize that if he is to read the material aloud properly, he must understand not only what the author has said but also the structure of the literary piece: its "builds" and climaxes, its forewarnings, and its character relationships. The student is thereby stimulated to make the close textual study of the literature needed to comprehend the material thoroughly. When he understands it, he almost invariably enjoys it.

---

[15] For a detailed discussion of tone, see pp. 69–70.
[16] *The Creative Mind,* trans. Mabelle L. Andison (New York: Philosophical Library, Inc., 1946), pp. 101–2.

PERSONAL DEVELOPMENT

Not only does Readers Theatre enrich the study of literature, but it also contributes significantly to the personal development of the participants. Since the readers have only their voices, the muscle tone of their bodies, and their facial expressions by which to convey the ideas, the emotions, and the attitudes expressed in the literature, they are motivated to develop rich, flexible, expressive voices and to free themselves from muscular tensions so that they can respond vocally and physically to the content of the literary material. For example, read the following poem, "High Flight," by John Gillespie Magee, Jr.

> Oh, I have slipped the surly bonds of earth
> And danced the skies on laughter-silvered wings;
> Sunward I've climbed and joined the tumbling mirth
> Of sun-split clouds—and done a hundred things
> You have not dreamed of—wheeled and soared and swung
> High in the sunlit silence. Hov'ring there,
> I've chased the shouting wind along and flung
> My eager craft through footless halls of air.
> Up, up the long delirious, burning blue
> I've topped the wind-swept heights with easy grace
> Where never lark, or even eagle flew;
> And, while with silent, lifting mind I've trod
> The high untrespassed sanctity of space,
> Put out my hand, and touched the face of God.[17]

In the poem, the reader can experience the exhilaration of flying: he slips, dances, climbs, wheels, soars, hovers, chases, and flings himself through the blue with the pilot. He senses the laughter-silvered wings, tumbling mirth, sun-split clouds, shouting wind, the eager craft, the delirious burning blue, and windswept heights as the author describes them. Through his muscles surge the vestigial movements of the wheeling, soaring, and dancing of the poem. His face reflects the pleasure of the speaker-in-the-poem; his voice quality conveys the emotion of the pilot and reconstitutes the tumbling mirth and the shouting wind. In giving the lines full meaning and vitality and thus projecting the life of the poem to the audience, the reader learns self-discipline. Anything he does to disrupt the audience's mental participation will break their empathic response to the literary material. Since an effective reading demands close attention to details, the reader must concentrate wholly on the meanings to be expressed and, in turn, must cause the audience to concentrate. Also, the stu-

---

[17] Pilot-Officer John Gillespie Magee, Jr., RCAF, "High Flight," reprinted from *New York Herald Tribune,* February 8, 1942, by permission of Mrs. John G. Magee and Mr. David B. Magee.

dent has the opportunity to portray a variety of roles within a single script; sometimes, for instance, he may be called upon to interpret three or four different characters within a few minutes—a challenge to his skill.

When students experience literature that gives them insight into their fellow human beings—their desires, their aspirations, and their frustrations—they gain a clearer understanding of the problems of others and are helped thereby to comprehend their own quandaries, to know themselves. *The Diary of Anne Frank,* the biography of Helen Keller, *Kon-Tiki,* and the poetry of Theodore Roethke will open fascinating doors and windows to the young and to the young in spirit.

Because it requires little, if any, scenic elaboration, Readers Theatre can be presented effectively in student centers, in banquet halls, in living rooms, around campfires, and in other places having no formal stage. This suggests its usefulness to those who work in churches, temples, summer camps, clubs, parent-teacher associations, and other community-centered groups, whether their purpose be religious, social, or recreational. Functioning from such a broad base and with so much potential for performing, Readers Theatre stimulates the student to master the techniques of effective oral reading in various situations, making him more confident, flexible, and creative.

CULTURAL ENRICHMENT

In a wide variety of ways, Readers Theatre can add to the cultural enrichment of the individual and the group. It appreciably enlarges the dramatic fare because it allows an interpreter to read aloud many plays for which a fully staged production would be too costly, or to read aloud individual scenes as the students study the plays in literature classes. In fact, the medium can broaden the entire literary spectrum, for it makes use not only of plays but also of poetry, narratives, letters, diaries, biographies, and other forms of literature.

Students at both university and secondary school levels enjoy participating in Readers Theatre and often arrange programs on their own initiative. Working alone or in groups, they adapt scripts from both serious and comic materials in their literature texts and from their outside reading, which not only exposes them to various types of literature but also forces them to study, analyze, and compare the selections they consider.

CREATIVITY

Especially important among the many values to be derived from Readers Theatre is the *creativity* it helps generate in students, the outlet it provides for their originative talents. This is particularly true when they are called upon to develop a script from more than one source. Combining the materials and effecting transitions allows them to be creative. Performance of the scripts also presents the readers with an opportunity to create—to create a believable character, a mood, or an emotion.

It can be seen that work in Readers Theatre accomplishes many of the commonly accepted goals for creative study: educating the emotions for controlled use, educating the imagination for creative self-expression, disciplining the voice and body for purposeful use, and expanding intellectual horizons to include aesthetic awareness. These are some of the benefits of participating in Readers Theatre: It is a stimulus for a close reading of literature which, in turn, leads to a fuller understanding and a keener enjoyment of the best that has been written. This approach to the study of literature results in a deeper understanding of life as a whole, an appreciation of human needs and desires, and a more penetrative self-knowledge. Readers Theatre provides, moreover, a strong and enduring incentive for mastering the skills of effective oral interpretation. Working in this medium, the interpreters develop more flexible, resonant voices and better diction as they strive to "read out" the full meaning and import of the literature; and they gain poise as well as agile, expressive bodies. They have a creative outlet. They become more sensitive in their responses to literature and to life.

Audiences, too, derive substantial benefits from their participation in Readers Theatre. For them, it provides the opportunity to explore the wide horizons of literature—great novels, memorable short stories, stirring poetry, and distinguished plays seldom produced in the theatre—and it challenges them to participate in the literary experience. In a very special sense, the audiences of Readers Theatre are also "readers"—those who love to read. Clearly, this oral-interpretational art performs a threefold service: for the reader, for the audience, and for the literature itself.

Having considered some of its benefits, let us now move in for a closer examination of Readers Theatre, a somewhat more detailed perspective in which we devote special attention to its origin, to its parallel development at both the professional and educational levels, and to some of the playwrights who have experimented with ways and means of creating performer-audience relationships which are similarly direct and participatory.

CHAPTER TWO

Readers Theatre:
Theatre of the Mind[1]

Readers Theatre has not only a varied nature, but also a dual origin. Its beginnings as well as portions of the form it takes parallel conventional theatre, but a Readers Theatre presentation differs from a conventional play in several ways.

READERS THEATRE AND THE STAGE

Readers Theatre is evocative, narrative theatre of the mind, requiring double-vision of the audience—they see both the readers before them on the stage and, superimposed on them, the characters in action in the world of the literature. Readers Theatre has the narrative point of view. Even in the reading of a play, a narrator usually tells the audience what it needs to know of the characters, the setting, and the action. In prose fiction, even if no narrator is used as such, the point of view is still narrative rather than dramatic. This is the major way in which Readers Theatre differs from conventional theatre. Also, Readers Theatre is not bound by time or space; the space is as limitless as the imagination, and the time can shift as easily as fog can slip in and out of a valley.

A Readers Theatre presentation also differs from a conventional play in that it demands stricter attention to the aural elements of the literature. The interpreter must express the emotions, the attitudes, and the actions of the characters by economically using his face, his voice, and his body as vocal and physical clues to meaning. Nothing he does should distract the audience's attention from the characters, the scene, and the action within

---

[1] Revised from Leslie Irene Coger, "Interpreters Theatre: Theatre of the Mind," *Quarterly Journal of Speech,* 49, no. 2 (April 1963), 157–64.

the literature. Overdoing these clues is "ham" acting and bad interpretation. Obtrusive gesturing is not acting as opposed to interpretation (it would be equally bad on the part of the actor); it is a lack of selectivity and the use of meaningless gestures on the part of the interpreter.

Yet another way in which a Readers Theatre production differs from a conventional play is in the type of participation which it requires of its audience. The oral interpreter gives to the audience, as does the actor in a play, the text and subtext of the literature—its inner essence; but the audience must generate its own visualization of the scenery, the costumes, the action, the makeup, and the physical appearance of the characters. In a play these components are usually presented tangibly on the stage.

In Readers Theatre, then, the majority of the action does not occur onstage with the interpreters but rather in the imagination of the audience. Through the artistry and skill of the readers, the audience is stimulated to experience the emotional impact of the literature as well as its intellectual content; and since so much of the performance depends upon the mental creativity and contribution of the audience, Readers Theatre may well be called the Theatre of the Mind—Theatre of the Imagination.

ORIGIN AND HISTORY

The form taken by this oral art is not altogether new, but the impetus of its revival and resurgency is comparatively recent. The roots of Readers Theatre can be traced to the dramatic practices of fifth-century Greece. According to Eugene Bahn of Wayne State University:

> There . . . arose in Greece . . . a recitative art. This was carried on by wandering minstrels known as "rhapsodes." The rhapsode spoke, in a measured recitative, portions of the national epics. Sometimes he read to the accompaniment of a lyre or other primitive musical instrument. . . . [T]here was a form of dialogue carried on between two characters, read by two rhapsodes. One would read, in the first book of the *Iliad*, up to the quarrel of the princes; then a second reciter would step forward and declaim the speeches of Agamemnon while the other read the part of Achilles. . . .
>
> The rhapsodes did not always confine themselves to the epic poems. They also read the didactic and gnomic poetry of such writers as Hesiod. . . . When these poems, which were read by one person, had more than one character in them, a type of activity which approaches the art of the interpretative reading of plays was developed. When . . . two characters were read by two different individuals, the drama began.[2]

One might add that when these two characters were read by two different individuals, Readers Theatre began. Bahn also referred to other Grecian

---

2 "Interpretative Reading in Ancient Greece," *Quarterly Journal of Speech*, 18 (June 1932), 434–37. Reprinted by permission of the author.

activities which are incorporated in Readers Theatre today. Writing of the dithyramb, the hymn sung to Bacchus and accompanied by dancing, he remarked:

> The dithyramb was performed by a chorus, and after it had sung a hymn in honor of Bacchus, Thespis stepped forward, out from the chorus. He came in front of the chorus, placed himself on an elevated stand and recited one of the religious stories or historical myths, just as any rhapsode would have done. When he had finished his reciting, the chorus again continued with its singing and dancing, and the rhapsode again disappeared. As time went on, the chorus began to take a part in the story of the rhapsode, giving an exclamation, offering an answer, or asking a question. . . . In this new art there was a combination of the arts of dancing, music, song and interpretative reading. However, the first three were always subordinate to the last, the element of speech.[3]

Drama and interpretive reading sometimes were united in medieval times, too.[4] Church liturgy was amplified by the addition of mimetic action, symbolic costume, and the suggestion of dialogue through antiphonal chant. While this would seem to describe the drama more than it does the Readers Theatre, it should be remembered that the Easter *trope* was at first "a simple chanted colloquy between voices of the choir, signifying the two Maries and the responding angel."[5] Viewed in this way, the *trope* and Readers Theatre have certain elements in common, and one can thus discern the two forms emerging from the same source.

From this and similar scholarly research, it can be seen that theatre and interpretive reading have a common background. In Readers Theatre they come together again. Today, artists in both theatre and oral interpretation are turning to this unique and challenging medium, experimenting with its possibilities, exploring its many facets. This dual approach to Readers Theatre is the source of some controversy regarding the form a particular presentation should take. Those teachers and directors who have an oral interpretation orientation usually require their readers to carry a written script and read aloud from it, whereas theatre-oriented directors agree on memorization of lines as the natural approach. Similar arguments arise over whether the readers should relate directly to one another and look at each other on the stage, and whether music, movement, and lighting should be used. Fortunately for the medium, there is no final arbiter on these questions, and lively experimentation is continuing.

---

3 Ibid., p. 438.
4 Eugene Bahn and Margaret L. Bahn, *A History of Oral Interpretation* (Minneapolis: Burgess Publishing Company, 1970), p. 174. "In the Middle Ages the nun, Hroswitha, wrote plays which were presumably read by a group."
5 Felix Schelling, *Elizabethan Playwrights* (New York: Harper & Row, Publishers, 1925), p. 7.

PROFESSIONAL READERS THEATRE

As another basis for discussing the nature of Readers Theatre, one may observe the form it has taken on the professional stage, both as to production methods and as to the literary material used.

Perhaps the first time the term "Readers Theatre" was used occurred in 1945 in New York when *Oedipus Rex* was produced by a professional group who called themselves Readers Theatre, Inc. Their stated purpose was "to give the people of New York an opportunity to witness performances of great dramatic works which were seldom if ever produced."[6] Historically, however, this type of group reading was in use as far back as the early 1800s.

> Another species of dramatic reading has of late years been practised in private companies assembled for that purpose. It differs from that just mentioned [one person reading a play] by limiting each individual to the reading of the part of a single character. In this entertainment, as on the stage, the characters of the drama are distributed among the readers according to their supposed talents; and each being furnished with a separate book, either the whole play, or certain select scenes from one or more, are read by the performers sitting around a table, whilst others of the company serve as the audience. The reading is performed by each in his best manner, the part allotted to each is often nearly committed to memory, and such gestures are used as can be conveniently executed in a sitting position posture. Higher efforts are here required in order to keep the auditors alive to the interest of the scene, thus divided and stript of all that aids delusion, and mutilated of its complete action.[7]

In 1951, a *Don Juan in Hell* production was given by a "drama quartet" which featured four well-known actors: Charles Boyer, Sir Cedric Hardwicke, Charles Laughton, and Agnes Moorehead. These artists sat on stools and appeared to read from scripts placed on lecterns, even though it was obvious they had memorized the material. In this seldom-staged third act of Shaw's play *Man and Superman,* the readers sometimes shifted their positions on the stools but in general used little movement. A 1973 revival of *Don Juan in Hell* at New York's Palace Theatre was again presented as a reading. The players, in evening dress, used microphones, lecterns, and high stools. Agnes Moorehead, twenty-two years after she was featured in the drama quartet performance of this two hours of Shavian philosophizing, read the role of Dona Ana, with Paul Henreid, Ricardo Montalban, and Edward Mulhare completing the cast of this so-called staged reading.

---

6 George Jean Nathan, *The Theatre Book of the Year, 1945–1946* (New York: Alfred A. Knopf, Inc., 1946), p. 234.
7 Gilbert Austin, *Chironomia* (London, 1806), pp. 203–4. From Alethea Smith Mattingly and Wilma H. Grimes, *Interpretation: Writer, Reader, Audience,* 2nd. ed. (Belmont, Calif.: Wadsworth Publishing Co., Inc., 1970), pp. 315–16.

In 1952 Stephen Vincent Benét's long narrative poem *John Brown's Body,* adapted and directed by Charles Laughton, was presented by three readers and a chorus of twenty. Raymond Massey, Judith Anderson, and Tyrone Power read the various roles. In contrast to *Don Juan in Hell,* in which each reader read the lines of only one character, each actor in *John Brown's Body* read many different parts. The chorus—which chanted, hummed, and produced other vocal sound effects—and a musical accompaniment composed by Walter Schumann were used not so much for background as for helping to carry the dramatic action forward as the chorus did in Greek drama. Considerably more movement was used in this production than in *Don Juan in Hell.* For instance, in the ballroom scene Miss Anderson moved about as if she were dancing. The only property was a three-foot-high railing used both as a place to pray and as a place to hide from the enemy. Occasionally the readers sat on or leaned against this railing. Lighting was used to enhance the mood.

Raymond Massey's account of his experience in this production demonstrates some of the striking and occasionally unexpected ways in which this art elicits audience participation:

> Thirty years of stage work before audiences prepared me in no way for what happened out front with *John Brown's Body.* It's frightening. They are so still. Nobody out there sees the same show. . . . Steve Benét's words do, indeed, cast a spell. Those people are enchanted. The quiet of our audience is an awesome thing. But the audience is not just sitting there, allowing itself to be entertained. We seem to have brought to them the key to that too-long-locked room where they had put away their own ability to imagine—to see, to do, to share.[8]

Massey mentioned Cyrus Drugin, a western critic, who in his critique described in detail a white picket fence. There was, of course, no fence of this kind on the stage, but he had been stimulated to see it so vividly in his mind's eye that he was positive that such a fence actually existed. According to Massey, Drugin remarked: "I daresay that no two people in the capacity audience formed just the same mental picture of what was going on in the drama of *John Brown's Body.* You formed your own image according to your imaginative resources and accordingly you were moved, amused, excited, enthralled."[9]

William Hawkins, in the *New York Mirror,* February 16, 1953, wrote of the same production: "The work is staged so nothing interferes with the poet's phrases, in their primary function of inciting you, the listener, to create image after image of your own." These comments by Hawkins and the others further emphasize the unique nature of the audience's role

---

8 "American Classic: *John Brown's Body* Is a Vivid Reminder of Our Heritage," *New York Herald Tribune,* February 8, 1953, Sec. 4, p. 3.
9 Ibid.

in Readers Theatre: that of creative participation in the production.

There have been many other professional productions which have employed the concepts and techniques of Readers Theatre and which have, in turn, made significant contributions to this medium of interpretive art. For instance, Paul Shyre, a New York producer, used it to present three volumes of Sean O'Casey's six-volume autobiography. In his first two productions, *Pictures in the Hallway* and *I Knock at the Door,* he employed six readers sitting on stools behind lecterns, reading in concert style.

Two projectors were used in this university production of Brecht on Brecht, *one of which projected the huge portrait of Brecht which was present throughout the performance on half of the screen, while on the other half titles of individual works and/or appropriate slides counterpointed the words of the selection being read or sung. Here, "Song of a German Mother."*

Each participant read many different parts. In planning his production of the third volume, Shyre decided to change the style of presentation:

> *Drums Under the Windows* will be staged as a sort of narrative panorama rather than as a formal reading with actors reciting from scripts. The actors will not sit behind lecterns this time; more characters will be represented, and there will be a lot of action. A narrator will link thirty-two scenes in which seven actors will play sixty roles. They will use the entire bare stage back to the brick wall. . . . *Drums Under the Windows,* which deals with O'Casey's intellectual and philosophical development in his twenties, called for a new form of presentation. The first two volumes concerned O'Casey and his family and were more sentimental. In this one, there is more Dublin and less O'Casey. It goes into the influences of Yeats, Shaw, and Darwin and incorporates a great deal of fantasy and tells the story of the 1916 Easter Rebellion. I don't think I could cope with all of this in a conventional reading which in itself imposes restrictions.[10]

For this project Shyre felt the need for movement and the accommodation of the entire stage space, but since he used a "bare stage back to the brick wall," the scene still had to be imagined by the audience.

Gene Frankel, in directing the New York production of *Brecht on Brecht,* used stools and lecterns but moved his six actors about a platform that had a large picture of Brecht hanging from the ceiling. Also, a few placards were lowered on ropes at various times during the performance. The program consisted of two parts. Part I, called "Life," was made up of poems, songs, letters, essays, and stories revealing the life of Brecht. Part II, called "Theatre," consisted of long speeches, songs, and scenes from some of Brecht's plays.

Another professional production, John Dos Passos' *U.S.A.,* was presented by a chorus of six readers who, as they stood in line before an abstract background, delivered expository comments from the book in the form of news flashes.[11] From their initial positions the readers moved into localized areas with simple properties, such as chairs and tables, and acted

---

10 Arthur Gelb, "Campaigner in the Cause of Sean O'Casey," *The New York Times,* September 25, 1960, Sec. D, p. 1.

11 This production had elements of a form of theatre called "Chamber Theatre." Its originator, Robert Breen of the School of Speech, Northwestern University, defines it in "Suggestions for a Course of Study in Theatre Arts at the Secondary School Level," presented at the Secondary School Theatre Conference, August 21, 1962, Eugene, Oregon: "Chamber Theatre may be defined simply as a method of preparing and presenting undramatized fiction for the stage, as written, the only changes being those to accommodate the limitation of time, physical stage set-up, or number of actors. . . . What an audience sees in a Chamber Theatre production bears some resemblance to a traditional play— there are characters speaking dialogue, expressing emotions in a plotted action, and giving all the evidence of vital immediacy. What distinguishes the production from a conventional play, however, is the use of the author's narration to create setting and atmosphere and, more important, to explore the motivations of the characters at the moment of action." See also *Course of Study in Theatre Arts at the Secondary School Level,* rev. ed. (Washington, D.C.: American Theatre Association, 1968), pp. 107–110.

out scenes from the novel. One or two long sections were given in a narrative manner directly to the audience.

Other Readers Theatre materials have been developed for and at the professional level: Dylan Thomas wrote a radio script, *Under Milk Wood,* subtitled *A Play for Voices,* which, when adapted for the stage, was most effective as a dramatized reading for eight readers developing some thirty characters; Lewis John Carlino created a "collage for voices" entitled *Telemachus Clay;* Jerome Kilty adapted the correspondence of George Bernard Shaw and Mrs. Patrick Campbell into a script for two which he called *Dear Liar;* a multiple reading of the compiled script *Chekhov's Stories* was presented off-Broadway with the readers using stools and lecterns; *Adam's Diary* and *Eve's Diary* were given as one part of a program at Town Hall in New York; and *The World of Carl Sandburg,* a program made up of Sandburg's prose and poetry, was presented in New York and on the road. *Spoon River Anthology* and *In White America,* presented professionally, won success and acclaim in New York as well as across the country.

In The Hollow Crown *the three scenes shown simultaneously in this composite picture were lighted one at a time. At Stage R, Henry VIII proposed to Ann Boleyn; stage C, Charles I confronted John Bradshaw, President of the Court; stage L, the Epilogue from the Morte d'Arthur scene was read. The reader/actors moved from one area to another as needed, the lights shifting attention from scene to scene.*

The Hollow Crown, presented by the Royal Shakespeare Company of London, used four readers sitting informally at a coffee table located on one side of the platform; on the other side a pianist sat at a piano, with a harpsichord close by. According to the program, The Hollow Crown is "an entertainment by and about the kings and queens of England—music, poetry, speeches, letters, and other writings from the chronicles, from plays, and in the monarchs' own words—also music concerning them and by them." Some of the material was read while the actors were seated, but for most of the program the actors moved about and took different positions on the stage. At times, two actors engaged in dialogue; at other times, one walked forward and told a story, read a poem or letter, gave a speech directly to the audience, or leaned against the piano while singing a song. In The Rebel, another presentation by the same company, the program was unified by the idea that the rebel is the man who says no. It was composed of prose, verse, and song—all expressing defiance of authority by the individual. The Golden Age, similar in format, presented the Elizabethan age in prose, poetry, and drama. In all three of these performances, the readers wore formal attire.

A Readers Theatre type production presented on Broadway during the 1966–1967 season was The Investigation by Peter Weiss, a cold and impersonal digest of the court record of the men tried for participation in the destruction of four million people at the German concentration camp Auschwitz between 1941 and 1945. The play is a distillation of the facts and words of the witnesses, the accused, the prosecution, and the defense during the Frankfurt, Germany, trial in 1964 and 1965, "a selective transcript, an evening of edited fact," as Walter Kerr described it. In the production, thirteen men played the roles of the accused, each maintaining his own identity throughout. The seven witnesses each played a variety of roles—all of them prisoners spared from death, but each representing a composite of hundreds of witnesses. The lines were memorized. The narration was provided by three actors portraying the judge, the defense attorney, and the prosecuting attorney, who sat at a table in the built-up orchestra pit area. The questions of the presiding judge moved the story along. The accused and the witnesses stood as they gave testimony; the judge and the attorneys either remained in their seats at the table or stood near their seats. The play had no conventional plot, a modicum of gesture, but had many dialoguelike speeches. The prisoners and witnesses sat in cubicles on the stage, each tier of cubicles elevated above that in front of it. The houselights remained on throughout the performance, and the audience intermission was announced to the courtroom as a ten-minute recess in the trial. In short, The Investigation was dramatic use of essentially nondramatic materials.

Each succeeding season in New York has offered several Readers Theatre type productions. In 1965 Nassau Community College commissioned Paul Shyre to write a dramatic work based on Walt Whitman material. As a result, *A Whitman Portrait* had its premiere at the college as part of a Walt Whitman Festival. That fall it was seen off-Broadway with Alexander Scourby as Walt Whitman. Robert Frost and his writings became *An Evening's Frost,* subtitled *A Portrait of the Poet,* on the University of Michigan Professional Theatre Program, and it moved to New York in the fall of 1965. Another work based on the life and writings of Frost was performed by The Theatre Group, University of California Extension, as a part of their 1965–1966 season. In 1966 Norman Rosten's *Come Slowly, Eden,* subtitled *A Portrait of Emily Dickinson,* was produced as part of the ANTA Matinee Series at the Theatre de Lys, Greenwich Village, with Kim Hunter as Miss Dickinson. The "play" was made up almost entirely of quotations from the poet's poems and letters, and was described by one critic as "a dramatic autobiography." In 1967 Dan Sullivan of the *New York Times,* reviewing *The Rimers of Eldritch,* revealed some of its Readers Theatre characteristics:

> The actors play out their drama on a setting of several bare platforms and a black backdrop. There are numerous scenes, some abrupt, some lengthy. . . . The actors remain on stage in various postures or with their backs to the audience while a scene is being played. At times they are called upon to mime little pieces of business—such as cooking or buying groceries. . . . There is nothing new in the fragmented voices and fractured time-sense of *The Rimers of Eldritch*—nothing that would surprise Joyce or Thornton Wilder or, in particular, the Dylan Thomas of *Under Milk Wood.* The seventeen members of the cast represent the seventy men and women who live out their sad little half-lives in Eldritch, Iowa. . . .[12]

The first musical to be done professionally in Readers Theatre style, *You're a Good Man, Charlie Brown,* opened on March 7, 1967, at Theatre 80 St. Marks in New York. Based on "Peanuts" by Charles M. Schulz, this delightful adaptation of the comic strip used suggested characters, settings, and costumes rather than realistic ones. Narration, sometimes just spoken but often sung, was directed to the audience. The locus for dialogue exchanges was onstage. Everything was memorized, yet everything was handled in the style of Readers Theatre. The sets were suggested rather than realistic. Lighting focused attention on whatever stage area was being used for a particular scene.[13] Charlie Brown struggled with an invisible kite on an invisible string. Throughout the performance the cast expected the audience to see what they saw, to believe what they believed. So the audience believed the undersized young man who played the dog Snoopy

---

12 "Theatre: 'The Rimers of Eldritch' at Cherry Lane," *The New York Times,* February 22, 1967, p. 18.
13 See pp. 87–88 for a description of the setting and lighting for *You're a Good Man, Charlie Brown.*

was Snoopy. The hundreds of productions of this musical and the thousands of performances, both professional and amateur, attest to the possibilities of memorized Readers Theatre.

Mention should be made of *Hamlet,* touring in 1970–1971 with Dame Judith Anderson in the title role. Most critics agreed that this "arrangement" of Shakespeare's masterpiece was a fiasco. But many practices and techniques of Readers Theatre were evident throughout the production, successful or not. This *Hamlet* consisted of a series of pictures with limited and simplified movement, on a stage with a central elevation surrounded by several steps and an arrangement of screens. There were no props. The arras was created by a gesture. Actors died by turning to kneel upstage, remaining motionless to the end of the scene, and then walking off. In this production, as in all of the evenings of theatre mentioned above, elements of Readers Theatre were prominent, not only in the arrangement of the literature, but also in the physical arrangement of the scenes, the use of narration, and the use made of the imaginations of the audience members.

This was also the case in 1970 and 1971 when Paul Sills and Story Theatre were much in the theatre news at the Mark Taper Forum, Los Angeles, at Yale University, and on-Broadway. *Grimm's Fairy Tales* in Los Angeles was reviewed:

> His [Sills'] technique is disarmingly simple: the actors work on a stage that has only the merest suggestions of setting and props. There is nothing for them to lean on. The atmosphere comes from lighting, music . . . sound effects (sometimes produced by an actor offstage), and the actors themselves, who must transform the basic setting into the fantastical world of the Brothers Grimm for an audience.[14]

Tom Prideaux, *Life* theatre editor, described Yale's Story Theatre: "Story Theatre commandeers your imagination and leads you into the fantastic world of dreams. . . . Here, at last, our imaginations are needed, and it is a delight."[15]

It is significant that these professional productions ranged in composition from four actors who used stools, lecterns, and written scripts to a much larger group of readers who memorized their lines, utilized tables and chairs as needed, and, in some instances, employed movement and physical action to develop or enhance their interpretation. Viewed collectively, these productions clearly indicate that (1) professional Readers Theatre is experimental, (2) it has no one established form of presentation, and (3) it uses all types of literature.

---

14 John Weisman, "Paul Sills Probes Theater and Finds a Storyline," *Los Angeles Times* Calendar, May 24, 1970, p. 14.
15 "New Blood from an Old Vampire," *Life,* September 18, 1970, p. 20.

The imaginative approach, the courage to experiment with new elements and techniques, and the eagerness to interpret a challenging variety of literary materials which have characterized the professional producer of Readers Theatre are also evident in his academic counterpart. In educational institutions the vision and energies of teacher-directors have also produced exciting and noteworthy results. In addition to developing in their students oral interpretive skills, they have used techniques of Readers Theatre in the teaching and learning processes and are involving their audiences in the experiencing of "live" literature. Often their progress has paralleled but in no sense imitated that of their Broadway counterparts. At the college and university level, Readers Theatre programs have ranged from the simplest forms of oral reading with little or no movement by the interpreters to more elaborate, even somewhat theatrical, presentations. Since Part II of this book contains summary-descriptions of many of these educational productions, a full-scale discussion of them will not be provided here. However, to suggest something of the energetic experimentation being carried out on campuses across the country and the freshness and originality with which these efforts are being infused, it may prove helpful to cite a few typical productions.

The term "Readers Theatre" was first used, to the best of our knowledge, by a professional group in New York, as was stated above. Previous to the midforties group interpretations usually were labeled, as were most interpretation recitals, as reading hours, play readings, or other such terms. In December 1948, William McCoard presented a group reading of W. H. Auden's Pulitzer Prize-winning long poem, *The Age of Anxiety,* at the Speech Association of America Convention.[16] At the 1957 Joint Convention of the American Educational Theatre Association and the Speech Association of America (now called, respectively, the American Theatre Association and the Speech Communication Association), Helen Hicks of Hunter College presented Book I of *John Brown's Body* with readers using scripts as they sat behind lecterns. At a subsequent meeting of the Speech Association of America, Wallace Bacon of Northwestern University, Albert Martin of DePaul University, and Natalie Cherry, a former Northwestern student, presented Henry James' "The Beast in the Jungle" in a similar manner. At the 1960 Convention of the Speech Association of America, Southwest Missouri State University presented Ray Bradbury's novel *Dandelion Wine,* with six readers using stools, lecterns, and scripts, and employing some movement. For "Imagination '62," a festival sponsored by the University of Kansas, this same group produced a script, *Ebony Ghetto,*

---

16 See William B. McCoard, "An Interpretation of the Times: A Report on the Oral Interpretation of W. H. Auden's *Age of Anxiety,*" *Quarterly Journal of Speech,* 35, no. 4 (December 1949), 489–95.

compiled from a narrative by Frederick Ramsey interspersed with poems by Langston Hughes and Fenton Johnson and interwoven with ballads by a folksinger. The physical arrangement consisted of one stool, two lecterns, and a bench. The storyteller sat on the stool while three other readers moved into a succession of different positions that suggested the changing relationships and moods of the characters. All but one of these readers carried scripts in small, easily managed notebooks; the guitar-playing folksinger rested his material on a lectern. Other productions given at national and regional professional conventions include *The Battle of the Sexes,* presented by Central Michigan University; Camus' *The Stranger,* by Southern California University; Fielding's *The Tragedy of Tragedies: Or the Life and Death of Tom Thumb the Great,* by Northwestern University; *Readers Theatre for Children,* by Southwest Missouri State University; *The Underground Alice: An Experimental Mixed Media Entertainment,* by Loretto Heights College; and *The Tandem Muse: A Postured and Tonalized History of Spoken Literature,* by the University of Southern California.

As a further reflection of the interesting and extensive interpretive activity being carried on at the campus level, it should be noted again that the Interpretation Division of the Speech Communication Association periodically prepares a report of college and university research in this field.[17] In one of its more recent summations, the Interpretation Division categorized twenty-one articles, dissertations, and theses written on various aspects of Readers Theatre and listed more than two hundred specific literary selections—prose, poetry, and plays—which had been presented in group readings from coast to coast.[18]

From this brief overview, it should be evident that earnest experimentation and creative effort are continuing and expanding on both the professional and educational stage. Although professional producers and directors, being more strongly oriented toward the theatre, tend to make greater use of memorization and physical movement, both groups are striving vigorously toward a mutual goal: to create for the widest possible audience the opportunity to experience a "living" literature—a literature that is emotionally and intellectually invigorating, that can probe man's interrelationships and interdependencies in new and revealing ways, and that can revitalize the human spirit.

READERS THEATRE AND EXPERIMENTAL PLAYWRIGHTS

The statement is occasionally made, and with some justification, that the writing which has been produced for Readers Theatre is adaptive rather

---

[17] Inquiries about the availability of the Annual Readers Theatre Bibliography should be directed to the Speech Communication Association, Statler Hilton Hotel, New York, N.Y. 10001.

[18] Clark S. Marlor, ed., "Readers Theatre Bibliography: 1960–1964," *Central States Speech Journal,* 17, no. 1 (February 1966), 33–39.

than original. Certainly, very few original scripts have been written exclusively for performance in Readers Theatre, though there is some evidence that writers are turning to this medium. The originality of the scripts lies rather in the selection and arrangement of the materials and the ways in which they can be made to invoke a special and direct relationship with an audience. While there are similarities between Readers Theatre and a stage play, there are also significant differences. Readers Theatre is not like a conventional play, nor is it like a revue; it is, as we have seen, an art form that seeks a more direct relationship between audience and readers. In realistic drama, playwrights worked to maintain what has been termed *a fourth wall* between those who were enacting their story ideas and those who were witnessing them. This indirect relationship between actors and audience was thought to be essential for a proper balance between the subjective and objective appreciation of the dramatic form. Put another way, the audience was "looking in" upon the actors, but the actors were not "looking out" at the audience.

Breaking the mold: Wilder and others

In recent years, several modern dramatists have been trying to break out of this mold and have been seeking means of creating actor-audience relationships which are much more direct and participatory. It is in this aspect of play-writing that creators of Readers Theatre scripts and the modern playwrights have a similar goal. Among the foremost of these experimenters is Thornton Wilder. In his play *Our Town,* Wilder used a narrator to unite scenes which lacked conventional settings and which used only the unadorned rear wall of the theatre as background and only such necessary properties as tables, chairs, and ordinary stepladders. In *Skin of Our Teeth,* he employed direct actor-audience contact. Archibald MacLeish used this principle of actor-audience contact in *J. B.,* and Robert Bolt employed it in *A Man for All Seasons.*

In the early 1970s, increased experimentation was evident in the professional theatre world, and much of it involved simplification. The "poor theatre" of Jerzy Grotowski, the Polish Laboratory Theatre, eliminated practically everything to which the theatregoer was accustomed—even more than Readers Theatre—texts, costumes, sets, music, and even lighting effects. Two essentials only were kept, actors and audiences. In the first few months of 1971 theatre audiences saw *The Night Thoreau Spent in Jail,* by Jerome Lawrence and Robert E. Lee, which dealt with civil disobedience and was presented in the style of a historical documentary, with the narrator as a key persona. However, *Pueblo,* by Stanley R. Greenberg, and *The Trial of the Catonsville Nine,* by Daniel Berrigan, were fresh from the courts, jails, and newspapers of the day. The latter concerned the testimonies of the nine defendants in the Catonsville trial, and was not a play in the sense that a play contains a story arranged in dramatic progression. Rather, "it was a political and philosophical discussion, a debate, written in the form of a radio scenario, and fleshed out with living actors who could just as effectively carry their scripts."[19] *Pueblo* was a dramatization, again Readers Theatre style, of the ordeal of Commander Lloyd Bucher that was revealed by a court-martial and a congressional investigating committee.

The Brechtian impetus

Bertolt Brecht also sought forms and devices that would break with traditional staging in order to develop a new relationship with the audience. Since they have striking similarities, an understanding of Brecht's Epic Theatre may help one understand more fully the form of Readers Theatre, or "Concert Theatre,"[20] as he called it, although his reasons for turning to a new form differed quite radically from those of the directors of Readers Theatre. Brecht invented or evolved his Epic form because he wanted his audience primarily to *think,* to become—above all else—intellectually involved. He wanted to prevent the audience from becoming so emotionally involved in the characters that they no longer evaluated the significance of the thoughts being presented. Readers Theatre likewise demands a thinking audience, but it also demands an emotionally involved audience.

William Menze of the University of Minnesota has pointed out, in mimeographed material distributed to his students, that Epic drama is a hybrid form of drama employing epic, dramatic, and lyric elements; and he added that, according to Brecht, Epic drama is "a narrator of events," operating from a stage that serves as a platform. To prevent emotional involvement by the audience, Brecht introduced what he called *alienating devices.* These bear a striking resemblance to methods used in Readers Theatre, the goal of which is total involvement, both mental and emotional, on the part of the audience. One means of alienation advocated by Brecht is a narrator or storyteller who talks directly to the audience and who interprets and comments on the events and incidents. This narrator verbally changes the scene, a device which is also used in Readers Theatre. Moreover, in Brecht's theatre there is an avoidance of the concept of the *fourth wall,* a convention commonly avoided in Readers Theatre, too.

Brecht also had his actors shift roles and play more than one character, as was done in *John Brown's Body, I Knock at the Door,* and other Readers Theatre performances. An example of Brecht's role-shifting technique

19 David C. Gild, "The Trial of the Catonsvilie Nine," *Educational Theatre Journal,* 23, no. 2 (May 1971), 210.
20 That Brecht was deliberately bringing the quality of a concert into his presentation is attested in a statement he made to Mordecai Gorelik about the set for *The Mother.* Said Brecht, "We'll place two grand pianos visibly at one side of the stage; the play must have the quality of a concert as well as that of a drama." See Mordecai Gorelik, "Brecht: I Am the Einstein of the New Stage Form," *Theatre Arts,* 41 (March 1957), 73, and Douglas Charles Wixson, Jr., "The Dramatic Techniques of Thornton Wilder and Bertolt Brecht: A Study in Comparison," *Modern Drama,* 15, no. 2 (September 1972) 112–24.

can be seen in his play *The Experiment,* in which three comrades return from China and report on their activities there. With the help of a chorus and an orchestra, they tell their story by acting it out. The three comrades play the roles of all those who enter into the narrative. This closely approximates the form followed by Charles Laughton for *John Brown's Body,* even to the use of a chorus.

Another alienating device used by Brecht was to have an actor step out of the scene to sing directly to the audience a song that comments on the action. He also made use of such devices as the projection of pictures, printed comments, and similar information onto a background screen; and he characteristically employed bare stage walls and minimal properties to keep the audience continuously aware of differences between real life and the stage.

Many of Brecht's dramas are made up of a succession of several scenes, each existing for itself instead of being linked to subsequent scenes. In short, Epic drama tends to consist of a series of relatively independent segments which, when taken together, present a broad overview of a sequence of events. This compositional form is similar to that found in *The World of Carl Sandburg* and *A Thurber Carnival.* The latter, incidentally, consists of short dramatic sketches on an uncluttered stage, with blown-up Thurber drawings projected onto a screen, storytellers narrating directly to the audience, and dancing couples who suddenly "freeze" and fling out Thurberisms.

Thus Brecht, in searching for a new relationship with his audience, used many of the compositional and presentational elements employed in Readers Theatre: he utilized a narrator to tie segments together, to verbally set the scenes, to comment upon and interpret the action; his actors portrayed more than one role; and his stage was a platform with few properties. Each scene existed for itself; but when the scenes were taken together, they presented a broad overview of a major premise. He, too, demanded a thinking audience; but contrary to the aim of Readers Theatre, Brecht sought to avoid emotional involvement on the part of the audience.

Key characteristics: a summation

What, then, are the unique and distinguishing characteristics of Readers Theatre? In most of the professional and educational productions surveyed in this chapter, certain elements have recurred frequently enough to be considered typical: scenery and costumes are not used or are only selectively implied; action or physical movement is merely suggested by the interpreter and is visualized in the minds of the audience; a narrator, speaking directly to the audience, usually establishes the basic situation or theme and links the various segments together; a physical script is usually carried by the reader or is at least in evidence somewhere; and, probably most important, there is a continuing effort to develop and maintain a closer, more personalized relationship between performer and audience—a relationship which, in Readers Theatre, requires a decidedly different kind of participation from that demanded by the conventional theatre. Specifically, the emphasis in Readers Theatre is upon the aural appeal, and the audience's attention is concentrated upon the literature. In both conventional theatre and Readers Theatre, the subtext of the material—the meaning underlying the words—is shared with the audience to the fullest extent possible; and, Brecht notwithstanding, the audience is emotionally involved.

The possibilities of this medium have not yet been fully realized or exploited. Relatively new on the contemporary scene, Readers Theatre is free for experimentation and open to the use of imaginative techniques for bringing literature to an audience. As Allardyce Nicoll has said, "Almost always we find dramatic genius flowering when a particular land in a particular age discovers a theatrical form that is new, adjusted to its demands, and hitherto not fully exploited."[21] Readers Theatre, it must be reiterated, is not a substitute for conventional theatre and is not intended to be. It is a different form, with a focus on the literary text, on words and psychological actions, rather than on physical movement. With few outside trappings, it centers the audience's interest on the words and the motivations underlying the words. Since it is not limited to the play form, it can bring to the stage a far greater range of literary materials than conventional theatre. Whether playwrights create new material or adapters arrange scripts from plays or other literary sources, they are seeking to stimulate the audience and are demanding of the audience a special type of creative participation. This, then, is the essence of Readers Theatre, which may properly be called Theatre of the Mind—Theatre of the Imagination.

---

21 *World Drama* (New York: Harcourt Brace Jovanovich, Inc., 1950), p. 933.

CHAPTER THREE

Selecting and Adapting Material for Readers Theatre

The range of literature suitable for Readers Theatre is limitless. As we have noted, plays, novels, short stories, letters, diaries, poems, and even some essays have been used successfully. Both serious and comic materials have been adapted. The following list of selections on which productions were based gives some idea of the infinite variety that is possible: Robert Frost's poem "The Death of the Hired Man," Philip Roth's short story "The Conversion of the Jews," Mark Twain's *Adam's Diary* and *Eve's Diary* (see pp. 233–238) and Karl Shapiro's poem "Adam and Eve," Norman Corwin's radio script *My Client Curley,* Oscar Wilde's play *The Importance of Being Earnest,* Peter Beagle's novel *A Fine and Quiet Place,* Addison and Steele's, essays *The Spectator Papers,* the letters exchanged between Mrs. Patrick Campbell and George Bernard Shaw, and even the comic strips of Jules Feiffer and Charles Schulz.

This wide range of appropriate materials places a challenging and somewhat complicated responsibility upon those who would prepare scripts for Readers Theatre. This preparation is basically a two-step process which involves, first, selecting materials with high literary values and strong dramatic potential and, second, adapting these selections for a script which —through its aural appeals—will secure the desired emotional and intellectual involvement of the audience. The task is not, however, as formidable as it may appear at first glance. Experimentation and experience have singled out certain qualities that the selector-adapter can look for as he goes about the job of finding and choosing his materials, and certain precepts that will aid him in adjusting and fitting the components together into a unified and fluid whole.

Adam and Eve in Karl Shapiro's poem "Adam and Eve" sit informally on a two-step platform unit as if on a grassy knoll in Eden. The narrator remains slightly back and at the side. All three of the characters are served by a concentration of light picking them out from the void.

SELECTING SCRIPT MATERIALS

Certain dramatic qualities and styles of writing should be looked for in any material being considered for Readers Theatre: *evocative power, compelling characters, action, enriched language,* and *wholeness.* The literature is evocative to the extent that it contains stimulating ideas and insights that leave the audience with a memorable, meaningful experience. It should deal with characters who compel interest not only in their mental and emotional conflicts, but also in their uniqueness. The text should contain definite action, usually psychological and emotional rather than physical action. It should have aesthetic value in the sense that its language is enriched with strong image-making wording, with aural reverberations. The selection chosen should present a complete episode rather than a fragment, an entity that is self-contained, so that the audience can experience the wholeness of the author's concept. If these criteria are met the literature should benefit from performance, be vitalized by a Readers Theatre experience. The literature thus presented, if carefully selected for the particular audience involved, should prove entertaining as well as stimulating.

Evocative power

Literature with strong evocative power pulls the reader deeply into the experience recorded so that its significance is felt and becomes a part of his vicarious life. Such significant literature has the power to stir the imagination and energize the intellect of the listener. In short, it deepens his involvement with and understanding of life. It tends to make him a more responsive and sensitive human being. Literature with the power to draw the audience member into its world and involve him in the action evokes a definite response: it makes him shiver, makes him cry, makes him happy. Such material often encompasses a "moment of truth" (Henry James' "The Beast in the Jungle"); provides an insight into a fellow human being (John Steinbeck's "The Flight"), into a complex problem

In James Clavell's The Children's Story, *a series of step units and a platform (a pyramid arrangement) enable the new teacher to sit at the top with the children grouped around and below her. The old teacher remains slightly back and to one side—an arrangement which makes it possible for the audience to see all phases of the presentation at one time.*

(James Clavell's "The Children's Story") or into man's relationship with a higher being (T. W. Turner's "Christ in the Concrete City"); or delineates a meaningful relationship with nature (Hamlin Garland's "Under the Lion's Paw"), or with society (Gerhart Hauptmann's "The Weavers"). In searching for material for Readers Theatre scripts, the adapter/director should choose literature with the power to stir the imaginations of the listeners, thus allowing them to have a meaningful, vicarious experience.

Interest-compelling characters

Some characters arouse interest and compel the attention of the reader far more than others. Literature for Readers Theatre needs the interaction of interest-compelling characters. The more strongly delineated the characters are, the more fascinating they will be. The more sensitive they are, the more intriguing they will be. The more involved they are with each other and with the situation—the action of the literature—the more involved the audience will be. Literature with little or no characterization and interaction of characters lacks elements vital for an engrossing Readers Theatre script. Many essays having only the writer (or speaker) and no other characters, and only the interaction that occurs between the writer and the reader, are difficult to adapt into a successful script for this medium. The same is true of fictive prose having only one persona. Action and interaction of interest-compelling characters are necessary ingredients in a theatre script, whether it be Readers Theatre or conventional theatre.

Many factors about a character compel our attention. We are caught by characters so familiar that we can immediately identify with them, by strangely unique characters, or by characters capable of surprising us convincingly. A familiar character in an unfamiliar situation is intriguing, such as the heroine in *Alice in Wonderland*. Or the reverse may be true, unfamiliar characters doing the familiar, such as the bears in "The Three Bears." Other interest-compelling characters are Walter Mitty, Lady Macbeth, the monk in Browning's "Soliloquy of the Spanish Cloister," Yank in O'Neill's *The Hairy Ape,* and the delightful detective Christophero in Peter Shafer's *The Private Eye.* All are strongly drawn, sharply etched, distinctive personalities. And although not people in the ordinary sense, the characters in Roald Dahl's *James and the Giant Peach* are fascinating, especially the Earthworm and the Centipede. Such characters stir the imagination and the creative instinct of both readers and audience and furnish an essential ingredient of an effective Readers Theatre script.

Action: outward and inward

In a script worthy of Readers Theatre, the characters need to be seen in action—action that is provocative, intriguing, stirring. This action need not be physical; a character thinking or feeling is a character in action, especially if the thinking or feeling is directed against a counter-sentiment or

In Maria, *an adaptation based on* West Side Story, *ladders, although used primarily for scenes played on the fire escape, also provided variety in scenes involving many readers. Additional elements of the setting: two platforms of different heights, short stools, and one chair. Offstage focus was used throughout.*

force. The conflict which induces dramatic action, then, may be either outward or inward. Action can be the result of a conflict between two or more people, as in the gang wars of *West Side Story.* Or an individual may engage in conflict with society, as in Ibsen's *An Enemy of the People,* where Dr. Stockman is in conflict with all the people in his town. The conflict may also be with a force in nature. In Jack London's "To Build a Fire," a man is trying to cope with the freezing cold. Or the conflict may be an inner one—for instance, a man in doubt, fighting his own conscience or making a difficult choice. This is the conflict in Hamlet, Macbeth, and the character in Frost's poem "The Road Not Taken." This element of man-in-action—be it inner or outer—is imperative in the material chosen for Readers Theatre. It should not be random or aimless; action is more interesting if it has a "going somewhere" quality. As Bacon and Breen point out in *Literature As Experience:*

> No piece of prose fiction lacks *an action*—that is, a progression from one position or one point of awareness to another. Someone must undergo a change in awareness because a story *cannot be* (though a poem *may be* and a pure lyric poem *is*) in this sense static. The change in awareness may or may not be in a character or characters within the story; it may be produced within the reader alone, while the characters remain unaware. But it is this

revelation . . . which is basic to the life of the story and which constitutes its design, its action.[1]

Since the action in a Readers Theatre production is usually suggested rather than literal, the written material must contain clear and vital action that the audience can visualize in a succession of mental images. This action must be concretely phrased, be couched in vivid, mimetic terms, and progress from one point of awareness to another. Action may be expressed in description, in narration, and in dialogue. It may be presented in scenes and in summarizing narration. For Readers Theatre, material rich in scenes as opposed to summary fulfills the requirements for the dramatic element essential in theatre. A scene dramatizes the action directly in time (now) and place (here), and is revealed in dialogue and concrete details of time, place, action, and character. Through words we are shown the characters in action as opposed to being told about them in summarizing narration. This is not to say that narration is not suitable to Readers Theatre. It is in fact quite effective, as has been stated previously, and is an essential part of most Readers Theatre productions. But it is usually easier for an audience to become involved with characters in close-up scenes because of the immediacy of their thoughts and feelings. Action, whether revealed in dialogue or in narration, is an essential ingredient in literature for Readers Theatre scripts.[2]

Enriched language

Not only should the material be thought provoking, provide a memorable emotional experience, and present interesting characters in provocative action, but it should also be written in language rich in evocative overtones, in language with a poetic cast—hence, in language that benefits from being "sounded," from being heard. Many elements are incorporated in the term "enriched language." One is auditory effectiveness, which is achieved not only by sound matching sense as in onomatopoeia, but also through repetition and rhythm; in other words, a felicity of expression results from the ordering of sounds. Though found most frequently in poetry, repetition is found also in prose having a poetic quality. Alliteration, assonance, and onomatopoeia are among the more common devices imparting a poetic quality to language; they are readily identifiable in the following brief illustrative passages:

1 Wallace Bacon and Robert Breen, *Literature As Experience* (New York: McGraw-Hill Book Company, Inc., 1959), p. 215. Reprinted by permission.
2 For a discussion of scene and action, see Norman Friedman, "Point of View in Fiction, the Development of a Critical Concept," *PMLA*, 70 (December 1950), 1160–84. For a discussion of action, see Jere Veilleux, "The Concept of Action in Oral Interpretation," *Quarterly Journal of Speech*, 53, no. 3 (October 1967), 281–84.

Alliteration:	The *r*umble of *r*everberation *r*ose to a *r*oar.
	The *b*lazing *b*rightness of her *b*eauties *b*ecame. . . .
Assonance:	A g*o*lden gl*ow* suffused the d*o*me.
	The l*o*wing herd wind sl*ow*ly *o*'er the lea.
Onomatopoeia:	The hissing of the skates on the slick ice. . . .
	The moan of doves in immemorial elms,
	And murmur of innumerable bees. . . .

In the above examples, onomatopoeia occurs when the sound of the words suggests the meaning. The recurring *s* sound imitates the skates on ice, and the *m*s suggest the murmuring sound of the doves and bees.

The repetition of words and phrases can delight the ear as well as make the meaning clear. Repetition of certain phrases or words can give cumulative power, as in this passage from Shakespeare's *The Merchant of Venice* (Act V, Scene i, lines 192–98):

> *Sweet Portia,*
> *If you did know to whom I gave the ring,*
> *If you did know for whom I gave the ring*
> *And would conceive for what I gave the ring*
> *And how unwillingly I left the ring,*
> *When nought would be accepted but the ring,*
> *You would abate the strength of your displeasure.*

Such repetition establishes rhythm which, in turn, stimulates emotion and reinforces the meaning of the language. Children's poetry, nursery rhymes, and children's stories make discerning use of this appeal to the ear, as in the Dr. Seuss stories.

Enriched language employs figures of speech (metaphor, synecdoche, personification) which extend the meaning by evoking comparisons, making substitutions, and bestowing lifelike qualities on inanimate objects, thus giving the writing stronger evocative power. Literature rich in sense imagery, as Ray Bradbury's *Dandelion Wine,* is especially effective for Readers Theatre. By re-creating the sense images in the material, the reader can fully experience the sights, sounds, smells, and other sensory details and thus respond more completely to the situation. Kinesthetic imagery also greatly enriches the experience for the reader and for the audience. In *The Order of Poetry,* kinesthesia is defined as

> the perception or feeling of movement. . . . [T]his term is usually reserved for that kind of imagery which appeals, not to our senses of smell, hearing, etc., . . . but to our residual memory or imagination derived from the nerves and muscles which govern bodily movement and physical attitudes. Through kinesthesia we get "the feel" of an action, whether perceived directly or described in language; on the basis of having moved or arranged our own bodies in the past, we can imaginatively identify ourselves with, or project ourselves into, the motions or postures of others. The use of "body-

English" in games like pool or golf acts out our kinesthetic identifications, which work more inwardly in our response to such poetic images as Keats's "limping and trembling hare."[3]

Kinesthesia is, of course, closely related to empathy, the imaginative projection of one's own consciousness into another being. In other words, we imaginatively identify ourselves with the motions of the characters in the literature. We can also empathize with, or "put ourselves into," a physical response to the emotions felt by others. Because this identification and empathy make the literature more real as well as more enjoyable to the reader and the audience, it is advisable to choose materials rich in imagery. Curtis Canfield, in *The Craft of Play Directing,* avers:

> The imaginative use of language . . . has but one object: to increase the listener's enjoyment of what he hears. The verbal effects . . . are means to that end. They add one more dimension to a form of communication that can also appeal by means of interesting plots, significant themes, and characters human and engaging enough to enlist our attention and entangle us emotionally in what they feel and do.[4]

Wholeness: self-contained entity

Another factor to consider in choosing material for Readers Theatre is the length of the selection: whether a scene or passage from a longer work or the total composition is used, the finished script must possess a wholeness, a sense of completeness; that is, it must have a beginning, a middle, and an end. This does not mean that a portion of a novel, short story, or play cannot be used. Rather, it implies that the adaptation or cutting must give sufficient introduction to the characters, setting, and action so that the script is self-contained, understandable, and can reach an ending dictated by the happenings in the beginning and middle portions, which may have been condensed from the original.[5] In other words, it must furnish a complete experience for the audience: they must not be left puzzled because they do not know who the characters are, what the action is or has been, or what occurs as a result of the character action and interaction. It is also important to select material that can be cut and adapted to fit into a reasonable time limit. In Readers Theatre, as in a play, there must be condensation and a telescoping of events and characters. The material needs to be structured so that the story moves along and comes to a focal high point. The maximum duration of Readers Theatre performances is usually sixty to seventy minutes, and many directors feel that it is difficult to hold

---

[3] Edward A. Bloom, Charles H. Philbrick, and Elmer M. Blistein, *The Order of Poetry* (New York: Odyssey Press, 1961), p. 154.
[4] New York: Holt, Rinehart & Winston, Inc., 1963, p. 106. For a further discussion of dramatic language, see Hardie Albright, Hubert Heffner, and Lee Mitchell, *Principles of Theatre Arts* (New York: Houghton Mifflin Co., 1968), pp. 41–45.
[5] For further information on adapting scripts, see pp. 45–60.

an audience longer than an hour and a half. However, the recent trend to adapt full-length novels and plays is tending to change this, and longer programs with intermissions are being given.

SELECTIVE CRITERIA FOR PLAYS

The selection of stage plays for Readers Theatre involves a number of special factors. As with all types of literature, of course, evocative power, compelling characters, provocative conflict, sustained action, vivid language, and wholeness are very important considerations. In addition, however, certain other elements should be taken into account. The plays selected ought to have an unusually lively interchange of ideas (*Major Barbara*); dialogue that reveals each character's motivation, personality, and depth (*The Cherry Orchard*); and strong emotional climaxes (*The Little Foxes*). Plays that are dependent upon a great amount of visual action, particularly farcical action (*Charley's Aunt*), lose much of their vitality when this activity must be either verbalized by a narrator or omitted. For example, murder mysteries dependent upon such special effects as bodies falling from closets or emerging from window seats, detailed movements of a mysterious or menacing nature, or a great deal of broad physical action do not readily lend themselves to Readers Theatre adaptation. For effective Readers Theatre, words are still a most important ingredient —words interpreted by sensitive, expressive readers.[6]

These, then, are the essential criteria for selecting materials appropriate for Readers Theatre: the literature should, above all, provide provocative ideas and interesting characters in intriguing action; it should contain rich language with evocative overtones; and it should be capable of being cut to a reasonable time limit and still preserve its essential entity, a wholeness of experience. Ideally, literature chosen for this medium will provide the audience with an enduring and significant experience.

ADAPTING THE MATERIAL

Once appropriate material has been selected, the next step is the actual adaptation for Readers Theatre. Basically, as we shall see, the form this takes is dictated by the material. However, such external influences as the time limit of the performance, the available talent, the nature of the occa-

---

[6] See Mark S. Klyn, "A Note on Farce in Readers Theatre," *I.I.G. Newsletter,* November 1966, p. 5. Professor Klyn experimented with three Chekhov short farces: "A Marriage Proposal," "The Bear," and "The Harmfulness of Tobacco." He found that sharpness of timing, characterization, and dialogue, upheld with the immediacy of a true ensemble, could offset the lack of physical dimension in Readers Theatre. "The production was successful, funny a good deal of the time, and the mad, nonrational mood of farce *was* achieved." The conclusion drawn was that farce can be successfully performed in Readers Theatre.

sion and the audience, the physical characteristics of the theatre, and the overall mood to be established must also be considered.

Although there are certain precepts and general procedures for adapting nearly all types of literature, their specific application will vary somewhat, depending upon the form and nature of the original material. For example, the problems encountered in adapting a humorous short story for Readers Theatre may differ appreciably from those involved in reshaping a serious one-act play; an approach that might be desirable in handling a lengthy narrative poem may not be particularly useful to the adapter who is trying to arrange and link a series of newspaper editorials around a central premise. In the discussion which follows, therefore, an attempt will be made to explore the techniques and problems of adapting each literary form, specifically the dramatic literature of the stage and radio play, the prose fiction of the short story and the novel, and the compilation of scripts derived from such materials as poems, essays, letters, diaries, and newspaper items. Brief comment will also be made concerning the creation of an original script. But first, since to adapt a script one must analyze the material, make decisions on the number of readers to use, and determine ways of revealing who is to be in the scene and how to make transitions from one segment to another, we offer a "shakedown cruise"[7] on how to go about these tasks. The selection on which we shall work is "Ballad of the Landlord," by Langston Hughes.

Landlord, landlord,
My roof has sprung a leak.
Don't you 'member I told you about it
Way last week?

Landlord, landlord,
These steps is broken down.
When you come up yourself
It's a wonder you don't fall down.

Ten Bucks you say I owe you?
Ten Bucks you say is due?
Well, that's Ten Bucks more'n I'll pay you
Till you fix this house up new.

What? You gonna get eviction orders?
You gonna cut off my heat?
You gonna take my furniture and
Throw it in the street?

Um-huh! You talking high and mighty.
Talk on—till you get through.

---

[7] This exercise is drawn from "Multiple Reading of Dialogue-Type Poetry," in Melvin R. White, *From the Printed Page* (Piedmont, California: S & F Press, 1964), pp. 13–15.

You ain't gonna be able to say a word
If I land my fist on you.

Police! Police!
Come and get this man!
He's trying to ruin the government
And overturn the land!

Copper's whistle!
Patrol bell!
Arrest.

Precinct Station.
Iron cell.
Headlines in press:

MAN THREATENS LANDLORD

.   .   .

TENANT HELD NO BAIL

.   .   .

JUDGE GIVES NEGRO 90 DAYS IN COUNTY JAIL[8]

Analysis: It is impossible for you to communicate a selection to an audience unless you understand it thoroughly yourself first, understand the intellectual content (what it means, what it says), and the emotional content (the feeling behind the material—what the author felt, what his attitude or viewpoint was when he wrote the poem).

The following outline will serve to guide you in your analysis:

1. Who is the speaker?
2. To whom is he speaking?
3. What is the setting: place and time?
4. What is the central thought, the basic idea?
5. How has the poet expressed this idea?
6. What are the varying moods?
7. Where are the climaxes?
8. Why does the central character act as he does?

In addition, it is useful to know something about the writer, when he wrote, what he wrote, why he wrote what he did. It is important for you to know, for instance, that Langston Hughes was a black writer, that he was in his day referred to as "the voice of his people." If we were to fill in the outline above for "Ballad of the Landlord," it might read:

1. Speaker: A renter.
2. Audience: His landlord.

---

8 From *Montage of a Dream Deferred*, published by Holt, Rinehart & Winston, Inc. Copyright 1951 by Langston Hughes. Reprinted by permission of Harold Ober Associates, Inc.

3. Setting: The Harlem section of New York City; time, the present.
4. Central thought: The place I rent from you is in bad shape, but you do nothing about it. When I complain, I end up in trouble.
5. Idea expressed: Through a renter (or renters) talking to the landlord.
6. Dominant mood: Anger.
7. Climax: The entire poem is one climax, but the renter's anger reaches its height on "If I land my fist on you," with "Police! Police!" perhaps attaining even greater emotional and vocal energy.
8. Motivation: The renter is motivated to his actions by the way the landlord has treated him.

You should also decide about the characters in the poem. What age are they? How much education do they have? What type of people are they? What kind of voices do they have? As you read the dialogue, you should suggest the character in your voice, in your face, and with all of your body so that your audience can see in their minds' eyes the person you want them to see.

"Ballad of the Landlord" obviously should—or at least could—be read by one reader. For our "shakedown cruise," however, it is easy to find several characters: a renter or several renters, a landlord, a narrator, and perhaps one or more newsboys. The class or workshop should divide into groups of five or six and, working as teams, each group should plan and rehearse a minimum of six different group readings of the poem. Arrange yourselves as you wish. Use onstage focus; use offstage focus; combine onstage and offstage focus. Use chairs, stools, benches, stands, stepladders, boxes, and what you will. But make each arrangement strikingly different. For example, one possibility would be to have five renters, a landlord, and three newsboys arranged as in Figure 1.

FIGURE 1.   One seating arrangement for *The Landlord*

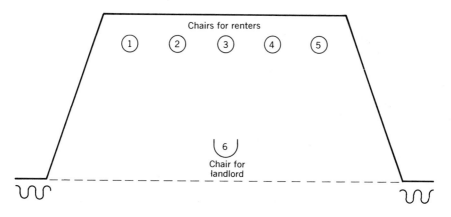

The landlord is seated, his back to the audience, in the downstage center chair. The renters are seated in chairs at the back, each chair representing a house or apartment. One by one, as they speak, the renters descend on the landlord until he is almost encircled by them. Finally, after the fifth complaint, the landlord stands up, comes around in front of his chair, and calls for the police. The dramatization ends with the three newsboys, seated in various parts of the auditorium, standing and singing out the headlines. As an alternative way of staging the production, with five chairs across the back, the landlord could stroll from stage right to stage left, being verbally abused as he walks past each imagined house. The possibilities are infinite, including such platform arrangements as these:

1.   #6
    #1   #5
            #2   #4
                #3

and with #6, Landlord, seated with his back to the audience.

2. #1   #6
        #2
            #3
                #4
                    #5
                        Newsboys

With this arrangement, you may wish #5 to move to or at least toward #6, Landlord, as he reads.

A few suggestions on voice arrangements—and keep in mind that each reader must make us see and hear a character, an individual, a definite person and personality:

1. Cast of three:
   a. Stanzas 1–5 read by one renter.
   b. Stanza 6 read by landlord.
   c. Remainder read by one narrator.

2. Cast of four or more:
   a. Same as above.
   b. Same as above.
   c. Stanzas 7 and 8 read by a narrator.
   d. Headlines read by one newsboy.

3. Cast of seven or more:
   a. Each of the first five stanzas read by a different renter.

b. Stanza 6 read by landlord.

c. Stanzas 7 and 8 read by one narrator, or read chorally by the five renters.

d. One newsboy on the three headlines, or three newsboys, one on each headline.

In short, be creative. Use your imaginations in deciding on assignment of lines to be read, on interpretation, on platform arrangements, on characterizations, and on movement. Use the platform area—or if you wish, the entire theatre or room. But make the material *live* as a group interpretation. Some of the ideas will work; some will not. But through experimenting you will see how one creatively approaches the task of adapting and presenting a literary selection in a Readers Theatre medium.

Adapting dramatic literature: the stage and radio play

Often the play is the easiest form to adapt because it is written expressly for oral presentation. The main problems are to cut it to an acceptable time limit and to translate the visual elements into words. In its original form, the typical play can be performed in approximately two hours or slightly less. For Readers Theatre, as previously explained, this running time is usually reduced to about an hour or an hour and a half. The intense concentration demanded by this oral art form makes it difficult to hold an audience much longer, even with an intermission. However, full-length productions are becoming increasingly popular, and some adapter/directors now use the time and length of a conventional theatre show with one or more intermissions. Recent full-length productions have been given of *The Mikado, Skin of Our Teeth, Lost in the Stars, Medea, The Visit, The Dybbuk,* as well as such Shakespearean plays as *The Merchant of Venice* and *The Taming of the Shrew.*

In adapting a play for Readers Theatre, the adapter usually assigns one role to each reader. However, if there are a number of minor roles, a reader may interpret more than one character satisfactorily by making each one quite distinctive. This requires skill in characterization. Through facial expression, body tonicity, vocal quality and rate, as well as what the character says and the way he expresses his ideas and feelings, the reader must make clear the identity of the character he is playing at any given moment. The goal is to distinguish the characters so clearly that there is no doubt in the minds of the audience that they are different characters. Since it is difficult for readers to remain unobtrusive, sometimes it is preferable to double up on small roles if the characters can be clearly projected, rather than to have a large number of readers on stage who seldom enter the action. The audience should accept the fact that a reader is playing more than one role. However, whether or not to double up is a decision for the director to make. The adapter cuts as many of the minor roles as feasible, and occasionally gives some of their lines to other characters, if this can be accomplished without harm to the text. Suffice it to say, there must be no doubt in the minds of the audience as to the identity of any character at any given moment.

In preparing the script, the adapter need not retain the act and scene divisions of the original play. The narrator can provide a bridge from one segment to another and describe the action that is not inherent in the lines. If an intermission is needed, the adapter or director should select a suspenseful or climactic point at which to break in upon the progression.

At the beginning of the script, the scene must be set, the characters introduced, and the information supplied for the audience to understand what is occurring. This is usually done by a narrator who may or may not be a character within the script. Often a minor character, maintaining the role he is to play, can fulfill the duties of a narrator. Some directors use two narrators. In *Under Milk Wood,* Dylan Thomas wrote two narrators into the script. For short scenes from plays, major characters may introduce themselves and set up the situation. For instance, in the famous wooing scene from *The Taming of the Shrew,* both Katherine and Petruchio could talk in character directly to the audience, giving the necessary information that would allow them to understand, visualize, and appreciate the scene. Whatever means are used to solve the problems of narrating the visual elements, making the transitions from scene to scene, and bridging any cut portions, the actual wording should be concrete, vivid, and written in spoken-English style. Moreover, the style of writing should be appropriate to the text itself.

To demonstrate how the problems of narration may be handled in an actual script, let us examine in some detail an adaptation of the Spanish play *The Women's Town* (or *The Woman Have Their Way*) by Serafín and Joaquín Álvarez Quintero. The character of Dieguilla served as the narrator; and since, in this instance, the original playscript had been cut to thirty minutes, this minx-like servant girl not only introduced herself and the other characters and set the scene, but also narrated the preliminary action. She provided this introduction in a storytelling manner and in character.

DIEGUILLA. (*To audience.*) Buenas noches. Good evening. My name is Dieguilla, and tonight we (*indicating herself and the others*) want to tell you the story of *The Women's Town,* or *Pueblo de las Mujeres.* It takes place in the Spanish house of my good friend, Don Julián Figueredo, the parish priest of the Women's Town. The action occurs in the combination patio and reception hall. (*With descriptive gestures.*) Here the ceiling is vaulted, and the floor is of red tile. It is a plain room with little furniture, but a large glass door leads into a beautiful garden with whitewashed walls, red brick walks, trees, and lovely blooming plants in pots all painted blue. The patio is a cozy enclosure, cool and very pleasant. It is night and in the month of June. The time, the present. (*Her manner and tone become confidential.*)

I work as a servant here. As I mentioned before, Don Julián is my very good friend. But his deaf sister, Santita—who lives here with her two daughters, Ángela and Pilar—is not such a buena amiga. She thinks me a little flirt and a little disobedient. (*Shrugs.*) And she is not a little wrong. (*Briskly; changing her tone.*) Now let us meet some of the people in *The Women's Town,* and then we'll be on to our story about how the women have their way. (*She approaches the various characters as she introduces each in turn.*) First, Don Julián and his sister, Santita. They are both more than sixty and less than sixty-five years of age. Don Julián hears all there is to be heard, since he confesses most of the women in the town; and Santita hears absolutely nothing, for she is deaf. But she understands gestures and lip movements perfectly. Just the same, her manner is one of constant observation and suspicion. Here we have Adolfo Adalid, a handsome young lawyer from Madrid and the hero of our story. Bueno, no? Concha Puerto, a very pretty lady but very meddlesome—in other words, the town gossip. Ángela and Pilar, the young, teen-age daughters of Santita. And Pepe Lora, a dark, suspicious youth, is the rejected suitor— rejected by (*indicating*) Juanita la Rosa, the rosebud of the town. Accompanying Juanita is her patronizing aunt, Doña Belén. (*In disgust.*) Ay, caramba! (*Shrugs, smiles at audience.*) Now, you have met the people who play a part in *The Women's Town.* And so, as I promised you before, our story. (*She moves to a new position and resumes in a narrational manner.*) Earlier this evening our hero, Adolfo, came to visit the good Don Julián and request a favor. It seems that Adolfo's uncle had recently died, and when he passed away, left all his papers badly mixed up. So Adolfo, being a lawyer, was summoned from Madrid to put his uncle's business in order. To begin this task, he had to have a letter of introduction, and this was the favor he asked of Don Julián. Although they had never met, Don Julián was very glad to be of service. However, as Adolfo was about to depart on an important errand, Don Julián pointedly mentioned a rumor he had heard in the town—a rumor that the handsome young lawyer had lost no time in finding some (*insinuatingly*) feminine diversion. Adolfo, all injured innocence, protested that he did not know of what or of whom Don Julián was talking. Don Julián replied that it was already apparent to many people that a certain girl who lives on the other side of the street—and who was accustomed to coming to Don Julián's casa evenings—had turned Adolfo's head with her pretty eyes. Adolfo, of course, denied this rumor, too. (*With a sly, amused chuckle.*) Little good it did him, though; for once the feminine population of the Women's Town make up their minds about something, that's the way it is. (*Suddenly peering off.*) Ay . . . but Concha Puerto, the town gossip, is coming now to visit Don Julián.[9]

Even easier to adapt than the conventional playscript is the radio play because, as in Shakespeare's plays, all the action and environment have

9 Serafín and Joaquín Álvarez Quintero, *Pueblo de las Mujeres* or *The Women's Town, Four Plays in English Version,* trans. Helen and Harley Granville-Barker (New York: Little, Brown & Company, 1928).

been included in the dialogue. Notice, for example, how Shakespeare skill-fully and swiftly sets the scene for Lorenzo's speech to Jessica in Act V, Scene i, lines 54–59, of *The Merchant of Venice:*

> *How sweet the moonlight sleeps upon this bank!*
> *Here will we sit and let the sounds of music*
> *Creep in our ears: soft stillness and the night*
> *Become the touches of sweet harmony.*
> *Sit, Jessica. Look how the floor of heaven*
> *Is thick inlaid with patines of bright gold.*

A radio script might reveal time and place in this manner:

NARRATOR. On Washington's Birthday, February 22, 1842, in Springfield, Illinois, Lincoln spoke to the people of that city.

In the radio play, environmental information might be provided as in the following passage:

NARRATOR. Yes, I remember the day very well. It was a bleak afternoon in November—one of those melancholy days when the sun and clouds inter-mingle reluctantly in a drab autumn sky.

Among the radio plays most frequently used for Readers Theatre are those of Norman Corwin, such as *Mary and the Fairy* and *My Client Curly,* and Archibald MacLeish's "The Fall of the City." Stephen Vincent Benét's delightful Christmas play, *A Child Is Born,* also makes an excellent script for presentation in this medium.

Adapting prose fiction

As seen above, the play and the radio script, having been written for oral presentation, are already in dramatic form, and to become a Readers Theatre script require only cutting to a manageable length and rewriting the portions of scenic embellishments, overt physical action, and perhaps some other scenes into descriptive narration. Preparing a script from prose fiction makes many more demands. Prose fiction is written to be read silently. It is told through narration, description, dialogue, inner mono-logue or "inner thinking," indirect discourse, and sometimes authorial com-mentary. Often the length is unwieldly for oral presentation. Just as a moviemaker selects and "orders" from the totality of the book, so the Readers Theatre adapter needs to decide on the portions of narration nec-essary to keep intact the story line, the theme or statement on life, the descriptive elements essential for painting the picture of settings and char-acters in the audience's mind, the necessary interior monologue as well as the outward dialogue, and the portions of the plot to be enacted. Some-times it is even necessary to rearrange the order of events. The guiding factor in these decisions is the point of view from which the author has chosen to relate his story. The point of view—the vantage point from which the events are seen—affects tremendously who tells what.

The first step in adapting prose fiction is to read the text carefully for its impact, for the type of response it draws forth; this response should remain the same for the adapted script. It is well to write down the original response so it will not be lost during the labor of cutting and molding the fiction into a form suitable for oral presentation. One should be aware not only of the attitude of the author toward what he has written, but also of what the story actually accomplishes through its comments on life, on truths, and on values. Keeping these facts in mind, the adapter's next step is to ascertain *how* the author has worked toward his goals. Here a major guiding principle is the point of view the author has chosen. This will guide the adapter in determining the function of the narrator and who will speak the various lines.

Determining the speakers. To determine who should say what words, it is necessary for the adapter to understand the various types of narrators and their points of view. The *function* of the narrator in the story is one of the most important elements in prose fiction and is of great importance in determining who shall say the lines. At times the narrator can be represented by more than one person to reveal different facets of his personality or to show him at different ages.

The position of the narrator also varies according to the *person*—first, second, or third—in which the story is written. Only first- and third-person points of view are frequently found in prose fiction. Both can take different forms, depending on the involvement of the narrator in the action. A major participant telling the story in first person is the protagonist and is usually fully dramatized. Such a narrator is found in Dylan Thomas' "A Christmas in Wales." A minor participant, such as the narrator in Melville's *Moby Dick,* is an involved witness, but may not be as fully characterized as the protagonist. A third type of first-person narrator is the witness who is a nonparticipant in the action, as in Faulkner's "A Rose for Emily." Often he is not strongly characterized and is less subjective about the events than the first two types because he merely observes the action.

There are also three major types of third-person narrators. The third-person narrator may be omniscient in that he can see into the minds of all the characters, as in Tolstoy's *War and Peace.* The adapter of the Readers Theatre script may allow the character himself to say those words of the narrator that reveal his own inner thoughts. A second type of third-person narrator is the one whose omniscience is limited because he sees into the mind of only the major character, as in Joyce's *Portrait of the Artist as a Young Man.* The third type is the objective observer, the "camera eye," who is outside the story. The narrator in Hemingway's "The Killers" is this type of objective observer. None of his lines may be assigned to the characters because they are completely objective.

The complexity of point of view, revealing as it does the positioning of the narrator in the story (whether central or peripheral to the action), his degree of subjectivity or objectivity, the importance he gives to the events, and the degree to which he is developed as a character, demands that the adapter make a close study of the narrator and the use the author has made of him. If he is truly to illuminate the author's work, the adapter must use the narrator as he is used in the story.

As an example of how the point of view guides the adapter in determining the speaker, look at a multiple-omniscient scene such as those found in Virginia Woolf's *To the Lighthouse*. Perhaps no narrator other than the characters themselves would be needed. Each character could read not only his dialogue, but those portions of the narration and description seen from his point of view. Or one might use a narrator for some portions and enter the minds of the characters in other portions. (See example, pp. 187–188.) Cognizance of the way the first-person involved narrator in William Carlos Williams' *The Use of Force* recalls an incident from his earlier days could lead the adapter to use two narrators in this story, one for the older doctor and one for his younger self. The director should be aware of the distancing of the older doctor's narration, the remembrance of time past having lost some of the emotional fervor of immediacy, and of the younger doctor's emotional and immediate involvement in the action of the event.

The answer to the question, "From whose intelligence are we receiving these words and insights?" will guide the adapter/director in assigning the portions read by each character and in determining how they are to be read.

This way of determining adaptation and presentation of prose fiction from the point of view of the narrator has been called "Chamber Theatre" by Robert Breen. As Breen defines it, this type of group theatre is the most similar to conventional theatre on the Readers Theatre continuum.[10]

The "A" position on this continuum is the most limited form of Readers Theatre—employing stools and lecterns, scripts in hand, offstage focus, and no overt movement, and aiming almost entirely at the imagination. The "Z" position, on the other hand, employs enacted scenes with onstage focus, memorized lines, minimal staging, and a narrator integral to the prose fiction script. How does this latter form remain in the realm of Readers Theatre, rather than conventional theatre or a dramatization of a story? It retains the epic mode; that is, it leaves in the narration, description, explanations, as well as dialogue, and it retains the past tense if that is how the original was written. It features the role of the narrator; thus those stories in which the narrator has a major role or is psychologically close

---

10 See Robert S. Breen, "Chamber Theatre," Supplement VII, *A Course Guide in the Theatre Arts at the Secondary School Level*, rev. ed. (Washington, D.C.: American Theatre Association, Inc., 1968), pp. 107–10. See also Bacon, *The Art of Interpretation*, pp. 416–25.

to the protagonist are most often used. Another distinguishing feature is that the characters often speak indirect discourse as though it were direct discourse. Although the characters in the scenes use onstage focus, the narrator often addresses the audience directly, using onstage focus only when he actively participates in a scene.

As has been noted above, there are ways of assigning lines to the readers other than having one narrator give all narrative and descriptive portions while individual readers interpret the dialogue of the characters. Mentioned previously was the method of assigning to the characters from whose points of view the ideas came the nondialogue portions—narration, description, and indirect discourse. Sometimes a narrator and a character can divide the narration, even splitting a sentence between them. For example, in *Henry and Ribsy* the narrator, speaking of Henry, says, "He began to think," and Henry, with a thoughtful look on his face, picks up the narration with, "If only he could keep the dog! He had always wanted a dog of his very own and now he had found a dog that wanted him." (See pp. 248–258 for complete script.)

In Henry and Ribsy, *Henry sits dejectedly on the bus, the dog Ribsy beside him, as the other passengers laugh at his expense. Note especially how the two lead readers employ facial and bodily expression to reveal characterization and viewpoint.*

The following cutting from Edith Wharton's "Roman Fever" shows how prose fiction as opposed to the play form reveals the complex motivation of characters, the descriptive elements which create setting and atmosphere, the descriptive elements which describe action, and the attitude and emotions which would be difficult to put into dialogue but which can be conveyed through descriptive narration. Note that the speakers often speak narration that reveals their thoughts.

MRS. SLADE. I horrify you.

MRS. ANSLEY. I wasn't thinking of you. I was thinking—it was the only letter I ever had from him!

MRS. SLADE. And I wrote it. Yes, I wrote it! But I was the girl he was engaged to. Did you happen to remember that?

MRS. ANSLEY. (*Dropping her head.*) I'm not trying to excuse myself; I remember.

MRS. SLADE. And still you went?

MRS. ANSLEY. Still I went.

NARRATOR. Mrs. Slade stood looking down on the small bowed figure at her side.

MRS. SLADE. The flame of her wrath had already sunk, and she wondered why she had ever thought there would be any satisfaction in inflicting so purposeless a wound on her friend. But she had to justify herself. (*To* MRS. ANSLEY.) You do understand I'd found out . . . and I hated you. I knew you were in love with Delphin . . . and I was afraid, afraid of you, of your quiet ways, your sweetness . . . your . . . well, I wanted you out of the way, that's all. Just for a few weeks, just till I was sure of him. So in a blind fury I wrote that letter. . . . I don't know why I'm telling you now.

MRS. ANSLEY. I suppose it's because you've always gone on hating me.

MRS. SLADE. Perhaps, or because I wanted to get the whole thing off my mind. (*She paused.*) I'm glad you destroyed the letter. Of course I never thought you'd become seriously ill.

NARRATOR. Mrs. Ansley relapsed into silence and Mrs. Slade, leaning above her . . .

MRS. SLADE. . . . was conscious of a strange sense of isolation, of being cut off from the warm current of human communion. (*To* MRS. ANSLEY.) You think me a monster.

MRS. ANSLEY. I don't know. . . . It was the only letter I had, and you say he didn't write it?

MRS. SLADE. Ah, how you care for him still!

MRS. ANSLEY. I care for that memory.

NARRATOR. Mrs. Slade continued to look down on her.

MRS. SLADE. She seemed physically reduced by the blow . . . as if when she got up, the wind might scatter her like a puff of dust.

NARRATOR. Mrs. Slade's jealousy suddenly leapt up again at the sight.

MRS. SLADE. All these years the woman had been living on that letter. How she must have loved him, to treasure the mere memory of its ashes! The letter of the man her friend was engaged to. Wasn't it she who was the

Monster? (*To* MRS. ANSLEY.) You tried your best to get him away from me, didn't you? But you failed and I kept him. That's all.

MRS. ANSLEY. Yes. That's all.[11]

It is the use of the narrator and narrative description which divorces Readers Theatre most convincingly from conventional theatre. There are many ways of handling the narration. The adapter may have a character pick up words of narrative description from the narrator and the two read a word or two together. This overlapping marks the transition into the mind of the character. Some narration and description may be given by a chorus speaking individually or collectively, as explained in the account of *Dandelion Wine* below. Assigning the speakers requires careful thought and a thorough study of the points of view revealed in the literature.

Cutting the material. After the overall meaning and theme of the fiction have been examined, the point of view determined, and decisions made on the manner of handling the narration and the number of narrators to utilize, the material must be shaped into a unified whole within a reasonable time limit for presentation. The most satisfactory procedure is to read it again with the idea of "cutting in" or marking those scenes and lines that must be included if the selection is to retain its full significance. Once these steps have been taken, the director may start "cutting out"— that is, omitting those scenes not essential to the basic meaning or scenes that can be summarized in narration for the sake of brevity. Often bridges must be written to retain continuity. These must preserve the style of the author and explain the time and place of the next segment if it has changed. The adapter should select carefully those details of description that will best stimulate the imagination of the audience to see the characters, their appearance and actions, and the setting in both its physical appearance and its mood values. Portions of the description may have to be cut. Proper names may sometimes be inserted more frequently than in the original as an aid to clarity. Some description of movement, gesture, or facial expression can be replaced with suggested action on the part of the reader. The adapter/director can use many such means of retaining the essence of the longer work in the cut-adapted version.

The adapter/director should remember that the vital script contains a number of fully developed close-up scenes. The term "close-up" is familiar to any moviegoer. In that context, it refers to a scene which is supposedly of special significance to the story and for which the camera is zoomed in very close to the actors' faces in order that the lens may not only capture minute details—the twitching muscle, the eyes widening in fear, the worried crease of the brow, the defiant thrust of the chin, the lips inviting a kiss—but may also *magnify* these meaningful manifestations. In

---

11 Edith Wharton, *Roman Fever and Other Stories* (New York: Charles Scribner's Sons, 1964), pp. 9–24. Copyright 1934, renewed © 1961 by William R. Tyler. Reprinted by permission of A. Watkins, Inc.

Readers Theatre the term "close-up" is used to describe a scene which is sufficiently infused with significant details to generate a strong empathic response from the audience and thereby assure its deep emotional involvement. A scene, in contrast to a summary, is filled with interaction of characters which is often predominantly written in dialogue, although it may be described. The length of time in a scene is normal time in that it lasts as long as it takes for the scene to occur, whereas in a summary time is condensed—many years may pass within a few sentences. Of course, in description of scenes and characters time stops and there is no forward movement, but in description of action the story progresses even though the time may be longer than the actual time required in the performance of the physical action.

The adapter should not select only strongly dramatic scenes. A balance of tense and relaxing, quiet and climactic scenes is needed to give light and shade to the performance. It is better to select fewer scenes and develop them well than to skeletonize the text. As mentioned above, long portions of the material must occasionally be cut and a bridge written to make a smooth transition from segment to segment. And to reiterate, enough narration and description must be retained to preserve the style of the author, to make the scene vivid, and to provide those special insights into motivations that can only be inferred in a conventional play.

The adapter/director, then, "cuts in," "cuts out," and "adds." He retains all elements essential to conveying the plot, character development, interaction, theme, and style of the author. He cuts out what is nonessential either through omission or through alterations achieved by summarizing, suggesting through action, or changing locale through movement on stage from one area to another. All of these changes from the parent material should be in the spirit of the text and should be unobtrusive.

Ray Bradbury's *Dandelion Wine,* which was presented at the 1960 convention of the Speech Association of America, can serve as a useful model to illustrate some of the basic principles which may be followed in adapting a novel. Bradbury's book is made up of a series of incidents that occur during one summer in a small town, and many of these incidents involve characters that are seen in only one episode. The main characters—those seen in successive scenes—are two young boys, Tom and Doug, who are enjoying summer and helping their grandmother make dandelion wine to brighten winter days.

Although this novel is too long to use in its entirety, there are several threads in the story which can be followed to make a unified script of the proper length. For instance, a number of episodes deal with machines: the time machine, the happiness machine, the fortune-telling machine, the trolley car, the Green Machine (as this forerunner of the automobile was called), and the machine for making dandelion wine. Another thread running throughout the story concerns time: the past which still lives in Colonel Freeleigh's head and the past that never was for old Mrs. Bentley, who the children said could never have been a little girl; there is the time for rug cleaning, for dandelion-wine making, for the first mowing, for saying good-bye, for dying. Another theme is that of rites and rituals. For Tom and Doug, the two young boys, all of living seems to be made up of rites and rituals. In the first of these symbolic rites, on the day after school is out, we see Doug standing in the third-story cupola bedroom of his grandmother's house, commanding summer to begin. This is followed by the ritual of making the first batch of dandelion wine, which is, in turn, followed by other rituals, including lawn mowing, rug beating, putting up the front-porch swing, lemonade making, and buying tennis shoes. Still another theme is that of discoveries and revelations. Doug discovers one day that he is alive. After the death of Colonel Freeleigh and Great-Grandma, he also discovers the saddening thought that someday he, too, must die.

Although any one of these threads could have been used as a unifying device in the adapted script, the one that seemed to enfold most of the others—and the one finally chosen—was the theme of discovering the joy in being alive and the saddening thought that we must eventually die. Accordingly, scenes were selected to develop Doug's declaration: "I am alive." Other scenes were chosen to bring out the antithetical thought: "I must someday die." These scenes were used as close-ups. The idea of rites and rituals, particularly of dandelion-wine making, was used as a secondary unifying device. As each episode in the story was concluded, another bottle of wine was placed on the shelf, lovingly labeled so that on some wintry day this bottle would recall this particular day of summer.

The script opened, as does the book, with Doug's ritual of awakening the town to summer and closed eventually with his sending the townspeople off to sleep on the last day of summer. Many of the book's scenes could not be worked into the adaptation, of course, but a few lines from excluded segments were selected and inserted at appropriate places in the final script. An example was Tom's delightful response to Doug's worrying about the way God runs the world. Tom, after thinking a moment, replied, "He's all right, Doug. He *tries.*" In its final form, the cast included: (1) the characters who handled scenes in dialogue; (2) a narrator who commented upon the story and the action and vocally set and changed the scenes; and (3) a group of voices that evoked moods, made comments, and narrated events somewhat in the manner of a Greek chorus.

An example of a bridge that was created to link two close-up scenes was the one leading from the death of Great-Grandmother to Doug's fever dream. This passage illustrates how the adapter may employ a variety of voices to present narrative material rather than assign long passages to a single reader. In this particular bridge, composed of dialogue between Doug and his thoughts, the thoughts were vocalized by the chorus, each member speaking alone, rather than in unison as in choral speaking.

DOUG. Here it is, all written down in my nickel tablet: "You can't depend on things because . . .

753336

VOICE ONE. Like machines . . . they fall apart or rust or run down.

VOICE TWO. Like tennis shoes, you can run so far, so fast, and then the earth's got you again.

VOICE FIVE. Like wine presses. Presses, big as they are, always run out of dandelions, and squeeze, and squeeze to a halt."

DOUG. "You can't depend on people, because . . .

VOICE FOUR. They go away . . .

VOICE FIVE. People you know die . . .

VOICE FOUR. Friends die . . .

VOICE SIX. Your own folks can die."

DOUG. So . . . (*with a big breath*) so . . .

VOICE ONE. So if wine presses and friends and near-friends can go away for awhile or go away forever,

VOICE TWO. Or rust,

VOICE SIX. Or fall apart,

VOICE FIVE. Or die,

DOUG. And if . . . someone like Great-Gran'ma . . .

VOICE FOUR. Who was going to live forever . . . can die . . .

DOUG. Then . . .

VOICE ONE. Then, you, Douglas Spaulding, someday must . . .

DOUG. Then I, Douglas Spaulding, someday must . . . no!

VOICE ONE. Colonel Freeleigh . . .

VOICE FIVE. Dead!

VOICE ONE. Great-Gran'ma . . .

VOICE SIX. Dead!

DOUG. Me! No, they can't kill me!

VOICE FOUR. Yes.

VOICE TWO. Yes.

VOICE SIX. Yes!

VOICE FIVE. Yes, anytime they want to . . .

VOICE ONE. No matter how you kick or scream . . .

VOICE TWO. They just put a big hand over you,

VOICE FIVE. And you're still.

DOUG. I don't want to die!

VOICE SIX. You'll have to, anyway.

VOICE ONE. You'll have to, anyway.

VOICE SIX. Write it in your notebook, Douglas.

VOICE FOUR. "I, Douglas Spaulding, someday must . . ."

DOUG. "I, Douglas Spaulding . . . someday . . . must . . . must . . . (*very small*) die."[12]

Placing all of the narration in the present tense heightened the immediacy of this particular story. Using many voices rather than a lone narrator in descriptive passages, as well as in part of the narration, made the pro-

---

12 Ray Bradbury, *Dandelion Wine* (New York: Bantam Books, Inc., 1959), pp. 142–43. For the complete script, see pp. 205–32.

duction more vivid, allowed for greater variety, and assured better balancing of the lines for the readers. Speeches ranged in length from one word to a page or more, although both of these extremes occurred infrequently.

Many vocalized sound devices were used in this production of *Dandelion Wine*. When Doug lay ill and the day seemed interminable, one voice ticked off the time while other voices told of the scenes going through Doug's fevered brain. The sound of this relentless ticking counterpointed the rising excitement in the other voices as the fever caused wilder and wilder ideas to surge through Doug's mind. The scene was climaxed by voices singing "Shall We Gather at the River?" in harmony at first, then in the discordant sounds that the feverish Doug was presumably hearing. Singing was also introduced when Colonel Freeleigh was recalling Civil War songs. As each song came to Colonel Freeleigh's mind, a voice sang a portion of it, as though far away.

This Readers Theatre script of *Dandelion Wine* was arranged for six readers, each reading two or more specific characters as well as being a voice in the chorus. The printed program, the contents of which are reprinted on page 204, listed the characters involved in each scene and named the respective interpreters reading those roles. Each scene had a title, as did the two major divisions of the script. Because it showed the basic structure of the adaptation and supplemented this with information about the author of the novel, the program was a useful guide to the audience.[13]

Other recent productions have been arranged of such novels as Peter S. Beagle's *A Fine and Private Place,* Carson McCullers' *Ballad of the Sad Cafe,* Don Robertson's *The Greatest Thing Since Sliced Bread,* and J. D. Salinger's *Franny and Zooey.*

These comments on cutting and adapting a novel apply also to the short story, which is probably the most popular type of prose fiction to be adapted for Readers Theatre presentation because of the ease of fitting it into a necessary time limit. The range of stories which have been adapted for Readers Theatre is wide: from Rainer Maria Rilke's "Gym Period," Sholom Aleichem's "Gymnasiye," and Stephen Leacock's "The Errors of Santa Claus," to the simple and touching "Leaves That Fall" from *Bambi* by Felix Salten.

Regardless of whether the adapter/director is working with the short story or the novel, his overall goal in preparing and presenting the script is to so illuminate, clarify, and vivify the literature that it becomes a meaningful, pleasurable, aesthetic experience for the readers themselves and for the audience.

---

[13] For an approach to another type of longer fiction, see Leslie Irene Coger, "Let It Be a Challenge—A Readers Theatre Production of *Up the Down Staircase,*" *Dramatics Magazine,* February 1969, pp. 11–14.

This university presentation of Ray Bradbury's Dandelion Wine *employed a five-level unit platform, a few stools, and a symbolic time-machine. In the top photo, Doug conducts the awakening overture; in the middle photo, he cries out during the fever dream; and in the lower photo, Pawnee Bill points out the buffalo herd.*

Adapting poetry, essays, letters, and diaries

Poetry, too, may be adapted for Readers Theatre. Long poems can furnish provocative and stimulating materials for a full-length program, and shorter selections may be interspersed with other literary materials or combined for an evening's entertainment built around the life and work of one author. An example of the latter is *An Evening's Frost,* presented off-Broadway in 1965. A very moving, effective, and fully rounded script can be developed from Peter Bowman's *Beach Red,* a story of war which describes the attitudes and feelings of soldiers with such intensity and vividness that both readers and audience become excited participants in this concentrated adventure. Milton's *Samson Agonistes* has been adapted to a fifty-minute script that, when presented, is vital theatre. Dante's *Inferno* also makes a stirring script, as does W. H. Auden's *Age of Anxiety*.[14] Many short poems likewise lend themselves admirably to group readings, among them Amy Lowell's "The Day That Was That Day," Robert Frost's "Home Burial," Roy Helton's "Old Christmas Morning," Christina Rossetti's "Goblin Market," Phyllis McGinley's "How Mrs. Santa Claus Saved Christmas," Robert Graves' "Not at Home," Sidney Lanier's "The Revenge of Hamish," and T. S. Eliot's "Sweeney Agonistes"—all of which tell a story through dialogue. Although there is no dialogue in Federico Garcia Lorca's "Lament for a Matador," it provides the basis for a powerful script; in fact, a whole program of Lorca's poetry is effective. For a program on Lincoln, Millard Lampell's *The Lonesome Train* is especially suitable and permits the inclusion of a ballad singer and square dancing, if desired. On the whole, poetry that tells a story with dialogue is easier to adapt to Readers Theatre, but nondialogue poems have also been read successfully in this medium.

Letters, essays, and similar materials require special handling if they are to be used successfully. To convert an essay into appropriate material for Readers Theatre, it is usually necessary to add characterization to the lines. In order to have some action or conflict or at least a degree of contrast, more than one point of view needs to be represented. This opposing attitude or outlook is also required when a script is read by more than one person. For example, the Corey Ford essay "How to Guess Your Age,"

---

[14] William B. McCoard, "An Interpretation of the Times: A Report on the Oral Interpretation of W. H. Auden's *Age of Anxiety,*" *Quarterly Journal of Speech,* 34, no. 2 (April 1948), 174–76.

although originally written as if it were spoken by one man, can be presented as though two men were standing in a bar, exchanging comments on how the world is changing. "The Ten Worst Things About a Man," from Jean Kerr's *The Snake Has All the Lines,* can in similar fashion be divided between the husband and the wife. (See pp. 278–282.) In adapting Addison and Steele's *The Spectator Papers,* a secretary can be added so that conversation can occur between her and Sir Roger de Coverley. Letters should be arranged to tell a story, to reveal a change in awareness between the recipients, or to allow the audience to perceive a progression from one state of awareness to another. *Eneas Africanus,* by Harry Stillwell Edwards, and *Dear Liar,* a professional production based on the letters of George Bernard Shaw to Mrs. Patrick Campbell, illustrate ways in which letters can be arranged to tell an entertaining story. Diaries also should contain a story line, reveal character progression or regression, or unfold successive new perceptions. Mark Twain's *Adam's Diary* and *Eve's Diary* have been combined to reveal the thoughts of the first man and the first woman on a series of identical topics, to manifest their growing awareness of each other, and to tell the story of their expulsion from the Garden of Eden. (See pp. 233–238.) More information on the use of these genres is contained in the next section.

COMPILING A SCRIPT

In the preceding discussion we have examined ways in which a Readers Theatre script may be built from a single source of prose or poetry. However, some of the most exciting Readers Theatre performances result from compiled scripts consisting of materials of various genres taken from many sources but given contextual cohesion. Many factors can unify the compiled script. It may explore a theme or idea, illuminate the dimensions of an author's work, provide insights into a period of history, class of people, or geographical section, or tell a story, as did *Chrestus Felix—Perspectives on a Spring Weekend Close to the Year 33* A.D., which told the Christ story through selected readings of prose and poetry.[15] The range is limited only by the creativity and ingenuity of the adapter/compiler. There can be a kaleidoscope of materials so organized that the contextual arrangement forms a gestalt giving a total effect greater than the sum of its parts. The juxtaposition of materials makes telling statements, provides insights, points up incongruities, and, through interaction of parts and interaction with the mind of the audience member, becomes a unified theatre piece. These elements—unification, cohesion, focus, and point of view—are necessary in the compiled script. If the performance is "theatre" it must be

---

15 Presented by Memphis State College at a Southern Speech Association convention.

given a dramatic framework, allowing for interaction of personae or of personae and audience. The script "What Shall I Tell My Children Who Are Black?" is a good example of a group of varied points of view given focus through the responses to the question asked by the persona of Margaret Burroughs' poem of the same title. The persona asks the question over and over, and each time someone gives her a different answer, selected from the works of various black writers. The *interaction* comes between the speaker of the poem and the speakers in the various pieces of literature. The voices of the past answering the cry of the present make this a dramatic script, make it theatre.[16] To create a dramatic framework, the adapter of "A Wilde Night," Sheila Reiter, created imaginary characters from the life of Oscar Wilde during his days at Trinity and at Oxford, plus an American who had heard Wilde lecture and a London society figure. Through research she found the opinions held by his classmates, the reactions of Americans to his tour, and the response of London society to his life and works. From this research she constructed dialogue revealing the pertinent information. To introduce Wilde's writings, she used letters to his friend Lord Alfred Douglas that expressed ideas and referred to happenings that could have inspired the writing of the fiction. This framework gave a composite picture of Wilde's life and writings from various points of view through the dramatic interaction of characters who had known him. It allowed the writings of Wilde to be explored and illuminated in a theatrical format.

Another factor needed for the presence of theatre in a compiled script is a sense of progression, a building to a point of awareness, an insight—what Bernard Beckerman would call an "ah-ha" moment of intuition. A compiled script whose cumulative power progressed to such a moment was entitled "A Casual Approach to Violence," and was presented at an American Theatre Association convention in Minneapolis by Macalester College. This script found its theme in an editorial by Norman Cousins in *Saturday Review* entitled "A Casual Approach to Violence." (See p. 99.) The various selections explored the way Americans in their choice of toys for children, in their advertisements, and in their popular songs take a very casual attitude toward killings, bombings, and other forms of violence. The materials came from varied sources. Among other pieces were an ad for Marlboro cigarettes, a song from the musical *South Pacific* explaining, "You have to be carefully taught to hate . . . ," a description of a prize in a cereal box, a newspaper account of the number of enemy killed, and the hymn "Onward Christian Soldiers." The readers, singers, and dancers, with the skill of a symphony orchestra expressing the nuances of sound, the softness and harshness, the languorous and staccato rhythms, thrust the theme home to the listeners, making them think and feel, sensitizing them

---

[16] For further information on theatre in Readers Theatre, see pp. 5–8.

by means of a vicarious experience. Materials with dramatic possibilities can be found in unlikely places, including any form or combination of poetry, prose, and drama, such as the short story, essay, dialogue, narrative poem, sermon, news item, and editorial.

One all but untapped source is the news column. Among the columnists whose materials lend themselves to adaptation for Readers Theatre are Russell Baker, Art Buchwald, Mike Royko, Goodman Ace, Ernie Hines, Al Hoppe, and Al Martinez. Their satirical columns dramatize easily, as do those of dozens of other such writers. These can be combined with other current materials by using cartoon quips, advertising slogans, newspaper headlines, and other such "from the press" comments for transition purposes. For example, a forty-five-minute program called "From the Printed Page," and various other titles, was performed over a period of several months, with old material dropped and new material added as local, state, national, and world events occurred. Three men and three women, all versatile readers, and all capable of suggesting many different characters and ages, brought the current events to life. Each reader was given a number, and the script opened like this:

(*All six readers stand.*)
FOUR. (*Dramatically.*) Americana 1972!
SIX. From printing press . . .
FIVE. In magazines and newspapers . . .
ALL. We hear America talking!
ONE. The old year's out . . .
TWO. The new year's in . . .
ALL. What gives? (ONE, THREE, *and* FOUR *sit; freeze.*)
SIX. Whatever became of Jack Paar? (SIX *sits; freezes.* TWO *and* FIVE *meet* DC, *Area Two.*)
TWO (REPORTER). May I ask you some questions, Senator?
FIVE (SENATOR). (*Pompous, stuffy, self-important.*) Certainly, young man.

The material for one performance of this ever changing script included the following longer skits: Dialogue from a Brickman "The Small Society" cartoon strip, a Senator with no mind of his own; Russell Baker, "A Day in Our Lives," man's acceptance of daily events which affect him; Ernie Hines, "Inter-Generational Noncommunication," the generation gap; Arnold M. Auerbach, "Love Finds Andy Hardy," heart-to-heart father-and-son talk about pot, the draft, and young marriages; Al Martinez, "Uncle Sam Wants Who?" the draft vs. enlistment syndrome; Art Buchwald, "The Consumer Conspiracy," consumerism; Al Martinez, "Sorry About That, Lord," bureaucracy; Russell Baker, "All Up in the Air," the 747 airplane; and Art Buchwald, "What Is It, Mrs. Perkins?" women's lib and the space program (see pp. 283–285). These nine different scenes, with caustic comment transitions, ended with an item concerning ecology called "Adam and Eve, Ltd.," and these final lines:

TWO. This has been Americana 1972!
FOUR. And all we can add now is . . .
ALL. (*Each holding out his hands in a questioning gesture.*) What next!?

Materials of this type are chosen by professionals as well as amateurs. Fred Allen in his "Allen's Alley" of years ago used timely topics on his radio series. Steve Allen more than a decade ago had great fun on TV with current events. More recently "That Was the Week That Was" had a successful season on TV, and "Laugh-In" has made effective use of short news dramatizations, single-line quips, and caricatures of newsworthy personalities. Current materials culled from weekly or monthly magazines, or daily papers, often more timely in content, should not be overlooked.[17]

Despite the fact that no two compiled scripts are alike, some guidelines may be useful. Psychological principles should be applied in arranging the material. Already mentioned has been the need for progression to a point of awareness. Other factors demanding care are choices of opening and closing materials. Attention should be captured in the opening selection. Something striking, startling, emotionally charged either humorously or seriously, should capture the audience. No bland statement will do this. The concluding piece should round out the script, point up the theme, be memorable, and conclusively elucidate the idea, emotion, and spirit of the total script. Since it is difficult to sustain attention for a length of time with short selections, some longer numbers will aid in achieving continuity and sustaining attention. Variety within the materials chosen makes a more interesting program. Transition material should lead the audience from one mood to another, as a sudden switch of deep emotion is jarring. Often original material has to be written to create the dramatic framework or to effect transitions from one literary selection to another. The exciting results justify the labor of finding and ordering the parts.

In recent years professional producers have been turning to compiled materials. Since the revival of interest in this format the productions of *Spoon River Anthology* and *John Brown's Body, The World of Carl Sandburg, Thurber Carnival, An Evening's Frost, A Walt Whitman Portrait, In White America, Brecht on Brecht,* and *Come Slowly, Eden* have been produced, among others. *Story Theatre* made effective, dramatic use of fairy tales.[18] And the delightful haunting musical *The Me Nobody Knows* was based on poems written by ghetto children. The interest is high and the variety wide. These productions attest to the fact that, while there is no one way to write, adapt, and produce a Readers Theatre script, the successful script calls for a cohesive, dramatic framework allowing for interaction among the personae and/or between the personae and the audience, for

---

17 For an example of how to dramatize a newspaper column, see Melvin R. White, "The Current Scene and Readers Theatre," *Today's Speech,* 15, no. 1 (February 1967), 22–23.
18 See Melvin R. White, "Story—Readers Theatre," *Dramatics,* 42, no. 4 (January 1971), 12–13, 24.

progression from one point of awareness to another, and for the application of psychological principles in the arrangement of selections.[19]

CREATING THE ORIGINAL SCRIPT

From the early years of experimentation in Readers Theatre up to the present time, most performances have been adaptations or compilations. However, thanks to the rapidly increasing interest in this art form, writers are beginning to create new materials especially for this medium. Cases in point are the original work *The Locomotive,* written by Frank Galati, a student at Northwestern University; "Four Women West" by Thomas Turpin, University of Southern California, Los Angeles; and "The Last Summer," by George P. McCallum, an original autobiographical work in the mode of *Dandelion Wine,* first produced at California State University, Hayward. *A Quiet Walk* by Howard Slatoff, also first produced at California State University, Hayward, is an impressive full-length script written especially for Readers Theatre. Another example of an original script was created by a group of students who wished to share with an audience their experiences while touring Europe with the musical comedy *Finian's Rainbow* for the American Theatre Association. This is an excerpt from the script:

VOICE THREE. Then quite unannounced and unexpectedly we were in Munich. Munich—that exciting, bustling city!

VOICE FOUR. Munich, where Hitler began his rise to power. I stood quietly a moment on the vast Nazi parade ground. I went to see the huge World War I Monument in the heart of the city, and the infamous Nazi Brown House that once held Hitler's elite storm troopers.

VOICE FIVE. Munich had everything we expected from an old German city: the royal palace of Ludwig I, with its spacious gardens and huge canals . . .

VOICE ONE. The Glockenspiel in the tower of the Rathaus or city hall . . .

VOICE TWO. The famous Hofbrauhaus and the new gigantic Mathausen Beer garden . . .

VOICE THREE. The pulsating open market place in Marianplatz . . .

VOICE FOUR. . . . And Dachau . . .

VOICE ONE. Dachau! As I stood alone on the grounds of the former concentration camp and heard the wind whispering through the stunted pines, I had thoughts of the thousands of Jewish people who had taken their last breath there. I sniffed at the air, and it was fetid and oppressive; I gazed at the open furnace pits, at the experimental hospital, and at the towering mounds of mass graves left just as they had been, undisturbed through the years. Atop one of the large mounds a tiny yellow flower blossomed. It

---

[19] For other examples of compiled scripts, see Part II, pp. 141–143, 151–154, 188–189, as well as Part III, pp. 286–291.

may have been my imagination or the twisting shadows of the approaching night, but for a moment it resembled the Star of David.

Instruction in the technical intricacies of scriptwriting is not the province or intent of this book. Suffice it to say, it is no more simple to write an original Readers Theatre script than it is to write a new stage play. Each requires creative imagination, literary skill, the insight to draw convincing characters, and the ability to write believable and purposeful dialogue— all imbued with that intangible something called "dramatic sense." But it is a challenging field of endeavor and one well worth the interest of enterprising writers.

PREPARING THE SCRIPT

One of the final steps in adapting material is the preparation of the typed script. This should follow the usual playscript format and should be as complete as possible, although no untried script is actually complete until it has been worked through in rehearsal. However, it is helpful to follow a procedure similar to this: Have a title page listing the title, author, and adapter. The time and place may also be noted. If the script is divided into sections, it is well to list these after the title page. The cast of characters should be provided, with a descriptive phrase identifying and characterizing each. The physical arrangement to be employed should be explained in as much detail as possible. A drawing of the arrangement may prove helpful.

In typing a Readers Theatre script, it is important that the character's name be made to stand out clearly from the dialogue. To ensure this, the character's name is customarily positioned on the left side of the page, and the dialogue extends from it toward the right. Usually the character's name is typed in capital letters. If more than one line of dialogue is used, the extra lines extend from the end of the character's name. They are not placed under it. Brief interpretive notes or suggestions are enclosed in parentheses *within* the passages of dialogue, and longer directorial notes are set off in separate parenthetical paragraphs *between* successive sections of dialogue or narration. Important technical cues are similarly noted. Double spacing is used throughout the manuscript, and the margins should be wide enough for readers' notes, as well as for any script revisions made during exploratory rehearsals. If the script is typed on booksize sheets rather than the usual 8½ by 11-inch typing paper it is much easier for the reader to handle, and it does not become a barrier between him and his audience. A small, neatly typed script with fairly short lines surrounded by space, and with readers clearly noted, is of great importance for ease in handling and reading.

From the foregoing discussion it should be evident that the preparation of a Readers Theatre script can take many directions and many forms, the choices being guided primarily by the nature of the material to be adapted, the time limit of the program, and the skill of the readers. The conventional play and the radio play, originally written in dialogue form for oral presentation, are comparatively easy to adapt, for they usually demand only a condensation in time and a verbalization of the action and setting.

Prose fiction—both novels and short stories—provides one of the largest sources of Readers Theatre material. Key passages must be selected carefully and connecting material or bridges must often be written to link the scenes together. Care must be exercised to retain the proper proportion of the original description and narration in order to reflect accurately the author's style of writing. Moreover, the scenes must be selected and arranged to ensure a rhythmical flow and alternation of tense and relaxed moments. Point of view is a very useful guide in determining who should be assigned the various parts of the script; frequently a character will be assigned the narrative portion that is told from his point of view instead of having an "outside" narrator relate the events. Sometimes, for the sake of variety and for psychological reasons, certain narrative and descriptive passages may be given by a group of readers, somewhat in the manner of a Greek chorus.

Poetry, especially poetry containing dialogue, may be used with good effect. Essays may be adapted, but this kind of literary material ordinarily requires the addition of characterization and more than one point of view. An exchange of letters, being similar to dialogue, can readily be arranged into a successful script; those letters having a strong personal element and a revealing story line tend to work best. Finally, regardless of the nature of the original material, the adapted script should provide insight into the characters and their reactions to the situations within the story; it should progress from one point of awareness to another; it should stimulate an empathic response from the listeners; and it should be self-contained, that is, it should have a beginning, a middle, and an end: a sense of wholeness for the audience. Above all, it should faithfully reflect the literary text(s).

CHAPTER FOUR

The Director Prepares

"This production was really vital—*alive!* Some reading programs I've seen have been so dull and uninspired. What makes the difference?" To no small extent, the answer to this question lies in the director: his knowledge, perception, and skill. A vital, unified, effectively paced presentation is essential to any Readers Theatre venture, and the responsibility for this achievement rests primarily in the hands of the director. It is just as necessary to have a creative director at the helm of a Readers Theatre production as it is in any other form of play production. It is the director who must activate and guide all the elements of the program into a cohesive whole, accurately analyzing the literature and infusing it with the interpretive spark, the pacing, and the "builds" that insure causal progression from its opening line to its final words. And it is the director who must mold the interpretive group into an ensemble that will bring the literature to life in the minds of the audience.

Framed in rather broad categories, the director's tasks may be considered as (1) his analysis of the literature (2) his decision on physical elements to illuminate the script and (3) his directing of the rehearsals. Each is heavily dependent upon the others; the meanings inherent in the literature will determine what must be done in staging and movement for the projection of these meanings. In this chapter, we will concentrate upon script analysis and the physical elements.

ANALYZING THE SCRIPT

It cannot be said too often that there is *no one way* of presenting a Readers Theatre script. No two pieces of literature are identical and no two productions can be alike. A director must explore the material to find its essential nature, form, and meanings and then experiment with many different approaches and techniques to express these by means of the interpreter/ actors in space. As William Archer, commenting on new drama trends in his *Playmaking,* said, "Any movement is good which helps to free art from the tyranny of a code of rules and definitions."[1] Only one rigid rule holds in this medium: the literature itself dictates the form the performance must take. One must be true to the literature.[2] Half the satisfaction and value in working with Readers Theatre is the experimentation with different approaches to find the form within the selection. This search for form has been compared to a sculptor working with his block of marble. He doesn't know what the sculpture will be until he finds it within his marble.[3]

As in all art forms, taste and discrimination will be guiding factors in the creative direction of the Readers Theatre script. And the fact that there are no rigid formulations for this medium does not mean that there are no basic principles and guidelines. There are. In his analysis of the script, the director may take a number of logical steps which will lead him to knowledge and insights helpful to both himself and his readers as they jointly strive to chart for their audience a fresh, meaningful, and memorable journey into the wide, enthralling galaxy of literature.

Determining the meaning

To achieve a successful production in this medium, the director may use many of the techniques of conventional play directing. His methods of studying the script, if it is a play, will be much the same. If it is prose fiction or some other form of nondramatic material he will have other factors to consider such as point of view. Of course, if he has made his own adaptation, he has already made a careful study of the point of view, structure, and meaning of the literary work. If he is not the adapter, he will need to study the total work from which the script was made and note exactly what the adapter has cut and retained to determine in his own mind how these omissions have affected the adapted script. If the script is a cutting of a longer play, the director again will need to study the whole. Even if the director is the adapter, as he begins the duties of directing he will think the script through again. In private, before meeting the cast, he must master the script, comprehend its many facets.

At first it is well for him to read it appreciatively, giving himself to the aesthetic experience. In the second reading, he should be analytical as he searches for the central or dominating idea, the theme of the work, the

---

1 *Playmaking: A Manual of Craftsmanship* (New York: Dover Publications, Inc., 1960), p. 32.
2 See Charles M. Sandifer, "From Print to Rehearsal: A Study of Principles for Adapting Literature to Readers Theatre," *The Speech Teacher,* 20, no. 2 (March 1971), 119. Sandifer reports on a director who said that he would change the spirit of some older works if he felt a contemporary audience needed such a change for the comprehension of theme.
3 Ibid.

principal premise which the author is trying to illustrate through the be-havior of the characters in their environment. He finds, for example, that in *Macbeth,* Shakespeare is saying, among other things, that excessive ambi-tion leads to a man's downfall; Maxwell Anderson, in *Winterset,* declares that love has a redeeming power; Ibsen, in *A Doll's House,* observes that a successful marriage rests on mutual respect; Sophocles, in *Oedipus Rex,* asserts that man cannot escape his predestined fate; Keats, in "Ode to a Nightingale," avers that man does not have immortality as does the beauty found in the song of a bird.

Often the author does not stop with illustrating a theme but may take a psychological, anthropological, sociological, or ideological position with reference to it. In *A Doll's House,* Ibsen was not only concerned with the need for conjugal respect; he was also seeking a reform in the then pre-vailing attitude toward marriage—an attitude which insisted that the woman was but the plaything of the man. The director must decide what the writer's subject is and what he is saying about it. A complex work or compilation may have many themes. The director needs to be aware of them all and of their relative importance. Only with this awareness can he hope to aid his cast in discovering these meanings for themselves.

Ascertaining the attitudes

One of the most important parts of the director's analysis is ascertaining the author's or speaker's attitude as expressed in the material, his attitude toward his subject and toward his audience. This attitude, sometimes called *tone,* is revealed in the author's choice of words—in the affective qualities of those words.

It might be well to pause at this point and define *tone* more fully. Some writers and practitioners use *tone* and *mood* interchangeably. For our pur-poses here we make this distinction: tone equates with *attitude,* mood equates with *atmosphere* or *emotional aura* (which we will discuss later). Recent writing and experimentation tend to reinforce this distinction. In *Understanding Poetry,* Brooks and Warren say:

> The *tone* of a poem indicates the speaker's attitude toward his subject and toward his audience, and sometimes toward himself. The word is, strictly speaking, a metaphor, a metaphor drawn from the tone of voice in speech or song. In conversation we may imply our attitude—and hence our true mean-ing—by the tone in which we say something. . . . Tone, in a poem, ex-presses attitudes.[4]

Armstrong and Brandes, in *The Oral Interpretation of Literature,* define tone

---

[4] Cleanth Brooks and Robert Penn Warren, *Understanding Poetry* (New York: Holt, Rine-hart & Winston, Inc., 1960), p. 181.

. . . as the attitude of the writer toward his material and his audience. Therefore, an analysis of the tone of a selection will lead the student to the emotions that the poet has used to surround his ideas. There is no limit to the shadings of tone that an author may choose from. . . . Tone may also be spoken of in the terminology used to classify emotions, for the poet may be angry, sad, joyful, hateful, proud, and the like.

We are continually taking attitudes toward what we say in our daily conversation, thereby imparting shades of meaning to what we say by our *tone* of voice.[5]

Before the director can hope to bring out the particular attitudes in a given work, he must first study the material to ascertain the author's attitude or tone and then decide how this may best be expressed. The author's attitude is usually revealed in his choice of words. For example, in *Hamlet,* Shakespeare establishes a tone of gloom by using metaphors referring to decay and corruption, both physical and moral. When the director starts rehearsing, he will make certain that his interpreters, through their use of the expressive human voice, through proper intonation and inflection, are able to "read out" or elicit the changing attitudes within the piece. Similarly, in reading Edwin Markham's "The Man with the Hoe," the interpreter must express the speaker's indignation, his outrage at those who have caused this unfortunate man to become the abject thing he is. In reading the poem "Departmental," the interpreter must manifest Robert Frost's satirical attitude. In Donne's "The Canonization," he will want to reveal the alternating tones of exasperation, irritation, ironic banter, and defiant tenderness.[6]

Although the voice is the main vehicle for communicating the attitudes in the text, it alone cannot always effectively convey them. The director must help his readers to become totally involved—both in mind and in body. The mind must comprehend the particularities of the experience, and the reader must so enter into the experience that his face and body manifest his inner feelings. For instance, the reader of William Rose Benét's "The Skater of Ghost Lake" might respond to the mysterious aura of the setting and events of the poem in the following ways: The reader leans forward as Jeremy skates with long, lean strides across the ebony ice; he tenses as Jeremy hears the faint, mysterious, whirring sound; he relaxes for a moment as Jeremy recognizes his sweetheart; he tenses again in response to Jeremy's vague, impinging fear; he hears the roar of water in his ears as Jeremy sinks down and down in the deep, cold lake. By thus em-

---

5 Chloe Armstrong and Paul Brandes, *The Oral Interpretation of Literature* (New York: McGraw-Hill Book Company, 1963), p. 255.

6 Cleanth Brooks, *The Well Wrought Urn* (New York: Harcourt Brace Jovanovich, Inc., 1947), p. 174. For a valuable discussion of attitudes, see also Don Geiger, *The Sound, Sense, and Performance of Literature* (Glenview, Illinois: Scott, Foresman and Company, 1963), Chapter 2 and pp. 83–84, 93.

pathically entering into the particularities of the poem, the reader has experienced it, has responded to it mentally, emotionally, and physically.

In analyzing prose fiction, the director must orient himself and his subsequent emphasis to the point of view from which the story is told and the relationship of the narrator to the events, as well as his attitude toward them.

Identifying the mood

The director should also take careful note of the predominant mood, the prevailing atmosphere, of the literary work. Although this atmosphere is determined in part by the setting or locale, it is more than that: it is the emotional aura which the work possesses and which guides the reader's expectations and attitudes. Ibsen's *Ghosts* opens in an atmosphere of gloom, which is intensified by the darkness and the cold rain. Poe's "The Raven" has a pervading mood of gloom and despair. The dominant mood of Stephen Crane's "War Is Kind" is bitterness; of "High Flight" by John Gillespie Magee, Jr., exultation. Although one mood will prevail, it may vary throughout the poem. Or the mood may change entirely. In Thomas Hardy's poem "When I Set Out for Lyonnesse," the speaker is at first lonesome and unhappy; gradually, however, this dissatisfaction changes to radiant joy. In other words, the emotional aura of the first stanza fades away and gives place to a new feeling in the third stanza. The author's choice of words and imagery sets up these moods. The director of the Readers Theatre script must first become aware of the emotional variations and then must induce the readers to ring out the varying moods through changes in muscle tone and vocal elements—tempo, pitch, intensity, volume, and quality. This variety maintains the attention of the audience and evokes from it an empathic response to the mood of the literary selection.

Analyzing the characters

One of the most important tasks facing the director is that of analyzing the characters through whom the author presents his theme. Not only must the director know what the characters are, what their personalities and potentialities are, but he must also be aware of what *makes* them what they are.

The first determinant in analyzing a character is his relationship to the situation and his emotional involvement in it. Is the character the protagonist or the antagonist? If he is neither, with which of these is he aligned? What has he to gain or lose by a change in the situation?[7] A knowledge of

---

[7] Curtis Canfield, *The Craft of Play Directing* (New York: Holt, Rinehart & Winston, Inc., 1963), p. 48.

the character's place in the action will elucidate many useful facts about him.

The second major determinant in analyzing a character is his motives. *Why* the character says and does what he does reveals more about the type of person he is than his actual words and actions. This *why* evolves from the major desire or desires of the character. Not only must the director know what this basic drive or major desire is, but he must also be aware of any obstacles in the character's path to achieving this desire, and he must understand how far the character will go to attain the goal. For example, Medea was so intent on taking revenge upon Jason that she killed her children; although this caused her pain, it was the surest way of hurting Jason. The character's potentiality for action and his basic desire determine the response he seeks from the other characters and provide important clues as to how his lines should be read.

Both the character's place in the action and his motives will, of course, shed light on his personality. In seeking further for the sources of these motivations, the director will want to study the character's educational and social background, his profession and nationality, age and sex. The director should be aware of the character's intellectual acumen, his emotional depth and stability, and his degree of maturity. He should ask what the character laughs at and what he is moved by. And perhaps the most important question he should ask is, "Does he change as a result of the action in the script—and how?" Answers to these and similar questions guide the director and the reader in interpreting the lines, in providing the degree of casualness or intensity needed to project the character's emotional responses to the situations in the script. Finally, having determined the character's place in the action, his motivations, and his personality traits, the director must, in turn, see to it that his readers clearly understand the characters and their interrelationships and convey them with maximum effectiveness to the audience.

If the character is the narrator in prose fiction, not only will the director need to know all of the above information, but he will also need to determine what type of narrator he is; that is, whether he is first- or third-person with their variations, how he functions in the story, and how reliable and unbiased he is in his telling of the story. The various types of first- and third-person narrators have been discussed above in adapting prose fiction. (See pp. 48–57.) The director must understand the precise nature of the narrator in order to guide the reader/actor playing this role. Directly proportionate to the degree of emotional involvement is the narrator's activity in the story. For example, the account of an accident told by the driver of the car involved would differ from an account of the same accident observed by a stranger from a third-story window. Both the physical involvement and the passage of time from the occurrence to the relating of the accident would temper the degree of emotional involvement of the narrator. The driver of the car would be more emotionally involved than the unaffected observer.[8] The narrator's reliability will guide the reader/ actor in the truth and believability with which he will deliver the lines. The narrator's use of the past or present tense will dictate the degree of emotional immediacy in the reading. In prose fiction the director will also study the author's use of inner monologue and his revelation of the motivations for action, and will see that the reader/actors convey these to the audience. Thus we see that the direction of prose fiction poses special problems for the director beyond those inherent in dramatic literature per se.

Studying the structure and author's style

The director should study the structure of the writing and become thoroughly familiar with the elements of the author's style. He needs to know each step in the plot development, the specific function of each component and its relationship to the entire script, the prevailing emotion of each portion and the emotional response it should engender in the audience. He needs to know where the high point of interest is, the factors that build suspense, the clues or forewarnings of the outcome that have been written into the material. In prose fiction he will note the ordering of the parts, the time sequence used—whether it is chronological, flashback, or projected into the future. He will note the author's use of description: how he introduces characters and setting and relates them, creates emotional responses to the characters, establishes the emotional aura of the scene, and advances or retards the action. The director's awareness of how the author achieves his effects will be made evident in the responses he elicits from the readers. Moreover, he will need to make a careful study of word choice, word order, and sentence structure. He must note how the author uses parallel sentences, periodic sentences, antithesis, figurative speech, sense imagery, and rhythm. Often the meaning and atmosphere of the piece are inherent in the recurring use of images and connected metaphors. The imagery can clarify and illuminate the work.

The director will need to be especially alert to the sound or auditory values in the script: the author's employment of onomatopoeia, alliteration, assonance, consonance, and other repetitive devices. He must be sensitive to the music made by words, the tunes and cadences within the language. Being aware of the images and the aural values of the author's special use of language, the director will encourage the readers to underscore them, to make these devices count with the audience. He will point out to them that rich verbal texture demands stylistic verve in the reading, that both the cognitive and connotative impact of the words must be projected. For instance, in Vachel Lindsay's "The Congo," the director must elicit from the readers strong rhythms, response to the images, a vocal montage. To achieve these goals, he must first recognize these elements in the writing.

---

8 See Joseph Satin, *Reading Prose* (Boston: Houghton Mifflin Co., 1964), p. 351.

In this respect the director's task is not unlike that of the symphony conductor or concertmaster. A significant part of the delight in Readers Theatre comes from this symphony of sound.

Outline for dramatic analysis[9]

For literature written from the narrative point of view these questions will guide the director in his analysis, and the answers will dictate his approach to animating the script in the Readers Theatre medium.

1. Who is the speaker?
   a. What are his physical, emotional, intellectual, vocal, tonal, cultural, and expressive attributes?
   b. What is his relation to the action? Usually he will be a first-person participant or nonparticipant—either major or minor character— or third-person observer or participant with or without omniscience.
   c. What qualities has the author bestowed on him?
      (1) Is he dramatized or undramatized?
      (2) Does he comment on the action or remain silent?
      (3) Is he reliable or unreliable?
      (4) Is he an observer or a narrator-agent?
      (5) Is he omniscient? If so, to what degree?
   d. The point of view may shift so that what is true about a speaker at one point in the story may change in another. Are there shifts in the point of view in the story you are analyzing?
2. To whom does the speaker speak: a general audience, specific audience, audience of the self, combination, some other audience?
3. Where is the speaker: at the scene of the action or someplace other?
4. When is the speaker speaking: at the time of the action, after the action, before the action?
5. What does the speaker say in the literature, be it a short story, novel, poem, letter, diary, journal, essay, or drama?
   a. Who is the "story" about and what is he like?
   b. To whom is the "story" directed?
   c. Where does the "story" take place?
   d. When does the "story" take place?
   e. What is the "story" about? What does it mean?
   f. How is the "story" presented?
   g. Why is the "story" presented?

Note that these questions concern the story that the speaker (narrator) is telling.

---

[9] For the ideas in this outline the authors are indebted in part to Geiger, *The Sound, Sense, and Performance of Literature,* and to Wayne C. Booth, *The Rhetoric of Fiction* (Chicago: The University of Chicago Press, 1961). For further discussion, see Paul Campbell, *The Speaking and the Speakers of Literature* (Encino, California: Dickenson Publishing Company, Inc., 1967).

6. How does the speaker say what is said?
    a. What genre does he use: lyric, epic, or dramatic?
    b. What are the characteristics of his style: diction, literary devices, implicit or explicit information?
    c. How does he use scene, summary, and description?
    d. Does he narrate (tell) or reveal the action through scene (show)?
    e. Are there any other special characteristics of his manner of relating the story?
7. Why does the speaker say what is said? For personal satisfaction? To present a moral? To teach? To shed light on human nature? For psychological, sociological, or historical reasons? To share insight, knowledge, or opinion? To entertain? For other reasons?

The depth and length of this analysis will vary with each piece of literature. Knowledge of this kind will help the director achieve a meaningful oral presentation of the narrator and other characters by improving his grasp of their motivation for action, the points to be made if the story is to be understood, the causal relationships of events, the tonal quality of the production, and the response expected from the audience. This information will influence decisions on the appropriate paralinguistic expressions (vocal intonations used in expressing the words), type of focus, movement (overt and/or covert), and form of staging including setting, costuming, lighting, use of properties, and possibly use of multimedia.

STAGING THE PERFORMANCE

During and after his intensive study of the literature, the director should consider the staging of the performance, the most effective means of conveying its content and value. It has been emphasized that choices in staging will be determined by the material itself—what will best illuminate the interaction of characters, their psychic and psychological makeup, the symbolic action of the text. The director must choose the type of focus, the type and degree of movement, and the visual and aural aspects such as setting, lighting, costuming, properties, and multimedia enhancements. The needs of the text will also guide the director in deciding the place he will choose on the continuum of Readers Theatre forms. This continuum ranges from placing readers on stools behind lecterns with manuscripts and off-stage focus to enacting all scenes but the narration with memorized lines and onstage focus. (See p. 50.)

Focus

It is the director's responsibility to determine the type of interpretational relationship and contact the readers are to have with one another during the performance. This is a realm of Readers Theatre in which imagination and experimentation are particularly valuable. A key factor in this contact,

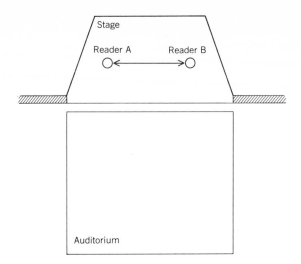

FIGURE 2.   Onstage focus

of course, is the eyes of the readers, for the eyes are what establish focus. The three possibilities from which the director can choose are onstage focus, offstage focus, and a combination of onstage and offstage focus.

Onstage focus means that the readers relate to each other on the stage, sensing each other's presence, sometimes even turning to the person being addressed and actually establishing eye contact. (See Figure 2.) It should be apparent, of course, that the larger the number of readers in a given scene, the more difficult it is to use onstage focus, because each reader has to be able to see and relate directly to all the others. Some directors believe that under these circumstances a semicircular arrangement of the readers provides the most workable solution, but they realize that the audience will have more difficulty in seeing all of the readers if they are placed in this fashion. Other directors feel that the use of various *levels* in the playing space affords a more satisfactory arrangement. Basically, the techniques employed by the director of a Readers Theatre production involving a large number of readers with onstage focus are quite similar to those used by the director of a conventional stage play.

Offstage focus refers to two techniques, the first by which the narrator looks directly into the eyes of the audience, and the second by which the readers envision the scene out in the audience, of figuratively placing the scene of action in the midst of those witnessing the performance. Wallace Bacon, in *The Art of Interpretation,* refers to this imaginary location as *locus.* Offstage focus requires that the character, in conversation, direct his words to the other characters as though they were out in the realm of the audience. The other characters, in turn, speak to him as though he, too, were similarly situated. When the readers are participating in a scene with offstage focus, their lines of vision intersect a hypothetical area about midway out in the center of the auditorium and slightly above the heads of the audience. (See Figures 3 and 4.) This midway point is more efficacious than the back wall because it focuses the scene closer to all segments of the audience. Also, it holds the narration closer to the scene which all of the interpreters are envisioning. Note that the characters are not looking into the eyes of the audience, but rather at the imaginary characters in a scene envisioned out in the realm of the audience. Of course, in some instances the script requires the characters to make contact with the audience directly. The narrator, on the other hand, usually looks directly into the eyes of the audience, but occasionally he looks at the scene, then at the audience, and then back to the scene, as though he were looking and then sharing what he saw with the audience. In addition to permitting the creative imaginations of the audience innumerable options in evoking the scene in their minds, the offstage focus also puts the readers in a full-front stance or posture in relation to the audience, which allows all of their facial expressions to be seen easily.

In The Unknown Soldier and His Wife, *the readers employed onstage focus, establishing eye contact with the other readers and keeping the action on the platform. Note the uniform costumes for all the men except the bishop, whose headgear was changed to indicate different time periods. Projections were used to show shifts of locale and time.*

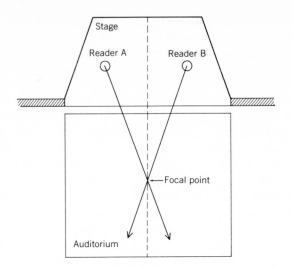

FIGURE 3.　Offstage focus; two readers

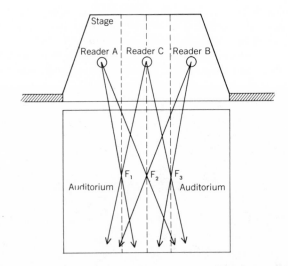

FIGURE 4.　Offstage focus; three readers. The focal point when A and B look at each other is F_2; for A and C, F_1; for C and B, F_3.

In employing offstage focus, the director must emphasize to his readers the necessity for keeping in mind that they are not seeing a specific point or spot somewhere in the audience; they are seeing characters doing something in a definite locality—a scene. The readers can help themselves establish this imaginary scene or picture if they will but fill in the details; that is, in their mind's eye they should be seeing how the imagined characters are dressed, how they are standing or sitting, what they are doing, how they are reacting—what the scene is. For instance, in Roald Dahl's delightful children's story *James and the Giant Peach,* when James first sees the Centipede the latter is lolling on his back with his legs crossed above his knees, a straw hat tilted rakishly to one side of his head. At one point in the script, these characters see tall, wispy men angrily throwing giant hailstones at them, stones that go "ping, ping, ping" as they sink into the flesh of the huge peach. The readers should experience this so vividly that their bodies react to the falling hailstones.[10] In this method of focusing, both the readers and the audience are creating the characters and the scene with their imaginations. In the use of both onstage and offstage focus for scenes, the narration is offstage, given directly to the audience. However, if the focus is offstage, it is imperative that the director make sure—from an outfront vantage point—that at a given moment all readers involved in a given scene are placing that scene in the same locality, that their eyes are consistently directed toward this area, that their focal gaze converges properly upon it. The reader cannot determine this for himself because he is not seeing the person sitting or standing beside him onstage but is reacting to the character role that person is portraying in the imaginary scene which is taking place out in the realm of the audience. The use of offstage focus makes great demands on the concentration and creative imagination of the readers. They must actually "see" the action in this imaginary world at the place selected for their focuses to cross.

As a third possibility, the director may elect *to combine* onstage and offstage focus. Marion and Marvin Kleinau of Southern Illinois University, in discussing scene location through focus, speak of productions that utilize the combination. Their contention is that the imaginary field in which the audience places the scene is a constantly shifting one that is determined by the nature of the literature being read. In descriptive material the audience is more likely to see the scene close to themselves in their imaginations, but in dialogue, with the two readers physically present, the audience probably places the scenes onstage with the readers. This, Marion and Marvin Kleinau say, is hypothetical, as is any theory of audience reaction, but they cite several examples in support of their point of view:

---

[10] For a discussion of kinetic and kinesthetic imagery, see Chapter 5.

Dr. Elbert Bowen of Central Michigan University, in a production of John Cheever's novel *The Wapshot Chronicle,* used change of focus to achieve variety in staging, to heighten humor, and to reinforce the author's use of point of view. Throughout the major part of the production, the readers placed the scene visually in the realm of the audience. But in a specific scene, a parody on industrial psychology which consisted of an interview between a doctor and a job applicant, the two characters seated themselves facing each other, and the scene was suddenly on stage. Dialogue at this point became more direct, with less intrusion by the author; the directness of contact between the two readers heightened the farcical elements in the scene.

Another example may be cited from a Readers Theatre production of *Othello,* directed by Dr. Wallace Bacon of Northwestern University. Some of the scenes were deliberately set on stage and some were set off stage. In the fight between Cassio and Roderigo, Act V, Scene 1, the readers focused toward the audience; but when Iago wounded Cassio *from behind,* without explanation of the stage business in the lines of the text, Iago actually ran up behind Cassio to deliver the thrust. *What happened* was the point here—not what was heard, not what the characters felt at the moment, but what actually happened. The eye was the significant witness at the moment; thus the scene was presented to the eye. Later, in the murder of Desdemona, the director felt that the significant action was the effect, on Othello, of his own action—not the deed itself, but what the deed did to the Moor. The actions were performed—the strangling, Desdemona's struggle—but the scene was focused toward the audience so that the major emphasis was placed upon

Onstage and offstage focuses are combined in Troilus and Cressida, *as the narrator focuses on the readers onstage while the characters envision the scene offstage—in the realm of the audience. Note how the body lines reveal relationships of characters.*

Othello's face and thus on his personal suffering. Here an interesting tension was set up between *physical cues,* which tended to draw the scene on stage, and the readers' focus, which acted to draw the scene into the realm of the audience. This tension, it may be assumed, acted to reinforce Othello's own struggle within the audience member.

Finally, in a Readers Theatre version of *Dark of the Moon,* produced at the University of Wisconsin, Dr. Jean Scharfenberg used focus to isolate and reinforce one of the main dramatic climaxes of the play. Throughout the production, the lines were directed forward toward the audience, but at the climactic moment in question, the two leading characters, Barbara and John, turned and looked directly at one another for the first time. It was a moment of awareness, and the director used the technique of focus in a way to make that moment unique. These productions . . . deliberately made use of the dynamic interrelationship between eye and ear to emphasize certain values and meanings found within the literature itself.[11]

In the final analysis, of course, the director must make the decision on the focus to be employed. Focus should always be handled with great care and subtlety; some directors contend that mixing styles of focus is distracting. If the switching from offstage to onstage focus jars the audience and calls its attention to what the readers are doing rather than keeping its mind on the literary experience being shared, the director is not accomplishing his goal of making the literature the foremost element in Readers Theatre. Through experimentation, the director should find the means that best illuminate the literature being presented.[12]

Perhaps the most important factors in guiding the audience to visualize and experience the scene are the concentration with which the readers themselves visualize the scene and the way they listen to one another. If the interpreters are truly seeing the characters in action in their minds, the audience is likely to do the same. It is this ability to be *in* the scene imaginatively that enables the readers to project that scene to the audience. No action or shifts in focus should break this concentration.

Action and movement

As has been emphasized, Readers Theatre requires *double vision.* Not only do the viewers behold the readers in a physical locale, be it a bare stage or a stage filled with scenic bits, but superimposed on readers and locale is the world of the literature with the special "event" of the text occurring within that world. Peter Brook describes this double vision as he discusses the effect of the use of language, particularly of image-provoking language, in the theatre:

---

11 "Scene Location in Readers Theatre: Static or Dynamic?" *The Speech Teacher,* 14, no. 3 (September 1965), 198. Reprinted by permission.
12 For an interesting theory of the use of focus to feature the text, see Joanna Hawkins Maclay, *Readers Theatre: Toward a Grammar of Practice* (New York: Random House, Inc., 1971), pp. 17–22.

When someone describes to us a street accident the psychic process is complicated: it can best be seen as a *three-dimensional collage* with built-in sound, for we experience many unrelated things at once. We see the speaker, we hear his voice, we know where we are, and at one and the same time, we perceive superimposed on top of him the scene he is describing: the vividness and the fullness of this momentary illusion depends on his conviction and skill. It also depends on the speaker's type. If he is a cerebral type, I mean a man whose alertness and vitality is mainly in the head, we will receive more impressions of ideas than of sensations. If he is emotionally free, other currents will also flow so that without any effort or research on his part he will inevitably recreate a fuller image of the street accident that he is remembering, and we will receive it accordingly. Whatever it is, he sends in our direction a complete network of impressions, and as we perceive them, we believe in them, thus losing ourselves in them at least momentarily.[13]

This psychic process of seeing outwardly and inwardly at the same moment provides the animation in Readers Theatre.

As a general rule, little movement is used when presenting a play in Readers Theatre form, for action would place the production in the realm of conventional theatre. In Readers Theatre based on prose fiction and other forms of literature, however, movement may or may not be used. A distinguishing characteristic (in addition to double vision, which is characteristic of all Readers Theatre) of Readers Theatre based on prose fiction as opposed to conventional plays is the accretion of details in prose fiction as opposed to the simultaneity of the total action in drama. In drama we see the successive stage pictures as a whole, the whole image at a moment. This is not true of the picture in narrative fiction; we see a detail at a time until we have the total picture. As Rudolph Arnheim explains, "A successful literary image grows through what one might call accretion by amendment. Each word, each statement is amended by the next into something closer to the intended total meaning. This buildup through the stepwise change of the image animates the literary medium."[14] This gradual accretion which calls for "closure" for completion produces expectation. Arnheim avers further, "These demands for over-arching connections create tensions that knit the sprawling length of verbal discourse together."[15] Accretion can be compared to a jigsaw puzzle. One by one the pieces interlock to reveal the total picture. These two special characteristics of the viewing of a Readers Theatre performance, the double vision required and, in the case of productions based on prose fiction, the gradual revelation of the picture through accretion, affect the degree, the quality, and the timing of movement.

---

13 *The Empty Space: A Book About the Theatre* (New York: Atheneum House, Inc., 1968), p. 78. Copyright © 1968 by Peter Brook. Excerpts from *The Empty Space* reprinted by permission of Atheneum Publishers.
14 *Visual Thinking* (Berkeley: The University of California Press, 1969), p. 249.
15 P. 250.

A third determining factor in the amount and kind of movement to use is the nature of movement in Readers Theatre. To evoke the mental imagery within the mind which may not be congruent with what is actually seen on the stage, the reader eschews literal movements for suggestive ones. He employs a "behavioral synecdoche." Through enacting a carefully selected portion of the total action the reader evokes on the mental screen of the audience member the action in its totality. Behavioral synecdoche is like the literary term. Instead of saying, "I see three ships on the horizon," the writer invites the participation of the reader in evoking the scene by saying, "I see three sails." No one sees only three sails standing isolated; he envisions the hull of the ships as well as the sails—the total picture. The full action is called onto the mental screen by presenting a selective portion of the total.

Keeping these three special characteristics of action in Readers Theatre in mind—double vision, accretion (in prose-fiction productions), and behavioral synecdoche—let us explore action more specifically. Action can range from covertly expressed inner tension to overt physical movement, depending on which best expresses the complexity of the text. In combination with onstage focus in the staging of scenes in prose fiction, pantomime and overt movement are sometimes used. The narrator often moves about the stage as his function in the text takes him in and out of the scenes. The types of action may take various forms as long as they evolve from the literary text. The extensive nature of action has been discussed above. (See pp. 35–37.) It is imperative that the reader find the proper behavioral synecdoches to parallel, point up, clarify, illuminate, or even contradict in order to establish the tensions, the movements, the gestures within the text. The text is filled with symbolic action—literary action suggesting the action of life—that must be tangibly experienced by both readers and audience. But movement for movement's sake is to be avoided. There need be no fear that readers sitting on stools will become monotonous if the action on the mental screen is sharp and varied, if it moves the minds of the audience from one character to another, from one locale to another, from one type of action to another.[16] The important feature is the action within the script. This does not mean that no overt physical movement may be employed in Readers Theatre, but it does mean that it is not essential to an action-filled performance. Movement in Readers Theatre is used to illustrate psychological relationships among characters, to illuminate symbolic action, and to provide behavioral synecdoches for the stimulation of the imagination of the audience.

In addition to muscle tonicity and facial expression, what types of movement may be used? Of first consideration are those essential to the script.

---

16 Jere Veilleux in "The Concept of Action in Oral Interpretation," *The Quarterly Journal of Speech,* 53, no. 3 (October 1967), 284, contends, "Creative physical action in ensemble interpretation is achieved by manipulating audience vision, not interpreters."

Getting characters on and off stage, or in and out of the scene, is a prime concern. The entrances and exits of the readers must necessarily be more symbolic, and in a physical sense more restricted, than in a conventional play. Of course, characters could come on stage as they would in conventional theatre, but this calls attention to their walking in, on stage, when the scene is actually in the mind. This can be jarring if there are many entrances and exits to be effected. A second way of making known which readers are in and which are out of the scene is to have those outside of the scene turn their backs. A less obtrusive alternative is to have those readers not in the scene sit with lowered heads until their entrances, at which time they raise their heads and "enter the scene." Readers who are immediately involved in a particular scene may stand while the non-participating readers remain seated. The "freeze"—readers holding a position without moving—may be employed to take characters out of a scene momentarily until they are needed again. This is useful if there are a series of short scenes being played in such a way that the action shifts back and forth rather quickly from one group to another. Singling out a set of readers by means of spotlights or other special illumination can designate those who are in the scene. These readers may or may not have moved

Proper muscle tone can give the suggestion of action. This picture of Nothing Gold Can Stay *shows how vivid action and movement can be combined in Readers Theatre with offstage focus. It also reveals the concentration of all of the characters in the scene.*

From Chitty-Chitty-Bang-Bang, *a children's story by Ian Fleming, these two pictures demonstrate the concept of suggested movement and readers' concentration on and participation in the imaginary offstage scene. In the upper photo, the two characters' sitting with their backs to the audience indicates that they have not yet "entered" the scene. In the lower picture, having entered, they now face front—a movement facilitated by the use of swivel stools.*

from one portion of the stage to another. Whatever method is used to convey the highly important information of who is in the scene to the audience, it is imperative that the reader "enter" the scene definitely and at exactly the right moment.

Fluidity of scene progression is an essential aspect of Readers Theatre. That is why the director must make clear where one segment of the story ends and the next begins. He must also make sure that in both an oral and a visual sense the scenes and segments are clearly and appropriately *linked,* that there are no distracting or unexplained gaps. The necessary bridges or transitions may be accomplished in a variety of ways. As has been suggested above, one means of pointing up temporal and spatial changes is through the use of lighting, by either dimming or changing areas that are illuminated. Sometimes a musical bridge is used, or a sound effect. An even simpler device is to have all the readers relax and slightly change their sitting or standing positions before starting a new scene. And, since the introduction of a new plot element almost invariably brings a change in the physical and psychological relationships between the characters, the director may have a set of readers rise or move to a different position on the stage as they lead into a new phase of the story. Clarity is the aim of transitions in both the written script and the production. Indeed, all action and movement should clarify meanings, reactions, and relationships.

PHYSICAL ARRANGEMENTS

As mentioned earlier, Readers Theatre styles of performance form a continuum ranging from readers on stools behind lecterns with manuscripts and offstage focus to readers enacting all scenes onstage, lines memorized except for, and in some cases even including, the narrator's. At one end of the continuum only suggestive action is portrayed through muscular tensions and facial expression. At the other end there is physical movement about the stage space, the major distinguishing feature between this and conventional theatre being the use of the narrator moving in and out of the action, and the retention of the descriptive narration that explores the complex motivations of characters which is found in prose fiction. The director, in determining the physical arrangement, probably will experiment with different approaches until he decides which serves the literature best. And he will consider what use, if any, he will make of settings, lighting, costuming, properties, and multimedia.

Settings

Because Readers Theatre is so much theatre of the mind, of the imagination, and because it is evocative rather than representational, concrete, explicit, and realistic, sets tend to limit the creative options of the audience. There are advantages in having a comparatively bare stage. The world of the literature needs to be created in the mind. No painted set could possibly create "the vast fields of France" on stage as can Shakespeare's words. No theatrical set has ever been designed that could begin to approach the dimensions of the individual imagination. As Peter Brook points out, the absence of scenery in the Elizabethan theatre was one of its greatest freedoms.[17] As in Readers Theatre, it allowed the dramatist effortlessly to whip

---

[17] *The Empty Space,* p. 87.

the spectator through an unlimited succession of illusions, covering if he chose the entire physical world. "The fact is that this theatre not only allowed the playwright to roam the world, it allowed him free passage from the world of action to the inner impressions."[18] The bare stage with its neutral areas allows the space to be not only any physical place, but also a psychic, inner world. No useless elements need absorb our attention at the expense of something more important—a basic tenet of Gordon Craig.

The keynote in staging Readers Theatre is simplicity, not to save money by forgoing elaborate sets, but to enhance and exploit the uniqueness of the form, its utilization of the limitless boundaries of theatre of the mind. A setting really needs only something to stop the eye and define a neutral space wherein the action and moods may be evoked. What form shall this simplicity take? Some scenic experimenters have made valuable suggestions. Gordon Craig, opposed to the realistic set, substituted for it masses of light and shade with different planes that provided a more adequate view of the actors; he asked for suggestive shapes rather than illusionistic details.[19] Terence Gray wanted masses of simple planes constructed of cubes of different sizes fitted together in varied scenic shapes, because to him the set "could be vested with significance only when the business of the stage was in action before and upon it."[20] Norman Bel Geddes contended that the designer should think only of abstract solids and voids. For Readers Theatre, if more than one level is needed to illuminate the text, one could well follow Bel Geddes' concept of space, shapes, platforms, and voids around them.[21]

An example of the use of this simplified, suggestive, abstract space staging is *You're a Good Man, Charlie Brown,* the first professional Readers Theatre-style musical. After an introductory series of solo remarks by various characters in the cast, punctuated by bits of music, the lights came on. "The stage is suddenly filled with light and we at last can see its contents: several oversized, brightly painted objects in simple geometric shapes, and six undersized, simply dressed people of straightforward, uncomplicated characters." As the musical continues, those shapes and areas of the stage become various locales as we are told what they are or see them used in a suggestive way. For example, Charlie Brown has his luncheon sitting on one, and remarks that the PTA certainly did a good job painting the benches. Schroeder is seated at a shape " . . . which slightly resembles a piano. He is engrossed in his playing." Later Charlie is looking at a large,

18 Ibid.
19 Allardyce Nicoll, *Development of Theatre,* 3rd ed. (New York: Harcourt Brace Jovanovich, Inc., 1946), p. 202. Also see Arnold Rood, " 'After the Practise the Theory': Gordon Craig and Movement," *Theatre Research,* 11, nos. 2 & 3 (1971), 81–101.
20 Nicoll, *Development of Theatre,* p. 203. Also see Graham Woodruff, "Terence Gray and Theatre Design," *Theatre Research,* 11, nos. 2 & 3 (1971), 114–32.
21 See p. 186 for a picture of *To Kill a Mockingbird* which illustrates this principle.

The director of Tolkien's Lord of the Rings *assisted his cast by providing a mass of simple planes of different sizes upon which the action could take place. With purposeful use of light, the result was an effective environment of space, shapes, platforms, and voids.*

stiff, brightly colored square of board, and when he says, "I think most of us take newspapers too much for granted," we know what the square board is. The largest object on the stage could easily be mistaken for a doghouse, and we know it is just that when Snoopy enters wearing a white turtleneck sweater, black pants, and sneakers. But if we don't, Patty's first line after he enters tells us: "Oh, Snoopy, you're such a sweet doggy." Pools of light direct our attention from one area of the stage to another, as they dim out in one section and come up on another; the dialogue identifies the scene as we enter it. Charlie Brown struggles with an invisible kite on an invisible string. A sign is flipped over, "The Doctor Is In," and Lucy sets up her psychiatric shop. The geometric shapes become desks when used as desks. The cast puts on baseball caps and gloves, and we know we're at a ball game. Sometimes we don't have to know exactly where we are, so we are not told. If the mood changes, the lights change: *"The scene is dimmed and spotted with evening colors, and airy music is heard.* LINUS *and* LUCY *wander on, looking at the sky."*[22]

---

[22] From Charles Schulz, *You're a Good Man, Charlie Brown* (New York: Random House, Inc., 1967, 1968). Copyright © 1967, 1968 by Clark Gesner. Reprinted by permission of the publisher.

Aristotle considered "spectacle" the least important of the six elements comprising theatrical experience. A few years ago, those interpretation specialists who pioneered in the birth—or rebirth, depending on the viewpoint—of Readers Theatre followed his precepts. Stripping their performing areas of sets, properties, curtains, and even lights, they placed upon it stools, lecterns, chairs, platforms, ladders, benches, crates, stacks of pillows, and other nonillusory scenic bits. These were not to *be,* but to *suggest,* a setting, by providing varying levels, varying heights, varying focal points, places to sit, spots on which to stand and to move. They were used for composition, for relating or separating characters, for focusing attention on key readers or for minimizing the importance of readers at times. A piano bench became a settee, a love seat, a davenport, a car, a bed, or whatever the literature told the audience it was. A longer bench became a train, a garden wall, or a dinosaur. A stool became a chair—or a chair became a stool. A ladder became a radio tower, a balcony for Juliet, a windmill, the top of the Empire State Building, a mountain peak in the Alps, or the top of a pile of turtles in "Yertle the Turtle." *Anything* or *anywhere* the readers told the audience it was when atop the ladder, it became. So it remains today with most Readers Theatre practitioners. Whatever is used should fade from the attention of the audience when the words of the readers transport them into the world of the literature, for it is the setting painted with words that is important.

An illustration of the way in which this neutral space achieves its effect is given by Peter Brook in an account of his experience on seeing *Crime and Punishment.* This account describes not only how the setting worked, but how Readers Theatre can evoke the world of fiction.

All the theatres in the war had been destroyed, but here, in this attic, when an actor in a chair touching our knees began quietly to say "It was in the year of 18– that a young student, Roman Rodianovitch Raskolnikov . . ." we were gripped by living theatre.

Gripped. What does that mean? I cannot tell. I only know that these words and a soft serious tone of voice conjured something up, somewhere, for us all. We were listeners, children hearing a bedside story yet at the same time adults, fully aware of all that was going on. A moment later, a few inches away, an attic door creaked open and an actor impersonating Raskolnikov appeared, and already we were deep in the drama. The door at one instant seemed a total evocation of a street lamp; an instant later it became the door of the moneylender's apartment, and still a second later the passage to her inner room. Yet, as these were only fragmentary impressions that only came into being at the instant they were required, and at once vanished again, we never lost sight of being crammed together in a crowded room following a story. The narrator could add details, he could explain and philosophize, the characters themselves could slip from naturalistic acting into monologue, one actor could, by hunching his back, slip from one characterization to another, and point for point, dot for dot, stroke by stroke, the whole complex world of Dostoevsky's novel was recreated.

How free is the convention of a novel, how effortless the relationship of writer to reader: backgrounds can be evoked and dismissed, the transition from the outer to the inner world is natural and continuous. The success of the Hamburg experiment reminded me again of how grotesquely clumsy, how inadequate and pitiful the theatre becomes, not only when a gang of men and creaking machines are needed to move us only from one place to the next, but even when the transition from the world of action to the world of thought has to be explained by any device—by music, changing lights or clambering on to platforms.[23]

Various devices may be employed to stop the eye and define the space. Sometimes the bare wall of the theatre is all that is needed. This was done off Broadway with the O'Casey script *Drums Under the Window.* It left the theatre free to be various places in the city of Dublin in quick succession. Nothing interfered with the freedom of the imagination. A scrim (a curtain with an open weave) with a dim light behind it gives a three-dimensional picture, and lighting on this scrim can change to help establish mood, to mark transitions, and to give variety. In a presentation of the children's script *Charlotte's Web,* by E. B. White, a huge spider web constructed of white rope was suspended behind the readers. Standing out clearly before black drapes, it was effective and appropriate to this story about a spider. In a production of Feiffer sketches, four reversible freestanding screens stood behind the readers. On one side were the names of the stories to be read. On the other was a cartoon sketch of the leading character in that story. As the story began the screen was revolved to reveal this other side. For a moment the attention went to the drawing, but then it came back to the world of the story. Thus these screens met the demands of purposeful scenic devices for Readers Theatre.

Scenery is effective, then, if it helps the audience enter the world described by the author, if it evokes the mood of that world, and if it makes its impact and then is forgotten. Simplicity in setting best accommodates the evocative nature of theatre of the mind.

Lighting

The purpose of Readers Theatre lighting is to reveal the readers and their environment. But it accomplishes this in many ways. Lighting can focus attention on different areas of the performing platform, produce dramatic effects, project images on walls, theatrical scrim, screens, or cyclorama to aid in pictorial composition, help establish mood, and make key readers stand out from others in a scene. Many who work in Readers Theatre believe that light is the most important single factor in production other than the literature itself and the readers.

---

[23] *The Empty Space,* p. 81.

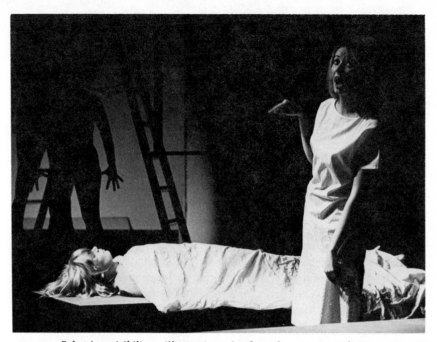

Selective visibility, silhouetting of other characters, realistic costumes, and memorized dialogue enhanced I Never Promised You a Rose Garden, *by Hannah Green.*

The presentational form of Readers Theatre, demanding as it does interaction with and the cooperation of the audience, suggests a further employment of light—light in the audience area. Often the house lights are left on, or are at least only slightly dimmed. The presentational, direct, storytelling nature of Readers Theatre calls for "feedback," for an overt response, from the audience. This interaction of readers and audience is one of the unique features of this type of theatre. Illumination of *all* the participants, both actor-readers and audience members (although it should probably be dimmer within the audience), more readily elicits complete involvement. This principle can be carried even further. Just as lights are subtly manipulated onstage, brightening, dimming, changing colors and areas, so could the degree of light within the audience vary with the degree of direct communication within a specific scene. Scenes composed primarily of descriptive narration would utilize more audience illumination than scenes enacted onstage with little or no descriptive narration. Many directors today are attempting to eliminate a division between audience and actors, and are tearing down the old "fourth wall." Readers Theatre dispensed long ago with that division.

Readers Theatre light is of two kinds, as is regular stage lighting: *specific illumination,* or shadow-producing light, and *general illumination,* or light which does not produce shadows. The problem of the lighting artist is to proportion and manipulate these two kinds of light during a performance.

Hunton D. Sellman divided the functions of stage lighting into five: *selective visibility, revelation of form, illusion of nature, composition,* and *emotional and psychological effects.* These same divisions are also valid for Readers Theatre lighting.

Selective visibility refers to the illumination provided so that an audience can see clearly everything the director intends it to see. It is used to light an area or areas either more brightly, or exclusively, so that the focus of attention is on that portion of the playing area and the readers occupying it.[24]

Revelation-of-form light is modeling light, added to give highlights, shadows, and variety in the distribution of light. General illumination tends to give readers, properties, and the settings, if any, a flat, uninteresting quality. Form is revealed by shadow-producing light, light from specific directions balanced by shadow, and areas of varying degrees of brightness.

Illusion-of-nature lighting, seldom used in Readers Theatre, is provided to create atmosphere by beams of light through windows and doors, imaginary or otherwise, accenting thereby important playing areas and objects, or spotlighting the interpreters. Some illusion can be provided by making use of the angle of the sun or moon, getting normal shadows from the readers and natural shadows from window bars and other architectural units. The more representational a Readers Theatre production becomes, the more illusion-of-nature lighting can be used.

Pictorial composition can be enhanced through a combination of specific and general illumination. This is accomplished by providing light sources which properly highlight objects and readers and produce shadows to form part of the design. It involves ensuring that everything is lighted from the best angle. Such lighting aids design, and is useful in focusing attention.

Emotional and psychological effects involve the symbolic use of colored lights, light and shade, variations in shadows, and the speed with which light changes are made.

Although general illumination, light which does not make appreciable shadows, is the most commonly used method of lighting in traditional Readers Theatre, as more and more theatricalism is being added to the presentation of the literature, more elaborate lighting effects are becoming common. Areas of the stage are picked out of the void to draw attention;

---

24 Norman Bel Geddes in his Elementary Lesson V, one of a series of lectures he gave in New York City in 1927, warned of the necessity for careful planning to control audience attention and mood. He emphasized that lighting has the ability to reveal certain things and conceal others—the power of concentration. For a summary of Geddes' theories and practices of stage lighting, see George E. Bogusch, "Norman Bel Geddes and the Art of Modern Theatre Lighting," *Educational Theatre Journal,* 24, no. 1 (December 1972), 415–29.

attention is directed to different areas by dimming the illumination on one portion of the stage as light is brought up on another portion. Individual readers are given total attention with pinpoint spots. Edward Albee's "The Zoo Story" at the University of Arkansas, for example, was staged with the two readers occupying stools some three feet apart, each singled out by a shaft of white light from a pinpoint spot overhead. As the play ended these spotlights were blacked out, and after a moment of darkness during which the two men made a hasty exit, red pinpoint spotlights singled out the two then-empty stools for perhaps five seconds before a second and final blackout. Projected scenery such as an oriental pagoda for "The Mikado," or a slide of a swastika, or a symbolic cross of light can indicate locale. Motor-driven "effects discs" on projectors create water ripples, fire, smoke, falling leaves, moving clouds, and other such effects. It should be remembered, however, that these can easily become distracting, and should be approached carefully.

Of Professor Sellman's five functions of lighting, selective visibility is the most often seen in Readers Theatre. For example, in the New York production of O'Casey's *Pictures in the Hallway,* the readers did not leave their places at lecterns. The stage lighting, however, focusing individually or collectively, softened or sharpened the impression in response to the mood of each scene. In "I, Diary," a documentary piece on human aliena-

In the scene from The Hollow Crown *in which Ann Boleyn writes to Henry VIII from the Tower before her execution, two playing areas of the stage were picked out of the void to concentrate attention, with lights dimmer in the third area, UC, yet with "the hollow crown" standing symbolically in the background.*

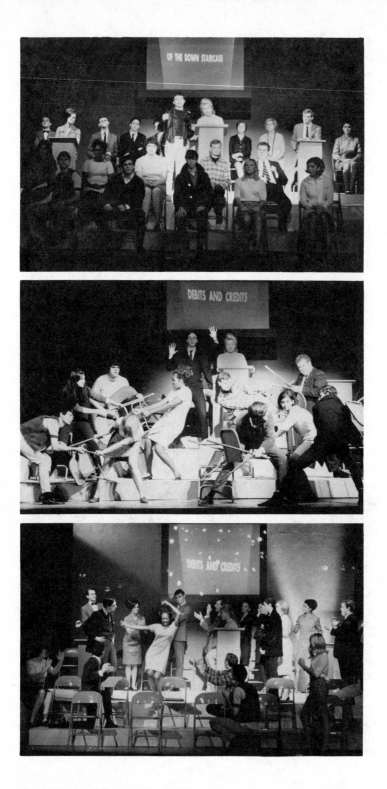

tion produced at Eastern Illinois University, isolated pinpoint spotlights were used in shadows to amplify a lonely face or a limp hand. "Raising and lowering a pinpoint spotlight on faces or forms accomplished a selectivity of image comparable to camera close-ups."[25] In a production of *Up the Down Staircase,* a revolving colored light wheel threw patterns on the stage during a dance scene.

> Lighting was used effectively to suggest mood, to focus attention on important characters, and to give variety to the stage pictures. . . . The three major areas could be lighted as needed. Dimming the lights as scenes changed allowed the projected title for the new sequence to be seen clearly. Spotlights on Alice and on Paul with the rest of the stage in darkness gave a special emphasis to each of them and their thoughts in their letter exchange scene.[26]

In Irwin Shaw's *Bury the Dead,* a spotlight singled out successive characters as they spoke. To emphasize the timeliness of Edna St. Vincent Millay's *The Murder of Lidice,* the readers stood for a moment in silhouette at the beginning while a swastika was thrown on the scrim behind them; then, at the end, the silhouette was repeated, but this time the hammer-and-sickle emblem was projected onto the scrim. James Clavell's "The Children's Story" utilized a similar device, but in this production the American eagle was replaced by a projection of the hammer-and-sickle as the young Communist teacher won the children to her ideology. In *One Flew Over the Cuckoo's Nest* (see pp. 176–177) the effect of shock treatment on the mind of an inmate of a mental institution was enhanced by a blinding white strobe light flashing on and off for the moment of contact, followed by a dull red glow to suggest the aftereffects of a muddled mind. The imaginary characters in the mind of the schizophrenic girl in *I Never Promised You a Rose Garden,* by Hannah Green, always appeared in a red light to separate her fantasies from the real world.

---

[25] Ray Schneider, "Readers Theatre: Experiment in Intimate Literature," *IIG Newsletter,* March 1968, p. 6.
[26] Leslie Irene Coger, "Let It Be a Challenge! A Readers Theatre Production of *Up the Down Staircase,*" *Dramatics,* 40, no. 5 (February 1969), 13.

Three pictures of Up the Down Staircase *show the use of levels, of a combination offstage and onstage focus, and of projection of scene titles on a simulated blackboard. In the top photo the two lower rows are students; on the middle platform Joe Ferone talks to the teacher; in the back row are seated the teachers and administrators. In the middle photo MacHabe breaks up a riot in the cafeteria. In the bottom photo Ella breaks into a dance at the party. A revolving mirror ball throws spots of light upon the scene.*

The atmosphere for this scene from The Murder of Lidice, *based on a poem by Edna St. Vincent Millay, was suggested by the hammer and sickle projected onto the scrim in the background.*

Formal attire for the men, a suggestion of period costumes for the women (with changes in the neck trim on the dresses to suggest character and period), and semistaging in a one-set general locale provided the environment for a compiled presentation, Shakespeare vs. Shaw.

To repeat: Lighting is the most common and most effective device to enhance Readers Theatre presentations, and experience has proved that productions can often be improved by special illumination. But the one essential factor in lighting is that the faces of the readers must be seen clearly. The eyes can help the ears to hear, and audiences can hear better when they can see the readers' faces. Not only must the face of the one who is reading be illuminated, but the faces of all interpreters who are "in the scene" and reacting to the speaker must also be lighted. Further, the presentational quality of Readers Theatre is often enhanced by illuminating to varying degrees those other participators in the production, the audience.

Costuming

The reader's apparel must, of course, be given careful consideration, for it can be very useful in reinforcing characterization. Although in Readers Theatre the audience takes a "double view," sees the reader tangibly before it while at the same time superimposing on him the character described in the literature, the reader's clothing should not distract from what is seen in the mind. Few programs call for special costuming; as a rule, the readers choose appropriate suits and dresses from their own wardrobes and avoid light-reflecting or jangling jewelry. This unobtrusive clothing is essential if one reader is interpreting many roles, as is sometimes the case. Attention should, however, be given to choosing appropriate colors: dark, sombre colors for very serious or heavily dramatic presentations; bright, cheerful material for light or humorous programs. Often the clothing worn by the readers is selected for its character-suggesting possibilities. For example, the group that presented *Spoon River Anthology* on Broadway used basic costumes which were changed by the simple addition of scarves, shawls, and hats; by wearing blouses and dresses with adaptable necklines that could be low for one character and high for another; by quickly altering hemlines by tucking up the skirts; and by using shawls either as a head-covering or as something to be thrown lightly across the shoulders. In a class production of the children's script adapted from Ian Fleming's *Chitty-Chitty-Bang-Bang,* the twins both wore red sweaters, the father a darker coat sweater, and the mother a plain dress. The interpreter who read the role of the green sports car, Chitty-Chitty-Bang-Bang, wore a green sweater. This made a colorful picture for this humorous tale, and at the same time helped suggest the relationship of the characters to the story and to each other.

Some formal literature, such as many of the classics, can be costumed in formal attire: dinner jackets for the men, with matching or contrasting floor-length evening dresses for the women. Another approach, still somewhat formal, is the stylized costume. Usually this reflects an element in the literature such as the period: a Greek play may have costumes with Greek characteristics, such as a long dress draped somewhat in the manner of Greek clothing but not actually reproducing it. For an Elizabethan play,

Ladies Lib *summarized and satirized woman's role throughout the years, and suggestions of period costuming increased the effectiveness of the presentation, as well as assisting in characterizations.*

attire might be tights and slip-on jackets for the men, with long skirts and blouses for the women—suggestions of the Elizabethan, yet not reproductions of true period costumes.[27] This stylization may find its motivation not only in the period, but also in the mood of the play, in the "color" of the literature.

To costume for Readers Theatre, it is well to think in terms of "costume for the mind," and to provide only that which will permit the audience members to see attire in the mind's eye, not characters on a theatre stage in a full-fledged, costumed, produced play. The major point to remember is that costuming should suggest the type of character and the spirit of the literature.

Properties

To use or not to use properties is another question the answer to which is found in the particular piece of literature. Will the use of a literal prop help illuminate the meaning of the story? Will a literal prop fit into the overall production plan? Will the use of a real fan, for instance, interfere in a performance in which the reader is holding a manuscript? Perhaps the

---

[27] For a helpful report on this type of costuming, see Alfred E. Rickert, "Costuming the Elizabethan Play," *New York State Community Theatre Association Newsletter,* May 1971, p. 2.

In Readers Theatre the scripts are often employed to simulate properties—fans, books, newspapers, dishes, and the like. In this case, the scripts are being used as machine guns in A Casual Approach to Violence.

answer is to handle the manuscript in such a way that it suggests a fan. For example, in a production of "A Casual Approach to Violence," the readers simulated machine guns, aiming their scripts at the audience. In this medium where much is left to the imagination, most properties are imagined, too. This does not mean that no literal props may be employed, but rather that only what will best serve to illuminate, clarify, and animate the literature should be chosen. When Baby in "The Death of Everymom" says about her breakfast, "It's on the floor," and then pantomimes picking up her plate and throwing it on the floor, the audience knows and reacts to what has happened. The imagination is a wonderfully creative faculty. With the use of proper behavioral synecdoches most properties will be clearly envisioned by the audience even though they are not actually on stage.

Multimedia devices

Many multimedia devices have been employed in Readers Theatre productions and experimentation with them in recent years has increased. Barbara Kaster writes:

Interpreters should consider using new techniques with the new literature. For example, the simultaneous use of voice, slides, film, and sound may do more to suggest the simultaneous nature of a text than a single reader can demonstrate for an audience. . . . But such techniques need not necessarily be eschewed even with entirely traditional literature. A careful use of slides, sound, and film can be used to help present the order, structure, rhythm, direction, and purpose of the text.[28]

Music and sound effects have been heard from the beginning in Readers Theatre productions. Vocal sounds such as humming or the sounds of a crowd muttering or exclaiming often add a dimension to the scene. However, these auditory elements should not dominate a performance; the author's material is primary. When used, the director must exercise great care and judgment in selecting the appropriate effects and then proceed to integrate them skillfully and subtly into the presentation as a whole. If any kind of auditory effect is to be used as background for the narration and dialogue, its loudness must be tested to make sure that the words of the readers can be heard above it. Well-known music may attract too much attention to itself, but a musical interlude, used with discernment, can often add a humorous note or underscore scenes of romance or tragedy. Elbert Bowen's production of *The Battle of the Sexes,* presented at a convention of the Speech Communication Association, used drums to punctuate and highlight segments of this compiled script. In Robert McCloskey's *Homer Price,* an intriguing original tune was introduced to mark transitions. For *The Reluctant Dragon,* lute music helped establish the ancient time in which the story unfolded.

Other multimedia devices include film, artwork, projections, modern dance, electronic sounds, tapes, or whatever media comes to hand and is purposeful. Care must be exercised, as has been emphasized, to avoid blurring the impact of the literature with these elements of spectacle. Only when the media reinforces the literature should it be employed. An example of effective use of dance was the production of Lorca's poem "Lament for a Matador" in which a dancer symbolically danced the bullfight and, on the lines describing the blood on the sand, let her black, red-lined cloak sink to the floor, red side revealed.

Judith Wray, formerly of Loretta Heights College in Colorado, has experimented extensively with multimedia and Readers Theatre. In a talk at a Western Speech Communication Association annual convention, she said:

I am personally excited about the many experiments in Readers Theatre now taking place across the country. Several years ago I was criticized by purists

---

28 "Massaging the Message: Marshall McLuhan and Oral Interpretation," *Southern Speech Communication Journal,* 37, no. 2 (Winter 1971), 198–99.

because I used sound effects, lighting, and minimal costuming in a production of *Winnie the Pooh* which was presented at the college where I teach. Despite the fact that the capacity audiences of adults and children were enchanted, the critics moaned, "But you were using *theatre* techniques, not Readers Theatre!". . . If audience members talk more about the slides, music, and dance and fail to talk about the poetry, then the program has failed. When staging mixed-media, we throw out more ideas than we end up with. In each case we return again and again to the question, "Does this presentation best portray the meanings and emotions of the poem?" If the theatrical effects begin to take on more significance than the literature we eliminate them. We use film, tape-recorded voices and sound effects, and live voices simultaneously to achieve what I call "fugue effects" with great success. But I stress again: it is the poet's intent that we work to express.[29]

To summarize: Mixed-media staging has both advantages and restrictions, and it cannot be emphasized too often that one's personal enthusiasm should not allow the theatrical elements to run away with the show. With judicious use of visual and aural effects, it is possible to expand sensory appreciation of literary imagery. The audience's delight can be increased by augmenting and enhancing the literature with imaginative effects. But only when sound effects, music, lights, dance, and other multimedia can be used to support, augment, and reinforce the text should they be employed. They must not become more important than the literature.

In any case, the oral interpreter must never forget that his most powerful tool is the human voice—the unamplified human voice. McLuhanesque slides, sound, and electronic gadgetry can, if not used properly, overwhelm the message, change the message. It is the voice and the body of the interpreter that can most deftly enfold, embrace, massage the message.[30]

Use of scripts

It has been pointed out that some directors require readers to memorize their lines and others require readers to use scripts which they carry in their hands during rehearsals and in performance. The script is a convention of the medium and, even though the material is memorized, is usually present. Each member of the professional group presenting *In White America* picked up his bound manuscript from a table in the center of the stage area, glanced at it a moment, put it down, and then spoke from memory. All of these readers were clearly using the manuscript as a symbol. Their material was factual; the presence of the manuscripts established the authenticity of the words.

Sometimes only the narrator will carry a script to show that he is telling the story, that all of the happenings are occurring as he sees them, from

---

29 "Readers Theatre: Advantages and Restrictions of Staging," paper delivered at the Western Speech Association convention, November 1968. Quoted by permission.
30 Kaster, "Massaging the Message: Marshall McLuhan and Oral Interpretation," p. 199.

his point of view. The other characters enact the scenes with lines memorized. It is the psychological principle behind the use of the manuscript that is important. First, as we have noted, it is a convention, just as omitting the fourth wall in conventional theatre is an accepted convention; second, it can show whose point of view is being revealed. For example, in *The Outsiders* (see p. 174), Ponyboy is the first-person narrator. In the end it is revealed that the whole book is the theme he writes for his English teacher. In one production of this novel, only Ponyboy carried a script and then only in retrospect. As he entered a scene as a participant in the immediate action, he left his script at his desk. The show began and ended with him at his desk, writing. The script in the hand may also be made to function meaningfully as a property. For example, it may serve as a letter, a fan, a shield, or some other object referred to in the text if it is used subtly and unobtrusively.

Regardless of whether the script is held in the hand, the material must be so completely mastered that it is memorized. Although the reader may glance at the book occasionally, he must use his eyes to establish his presence in the imagined scene or to establish contact with the audience in narration. He cannot keep his eyes glued to the page nor can he be groping for the words that come next. Mastery—*complete familiarization*—is essential.

If a script is used—and it usually is—some uniformity in size and color is desirable; and if it is to be held in the hand, a small notebook is less obtrusive and easier to handle than a large one. Moreover, a small notebook does not hide as much of the reader's body. Of course, if the script is to remain on a lectern the size does not matter, but if not, it should be firmly backed and bound in such a way that the reader can hold it open in one hand, leaving the other hand free for gesturing. The script should be held out slightly, away from the reader's body, and angled so that the light falls upon it but does not reflect from the white page and distract the audience.

Not all of the readers should turn the pages at exactly the same time, for this, too, may prove distracting. If a character is out of the scene for a long interval, the reader can clip together the pages of the script for those episodes or segments in which he does not participate—or even remove them. However, it is well for him to insert a warning signal at least a page before he is to resume reading so that he will be ready for his cue to reenter the scene.

A presentation of *Iphigenia in Aulis* illustrates how certain physical elements can be synthesized. In presenting this Greek classic, a chorus of three readers wore robes of three different colors that made a pleasing, harmonious picture. Iphigenia was a striking figure in rich red. There were platforms at two levels, with two columns—one on either side—positioned on the upper level to provide a suggestion of the scene. A scrim curtain, serving as a background behind the pillars and platforms, was indirectly

The actor/readers in Clever Gretel *found the small notebooks permitted freedom of movement appropriate to the text.*

lighted. The three readers in the chorus stood on the upper level and read from attractively bound manuscripts which were identical in size and color, and Iphigenia read from the lower level. In this way, the suggested costuming, setting, lighting, and other physical elements generated a visual stimulus that appreciably enhanced the aural stimulus of Euripides' words.

These, then, are the physical elements of a Readers Theatre production: the focus, action and movement, settings, lighting, costumes, properties, multimedia devices, and script. When the director has carefully and discerningly combined them with an effective reading of the lines, he can so illuminate and animate the literature that the readers will have a better chance of bringing out the best that is in the literature of the script and evoking the desired audience response. Whatever is done in the way of using and combining costuming, music, lighting, and set pieces on the stage, everything should be in harmony with the text, and should be utilized to provide insight into the material. The suggestive rather than the explicit, the nonrealistic rather than the realistic, should be employed, as the nonrealistic often allows more options for creativity and greater use of the imagination. The strength of Readers Theatre is that it is, indeed, the theatre of the mind. The goal is to stir the audience members' imaginations, to create in their minds all that the words imply. The very nature of this art form—often with a few characters taking many roles and with scenes shifting as facilely as the written word—precludes rigid realism.

CHAPTER FIVE

Casting, Rehearsing, and Performing

Once the director has analyzed the script for point of view, meanings, attitudes, style, and characterization and has determined tentatively how to handle the various physical elements in staging the production, he is prepared to cast the show and start rehearsals. Much of the movement, of course, will evolve during the exploratory rehearsals.

CASTING THE CHARACTERS

In selecting the readers, the director's prime concern is not their specific physical appearance. Physical type-casting is helpful to audience members in that it aids them to "see" the characters they hear; but of greater importance are sensitivity, a flexible voice and body, and an expressive face. Mobility of facial expression and responsive body tone are essential factors in the reader's ability to project the emotional and intellectual elements of the literary material to the audience. The personal tonality of the reader is another factor. Some readers almost invariably provoke laughter in fellow readers and in the audience and are unable to read a serious role effectively. A story is told that the late Zazu Pitts, an actress whose trademark was her fluttery hands, was once cast in a serious role in the motion picture *All Quiet on the Western Front*. Unfortunately, the film had to be remade with a different actress because the audience automatically laughed whenever Miss Pitts appeared on the screen. The ideal interpreter for Readers Theatre is one who can adapt to the needs and nature of the material, whether it is serious or comic, one who is capable of projecting the "essence," the totality of the character. The reader especially needs a wide vocal and emotional range when he is to play many roles in one script, as is sometimes the case in this medium. The director should, therefore, choose readers who can project variety in vocal quality, thus assuring contrast between successive characters as they are depicted in the text. And, as in casting for any artistic and interpretive endeavor, the reliability of the reader and his enthusiasm for the script are two elements essential for effective rehearsals and performances.

THE AUDITION

To expedite auditions, the material to be read should be furnished to the student. It should be explained clearly that the reader is a talent with many voices, that the purpose of the audition is for the director to learn what voices each reader has, what characters and emotions he can suggest effectively, and that each student is not expected to be successfully all the characters indicated, or to handle with equal skill all of the emotional states requested. But all should be attempted.

Two copies of the information sheet and audition blank on pages 105–108 can be given to each student, one to fill in at the top and return to the director, the second to use during the audition. The audition should not be private; individual readings should be heard by the tryout group.

INFORMATION SHEET & AUDITION BLANK

NAME _____ ADDRESS _____

City _____ Zip _____

Phone _____(home)_____(office)

Sex _____ Marital status _____ Age _____

Profession _____ Height _____ Weight _____

In which aspects of Readers Theatre do you think you are (or will be) especially interested: Writing _____ Acting _____ Directing _____

If employed, where do you work, and what are your hours? _____

_____

Your major _____ Your minor _____

_____

DO NOT WRITE BELOW THIS LINE

_____

NARRATOR: (*Storytelling quality.*) The year was 1944, and the month was October, and Johnnie Hooper III was nine years old, and he was in love with Veronica Lake. He also was in love with a girl named Suzanne Soares (her hair was also long and blond, and sometimes it fell over her left eye, too), but his love for Veronica Lake was much stronger. Suzanne Soares was only eight, and he saw her just about every day. These things made a difference. And anyway, sometimes Suzanne Soares was an awful pill.

CHARACTER NARRATION, MALE: The score was tied—five to three—in favor of us. We needed six runs to win. I was playing second base and right field, as I was too good for one position. My manager says to me—"Mr. Spalding" (I went under the name Spalding in those days; saved me autographing baseballs), he says, "You're next at bat." So I turned to our little batboy, Gerry Nugent, and says, "Gerry . . . " He says, "What is it, Mr. Delehanty?" I says, "Bring me my bat." So Gerry and three other fellows carried my bat over for me.

CHARACTER NARRATION, FEMALE: Last night I dreamt I went to Manderly again. It seemed to me I stood by the iron gate leading to the drive and for a while I could not enter, for the way was barred to me. . . . Then, like all dreamers, I was possessed of a sudden with supernatural powers and passed like a spirit through the barrier before me. . . . The drive wound away in front of me, twisting and turning as it had always done, but as I advanced I was aware that a change had come upon it. I looked upon a desolate shell—with no whisper of the past about its staring walls.

CHILD (*very young*): But Mommy, I don't want to go to bed. (*Whimper.*) You let Jimmy stay up and watch television!

ADOLESCENT: All right for you! I don't care if you do go out with her (him), because I'll never have another date with you as long as I live!

BELLOWING CHARACTER: Get out of here! And don't you ever dare come back! Do you hear me? Get out! !

FRIGHTENED CHARACTER: Who's there? Don't come in here. . . . Don't come near me. (Screaming.) Help! Help! Someone help me!

MIDDLE-AGED MOTHER: (Calling.) I'm here in the kitchen, Jody. (To small boy who has entered the kitchen.) Oh, the Monkey Ward catalog came. Don't lose it, Jody. Your father will want to see it. Oh, Jody, your father wants to see you before you go to your chores.

MIDDLE-AGED FATHER: (Sternly.) I wanted to see you, Jody. Billy here says you took good care of the pony before it died. Billy says you have a good patient hand with horses. . . . If you could have another horse, would you work for it?

UNEDUCATED RANCHHAND: Go outside, Jody. Go outside, I tell you. It'll be too late. (Sharply, loudly.) Turn your face away, damn you, turn your face! (Shouting.) Damn you, will you go now for the water? Will you go?

OLD MAN OR OLD WOMAN (very old): That's how it was in 1875 . . . out there in the wilderness. . . . The smell of bacon and hams ready for travel . . . heavy feel of wagons, ships floundering with goods. . . . Dogs running out to the edge of the wilderness ahead, and, fearful, running back with a look of empty space in their eyes. . . . This is how it was, going West.

CHARACTER HYSTERICAL WITH GRIEF: Save me!
Save me! I didn't mean to kill him! He's my
son . . . why would I kill him? Don't you hear
me . . . he's my son!

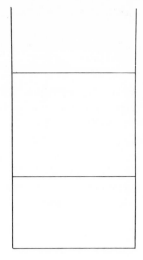

CHOOSE FOUR DIFFERENT CHARACTERS AND
READ THE FOLLOWING FOUR TIMES: Why
are you always picking on me? Can't I do anything
to please you?

Choose a short poem (not a narrative poem)
and interpret it.

INITIAL AND EXPLORATORY REHEARSALS

When the director is satisfied that he has a capable cast, he calls the first
rehearsal. In introducing the script, he may read it to the group, or he may
ask that the cast read it aloud. A good reading by the director does much
to reveal the possibilities within the script and to arouse enthusiasm for it.
However, there is a danger in this procedure, for the readers may think this
is the way each role is to be read and try to imitate the director's interpretation. On the other hand, an "at sight" reading may leave the group
unimpressed with the beauty and strength of the writing. Perhaps a combination of telling the story or plot and reading excerpts from the script is the
best approach; this seems to preserve the excitement of discovery while at
the same time decreasing the dangers of imitation.

It is extremely important that all readers be thoroughly familiar with the
whole script and its original source(s). If the script is a cutting of a longer
work, the readers should familiarize themselves with that work in its entirety. In the selective process, passages may have been cut that could guide
the readers in their interpretation of lines that have been retained, and their
study of these excised passages could give them a deeper insight into the
characters whose lines they will be reading.

On the first reading and for several readings thereafter, the cast should
read in an exploring manner. In other words, they should read with a minimum of expression until they discover the most desirable and effective
expression. Otherwise they may form erroneous vocal and interpretive
patterns that can be difficult to eradicate later. For instance, at first reading
a given character may seem quite gay and merry, and the interpreter will
read the lines with a corresponding emotion. Later, he may discover that
the character actually is heartbroken but is attempting to put up a brave

appearance. Thus, the light-hearted reading would be misleading. This is why it is better to read exploringly, with little expression, until the meaning and emotion back of the words are correctly determined. The director can do much to insure a unified performance if he and his readers explore the script together in this way, with the cast remaining free to express ideas and to ask questions. Each reader should apply the dramatic analysis on pages 74–75 to the script. Then all should discuss their views and come to a decision on the correct approach for this cast to pursue in animating the literature. These discussions should continue throughout the exploratory and growth rehearsals. Changes will usually be made as further insights are achieved.

In trying to determine how best to express the meaning, the readers should thoroughly explore the author's choice of words—their meanings and connotations—and the allusions in the script. A rewarding and oft-repeated question is "What does the author gain by using this word rather than some other?" Note, for example, the varying positive or negative feelings associated with these words: *fastidious, finicky, delicate, scrupulous, hypercritical.* Although their literal meanings are similar, each word carries a different degree of approval or disapproval. These first readings are tremendously important, and with each additional reading the interpreter should develop a more sensitive perception of the material he is reading, a deeper insight into the character he is developing, and an increased awareness of the significance of the action.

REHEARSALS FOR GROWTH

The growth period will require many rehearsals. During these developmental sessions, the readers should continue to evolve their characters, to ascertain motivations, to discover the basic ideas and conflicts, to respond to the imagery and emotions, and to experiment with different ways of expressing them. As the work proceeds, the director will, of course, encourage an interplay among the characters, a verbal hitting back and forth. In a figurative sense, this interplay is somewhat like a tennis game in which the ball is knocked back and forth between the players. The emphasis is upon returning the ball or—in Readers Theatre—upon answering the idea, or registering the character's response to the words he has heard. This interaction is one of the most important elements in bringing a script to life on the platform. Attention will be given to the interaction of the narrator(s) and the audience. Decisions will be made on which portions of the narration should be given directly to the audience and which given looking at the imaginary scene all participants are envisioning offstage in their mind's eye, which portions of narration spoken by characters will be treated as inner monologue and which treated as direct communication with the audience. Experimentation will be made in the type of movement necessary to clarify the events in the story; behavioral synecdoches—physical suggestions of movement—will be selected, or in some instances overt physical movement will be found more effective. Advantages of onstage or offstage focus will be evaluated. As the growth rehearsals continue, the director stimulates, encourages, asks leading questions, and suggests new approaches for the creative activities of the readers. Many exercises for vivifying the reading will be employed. (See pp. 112–115.)

During these rehearsals for growth, the director and the readers should concentrate on *segments* of the material rather than working on the total script over and over. Working in depth on a unit that can be read more than once in the rehearsal period allows more time for ferreting out the meaning. In aiding the interpreters to find symbolic meanings, the director may ask questions or make suggestions that will evoke new insights into the lines, making it possible for the reader to express the meaning and emotion inherent in the words. Once the segment has been analyzed and worked on for details in this manner, it should be read through again without interruption to develop the rhythmic flow, to reemphasize the cause and effect, to allow a build-up in emotion, to create a give-and-take among characters, and to enable the readers to sense progression in the scene.

Usually the script will have sentences and passages which build to a climax, and often these will be divided among several readers. In rehearsing materials of this type, the interpreters should read the total passage *together* until they sense the flow, the movement, and the "build." Then each individual reader should speak his assigned portion of the passage, meanwhile making sure that he retains the special qualities of flow and movement necessary to sustain the ascendancy of the work as a whole. Admittedly, this is difficult to do and requires patient drill.

As an illustration of this principle of reading first with "togetherness" and then with individuality, notice how the following lines from James Thurber's "The Last Clock" were divided among the townspeople:

VOICE ONE. Factories and schools remained closed.
VOICE TWO. Church bells no longer rang,
VOICE THREE. Because the bell ringers no longer knew when to ring them.
VOICE ONE. Dates and engagements were no longer made,
VOICE THREE. Because nobody knew when to keep them.
VOICE TWO. Trains no longer ran,
VOICE THREE. So nobody left town.
VOICE ONE. And no strangers arrived in town to tell people what time it was.
VOICE TWO. Eventually, the sands of a nearby desert moved slowly
VOICE THREE. And inexorably
VOICE TWO. Toward the timeless town,
VOICE THREE. And in the end it was buried.[1]

---

[1] James Thurber, "The Last Clock." From *Lanterns and Lances* (New York: Harper & Row, Publishers, 1961). Originally printed in *The New Yorker*. See pp. 259–267 for complete script.

In rehearsing passages like this, the director will wish to experiment, asking various readers to express the lines until the best "symphony of sound," the best vocal montage, has been gained. Thus the director works with the interpreters so that their voices bring out the full aural values of the material.

The director may frequently have to remind the cast to keep the imaginary scene consistently in the same area of the auditorium. If offstage focus is being used—that is, if the imaginary scene is placed in the midst of the audience—it is helpful to divide the cast into two groups, placing one in the middle of the auditorium and the other onstage. The readers onstage will note that the readers in the auditorium are not concentrated in one tiny spot; that is to say, they are not merely a theoretical dot or pinpoint in space, but physically occupy a visual area of several square feet. Therefore, the readers on the stage will find that they must aim their gaze directly at one of the auditorium characters and then *re-aim* it slightly in order to look at another character in the same group. (See Figures 3 and 4, p. 78.) This adds a very necessary sense of *dimension* to the offstage focus. After seeing actual characters grouped in the auditorium and rehearsing with them in that location, the readers will often find it easier to imagine or visualize them there in later rehearsals and in performance.

The reader should know that his eyes are his most expressive feature and that he must use them to help convey the intellectual and emotional meanings of the writing. The eyes are the main determinant of facial expression, and facial expression is needed in projecting characterization and attitudes. Furthermore, the eyes are used in revealing the reaction of one character to the words of another. Thus, to sustain the desired concentration and visualization by the audience, the readers should not direct their eyes constantly at the script. Moreover, if the eyes are kept continuously on the page, the reader tends to turn his whole face downward, and as a result the sound waves are directed toward the floor and are difficult to hear. The reader should, therefore, keep his eyes as free of the script as possible. This does not mean that he is to ignore the script; rather, he must train himself to grasp the words in a quick glance so that he may use his eyes for expressive purposes.

During these rehearsals, the readers must learn to enter the scene at exactly the right moment. To do this, they must follow the progression of the action and events closely at all times. Each reader must know *why* he is entering, what his mood is, how he feels toward others in the scene, and how he will adapt to them and to "what is going on." Like the actor, the reader must not allow the tempo and volume of the scene to drop on his entrance. To mark a new scene—and the entrance of a character does begin a new scene in that it changes the existing character relationships—the reader scrupulously avoids picking up and imitating the tempo, volume, and pitch of the interpreter who has been speaking immediately prior to his entrance. To enable readers to hear themselves, a tape recording of

In Readers Theatre, the interpreter takes advantage of his entire physical aspect to convey feelings and ideas appropriate to the story. In this scene from the compiled script Mother to Son, *note how the readers employ flexible facial expression to reveal characterization and attitude.*

their performance near the end of the period devoted to growth rehearsals is of great value.

Vivifying the reading

Reading that is alive—vivid—must be the mutual goal of the director and the readers. If the cast is inexperienced, it may be necessary during the rehearsal period for the director to assist them in improving their interpretive skills. In order to bring the script to life, the readers must bring out each nuance in the writing, each significant shade of meaning.

Responding to the image. One way to accomplish this is for the readers to make the descriptive passages come alive so vividly in their own minds that, through their concentration on the mental images of the scene, they will cause the audience to experience very similar images. The audience will tend to think with the reader, being guided by the manner in which he interprets the lines. This responding to the image or "thinking with the senses," the term used by Lowrey and Johnson in their book *Interpretative Reading*,[2] helps the reader gain an empathic response to the literature, which in turn stimulates the audience to a similar response.

In "thinking with the senses," the reader imagines, at the moment of

---

[2] Sara Lowrey and Gertrude E. Johnson, *Interpretative Reading* (New York: Appleton-Century-Crofts, 1953), p. 30.

speaking, that he is experiencing with his own senses the sights, smells, sounds, tastes, tactile sensations, and movements described in the text. He smells the roast pig, the honeysuckle, the ether. He tastes the sauerkraut, the lemon juice, the fudge. He springs through the air on his Para Litefoot tennis shoes. He strains to release the ropes binding his wrists, and he plunges through the line, carrying the football. The readers, responding to the images within the material, express the words with intonational and inflectional patterns that are believable and capable of drawing the audience empathically into the situation so that they, too, experience the literature in this way. "Thinking with the senses" helps the reader to concentrate, for it gives him something definite upon which to center his attention. Since in Readers Theatre the characters move within a setting created in the minds of the audience, it is of paramount importance that the reader first create this scene in his own mind, that he see the characters in action within this mentally visualized setting. In so doing, he can appreciably help the audience re-create in *their* minds the scene, the characters, and the event.

While the reader, as we have noted, thinks in terms of the traditional five senses—sight, sound, smell, touch, and taste—the senses of greatest importance to him as an interpreter are the kinetic and kinesthetic. The kinetic sense is an *overt* muscular response to the action inherent in the words. It is the muscular response to leaping into the air and plunging downward as one says, "He leaped into the air, arched his body, and then glided down, sliding into the water with scarcely a sound." Kinesthetic imagery calls for a *covert* muscular response to the emotion within the lines. To demonstrate this to yourself, read the following line aloud, responding to the images as you do so: "As she stood at the window, watching the children play, she wished desperately that she had not left home." If you were aware of a tensing of your muscles, you were responding kinesthetically. Similarly, a pleasant kinesthetic image would cause a relaxing of the muscles, as in this line: "Just seeing him move toward her across the lawn made her ecstatically happy." Not only must the interpreter respond with his total body to the imagery of the writing, but he must also concentrate on the images until an emotional response is evoked and externalized—made audible and visible to the audience.

Warming-up exercises. The director will need to achieve a climate of creativity if the reader-actors are to do their best work. Often a warming-up session is held at the beginning of rehearsals and before performances to release physical tension and focus attention on the rehearsal or performance—to prepare the readers physically and psychologically for concentration on the literature. In a sense, this corresponds to a singer's vocalizing. Taking from literature some words and passages that demand an emotional, sensory response, the director asks the readers to express them, giving full vocal and bodily response. Here are examples of words and phrases that might be employed:

miserable	happy	gay
tired	hot	cold
dejected	elated	delicate
hard	soft	swashbuckling

He slid into third base.
Leaping from rock up to rock.
Crouching miserably in fear.
Released from all cares, I swing into action.
I held still, not moving a muscle.

This warming-up phase should also include vocal-projection exercises. Vocalizing words with open vowels, such as *home, hold, hark, tone,* and *dawn,* the reader may figuratively take the word in his hand and bounce it high on the back wall, "following through" on the throw with his whole body. In exercising with words having an initial *h* sound, the reader should try to project the words forward through the mouth. Just as the voice needs warming up, so, too, do the muscles of the body. The football coach has his men flex their muscles and do other body-conditioning exercises before a game; the director instructs his readers to tone their muscles before rehearsing or performing. The right kind of physical activity helps tone up the muscles, and good muscle tone is important in producing full vocal tones. Stretching, leaping, and alternately expanding and contracting the body will result in the good muscle tone needed for an energetic, "alive" rehearsal or performance. Improvising actions found in the script is also effective. See page 134 for an example of the use of improvisation to vivify a scene.

Responding to the verbs. If the reader will reexamine the warming-up sentences described above, he will notice that *verbs* or action words were given considerable emphasis. The verb supplies the action in Readers Theatre. In the oral interpretation of literary material, the verbs must be as definite and specific in their suggestion of movement as the actual physical movements which characterize the conventional stage play. Through his empathic response to the inherent movement in these verbs, the reader vivifies for his audience the action in the script. For example, if he is responsive to the following phrases, he should note a slight muscular involvement as he reads them:

Striding and striding
Leaning into the wind
Slinking quietly to the door
Pouncing upon the unsuspecting victim
Turning around and around giddily, dizzily, happily
Jerking the handkerchief from off her face
Sweeping into the room in full sail
Sitting quietly, miserably, unable to help in any way

In narration the forward movement of the action is carried from verb to verb. A crisp handling of these verbs by the reader will endow the production with a strong sense of progression, a sharp and well-defined impression of action that is going somewhere exciting.

Vivifying through acting. Another way of securing vivid reading of the lines is similar to the one above in that it, too, calls for an empathic response to the words, particularly to the verbs. In this method, however, the readers first completely enact the scene, giving full movement as called for by the script. After sensing the movement in the muscles of the body through acting out the scene, the readers then retain the muscle tone demanded in the full action, without performing the action. In other words, the interpreter reads the words without the action but with the same inner bodily response that he had when he acted it out. Although this is an *internal* response, there will be some vestigial movement. For example, while working on *James and the Giant Peach,* the interpreter reading the role of James literally crawled through a small opening made with chairs, bumped his head, and then saw the Centipede, Earthworm, Spider, and the other characters sitting together as the book suggests. In this way, the readers achieved a sense of physical action and real interplay which carried over to the next reading when it was placed in the imagination. The same group actually rehearsed the ocean scene in the Atlantic Ocean at Vero Beach; they huddled realistically together as called for in the script and reacted to the expanse of water, the clouds floating by, and the moonlight. Later, as they read their lines and recalled their earlier muscular response, they seemed actually to be experiencing the situation at that moment. Once the elements of the scene had been truly experienced, the muscle memory—as well as the emotional memory—enabled the readers to re-create the scene fully.

Correcting faulty line reading

In correcting faulty line reading, the reader may combine two approaches: one is to develop a fuller understanding of the line, and the other is to use specific techniques that will lead to a more sensitive reading. Checking grammatical structure and paraphrasing are frequently helpful in achieving total comprehension of especially difficult or complex lines.

Checking grammatical structure. When the reader finds the subject and the verb, he should identify the object, if any, and the qualifying phrases and clauses. He should then analyze the relationship of these phrases and clauses to the main idea. For instance, in this sentence, "Irks care the crop-full bird?" the student will discover that the subject is *care* and the verb is *irk,* with the object *bird* modified by the adjective *crop-full.* Rearranged, it reads "Does care irk the crop-full bird?" Having ascertained the correct meaning in this way, the reader can then convey it to the audience through his intonation pattern.

Paraphrasing. Another method for determining meaning is to paraphrase the passage. Choosing words that have not been used over and over will demand a fresh appraisal of the thought. The sample sentence in the above paragraph could be paraphrased in this manner: "Can anxiety bother the bird that is satiated with food?" or "What does the well-fed bird have to be unhappy about?" Having discovered the meaning by restating the thought, the interpreter will vocally lift or emphasize the words *care* and *irk* in such a manner that the listener will comprehend the meaning the instant he hears it. If in this or some other way the director can guide the interpreter to voice whole thoughts, he will find that a number of other persistent faults in reading may have been eliminated. Skill in phrasing complete thought-units is a "must" for natural, meaningful reading, whether it be in Readers Theatre, in solo reading, or in acting.

Packaging ideas.   Quite often in a script, a long series of sentences must be vocally combined or "packaged" together as a unit, with a "build" to the important idea and a proper subordination of the qualifying elements. Packaging means revealing the relationship of a series of ideas that together express one thought. It binds together the phrases, clauses, and sentences that amplify an idea.

In the following passage (Act I, Scene vii, lines 12–28), for example, Macbeth is enumerating to his wife the reasons for not killing Duncan. He begins with two reasons: first, he is a blood relation and Duncan's subject; second, he is Duncan's host. But, as another argument, he adds that Duncan has been so humble and blameless as king that his virtues will cause people to decry his murder, and pity will cause all the people to weep for him. The relation of these ideas must be brought out in the reading.

> *He's here in double trust;*
> *First, as I am his kinsman and his subject,*
> *Strong both against the deed; then, as his host,*
> *Who should against his murderer shut the door,*
> *Not bear the knife myself. Besides, this Duncan*
> *Hath borne his faculties so meek, hath been*
> *So clear in his great office, that his virtues*
> *Will plead like angels, trumpet-tongued, against*
> *The deep damnation of his taking-off;*
> *And pity, like a naked new-born babe,*
> *Striding the blast, or heaven's cherubim horsed*
> *Upon the sightless couriers of the air,*
> *Shall blow the horrid deed in every eye,*
> *That tears shall drown the wind. I have no spur*
> *To prick the sides of my intent, but only*
> *Vaulting ambition, which o'erleaps itself*
> *And falls on the other.*

The first fourteen lines must be given as a package because, as a *whole,* they tell why Macbeth feels he should not murder his king. To communicate these reasons clearly and effectively to an audience, the reader must show their relationship to each other and tie them all together. To accomplish this in a sustained and vocal context is no casual task.

Projecting lines and meanings. Not infrequently, faulty reading results because the reader mumbles his lines. To overcome this, the interpreter needs to become more aware of the importance of the words. He must comprehend the idea and project, both mentally and physically, the key words which express that idea. He needs to be aware that thinking must always precede and accompany his speaking the words, and that the thought-carrying words stand out from words of lesser importance.

Marking transitions. Failure to mark the beginning of a new thought or a change in emotion will make the performance seem either unnecessarily slow or pointlessly rushed. Here again variety is basic. Quite often the problem is not in the pace itself but in the monotony of the reading. If the readers will establish and sustain the forward-moving pattern of the plot by emphasizing the shifts in thought and emotion, they will inject the necessary variety and avoid the monotonous pace which characterizes the "dragged out" production. Every change of idea and feeling in the text demands a difference in pitch, intensity, tempo, and sometimes tone. The readers must mark the beginning of a *new* incident, idea, or phase with a different tempo, a new pitch level, a change in atmosphere, or by a physical relaxing of their muscles and a slight shift in their positions with reference to each other and to the audience. This variety, so necessary for meaningful line reading, is also of great importance in providing proper balance for the series of scenes in the script. If the climax is not the highest point in the production, in all likelihood the preceding scenes are being read at too high a pitch, with too much intensity, or at too fast a pace. It is as important to conserve mental and physical energy in minor scenes as it is to unleash it at peak moments. Temper the reading of these secondary or transitional scenes, and the climax will take on added excitement.

Using the tape recorder. Perhaps the most effective means of improving line reading—and certainly one of the quickest and most efficient—is for the reader to listen to himself on a tape recorder. Despite all the director may have said about the line and its interpretation, many times the reader does not really understand what is wrong with his reading of it until he actually hears himself. While listening to the recording of his interpretation the reader becomes aware that he is not expressing the ideas and emotions he thought he was. He becomes cognizant of false emphasis, monotony in pitch and in pacing, lack of emotional coloring and vitality in the reading. Once the reader is aware of these deficiencies, most of the difficulties can be eradicated promptly, and a vastly improved interpretation will be the result.

To improve or correct faulty line reading, then, one must develop a fuller understanding of the line by analyzing it, by studying its syntax, and by paraphrasing it. The reader may employ a variety of useful procedures:

"packaging" the series of related ideas; attaining proper vocal and physical projection of thoughts and feelings; marking transitions for shifts in meaning and emotion; and obtaining "feedback" from tape-recording sessions.

EVALUATIVE REHEARSALS

As the time for performance approaches, the director should conduct a rehearsal in which he evaluates what has been accomplished by the readers thus far in order to determine what remains to be done for an effective, illuminating production. First, he should ask himself if the meaning of the script as a whole is clear, if the author's attitude has been clearly represented. If not, is the trouble in the reading, or is the adaptation inadequate? Does the descriptive narration evoke mental images? Does the movement of the story have causal progression? Does it move along at the proper pace to its high point of interest? This matter of pacing is, as we have stressed, tremendously important to an absorbing production. Cues must be picked up promptly. The tempo must be varied as demanded by the script. Climaxes must be reached and clinched. The performance must have a definite ending; it must culminate, leaving no doubt in the minds of the audience that this is, indeed, the end.

Many productions fail to achieve their full impact upon the audience because this sense of finality is lacking, because the ending is inconclusive. The listeners do not know whether they should applaud or not. The director can avoid this by making sure that the readers give concluding passages a special definiteness, a tone of finality. Also, the final physical positions or bodily attitudes of the readers must be given careful consideration. In a Readers Theatre production of Fielding's *The Tragedy of Tragedies: Or the Life and Death of Tom Thumb, the Great,* directed by Charlotte Lee of Northwestern University, the interpreters, representing dead bodies, leaned far forward over their lecterns. There could be no doubt that this was the ending. In an adaptation of Wilbur Daniel Steele's short story "So Beautiful with Shoes," the production opened and closed with music as the characters stood in silent silhouette for a moment. This visual framework added definiteness to the ending. In some scripts, especially appropriate endings may be drawn from the original literary source. This is exemplified in the ending of Ray Bradbury's *Dandelion Wine.* (See pp. 231–232.)

As the evaluative rehearsal proceeds, the director will want to ask other useful questions. Has the proper mood been established? Are the emotional elements of the material projected? Do the scenes reach the emotional climaxes found in the text? Are the transitions in time and place clear and definite? Has the production achieved its essential rhythm? The director should also examine the characterizations: Are the characters interesting and believable? Do the reader/actors reveal the characters' thoughts and feelings through their muscle tensions and body tone, as well as through their voices and facial expressions? Do the readers *listen* "in character"

In this scene from Jules Feiffer's story Passionella, *note the use of syncopated motion suggested by the three characters constituting the chorus. In this pose, Passionella is the glamorous movie star. As the chimney sweep, she slumped over; her knees were not crossed; there was a dull look in her eyes; and her mouth hung stupidly open. The narrator is observing the scene which is supposedly occurring offstage.*

and "in the scene," and *react* to what the others are saying? This staying "in character" is of great importance in keeping the total scene alive and unified. The readers must respond to all that is happening. They must not look directly out at the audience or consistently down at their books while they are supposed to be participating in the scene. Is it clear who is "in the scene"? Do the readers combine energy with ease; that is, do they project vitality without strain? Are they alive? The director should recheck the reading of the individual lines, especially those which have proved troublesome. Is the meaning clear? Are the thoughts properly phrased? Are the key words and thoughts unmistakable? Do the voices carry easily? Do they provide sufficient variety and contrast? Is the quality pure, unless it is intended to be otherwise for a special effect? Is the diction uniform and consistent with the characters being presented? If movement is used, does it illuminate points in the text? Does the production cohere?

POLISHING REHEARSALS

If the director, after evaluating what he has accomplished, is satisfied with the results and is confident that all elements are contributing to an organic and dynamic whole, then he can continue with the "setting" or polishing rehearsals. These final rehearsals should be a series of run-throughs with no interruptions, stressing a well-sustained pace, an ebb and flow of intensity, and unbroken concentration. No new elements should be added at this time. The performance should be allowed to take form, to solidify.

If possible, these final rehearsals should be held under the same circumstances as the performance, even to the clothes the readers will wear. The exact lighting should be used in order that the director can make certain that readers' faces are easily discernible. If there are music and sound effects, these too must be checked for proper cueing and for optimum volume. The presence of a small audience during these culminating rehearsals will help the readers get the feel of an audience, note reactions, and learn to hold for laughs. As part of the polishing procedure, the cast should practice their initial entrances and final exits; it is imperative for them to know the exact order in which they are to enter and leave the stage, and the cues for so doing. At the end of the performance, the readers should not drift aimlessly off or collapse into the nearest chair. The acts of walking on and off the stage should be done with definiteness, as if they were part of the performance, which of course they are.

PERFORMANCE

In these last rehearsals and before each performance, the director prepares his cast psychologically. For the "aliveness" essential to an infectious, audience-stirring performance, the director will need to evoke fresh enthusiasm in his readers. He may hold warming-up sessions before each performance in which the readers run through stretching and relaxing exercises to achieve the physical tone necessary for mental alertness; he may have them improvise scenes from the script in order to instill ebullience and immediacy in the reading of the lines. Above all, the director desires for his readers the joy of achievement, the stimulation of knowing an audience is completely engaged in the performance. He must convince them, through his own positive attitude, that they will entertain those who have come to hear them. Confidence in their ability to present a successful performance will encourage the readers to maintain the proper alternation of heightened tone and relaxation which they will need to do their best work, while at the same time experiencing a sense of ease and enjoyment.

In the well-directed Readers Theatre production an aura of contagious enthusiasm prevails. The performance has freshness and spontaneity—"the illusion of the first time." It has cumulative power with strong characterizations, vivid descriptions, forward-moving narration, and indissoluble unity. And in its final form it creates a memorable event for the audience, an event in which they are creative participants.

In an educational situation, the director's function does not end with the final dress rehearsal, of course. If Readers Theatre is to be a genuine, enduring experience, one which will contribute to the readers' intellectual and emotional growth and sharpen their interpretive perception and skill, the director must evaluate what is happening during the performance in order to improve subsequent presentations. Serving as an impartial observer insofar as is humanly possible, the director will witness the event in its uninterrupted totality and attempt to determine where he and the readers have succeeded and where they have failed. He will try to judge as fairly and honestly as he can the many facets and elements of the production, addressing himself primarily to the elucidation and evocation of the literature, to the validity and usefulness of the staging, and to the effectiveness of the script as literary-presentational material intended to evoke from the audience the intellectual and emotional responses necessary to their experiencing the literature in that most exciting of all places—the theatre of their minds. The director and others interested in critiquing the total experience —the adaptation as well as the performance—may find the following evaluation chart useful.

THE DIRECTOR'S CHECK LIST

Evaluation of Readers Theatre script and production

A. Adaptation
   of Script

1. Does the material evoke a definite response from the audience? Is it likely to give the audience a "memorable experience"?
2. Does it have "wholeness"? Does it leave the audience with a sense of having participated in a complete experience?
3. Are the story line and characters clear?
4. Is the division of lines meaningful? Do the characters have lines that would have been more effective if given by the narrator? If a character speaks narration or description, is the material clearly from his point of view? Does the narrator have lines that would have been more effective if given by characters?
5. Does the script have "close-up" scenes—scenes that reveal details of emotion, of motivation, of environment, of characterization?
6. If it is a compiled script, has it been given dramatic unity—made into a "theatre piece"?

B. Staging

1. Are the readers arranged so that all faces can be seen clearly?
2. Are the readers arranged for the best psychological effect?
3. Is the arrangement of the readers pictorially effective?
4. If levels are used, do they seem appropriate?
5. Are the readers sufficiently close together for the audience to see the reaction of other characters to the speaker?
6. If movement is used, does it serve a definite purpose for showing psychological relationships? For marking

a transition of time or place? For illuminating the action in the text?

7. Is the lighting effective? Can the faces of the readers be clearly distinguished? If lighting is used to pick out scenes and to mark transitions, is it handled smoothly?
8. If music or other sounds are used, do they add to the total impact of the performance? Does the music interfere with audience comprehension of the words?
9. Does the clothing of the readers aid in unifying the production? Does it contribute to pictorial effectiveness? Does it aid in suggesting who the characters are?
10. If properties are used, do they help the audience envision the scene, or are they distracting?

C. Performance

1. Does the performance have an overall unity?
2. Is the meaning of the script projected?
3. Does the performance have flow and effective pacing? Does it move from segment to segment with a sense of progression? Does it build to a high peak of interest?
4. Does the performance have a spontaneous "first-time" quality?
5. Is the narration delivered in a manner making it an integral part of the script and the performance (or does the action stop for the narration)? Is the narration vivid? Does it reveal the speaker's attitude? Is the point of view clear? Does the narration seem to create images of scenes and action in the minds of the audience?
6. Does the narrator use a storytelling manner, relating directly to the audience? Does the narrator seem to visualize the imaginary scene when he is not speaking? Does the narrator make clear his function in the story?
7. Do the readers project distinct and believable characters?
8. Do the characters change as dictated by the literary experience?
9. Are the readers "thinking with the senses" and creating mental images as they speak the words?
10. Do the readers possess an aliveness? Do they have projective energy—a reaching out to the audience—in their reading and action?
11. Do they *listen* when they are in the scene? Do they *react* through facial expression and muscle tone?
12. If an interpreter reads lines for more than one character, does he use voice and body tone to make a clear distinction among the various characters?
13. Is it clear at all times which readers are in the scene? Are the readers who are not in the scene sufficiently unobtrusive?

14. Do the interpreters handle their scripts efficiently and unobtrusively?
15. Is there consistency in the focus of the readers? Do all the readers locate a given scene in the same area?

D. Evaluation of Script in Performance

1. How would you rate the script? Very interesting_____ Interesting_____Moderately interesting_____Dull_____ Very dull_____
2. What degree of empathic response did it evoke from you? Very strong_____Strong_____Medium strong _____Weak_____None_____
3. What degree of intellectual response did it evoke from you? Very strong_____Strong_____Medium strong_____Weak_____None_____
4. To what extent did the readers cause you to experience the situation, to see and to hear it? Excitingly so_____ Experienced it_____Moderately experienced_____ Didn't experience it_____

CHAPTER SIX

Readers Theatre
Is for Children, Too

Readers Theatre has proved a delightful way to enrich the cultural life of children. Wherever it has been tried, the results have been gratifying. Rudyard Kipling's "The Elephant's Child" proved attention capturing, and delighted the first, second, and third grades at elementary schools in Castro Valley and Hayward, California. Kindergarten and first-grade children were spellbound by Mary E. Wilkins' "The Pumpkin Giant" in Hilo, Hawaii. At Brooklyn College, a curtain-raiser presentation of Dr. Seuss's *Thidwick: The Big-Hearted Moose* proved more intriguing than the main feature, a puppet-show arrangement of "Cinderella." Nineteen seventy-one was the fourth season for "Nursery Rhymes and Fairy Tales" at East Tennessee State University, a touring show for elementary schools with a new script each year, playing to over four thousand youngsters each season. One of the first widely known productions of a children's story was *James and the Giant Peach* by Roald Dahl, presented at the 1965 convention of the American Theatre Association. The production resulted in tremendously increased activity in this method of providing effective entertainment for children. In the fall of 1966, Alabama College devoted an advanced oral interpretation class to a pilot study of Readers Theatre for children. The course proved a challenging period of discovery for all concerned:

> Readers Theatre for children—which has the same relation to children's theatre and interpretation that chamber or concert reading has to adult theatre and interpretation—is an effective and practical way of creating living drama for young people. . . . [It] forced and encouraged them to use their imaginations—something not always encouraged by the professional television and stage productions.[1]

---

[1] Charles Clayton Harbour, "An Experiment in Readers Theatre for Children," talk given before the Southern Speech Association, Little Rock, Arkansas, April 7, 1967.

Carrie Rasmussen, well-known author of *Speech in the Elementary Classroom* and *Poetry for Children,* asserted in a letter to the authors, "I find storytelling does not seem to be used as much now as previously. This [Readers Theatre] is another way of bringing good literature, both old and new, to children. I . . . tried it out with children in Madison, Wisconsin, and found it very successful."

VALUES AND ADVANTAGES

Readers Theatre for children has many of the same values as storytelling to the young. Probably of foremost importance is its worth as sheer pleasure —as fun for fun's sake. For adults, as we have noted, this form brings dramatic joy and charms the mind. For children, these satisfactions are multiplied. As an interpretive and participatory art, Readers Theatre quickens children's imaginations. It not only gives the child a keener awareness of the emotional thrust that is experienced through literature, but it also develops his imagination in the role of spectator. His capacity to

By their bodily response to this offstage scene from James and the Giant Peach, *a children's story by Roald Dahl, the readers epitomize the sense of "aliveness" so essential to good performance. Note, too, the ease and naturalness with which they handle the scripts.*

imagine is extended. Hearing well-written stories reinforces his use of language skills, encourages him to read with avidity, and stimulates concentrated listening. For their growth in maturity it is important for children to hear various kinds of literature at ever-higher levels of intellectual and emotional complexity. Hearing literature that is mature in theme and content stimulates changes in thinking and feeling. Hearing inventive literature as opposed to the practical develops creativity by juxtaposing ideas in new relationships, and increases image-making powers, called "healthy hallucinating" by one psychologist. Hodgson and Richards define the dramatic experience as

. . . an intensification of living experience, realized by the selection and recording of significant moments, [which] exists in the communication between actors and audience physically present in one place. This communication takes place at every level: mental, emotional, physical, visual, aural, and aesthetic.[2]

Although the authors are speaking of conventional theatre, Readers Theatre has similar results. Since stories and poems as well as plays are read and interpreted in Readers Theatre, it is one of the best ways to introduce children to the world's wealth of literary materials. With such an introduction the child can be motivated to read and explore on his own initiative.

Those who perform for children are also enriched by the experience. Since children respond freely, frankly, and audibly, the readers develop an *audience radar,* a detecting device for measuring audience reaction. In addition, they learn how to cope with this feedback. They improve their ability to hold for laughs, to "come in" over audience reactions, to concentrate so fully on their material that they almost hypnotize the audience into listening. The uninterested child does not listen; the performer has to reach him, engage him, and involve him in the magic of the literature. Reading for children, although demanding, is highly satisfying, as the feedback is a potent stimulant. Performing for children of various ages and in different physical surroundings sharpens the reader's ability to adjust. Youthful audiences are among the most eager, attentive, appreciative, and spontaneous; reading for them is a highly gratifying experience.

Clearly, Readers Theatre affords significant advantages both to youthful audiences whose emotional and intellectual lives are enriched by the experience and to interpreters who find challenging opportunities to deepen their perception of audiences and to sharpen further their own skills and techniques. And there are still other advantages in using this particular medium with young people: productions can be physically accommodated in classrooms and areas where standard stage plays could not be presented, and an interpretive program of this kind is in several ways less costly than

---

[2] John Reed Hodgson and Ernest Richards, *Improvisation: Discovery and Creativity in Drama* (London: Methuen and Co., Ltd., 1966), p. 14.

a conventional children's theatre production, which often demands elaborate costumes and settings.

SELECTING SUITABLE SCRIPTS

In Chapter Three we discussed literature suitable for group reading and criteria to use in selecting it. These same considerations are to a great extent applicable to the literary materials to be chosen for a young audience. But there are certain special qualities in writing for which to look in literature to be shared aloud with children. The stories selected should create wonder and laughter, offer action and dramatic excitement, appeal to the imagination, and inspire a love of beauty both through the quality of the characters and through the beauty of the language. In addition to interesting and unique characters in provocative situations, look for repetition of sounds and actions, for verbal imagery, and for qualities in stories that make one wonder, that show unfamiliar characters doing everyday things or familiar characters tinged with mystery. Such stories fascinate children.

Libraries are full of intriguing folk tales, fairy tales, family stories, and fantastic epics. For example, Roald Dahl's delightful *James and the Giant Peach* is an imaginative story of magic crystals that cause all they touch to grow large so that a peach becomes as large as a house, and centipedes, ladybugs, spiders, and earthworms grow as large as people. With a young boy named James they all make a perilous journey across an ocean within the peach, harnessed to five hundred sea gulls, until a passing plane cuts the strings and the peach plummets to the top of the Empire State Building, where it is impaled for all New Yorkers to see, gasp, and wonder at. It makes an entrancing script not only for the truly young, but also for the young at heart. Other wondrously imaginative stories are Norton Juster's *The Phantom Toll Booth,* James Thurber's "The Last Clock" (see pp. 259–267), William Pène Du Bois' *The Great Geppy,* and E. B. White's *Charlotte's Web* and *The Trumpet of the Swan.* Lavinia Russ, children's editor for *Publishers' Weekly,* has described the types of characters and actions that delight children in this way: "Books should be about people (or animals, goblins, ghosts, and trolls imitating people) and the silly, wonderful, cowardly, valiant, wild, heroic things that people do."[3]

Children enjoy the old and familiar story, as well as the new. As we can probably recall from our own childhoods, three favorite children's stories are "The Three Bears," "The Three Little Pigs," and "Little Red Riding Hood." In each of these something is constantly happening; the events are familiar but still a bit strange, and the stories are full of repetition. These

---

[3] *The Girl on the Floor Will Help You* (New York: Doubleday & Company, Inc., 1969), p. 35.

special qualities can serve as useful guides for seeking and selecting materials for Readers Theatre scripts to be presented to young audiences.

Stories are more easily and effectively adapted to Readers Theatre than plays because children's plays generally call for much overt physical action. If a short program is to be given, it is often difficult to cut a play without its becoming episodic. Moreover, the "storytelling" quality of a story, told by a narrator (the storyteller) and brought to life by the characters of the story, gives it tremendous advantages with younger audiences.

Poetry may also be used successfully in programs for children. Ruth Strickland, in her book *The Language Arts in the Elementary School,* says: "Being required to read poetry tends to decrease interest and build bad reading habits, while *listening* to poetry is, for most children, a pleasant and satisfying experience."[4] (The italics are ours.) May Hill Arbuthnot also attested to the value of poetry in a child's life. Poetry, because it heightens, deepens, and enriches experiences, "becomes a shining armor against vulgarity and brutality—taking as it does the experiences of the child's everyday world and giving them a new importance, a kind of glory that they did not have when they were just experiences."[5] Children enjoy the singing quality of poetry, the rhyme, the rhythm, the repetition of sounds, words, and phrases, the "playing with words." They also enjoy a good story element, and the stimulation supplied by colorful and evocative words. They receive great satisfaction from humorous poems such as Phyllis McGinley's "How Mrs. Santa Claus Saved Christmas," A. A. Milne's "The King's Breakfast," and Eleanor Farjeon's "Hannibal Crossed the Alps." Even old ballads like "Get Up and Bar the Door" delight them.

ARRANGING READERS THEATRE SCRIPTS FOR CHILDREN

A single story may be used, or variety can be achieved through combining various types of children's literature in one unified script. The best way to illustrate this is to describe two such performances, one that could be given anywhere and one that needs to be staged.[6] The first was prepared for use at library story hours and was entitled appropriately *The Wonderful World of Words in the Land of Books.* An original opening and closing were written, and new words to an old tune were used as a linking, transitional device between a series of children's stories, poems, riddles, and word games. With a group of seven students reading, the opening went like this:

---

4 Boston: D. C. Heath and Company, 1951, p. 301.
5 *Time for Poetry* (Glenview, Illinois: Scott, Foresman and Company, 1961), p. xxiii.
6 Much of the following material is excerpted from Leslie Irene Coger, "Let's Bring Children and Books Together Through Interpreters' Theatre," a talk given at the Speech Communication Association Convention, New Orleans, December 1970.

NARRATOR. Come with us to the wonderful world of words which is found in the land of books! *Words are beautiful—*
READER 1. vermillion,
READER 2. mellow,
READER 3. fairy,
READER 4. shallow,
READER 5. wonder,
READER 6. cellar door.
NARRATOR. *Words are magic—*
READER 2. aba-ka-dabra,
READER 4. Rumpelstiltskin,
READER 6. fee-fi-fo-fum,
READER 3. double, double, toil and trouble, fire burn, and cauldron bubble.
NARRATOR. *Words are fun—*
READER 5. sachet,
READER 1. moisty,
READER 6. dingle,
READER 4. pebble,
READER 2. serendipity,
READER 3. pumpernickel,
READER 5. swashbuckling.
NARRATOR. *Words make up the wonderful world of books which are peopled with all sorts of characters—*
READER 4. kittens,
READER 1. frogs,
READER 3. geese,
READER 6. lions,
READER 2. elephants,
READER 5. and even hippopotamuses.
NARRATOR. *And books take you everywhere—*
READER 3. Petunia's farm,
READER 4. brier patches,
READER 1. Lake Okeefinokee,
READER 6. circuses,
READER 2. and faraway jungles.
ALL SING. *World of books, world of words,*
Bestest books you've ever heard,
With a nick, nack, paddy-wack, fetch another book,
Come with us to our story nook.

The stories involved the characters found in the locations mentioned. First there was Petunia, the goose, who learned that carrying a book under one's wing is not enough. One must know what is in it to be wise. Then there followed "The Wonderful Tar Baby"; "Veronica," the hippopotamus who goes to Petunia's farm; "Millions of Cats"; "Goliath II," the small elephant who scares a mouse; "The Three Wishes," in which the characters see that what they thought they wanted is not all they thought it would be;

"Mrs. Welladay's Tabby Cat," who turns out to be a lioness; and a poem entitled "Sparkle and Spin" which answers the question, "What are words?"

> Words are how what you think inside comes out,
> And how to remember what you might forget about.

Another poem used was that delightful play on words called "Metaphors."

> Where can a man buy a cap for his knee?
> Or a key for the lock of his hair?
> Can his eyes be called a school because there are pupils there?

The program came to a close with the song, but with a new last line:

> World of books, world of words,
> Bestest books you've ever heard,
> With a nick, nack, paddy-wack, fetch another book,
> Goodbye from our story nook.
> Goodbye, goodbye.

One performance of this show was given for a group of mentally retarded youngsters. The performers were warned the response might not be good, that the children had an attention span of only fifteen minutes. The forty-five-minute show held them quietly for its full length; that afternoon many of the children were heard repeating phrases from the show and singing the song. The show had met a hard test and passed it.

A second example of how to devise an imaginative, creative program may be found in a production created by Helen Cermak that had to meet the test not only of a mixed adult and child audience, but of a professional reviewer. *The Wind Is a Color* consisted of various types of literature: books, stories, poems, songs about color and the wind, all seen from a child's viewpoint. Ten readers using a colored jungle gym and many colored lights evoked pictures of the materials with words and actions. The performance started with a dance of actors, each representing a particular color, to the song "The Beautiful Land" from *Roar of the Greasepaint,* with its descriptions of yellow and green. Next each actor-color in a pool of color from a spotlight read from *Hailstones and Halibut Bones* with its childlike, unexpected reactions to colors. For instance, *purple* is described as the great-grandmother of *pink.*

The evening was filled with interesting characters. There was that bungling apprentice to Pittidoe, the Color Maker, who mixed all the colors together and lost them all until, brought to tears by his troubles, he found the colors again in his tears and got them all back. "The Big Yellow Balloon" told of a cat who wanted to scratch out the sun so he could sleep longer. Roger, the boy with the balloon, soon attracted a whole procession of characters: the cat who followed the balloon because he thought it was the sun, the eager little beagle who chased the cat, the dogcatcher who chased the beagle, the little old lady who chased the dogcatcher, the thief who attempted to snatch the lady's handbag, and the policeman who followed the thief. When finally the balloon caught in a tree and the cat's claw popped it, all sorts of happenings occurred at once.

In another story, Mr. Pine, who wanted his white house to be different from all the other white houses on the street, planted a tree, but his neighbors all did the same. He planted a bush, but all the neighbors did the same. Then, desperately desiring to be different, to establish his own identity, he painted his house purple, and all the neighbors painted theirs yellow, red, green, and blue, so that they lived on the most colorful street in all the town.

The tender story-poem "What Color Is Love?" described concrete images in terms of colors, stating that colors are *outside things* and feelings are *inside things,* and asked in stark simplicity, "What color is love?" This haunting combination of childlike ideas and adult perceptions was not only read aloud but was conveyed also in intriguing sign-language gestures. It told how an apple is red and an orange is orange, and how, though different, they can live happily side by side.

Other stories were "The Important Book," which proclaims that the importance of you is that "you are you," "Little Blue and Little Yellow," and "The Wishing Tree." Groups of poems by E. E. Cummings, Rod McKuen, and other poets blended many moods. The performance ended with Joseph Pintauro's book of poems, *One Circus, Three Rings, Forever and Ever Hooray!*

The stories and poems were imaginatively staged on a multicolored jungle gym by a group of performers dressed in neutral-colored pantsuits, each with a large square silk scarf of his particular color—red, yellow, blue, green, orange, and all the other colors of the spectrum. These were used in many ways: as aprons, scarves, sashes, and flowers. In "The Important Book," the red scarf was caught up in a ball to be an apple, and the yellow was used as a daisy. In the story "Little Blue and Little Yellow," the child of Mama and Papa Blue had a blue scarf, the child of Mama and Papa Yellow had a yellow scarf. But when they hugged each other tightly their colors blended and presto! their scarves were green.

Colored lights were imaginatively employed. A large eye, an opening in the back, turned a beautiful lavender when the flowers mentioned above fell in love. When the strong wind came, the eye turned a deep magenta. Music was also included in some of the segments.

When the production was presented to the general public, the professional reviewer for the Kansas City Star, Giles M. Fowler, wrote:

> The creator of *The Wind Is a Color* and the ten students who perform it at the University of Missouri, Kansas City, playhouse all seem to be young enough to believe in things like love, melancholy, the meaning of the seasons, and the inference of colors.
>
> It may be their commitment to these beliefs, or perhaps the kids' own at-

tractiveness as they revel in sheer verbal imagery, but whatever the cause, the show is charming. Charming and touching. . . . The production is the creation of Helen Cermak, whose goal is to wake us all up—yes, even jaded old reviewers—to the ability to feel things the way we felt them as kids ourselves.

To this end she has arranged a collage of Readers Theatre, music, mime-dance, poetry, and general fun and games. And she must have plundered half of English literature to come up with such a variety of material dealing with colors. The show is a rainbow of color images. The players also represent particular hues and wear identifying scarves as they roam over, crawl through, sit on, and play around a vividly painted jungle gym, the only setting.

Many of the funnier elements would appeal to children, though I found myself as hooked by them as my five-and-one-half-year-old guest. Other passages are more mature, more serious, but there is always some quality of wonder. And the text, compiled from many sources, is full of linguistic beauty.[7]

This is testimony of the appeal of Readers Theatre to all ages. However, to have this appeal Readers Theatre must not only be composed of carefully selected literature unified in an interesting format, but it must also be skillfully presented. Meanings in the literature must be explored, moods must be determined, the spirit must be captured, and all of these must be illuminated and projected by the readers by means of vocal intonations, facial expressions, physical tensions, and movements. The vocal intonations and behavioral synecdoches must be presented to the audience with such clarity, definiteness, and verve that they evoke the world of the literature in which, for a while, all the participants live and know the fictive experience. The readers must have mastered the material for this to happen; they must also have developed flexible, expressive bodies and voices capable of projecting the subtle nuances as well as the broader manifestations of attitudes and actions. Imaginatively directed and skillfully presented, a Readers Theatre production makes of the literature a memorable experience for those reading, as well as for those listening. It is a happy way of introducing children to literature so that they love it and enjoy it. From a lively production, the children are easily led into discussion and criticism resulting in deeper appreciation. If the adapter chooses literature beyond the child's reading level, he stretches the child. If he chooses literature that is inventive rather than practical, he nurtures the child's creativity, and if he chooses literature with which all can have fun, he creates a world of delight that the child will remember and will turn to for further enjoyment. Readers Theatre well-presented can result in children becoming attentive listeners, creative participators, and, hopefully, creators.

---

[7] From "Theatre in Mid-America," *Kansas City Star,* March 26, 1970, p. 26. Reprinted by permission of Giles M. Fowler.

Response of all of the readers to the offstage scene is shown in this picture of the delightfully heart-warming children's script Henry and Ribsy.

DIRECTING THE SHOW FOR CHILDREN

The director approaches a Readers Theatre production for children in the same way he does material for adult audiences: he allows the text to guide him. Literature for young people usually depicts strongly drawn characters; the plots are highly imaginative and filled with strong action; the language has pronounced rhythmical patterns, abounding in concrete imagery and rich in sound devices, such as assonance, alliteration, and onomatopoeia. The interpreters should emphasize these qualities in their reading of the lines. The characters may be broadly drawn, even exaggerated, both in their personality traits and in their reactions to the events of the story. The readers may mimic the voices of the characters and utilize broad facial responses and strongly suggested movement. For example, the insect characters in *James and the Giant Peach* can slump their shoulders, draw in their heads, and try to make themselves small as they attempt to escape being hit by the hailstones hurled at them by the Snow Men. When the peach in which they are riding falls on top of the Empire State Building and is spiked upon its slender needle with a "squelch," all the readers may jolt backward and forward again as though they had suddenly stopped. When the huge peach tilts, causing these same characters to slide across the room, the readers may lean to one side and then draw themselves sharply upright as the insects supposedly collide with the opposite wall.

To achieve vividness the director of *The Wind Is a Color* used an imaginative approach with her actor/dancer/readers. Much of the action in the stories and poems grew out of improvisations. Although these improvisations were used primarily as warm-up sessions to establish a climate of creativity, much of this improvised movement was retained in the final program. For example, one set of poems contrasted the feeling of children maturing with a garden growing. The group improvised flowers coming from seeds, and flowers growing and climbing toward the sun. Some of the readers trailed around the jungle gym, some entwined with each other. Then a brutal wind came. Only the strongest flowers survived. Others were beaten to the ground, were broken. In the preparatory rehearsals, this was improvised to gain the feeling and the emotion of the words, but the pantomime proved so effective it was retained in the show. (See pp. 112–115 for further warming-up exercises and means of vivifying the reading.) An imaginative director, working in a climate of creativity, can evoke the essence of the text for the readers and the audience.

Drawing the audience in on the act

As children witness the performance, not only are they drawn into the action of the piece through empathic responses, but they may literally be invited to participate in the action itself. For instance, during a reading of Bernard Waber's delightful "How to Lay an Egg," the children were asked to stand up to see if they had laid an egg. This delighted the youngsters and allowed them to rise and stretch. This "squirming" pause—a moment to wiggle a bit and relax—is necessary for young audiences; children can sit still only so long before they need to move. The knowing adapter will write passages into the script that will allow, even demand, this relaxing moment for his audience.

The young audience may not only participate in the movements but sometimes may also participate in the sounds of the script. In a performance of "Toad the Terror," taken from Kenneth Grahame's *Wind in the Willows,* the adapter of the script had added many "Peep, Peep's" for the horn of Mr. Toad's car. Each time Mr. Toad blew his horn, the children delightedly repeated these sounds with the reader. Brought joyously and excitingly to life, children's literature invites self-identification with the characters in their interesting adventures.

Requisite skills for the reader

If youthful listeners are to be successfully involved in this heightened participation, the interpreters must first empathize with the text; they must embody the characters so vividly that the youngsters will be utterly convinced that these characters are indeed breathing, thinking, feeling, and moving with their bodies as genuine people do. If the readers themselves can activate and respond to the literature in this manner, if they can re-create the imagery, identifying with the flesh-and-blood characters and embodying their respective emotions and thoughts, they cannot fail to endow the literary material with pulsating life, to make of it a truly rewarding and unforgettable experience both for themselves and for their young audience.

As in any Readers Theatre performance, the voice must be animated, alive, and expressive, and the interpreter should make effective use of pauses to "dig a hole" for an important idea or event before he "plants" it. Readers for children will find it useful to cultivate a "once upon a time" vocal quality which is characterized by tones of wonder, enthusiasm, and suspense. A sense of sharing which comes from direct eye contact is highly essential, but there must be no talking down to the audience. Excitement and a suggestion of something important about to be revealed must be reflected in the voice, the face, and the body, but the reader must not be overly dramatic.

The reading of each part of a story demands the same consideration as any Readers Theatre interpretation. Dialogue must create a believable character, and the reading of description must evoke mental pictures in the listener's mind, some close-up, some panoramic. The reading of narration must be very direct, warmly personal, and have a sense of progression—a quality of being "headed somewhere." For children especially, the narration ought to be touched with a hint of suspense, a suggestion of something marvelous about to occur.

Proximity—that is, a feeling of being physically close to people and events—will increase the degree of participation for the child audience. Just as children enjoy a play more if they can be close enough to see all the facial expressions, so they enjoy a Readers Theatre performance more if they are close to the interpreters. For this reason, it is often advisable that one or more of the readers make their initial appearance by approaching the stage through the audience. In this way they psychologically take the children onto the stage with them.

READERS THEATRE IN THE ELEMENTARY CLASSROOM

Children enjoy and profit from participating in this activity themselves, as well as being entertained by it. It is advisable not to burden the very young with many lines. This can be accomplished by the classroom teacher's serving as the storyteller, and by selecting stories such as Rudyard Kipling's "The Elephant's Child" or Harold Courlander's "Talk," stories told primarily by a storyteller but involving many characters with few individual lines which may be distributed among the students. Stories with repeated lines are ideal for this classroom activity. In a multireader, classroom reading of "Talk," for example, the teacher assumed the major task of narration. In this tale told by an Ashanti of Ghana, the lines of dialogue are short and are repeated many times, and the characters remain in one spot with few exceptions (in their regular classroom seats, if desired). Children find delight in portraying such amusingly imaginative roles as a yam, a dog, a palm tree, a palm branch, a stone, a fisherman's trap, a bundle of cloth, a river, and a stool, as well as such humans as a fisherman, a weaver, a bather, and a chief. The farmer, who is the narrator, moves from one reader to another, and is joined eventually by the various humans, who accompany him until they all tell the village chief about the talking inanimate objects. He thinks their report is a wild story and orders them to go back to work—but is in the end upset himself when the stool on which he is sitting laughs and says, "Fantastic, isn't it? Imagine, a talking yam!"[8]

"Mini-Readers Theatre" programs with group or ensemble readings of stories, plays, or poetry, useful in the teaching of elementary school literature, often can be given in school assemblies, in other classes "on tour," and at PTA meetings. Of course such performances call for rehearsals, for a degree of performance perfection not necessary when used in classes to vitalize the literature and provide oral reading activity for the students. "In ensemble reading, readers can be assigned parts commensurate with their abilities. Poorer readers, for example, can be given small, easy parts which insure their success, and at the same time they will not be slowing down the more gifted readers."[9]

Even from the brief overview provided in this chapter, it should be apparent that Readers Theatre can be a highly dynamic and enjoyable way of broadening the lives of young people by allowing them a keener understanding of the world about them, of their fellow human beings, and of themselves. It introduces them to the wealth of literary materials that have been written especially for them. When vividly interpreted, this living canvas of literature creates for them an aesthetic adventure—a brush with beauty. Only now are educational, religious, and recreational leaders beginning to discover the vast potential in Readers Theatre for children. In the years immediately ahead, we believe it will find an ever widening use in schools, libraries, churches, youth camps, and recreational centers.

---

[8] Harold Courlander, "Talk," in *The Cow-Tail Switch and Other West African Stories,* ed. Harold Courlander and George Herzog (New York: Holt, Rinehart & Winston, Inc., 1947), pp. 25–29.

[9] Robert M. Post, "An Oral Interpreter's Approach to the Teaching of Elementary School Literature," *The Speech Teacher,* 20, no. 3 (September 1971), 170.

PART TWO

This Is the Way
It Was Done

Probably the most effective way to learn how to work in Readers Theatre would be to see many different programs directed by many different directors. Ideally this observation-analysis procedure would involve the same material, adapted and directed by various directors, for Readers Theatre is, above all, creative. As we have emphasized, what is done with the selected material depends on many factors: the imagination of the director and his readers, the material they are interpreting, the room or auditorium where it is to be performed, and the point on the continuum between interpretation *per se* and theatre *per se* from which the director wishes to operate.

Unfortunately, opportunities to observe the work of others are often limited. Hence, we have provided here a number of descriptions, some brief and some detailed, of "how it was done." These descriptions are not intended to imply that this is *the* way in which a given presentation must be handled; rather, they are intended to show *one* way, *one* method chosen by *one* director because of the nature of the material. In some instances, the particular mode of staging was determined by arbitrary limitations, such as the available room, stage, or auditorium, the number of readers to be included in the cast, the required length of the program, the desired simplicity or elaborateness of presentation, and related considerations. In a few instances, different productions of the same material are discussed to demonstrate further the wide range of possibilities offered by this highly flexible medium.

Many Readers Theatre presentations have already been referred to in Part One in order to enlarge a concept, illustrate a principle, or explain a particular method. For instance, as an illustration of the way in which introductory material may be given by a reader "in character," see again the account of the reading of *The Women's Town,* or *Pueblo de las*

Mujeres, pages 46–47. For suggestions on cutting a novel, restudy the notes on Ray Bradbury's *Dandelion Wine,* pages 54–57. "What Shall I Tell My Children Who Are Black?", a script in which various responses are given to the question asked in Margaret Burroughs' poem of the same title; "A Wilde Night," a composite picture of Wilde's life and writings; and "A Casual Approach to Violence," a script based on a Norman Cousins editorial, are described on page 61. A possible presentation for *Iphigenia in Aulis* can be found on pages 102–103. Shorter summaries of various Readers Theatre productions have also been cited in Part One.

In the descriptions to follow, certain terms introduced in previous chapters are employed. For instance, *offstage focus* means that the readers placed the action in the midst of the audience; *onstage focus* means that the readers kept the scene on the playing area or stage, turning to the actual person being addressed and making direct eye contact with him. If both onstage and offstage focus were used in the same presentation, this is noted. Unless otherwise specified, all readers stayed within view of the audience at all times and made their exits and entrances by such suggestive or symbolic devices as rising from chairs and stools and returning to them, lowering their heads in order to disappear from a scene, or reversing the process by raising their heads, standing, or turning front —as the nature of the material and the style of the production required.

To clarify and simplify these descriptive summaries, certain established stage directions or "geographical" terms are employed. The chart below will help in visualizing the physical elements of the various productions. *Downstage* refers to the front of the stage or the playing area nearest the audience; *upstage,* to that part of the stage farthest away from the audience, toward the back wall. The chart indicates nine conventional divisions of the stage, with C meaning *Center;* DC, *Down Center;* UC, *Up Center;* R, *Right;* UR, *Up Right;* DR, *Down Right;* L, *Left;* UL, *Up Left;* and DL, *Down Left.*

FIGURE 5.   The geography of the playing space

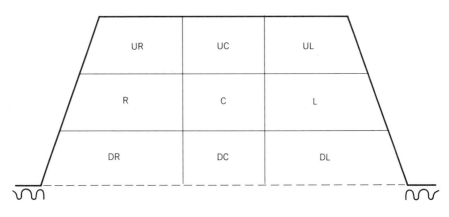

The selections included here were chosen because they represent various types of literature, because they illustrate different methods of adapting material, because they show a wide variety of approaches in presentation —for example, in staging and in lighting and costuming—and because each has proved successful in actual performance.

For the convenience of the reader, the following summary-descriptions are arranged alphabetically by title.

Almost Ancestors

An anthology for Readers Theatre of native American literature, assembled and directed by Richard Bagwell, and presented at the College of Holy Names, Oakland, California.

"Almost Ancestors" was compiled from the words, the oral literature, of native Americans, and featured stories, myths, legends, ritual poems, songs, magic spells, and oratory. The sources ranged geographically from Alaskan Eskimos to Peruvian Indians, but most of the material came from what we now call the United States. The production was staged in an outdoor setting, an Indian campsite where, carefully preserved, were mortars once used by local Indians to grind their acorn flour and some of the rocks from a well-used council fire found when the land was cleared. The production included masks, puppets, authentic Indian dances, and Indian motifs for properties and costumes. The material was memorized, and included solo reading, storytelling, duo-reading, and choral reading. Much use was made of Indian artifacts—tomahawks, peace pipes, masks, headbands, moccasins, and beads. The more theatrical elements of the presentation were found in storytelling dance-pantomimes and in Indian chants. The outdoor setting—the authentic campsite, trees, grass, shrubs, night birds, and insects attracted by the campfires (augmented by selective spotlighting)— resulted in fascinating entertainment, as well as an educational evening of most unusual material. A program note emphasized the title of the program:

> Perhaps it's appropriate for us to remember, briefly, that each of the pieces in "Almost Ancestors" had an author, just as did, for instance, the *Iliad;* an individual whose creative spark still is warm on the stage in front of you today. They are gone now, our almost ancestors, but we think it important that our voices should provide the next link in the chain of transmission.[1]

---

[1] Program note by Richard Bagwell for "Almost Ancestors," April 3 and 5, 1971.

> *A multimedia production, adapted and directed for Readers Theatre by James W. Carlsen, and presented at the United States International University, California, Western Campus, San Diego, and at the 1971 Desert Interpretation Festival, Tucson. The following information was provided by Mr. Carlsen.*

"America: Love It or Leave It" was a compilation of contemporary literature, music, and visuals meant to convey the changing moods in the American scene today. This collage depicted the contrasting values in our society, and the youthful revolution against war, poverty, prejudice, and societal injustice. The script included selections from Charles Reich's *The Greening of America,* E. E. Cummings' "next to of course god america i love you" and "poem, or beauty hurts mr. vinal," Janis Ian's "Society's Child," Gordon Lightfoot's "Black Day in July," Rod McKuen's "Methinks Thou Dost Protest Too Much," Buffy Sainte-Marie's "The Universal Soldier" and "Now That the Buffaloes Gone," Phil Ochs' "I Ain't Marchin' Anymore" and "Changes," Bob Kaufman's "Benediction," Leslie Woolf Hedley's "Chant for All the People," and others.

The cast included seven women and five men who interpreted the literature as a group through dialogue and choral reading, individually read selections, and sang songs individually and as a group. Two guitarist-readers provided introductory and background music, and interesting counterpoint to certain readings and songs. Some of the songs were played by a guitarist while the lyrics were read by another member of the cast, as in "Society's Child." "Suicide Is Painless," from the motion picture *M*A*S*H,* was sung by one guitarist and then softly accompanied the reading of the poem "Benediction," by Bob Kaufman. This blending of the musical lyric and the poetic statement provided an even greater emotional impact.

The staging of this multimedia compilation placed primary emphasis on the literature and its message. The platforms were decorated with red, white, and blue crepe paper, and the readers all wore some combination of red, white, and blue to enhance the visual effect of the staging. The readers sat on stools and on platforms two feet high upstage and one foot high downstage (see Figure 6) to create variations in height and placement, and to allow for the projection of visuals behind and above them on the cyclorama. Stage movement was kept to a minimum so as not to distract from the readings, songs, and slide projections. At certain times specific areas were lighted for individual readings to provide contrasts between the group, individuals, and visual effects.

The use of multimedia in the presentation allowed for an effective blending of verbal, musical, and visual "poetic" messages. Slides depicting war atrocities, racial unrest, riots, and societal oppression were flashed upon the cyclorama behind the readers and coordinated with the idea or emotion of the reading or song. The literature, music, and visuals combined to make a powerful poetic protest relevant to the underlying mood of change in our society today.

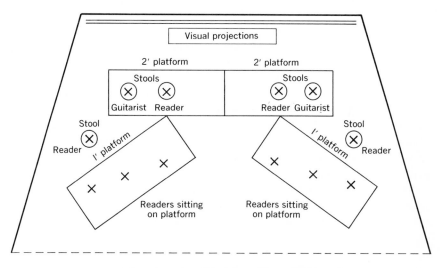

FIGURE 6. *America: Love It or Leave It* floor plan

America: Love It or Leave It combined visuals, guitarists, singers, and readers. The platforms were decorated in red, white, and blue; the readers were costumed in combinations of red, white, and blue. Visuals were projected on a cyclorama above and behind the cast.

The Boarding House   by James Joyce

A short story, adapted for Chamber Theatre, directed by William E. McDonnell, and presented at Wisconsin State University, Eau Claire. Mr. McDonnell provided the following information about the production.

"The Boarding House" used a minimum of set properties: three music stands, three stools, a coat rack, and a simulated bed. The cast included two men and two women. The production was designed for presentation on a thrust stage. (See Figure 7.) Costumes which seemed appropriate to the characters were employed: Mrs. Mooney wore a frumpy print dress; Polly, a sexy-looking mini; and Doran, dull tweeds. The Narrator, however, was quite stylish with a double-breasted striped sport coat, bell-bottomed slacks, dark-colored shirt, and bright tie. The Narrator carried a script which served as a prompt book and director's notebook. The other performers did not use scripts.

The production employed the device known as *trompe l'œil* (literally, a trick or deception of the eye). The performers, who were later to assume the roles of Mrs. Mooney, Polly Mooney, and Mr. Doran, came onstage as themselves to the strains of "Courtin' in the Kitchen" and, after preliminary greetings, sat down on their stools, reversed to form makeup tables with imaginary mirrors, and pantomimed putting on makeup. They were joined shortly by the Narrator, who functioned also as Stage Manager and Director. He proceeded to check the makeup of each actor in turn, pausing finally behind the actress playing Mrs. Mooney. Improvised dialogue between the two followed, with Mrs. Mooney wondering if her base was perhaps too dark and the Narrator, after checking his script, reassuring her that it was fine because "Mrs. Mooney was a butcher's daughter. She was a woman who was quite able to keep things to herself." To which the actress, as if to add qualities she had found in the character, straightened her posture, looked at herself in the "mirror" and stated, "A determined woman." Thus lines were divided throughout between the Narrator and the actor-characters, with care taken to present the story as written, to preserve the author's style, tense, and point of view. The *trompe l'œil* device of a play within a play provided motivation for the exposition and prepared the audience for the narrator-character role the performers were to assume throughout.

The idea of using imaginary mirrors grew out of the script, as Joyce at various times in the story describes all three of the characters looking at themselves in mirrors. Another line from the story which became stage business was the observation that Mrs. Mooney "counted all her cards again." This became a literal card game between Mrs. Mooney and the Narrator, with the music stand becoming a card table. (See picture on p. 11.) Later, when Mr. Doran went downstairs to "face the music," Mrs.

Mooney gave him a hand of cards, and by pushing the music stand (card table) to its lowest height forced Doran to kneel to play out the final hand.

Both offstage and onstage focus were employed. As was mentioned, the Narrator served at times as the Director, moving the performers about the stage. In one scene, for example, he brought Polly to Mr. Doran's room and coached her as she confronted Doran and told him of her "confession" to her mother of their affair. The two actors were facing each other at this moment, but when "he remembered well" (their first bedroom encounter), both actors turned outward and "saw" each other offstage. As the "re-lighting of the candle" episode continued, Polly and Doran slowly turned toward each other once more. In fact, they seemed about to embrace when the Narrator cleared his throat and directed them to another location to summarize more of the courtship. Later, when Polly and Doran did kiss, the Narrator turned to the audience and told them "he remembered well her eyes, the touch of her hand, and his delirium. . . ." Joyce's ellipsis again seemed to indicate action, so the kiss was exaggerated in performance and prolonged to the extent that Doran was late for his next line, "But delirium passes." In fact, the Narrator, after repeating the cue line, was forced to separate Doran from Polly before the action could proceed.

One character mentioned prominently in the story, Polly's bruiser brother, Jack Mooney, also was read by the Narrator, who after physically assisting Doran down the stairs—"a force pushed him downstairs step by step"—assumed the "thick bulldog face and a pair of thick short arms" of Jack. The emotional tone of Jack had already been provided by Joyce

The narrator surveys the performers in The Boarding House *pantomiming applying makeup.*

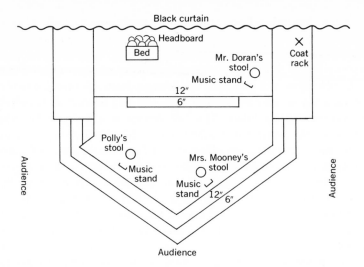

FIGURE 7.   Floor plan for *The Boarding House,* a thrust stage

with the warning that "if any fellow tried that sort of game with his sister he'd bloody well put his teeth down his throat, so he would." Since the above line was written by Joyce in indirect discourse rather than spoken by Jack directly, it seemed appropriate that the Narrator should take on Jack's qualities.

"The Boarding House" was combined with Mary McCarthy's "Cruel and Barbarous Treatment" for an evening of Chamber Theatre under the encompassing title "The Weaker Sex?"

The Contrast   by Royall Tyler

A representative early-American play in five acts adapted for Readers Theatre and presented at the University of Michigan, Ann Arbor. L. LaMont Okey provided the information about this presentation.

The chandelier-lit drawing-room atmosphere of the Clements Library, housing the University of Michigan's collection of literary Americana, proved to be the ideal setting for a production of the first native comedy of the colonial United States. (Because of its antiquity, *The Contrast* requires no royalty fees.) Since this play was initially staged on April 17, 1787, at the John Street Theatre in New York City by the American Company, the script offered some interesting challenges for the readers in terms of presenting stock characters using the stylized conventions and broad reactions of another period, such as direct asides to the audience and difficult diction patterns in long, flowery sentences.

The script underwent three revisions in order to render the language manageable, yet retain the flavor of the period. In its final stage of adaptation, ten readers emerged: two Narrators, who provided historical context and plot transitions; Colonel Manly, the hero; Dimple, the foppish dandy; Jessamy, his manservant; Letitia and Charlotte, two coquettes; Maria, the heroine; and Jonathan, the shrewd though uncultivated New England farmer who was the prototype for the "Stage Yankee" so popular in later productions.

The Narrators stood to the right and left of two groupings onstage. These groups represented, roughly, the main plot and the subplot of the play, and also suggested its thematic statement: the contrast between the superficialities of stylish foreign manners and the honest, homespun American virtues of character. All of the readers sat on stools, rising with black notebooks and stepping forward to come "into the scene" when the script indicated their entrances.

Only the suggestion of costume was used. The women wore street clothes tending toward the frilly, and each chose an accentual touch which reflected her character. One carried a fan, another a lacy kerchief, and a third wore a ruffled cap. The two male leads wore waistcoats over street clothes, another man was provided with a jabot, and the manservant wore a tricolor. These "costumes" were claimed from an early American trunk placed in the center of the stage before the performance began. Actors came onstage informally, selected and donned their finery, and assumed statuelike poses on their stools until distance was established and the audience quieted.

Each member of the audience received a personal invitation and was admitted by a special ticket. Programs were provided which carried not only the names of the students performing that evening, but also the names of the original actors who had first opened the play in 1787. After the performance, actors and audience mingled in conversation over tea and coffee from an antique silver service of the colonial period.

The Dissent of Dominick Shapiro   by Bernard Kop

A novel of adolescence, adapted and directed for Chamber Theatre by Elbert R. Bowen at Central Michigan University.[2]

This novel has sometimes been described with oversimplification as a "British-Jewish *Catcher in the Rye*." We wished to convey in our one-and-one-half-hour cutting the intimacy and universal fun of the novel. Lacking

---

2 From Elbert R. Bowen, "A Chamber Theatre Production," *IIG Newsletter,* November 1968, pp. 19–20. Reprinted by permission of Elbert R. Bowen.

a small theatre, we used a lecture room seating 380. The hall had an eighteen-inch platform, twenty-five feet wide and eight to twelve feet deep. We decided to use the entire hall for playing: the platform, all aisles, all doors. The Narrator moved freely with his manuscript in hand in the wide aisle between the platform and the audience. His approach was that of an informal storyteller, addressing the audience directly, sitting on the edge of the platform at times, and turning to watch the action with the audience.

All characters with the exception of Dominick emerged from the group of readers seated on boxes of various heights about a low lectern UR. All performers except the Narrator memorized all their lines. Only Dominick was always visibly in character and in the scene. His major side of the platform was L. On that side was a two-foot high platform representing his upstairs bedroom, although it was only large enough for him to lie upon. Although he might lead his entourage of Beats about the hall to suggest their pilgrimage out of London, Dominick essentially belonged L. His father, Lew, the second major character, occupied R primarily. The Narrator, who was interested in these two almost exclusively—never entering the mind of any other character and always relating events as they were seen by one or the other—moved laterally as his interest in these two alternated.

As is true of most Chamber Theatre, the Narrator was a powerful force in the performance, and his presence was always felt, if not always consciously attended to. Narrative portions of the script, which were never sacrificed to the dynamics of dialogue, were divided between the Narrator and the actors playing Dominick and Lew. Any line which could be interpreted as a thought of either of these characters was assigned to the actors, who addressed them to the audience as if sharing their thoughts with the audience. . . .

Readers moved out of the chorus to enact scenes only when they came into close psychological relationship with either Dominick or Lew; otherwise they gave their lines from the group of readers. Direct-focus–stage-locus was used when characters interacted with other characters; otherwise indirect-focus–audience-locus was employed.

Staging was very simple. The instructional austerity of the platform was softened by a backdrop of black. Boxes, stools, and platforms of red, yellow, and black served as the only props. Three huge, gaping glass screens for rear screen projection high behind the platform were lighted from behind: one with a Union Jack design and the others with different colors for the establishment of appropriate moods. Costuming was only slightly suggestive of character with one exception: a ridiculous old Russian overcoat and fur hat worn by Dominick through much of the book were provided as obligatory assistance to the audience's imagination. Spotlighting from two tripods at the sides helped establish a theatrical atmosphere.

A compiled script, arranged and presented by Judith Ten Eyck and Leslie Irene Coger at Southwest Missouri State University.

This program, a two-hour Chamber Theatre production, was prepared for a teachers' education association convention. The timely title, *Education Is a Riot,* was selected first. The material was then chosen to develop the theme. Irene Kampen's autobiographical *Due to Lack of Interest Tomorrow Has Been Cancelled* was discovered in the search. In this novel an older woman returns to a college campus and meets demonstrators, hippies, the Big Man on campus, and other campus types. She comes, through her association with these young people, to the understanding that it is not the outer appearance of strange clothes and long hair that matters, but the inner man, the "inner aura," as the young people say.

It was found that Irene Kampen's characters could be employed to represent all the differing facets of education. A title song was written for opening and closing, and a poignant song, "Over Thirty," was composed for the older woman back on campus.

The staging of the script was inspired by the idea of the "inner aura." Hanging above the three-leveled stage (see pictures on p. 150) was an orange-red circular aura just above the heads of the chorus of six who represented the opinions and attitudes of the younger generation. This chorus remained on stage at all times, observing and commenting on the activities of the campus characters—administrators, teachers, and students—who enacted the various scenes on the two lower levels of the platform. Various areas were lighted as scenes shifted facilely from the woman's apartment to a journalism laboratory, from the dean's office to the gymnasium and the football stadium, for events such as dances, banquets, sports events, "be-ins," and classes.

Only the Narrator, the older, returned woman, the journal of her year's experience in her hand, did not change costume as she told her story from her point of view. The other members of the cast were costumed, changed attire often, and spoke from memory. Although most scenes utilized onstage focus, properties were imagined.

A setting suggestive of the theme of Education Is a Riot—*that a person's inner aura is more important than his outward appearance—is seen in these pictures with the suspended circle representing the "aura." Both onstage and offstage focus were used, as illustrated in the photos.*

A compiled script, arranged and directed for Readers Theatre by Chloe Armstrong, Baylor University. Professor Armstrong furnished the notes on this production.

The idea behind this script was to introduce the literary works of Eudora Welty and to show how a group of selections may be collocated into a unified program. Two short stories, "Lilly Daw and the Three Ladies," and "Why I Live at the P.O.," and a novel, *The Ponder Heart,* offered contrasts in content, mood, and characters.

The basic stage arrangements were simple and easily achieved. The stage itself, with the addition of a few steps, gave three different levels. Lecterns and revolving stools were used by the readers, who were augmented by an occasional "walk-on" reader. A large book with the title "An Evening with Eudora Welty" printed on the cover stood on an easel at the back of the stage. The physical presence of the book not only helped in making transitions from one selection to another, but also was a subtle reminder to the audience that they were listening to a reading of stories by Miss Welty. All readers used scripts throughout the evening. No special makeup or sound effects were designed, but lighting effects to achieve "fade in," "fade out," and transitions of time and place were employed. Although the readers were not costumed as characters, attention was given to the choice of colors worn by the readers to achieve contrast and to reflect the emotional content of the literary materials.

The role of the Narrator was very important in each story. In "Lilly Daw and the Three Ladies" the Narrator walked onstage after the other readers had taken their places on stools behind the lecterns, with Lilly Daw seated on a small stool downstage in front of the three ladies. The Narrator turned the page of the book to the title page, "Lilly Daw and the Three Ladies," and then walked downstage and stopped on the steps to address the audience. She moved about the stage as she gave narration and description, and kept in the background when other readers were reading dialogue. Individual readers interpreted Mrs. Watts, Mrs. Carson, Amie Slocum, and Lilly Daw. Two women read the dialogue of all other female characters, while two male readers read the dialogue of the male characters.

The character Sister in "Why I Live at the P.O." served as the Narrator, telling the story in the first person. As in the previous story, she came on stage after the other readers were seated on their stools, turned the pages of the book to the title, "Why I Live at the P.O.," and took her place with the other readers on the stools. Each of the three female and two male characters in the story was read by an individual reader.

Since a brief intermission followed the second of the three stories, there was time for slight changes in the stage arrangements, and for one of the readers to turn the pages of the book to the last title, *The Ponder Heart.* Twenty-five readers appeared in this presentation, so only those necessary for the first part of the story took their places on the onstage stools for the opening of the program.

One of the characters in the novel, Edna Earle, told the whole story, but to have a balance of material and to create a dramatic effect, three narrators were used in this script. There were two Edna Earles, one who read the narrative and descriptive material, and one who read the actual dialogue of Edna Earle. When the lights came on, two women readers came walking down the aisle, talking with each other, and took their places on the steps of the stage. One was Edna Earle, the other an improvised neighbor. With a little rearranging of the material, the scene was created as the conversation of two women, one telling the history of the "Ponders," and the other, an enthusiastic listener, punctuating the conversation with questions and comments. The third narrator, or storyteller, was the Edna Earle who read the dialogue. Stage lighting was used to "fade out" the narrators sitting on the steps and to focus on other readers seated on stools during actual direct dialogue. Individual readers were used for the main characters such as Uncle Daniel, Edna Earle, Grandpa, Judge, the lawyers, Bonnie Dee, and Narciss. Other readers assumed multiple roles. One group of readers, with some slight rearranging for each, served as townspeople, the jury, and spectators at the trial.

A minimum amount of movement and action was used. When the Narrator began relating the trial the readers participating in the court scene, such as the Judge and the lawyers, came onstage and took their places on stools. Each witness walked on as he or she was called to the witness stand, and left as dismissed by the Judge. The production concluded with two Narrators sitting on the steps. As Edna Earle explained she would call Uncle Daniel, he responded, turned around, and the light focused on the two Narrators and Uncle Daniel.

As the readers walked off the stage, one member of the cast closed the book, "An Evening with Eudora Welty," thus ending the presentation.

Every Face Tells a Story

A compiled script, arranged and presented by Leslie Irene Coger and her Readers Theatre class at Southwest Missouri State University.

Essentially a framework to show how miscellaneous selections may be incorporated into a unified program, the final script contained a comic essay, a poem, three short stories, and a passage from a novel. A train conductor unified the materials by commenting on the faces of the people riding in a railroad coach car. One reader from each "story" sat in the train, which was represented by two parallel rows of chairs at L. As the program began, the readers for the first selection, "Mrs. Bentley's Story," were seated on stools at C (except Mrs. Bentley). A spotlight came up on the area at R to single out a man in a conductor's hat. He looked at his watch, listened for the whistle of a train, nodded, and began to speak.

CONDUCTOR. Hello! Yep, she's right on schedule. I'm the conductor on that train over there, have been for thirty-five years. I was once asked why I like my job, and the first thing that popped into my head was—faces. As I take tickets, I like to look into the faces of the passengers, and sometimes I feel that each face wants to tell me why it is happy or sad. A person can fool his heart and his head, but he can never conceal his true feelings from his face. Every face has its story! Sometimes I pick out an interesting face and just let my imagination go. (*Train whistle is heard.*) Well, it's time to get aboard. This way, please. All aboard! (*Music comes up under his words.*) Take this little old lady, for example—that faraway, dreamy look. Do you suppose she's thinking of a new recipe for Thanksgiving, or is she remembering . . . remembering a yesteryear more important to her than today?

(*The lights come up on* MRS. BENTLEY *as she rises, walks from L to C, and joins the other* READERS *involved in her story. The music fades out.*)

READING: "Mrs. Bentley," from *Dandelion Wine* by Ray Bradbury.

(*As the story ends, the lights go off; in the darkness,* MRS. BENTLEY *and her* READERS *return to L; the stools they have been using are removed; a table and two chairs are brought in and arranged at C;* TWO LADIES *rise from their seats at L, cross to C, and seat themselves in the chairs. Meanwhile, the spotlight comes up again on the* CONDUCTOR *at R.*)

CONDUCTOR. Those two ladies ride this train at least once a week, but they usually ride in the club car. Wonder why they're riding in my car today? (*The lights come up on the* TWO LADIES *at table C.*)

READING: "How to Guess Your Age" by Corey Ford.

(*At the conclusion, the lights go down on the* TWO LADIES; *they return to their seats at L; the table and chairs are removed; a* MAN *enters to C, and the spotlight comes up on the* CONDUCTOR.*)

CONDUCTOR. Once this woman's face was happy, but it hasn't been the same since she lost her child.

(*The lights brighten on the* WOMAN *as she rises from her chair in the "train" at L, and crosses to the* MAN *at C.*)

READING: "Home Burial" by Robert Frost.

(*The lights go down on the* WOMAN *and the* MAN, *who remain at C. Three stools are brought in and positioned at C. Meanwhile, the spotlight comes up on the* CONDUCTOR.*)

CONDUCTOR. Here's an interesting face. This old boy looks as if he's just put something over on somebody. There's age in that face, and I'll bet he's enjoying every minute of his life.

(*The lights pick up an* OLD MAN *as he rises from his seat in the "train" at L, walks to C, and joins the* MAN *and the* WOMAN. *The three seat themselves on the stools.*)

READING: "Heyday of the Blood" by Dorothy Canfield Fisher.

(*When the reading is concluded, the light dims on the* OLD MAN, *the* WOMAN, *and the* MAN. *In the darkness, the* MAN *disappears; the* WOMAN *and the* OLD MAN *cross to L and resume their former seats on the "train." A* BOY *and a* GIRL *enter and take positions at C. Meanwhile, the spotlight comes up on the* CONDUCTOR.)

CONDUCTOR. Now here's a young man who doesn't look too happy. My guess is there's a girl in this boy's story somewhere. And from the looks of him, I'd say his plans didn't exactly work out.

(*The spotlight comes up on* ANOTHER BOY *as he rises from his seat at L, walks to C, and joins the* BOY *and the* GIRL.)

READING: "Love Is a Fallacy" by Max Shulman.

(*The lights fade out on the group at C. In the darkness, the* BOY *and the* GIRL *disappear;* ANOTHER BOY *returns to L and resumes his seat; and* FIVE MEN *and the* SECOND WOMAN *enter and take positions at C. Meanwhile, the spotlight comes up again on the* CONDUCTOR.)

CONDUCTOR. Here's a face that epitomizes drudgery, toil of the earth; yet, there's something in this plain face that shows that the girl has been touched by beauty.

(*The light comes up on the* SECOND GIRL *as she rises from her seat on the "train" at L, walks to C, and joins the* FIVE MEN *and the* SECOND WOMAN.)

READING: "So Beautiful with Shoes" by Wilbur Daniel Steele.

(*At the end, the lights fade out on the* SECOND GIRL, *the* FIVE MEN, *and the* SECOND WOMAN; *and the spotlight comes up on the* CONDUCTOR. *There is a long, mournful sound of a train whistle. The* CONDUCTOR *glances at his watch with an air of finality.*)

CONDUCTOR. Yep . . . right on schedule. (*The train whistles again.*)

God Bless You, Mr. Rosewater, or Pearls Before the Swine   by Kurt Vonnegut, Jr.

A novel adapted and directed in Readers Theatre form by Elbert R. Bowen at Central Michigan University for a faculty presentation. The following remarks were provided by the director, Dr. Bowen.

The form of a production, its design and style, must derive from the literature itself. When the narrator can figure in the dramatic action of a production of prose fiction, we call that type of Readers Theatre "Chamber Theatre." It is admittedly so much fun to work with the narrator as a character that we sometimes forget that prose fiction can often be presented effectively with an undisguised narrator. Let him be a narrator and nothing else! Such is the case with the narrator in Vonnegut's novel. This storyteller is blatantly sarcastic, almost sardonic, about the major character, Eliot Rosewater. Furthermore, he speaks at great length. In our production the narrator became *three* narrators—three men, sitting side by side on tall stools behind reading stands, batting out the story with three interesting varieties of cynicism. They were fast and they were noisy, blasting the audience with Vonnegut's black humor. The narrators were interesting enough as personalities to hold attention well, but, while listening, the audience could also watch three readers—also on stools behind stands—who represented the major characters: a talented young woman who read all female roles of the novel, a man who read the role of Senator Rosewater, Eliot's reactionary father, and, seated center stage on a toilet seat, a man who read Eliot Rosewater, a fat man in long underwear as described by the novel. The readers never left their places; they read from manuscript, but they read dramatically. The audience and the novel needed no further assistance.

Costumes and properties as described in the novel God Bless You, Mr. Rosewater *add to the black comedy in the performance. Here Eliot Rosewater, a fat man in long underwear, is seen C on a toilet seat.*

A "New Theatre" one-act play, adapted and produced for Readers Theatre by E. Annette Mazzaferri at Kutztown (Penna.) State College. This report was furnished by Dr. Mazzaferri.

This one-act play with its stress on lack of communication in our society was presented on a small thrust stage in the Little Theatre. Focus varied from offstage to onstage; movement varied from psychological to overt gross movement encompassing the audience; scripts were used for "gesture expression." The speaker's attitude was demonstrated by the way he used his book: if hesitant, he turned a page hesitantly; if angry, he gripped the book with tension. The scripts also served as props; readers treated them as portfolios, hors d'oeuvres trays, or purses. The aim of the production was to create in the audience a sense of the chaos, impersonality, and futility of our current society.

Initially three interviewers faced front on three high stools lined up horizontally. They were dressed in navy blue pantsuits and sat rigidly holding large black leather books. On a horizontal line upstage, four interviewees stood flanking the stools. Each interviewee dressed individually to *suggest* a painter, a bank president, a cleaning woman, and a governess. Each held his or her book as a prop. When out-of-scene each faced the rear; when in-scene, the front.

Scene 1 consisted of interviews. When the interviewees became angered by questions, they stood downstage between the stools (see Figure 8). In-

FIGURE 8.   Floor plan for *Interview*

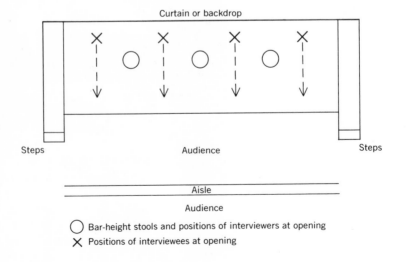

○ Bar-height stools and positions of interviewers at opening
✕ Positions of interviewees at opening

terviewers examined the applicants by rising and moving in a snake line in and around them.

Scene 2 began with interviewers and interviewees moving offstage through the center aisle of the audience, as one reader became "stranded" onstage. In her speech on being lost she addressed various readers who ignored her and kept moving across stage and through the audience.

Readers adapted stools and scripts to suggest a subway, a telephone switchboard, a cocktail party, and a confessional. At the end, the priest, who with his back to the audience had sat on a high stool DL while the penitent knelt at the base of the stool and all others stood with bowed heads in a line C stage to DR, became the politician and confronted various members of the audience as he moved out of the room. The remaining readers flopped down on the edge of the stage, becoming his admiring fans.

The Last Summer   by George P. McCallum

An original full-length play written especially for Readers Theatre, and presented at California State University, Hayward, as well as at the Banff School of Fine Arts, University of Calgary, under the direction of Melvin R. White.

This nostalgic look at a bygone era, the depression, in 1932, in Salmon Bay, Puget Sound, tells the story of a city-oriented family at their summer residence, a farm. The action covers an entire summer, and takes place in many different spots: the family home, a strawberry patch, an island in the sound, a Sunday school picnic, a highway, a pasture, and dozens of other places—all of them in the mind of the Narrator, who recalls his last summer at Salmon Bay with his grandparents.

The various scenes were developed around the Narrator, who, except when telling his story to the audience, sat in a chair C. Next to him was a chair for Petey, actually the Narrator at age twelve in 1932. A double row of chairs facing away from the audience at R accommodated readers who were not members of the family; the family occupied chairs arranged similarly at L. From these positions readers moved into and out of the many scenes as needed. Family scenes occurred in Area #3; away-from-home scenes in Area #1. When friends came to see the family, they moved to Area #3. When family members went away from the immediate vicinity of home, they crossed to Area #1. If large numbers of characters were involved, Area #3 spread into the center, Area #2, as did Area #1 when more space was needed. One exception was made. The Sunday school incident was staged in the auditorium, with the children and the teacher sitting in the audience near the front, taking their seats as if they were there to see the show as the first audience members were admitted. The teacher stood

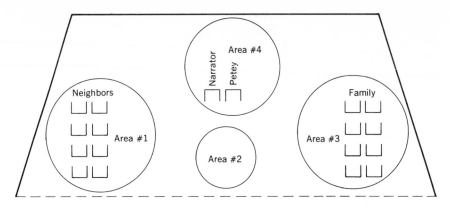

FIGURE 9. *The Last Summer* floor plan

as the scene started, using the entire front section of the audience as her class. Then, during the intermission following Act I, the children went backstage, ready for the Sunday school picnic scene which was played in Areas #1 and #2.

Petey moved back and forth from UC (the present), Area #4, where he talked with the Narrator, to all parts of the stage, participating actively in the events of 1932—or, in some instances, watching them along with the Narrator as they occurred.

In one production, area lighting was arranged which concentrated attention on the particular playing area or areas in use. Although this added to the theatricalism of the production, and perhaps assisted the audience members in shifting their imaginations from one scene to another, it was difficult to handle because of the intermittent exchanges between the Narrator and Petey, some of which were only a sentence or two in length. This problem was resolved, although not entirely satisfactorily, by retaining some space lighting in Area #4 throughout the performance.

The readers wore their own or borrowed clothes, with appropriate maturity in costuming for older characters such as the grandparents, some slight degree of character suggestion for farmers, the sheriff, and the Sunday school teacher, and more juvenile-appearing attire for children. Assistance was given the readers through the colors of costumes, too—somber for the sober, gay and bright for the children and the ex-actress, dark and faded for the older folk and working men. But most differences in ages and personalities were achieved through characterization rather than through makeup, hair arrangements, and costume.[3]

---

[3] For information on production rights to *The Last Summer,* write Dr. Melvin R. White, 583 Boulevard Way, Piedmont, California 94610.

In The Last Summer *the narrator remembers his past as the Sheriff tells Petey, the ex-actress, and the grandfather about the bootleggers he is trying to catch.*

Lazarus Laughed   by Eugene O'Neill

A stage play, adapted and directed as a Choral Theatre production by I. Blaine Quarnstrom, and presented at Central Michigan University.[4]

Eugene O'Neill's "philosophical pageant," *Lazarus Laughed,* was written in 1927, and received its first and only professional production at the Pasadena Playhouse in 1928. Since that time there have been only scattered productions of the play by colleges and universities. One of the major reasons for the scarcity of productions is undoubtedly the tremendous technical demands called for by O'Neill in the script. The large cast with its many choruses, the detailed masks suggested by the script, and [the] very difficult sustained laughter which the play calls for are all possible inhibiters.

---

[4] From I. Blaine Quarnstrom, "A Choral Theatre Production," *IIG Newsletter,* November 1968, pp. 20, 23. Reprinted by permission of I. Blaine Quarnstrom.

Lazarus Laughed, with its philosophical discussion of "love," "peace," and "war," presents ideas which are particularly timely for contemporary audiences. Our experimental theatre production of the play at Central Michigan was motivated by this fact. The play was presented in a 1400-seat theatre with a cast of twenty-five. The production employed a considerable amount of lighting and sound effects. Five solo performers portrayed the principal roles of the play in front of a chorus of twenty. The chorus used indirect-focus–audience-locus, and they moved about on an arrangement of platforms and step units during the course of the play. The voice choir proved to be a very exciting element in the production, and succeeded in communicating effectively the laughter which runs throughout the O'Neill script.

Costumes for the chorus consisted of black turtleneck shirts and trousers. Each chorus member wore also a string of "love" beads. The three male principals wore Nehru jackets—white for Lazarus, deep red for Tiberius, and green for Caligula. The Lazarus costume also included a large gold medallion of a peace symbol inlaid with multicolored stained glass. [The] Tiberius and Caligula costumes included several metal necklaces with medallions. The two female roles were costumed contrastingly to suggest the characters. Miriam's costume was gray wool with a Nehru collar and a strand of "love" beads. Pompeia's costume was mini-length, made of yellow chiffon, and trimmed with rhinestones.

Theatrical lighting was used to suggest locale and create a mood. The stage was draped in black and the only scenery other than platforms and stairs [were] rays of Saran Wrap which extended from the UC platform into the loft. This fan of translucent rays provided an interesting background on which the lights could play. Two scenes in particular were enhanced by unusual lighting. The battle scene which follows the revelation of Christ's crucifixion was very effectively communicated by the use of flashing green and purple lights. The sound of the chorus and [the] visual effect of the flashing color succeeded in communicating to the audience the desired effects of tragedy and battle. A second scene which became unbearably exciting was the final one in which Lazarus is burned at the stake in a Roman amphitheatre. The chorus was arranged in a semicircle behind the solo performers who focused directly toward the audience. The auditorium became the amphitheatre as Lazarus from offstage spoke his lines through a multi-speaker amplification system. The added sound of the jeering chorus and the visual effect of the intense red flickering lights which suddenly changed to white at a strategic moment succeeded in causing the audience to deeply contemplate O'Neill's thesis that "there is no death."

The production received excellent audience response. The numbers increased at each performance, with a surprising number of individuals returning a second and third time, expressing after each hearing a greater interest in and appreciation of the play.

Lisa and David   by Theodore Isaac Rubin

> *A novel adapted for arena-theatre style Readers Theatre by James Jewell, and presented at Illinois Valley Community College. The information on the production was provided by Mr. Jewell.*

Lisa and David is a novel written in the form of two intertwining case histories of children in a residential home for the emotionally disturbed. Because the segments of the story alternate and take place in different rooms, the performance was staged "in the round," or in a figure eight, with one area serving as Lisa's room and the other as David's. Neither Lisa nor David have particularly close contact with each other or with the other characters in the story; this manner of staging kept them separate, while at the same time maintaining a proximity with the audience.

Case history and background material were presented by six interpreters performing as interns and nurses who were located around the edges of the figure eight. Each was free to direct his part of the narration directly to the audience, while Lisa and David largely ignored the audience, in keeping with the nature of their disturbances.

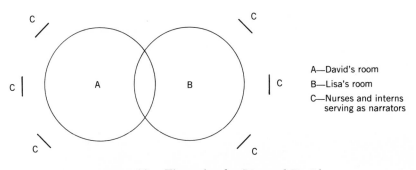

FIGURE 10.   Floor plan for *Lisa and David*

The two sections of the figure eight overlapped (see Figure 10), although neither had a definite boundary in staging. This overlapping was important in the final scene in which David overcomes his fear of being touched and Lisa stops talking in rhymes. They agree to go for a walk, and David asks Lisa to take his hand. The scene was played in the overlap area, as their worlds were no longer separate.

Lost in the Stars   by Maxwell Anderson

A stage musical based on Alan Paton's novel Cry the Beloved Country, *adapted and arranged for Readers Theatre with choral reading by Lucille and Bren Breneman, directed by Lucille Breneman, and presented at the University of Hawaii. It was subsequently shown on ETV in Hawaii. Mrs. Breneman furnished the following information.*

Twenty-seven readers performed this one-hour-and-twenty-minute cutting of the musical. Since much of the material was appropriate for choral reading techniques, a black chorus and a white chorus contributed significantly to the total effectiveness of the production. In addition to heightening the mood, the choruses carried some of the narration. However, one Narrator presented all of the other necessary transitions, as well as changes in setting.

The choruses were arranged R and L on steps set on the auditorium floor, progressing in elevation to the stage apron. Onstage elevation was continued through the use of platforms and chairs. The stage itself was only eight feet deep. The Narrator stood on the auditorium floor, R or L, always between the choruses. Readers interpreting individual characters were positioned in chairs or stood at the top where they could easily move into different areas on the stage for the fifteen different scenes. One stool was utilized in different positions for different purposes. One large, immobile, wooden lectern DL was used by the Judge in the court scene, and again by Kumalo as the pulpit in the church.

Vows are taken in Lost in the Stars.

The focus was offstage during most of the presentation; however, exceptions were made in a few scenes involving only two people, and in two larger scenes. For example, onstage focus was used by Irina and Kumalo in Irina's hut. The only time the choruses used onstage focus was when they turned toward Kumalo at the pulpit and he addressed them as a congregation. Onstage focus was also employed in the large "dive" scene, which involved six women and three men. In this scene no scripts were in evidence, as the girls moved, danced, and spoke to rhythm, sometimes in unison, sometimes solo.

Dress was suggestive of mood and character. All of the women's dresses were of the same style, cut from the same pattern, but of different colors. Irina wore blue; the six "dive" girls, hot pink, orange, gold, green, pumpkin, and fuchsia; the Narrator, beige. All other women were in black or white, depending on their chorus affiliation. Except for the young blacks who were in turtlenecks, the men wore dark suits and ties.

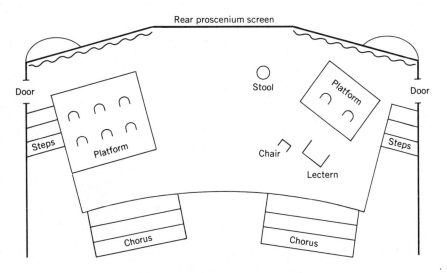

FIGURE 11. Floor plan for *Lost in the Stars*

Audiovisual effects contributed greatly to the overall success of *Lost in the Stars*. Area lighting and intensity changes coordinated with appropriate music helped create mood and unify the story. During the introduction six colored slides of scenes in Africa were projected on the large screen at the back of the stage. These depicted the contrast of the "green, rich veld" and the "poor, brown earth" in Africa, the settings for the book and the play.

This presentation of Pamela Travers' Mary Poppins *employed a number of suggested settings, two of which are shown here. The lower photo illustrates the ingenious handling of the "hanging from the ceiling" scene.*

Mary Poppins   by P. L. Travers

A children's story, adapted by Charles Closser, Jr., and presented at the University of Missouri. Frances McCurdy provided the information about this presentation.

Except for the roles of Mary Poppins, Michael Banks, and Jane Banks, the readers assumed multiple roles. Suggestive costuming was used: Mrs. Corry's daughters wore aprons over the black skirts and white blouses that formed the basic costume for all the girls, and the policeman wore a coat and policeman's cap in the park scene. On stage throughout the performance was the suggestion of a nursery setting, consisting of an elevated platform with stools and a large cutout of a bureau; but from time to time other cutouts were dropped from the grid or rolled on from the wings. A merry-go-round, with silhouette horses and a platform that could revolve on wheels, was rolled on for the scene where Mary Poppins leaves and afterwards was rolled out through the back curtains.

In the scene where Mary and the children visit Mr. Turny on the ceiling, the participants hung upside down on four firmly based chairs. In this position, of course, the readers had to exercise special care to make their words understandable to the audience. At the opening of each scene, Mary Poppins crossed to a large "book" at the side of the stage and announced the impending episode as she turned a page and placed a card with the title of the scene in a special slot. The readers did not use scripts, but delivered their lines from memory.

The Mikado   by Sir William S. Gilbert and Sir Arthur Sullivan

An operetta, adapted for Readers Theatre by Melvin R. White, and produced at Brooklyn College and the University of Arkansas.

Except for the overture, which provided aural atmosphere before the show started, this reading version did not include any of the music of *The Mikado;* instead it concentrated on the lines, the characters, and the plot as the important ingredients. Presented first at Brooklyn College in a one-hour version, it was done very simply. The script called for a cast of eight leads (four men and four women), a male chorus, and a female chorus—both small in number. Because the reading was presented in an auditorium with a narrow stage and no backstage space, only the leads were provided with chairs on the stage; the choruses had chairs out front in the auditorium itself but as close to the right and the left sides of the stage as possible. For this formal and simple reading, all the men wore business suits, and the women street dresses. No physical action was used, other than having the interpreters stand when "in the scene" and sit when not. Consequently no special lighting was designed; the reading area had only general illumination, and the houselights remained on throughout. No scenery changes were involved, and no props were provided.

At the University of Arkansas, *The Mikado* was offered as a modified stage production which involved the use of scripts, simple sets, colorful attire, and elaborate stage lighting. To enhance the production's effectiveness, oriental "rainbow" colors were chosen for most costumes. The chorus of men wore light summer trousers with knit shirts of many colors; the chorus of women wore bright summer dresses. The Mikado was attired in a green summer suit and a brilliant, red shirt. Katisha was garbed in a dull, unattractive brown dress in order to add to her size and apparent maturity. Ko-Ko wore black trousers with an off-white shirt. Pooh-Bah also wore dark colors. No suggestion of oriental costuming was attempted, merely the overall effect of bright, splashy colors. Oriental costuming can be used, however, to good advantage. For instance, in another performance of this adaptation, given at Southern Illinois University, the entire cast was costumed in kimonos and wore Japanese wigs and makeup.

For the Arkansas production, an oriental, simple and inexpensive, yet very effective set was designed. (See the illustration on page 167.) Each of the screens was made from four regular-sized flats, painted in yellow-gold with designs of Japanese trees as decor. The back wall and the two chorus platforms were painted black, as were the seven benches—two on each of the chorus platforms, one long one DC, one short one DR, and another short one DL. However, simple designs in gold and red were painted on the fronts of the three main benches, those at DC, DR, and DL.

FIGURE 12.   *The Mikado* floor plan

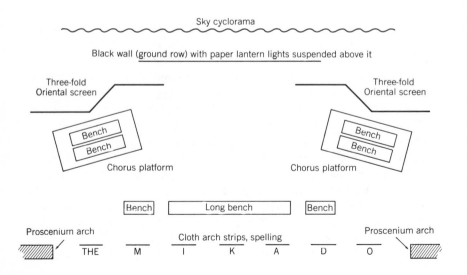

Imaginatively but simply mounted and costumed, this production of the Gilbert and Sullivan operetta The Mikado *employed dual platforms and a series of low benches. The swift grouping and regrouping of the performers helped sustain a lively pace throughout.*

Above the back wall were three huge paper lanterns suspended from a bright-colored, pagoda-shaped halter. Hanging in the place of the front curtain were seven separate strips of material, each in a different bright color and each with one of the letters of the title, *THE MIKADO.* During the overture, as the houselights were dimmed out, spotlights singled out the letters; and then, when the cast entered, these title-strips were pulled up out of sight. Dark drapes at the sides of the stage masked the backstage area and permitted entrances and exits.

Stage lighting was used to focus attention on the most important area or actor at all times and to enhance the rainbow effect. The chorus platform-areas were illuminated when the choruses were reading and were dimmed out when they were not "in the scene," but were sitting quietly with bowed heads. In short, conventional stage lighting was used, adding to the beauty of the reading environment and the visual appeal of the actors. No conventional properties were employed in either the Brooklyn or the Arkansas production. For example, when the death certificate was mentioned, the reader merely held the top page of his manuscript above and away from the rest of his script, thus suggesting rather than using an actual certificate.

In each production, consistency was the important thing. The completeness of the sets, costumes, makeup, lights, and properties depended upon the extent to which the director wished to elaborate his production. In one instance, the reading was a simple one with ordinary chairs, everyday suits and dresses, and no special lights; in the other, it was a rather completely staged affair with many theatrical effects. But in each case, the director decided exactly which style he wanted to follow, and the presentation was consistent with that decision.

Moby Dick: Rehearsed

A novel by Herman Melville, adapted by Orson Welles, and directed by John Rude for presentation at the University of Missouri, Columbia, as a project in a Readers Theatre class. Frances McCurdy provided the information about this presentation.

Orson Welles' adaptation of Melville's novel is ideally suited to Readers Theatre. Since this production was offered in the University Theatre as a part of the 1971–1972 theatre season, the director, John Rude, provided more scenic effects than would customarily be used in Readers Theatre. Actually, the script could be staged with no scenery other than platforms and benches.

The Narrator, Ishmael, tells the story as a completed journey, yet recreates that journey as if it were happening in the present. (See top picture, opposite page.) The roles of Ahab, Starbuck, Pip, and the Narrator were each played by readers who concentrated on only one part. All others in the cast played multiple roles. Parts were memorized, but the Stage Manager, who was a part of the action and who furnished some stage effects in view of the audience, held a script.

Several scenes, including the sailors' chase of Moby Dick, were played behind a scrim curtain with lighting effects; however, Captain Ahab's battle with Moby Dick was enacted in a pool of light DC. (See middle picture, opposite page.)

One player suggested his change to the role of the Carpenter by tying a handkerchief around his head and making an apron from a scarf. He brought his bench with him as he moved into the scene. Pip was played by a young black woman rather than a small boy. (See bottom picture, opposite page.)

The atmosphere in this university production of Moby Dick *was enhanced by selective visibility and special scenic and lighting effects. The middle photo illustrates the imaginative use of a scrim curtain.*

A compiled script, arranged and directed by Fran Tanner, and presented by the College of Southern Idaho for the Interpreter's Theatre Alliance Festival at the University of Montana. Professor Tanner provided the following information.

Material was compiled to show in thirty minutes a humorous yet thought-provoking program on how man is becoming so increasingly mechanized that effective individualism is difficult to maintain.

Selections used, in order, were "Dirge," by Kenneth Fearing, "Observer: Person at Bay," by Russell Baker, two modern jokes, "The Man Who Can Do It Himself," by Reed Whittemore, "R U There, Madam?" by Martin Levin, "The Machine," by Carl Sandburg, "Dolor," by Theodore Roethke, "Death of a Student Hopelessly Failing My Course," by George Cuomo, and "Portrait of a Cog," by Kenneth Fearing. (All are poems except for Baker's essay and Levin's short story.)

To effect transitions and provide unity throughout, theme lines from the first, second, and fourth selections were repeated in cumulative fashion after each piece. Hence, "Zowie did he live and zowie did he die," from "Dirge," was inserted again after the second selection. "Help, I'm a person," from "Observer," followed. "This is a business machine card. Do not staple, fold, or mutilate," from "R U There," provided the third tie-in.

Readers moved into specific blocking for each selection. Scripts were used throughout, as was offstage focus, except for Sandburg's "The Machine." To introduce this selection readers put down their scripts, arranged themselves on and around a set of steps, and "became" the machine with its movements and sounds. They recited the first half of the poem while rhythmically foot tapping, then once again enacted the machine as it sped up and finally broke down.

Costumes suggested a mass-production effect, with all of the readers wearing identical gold jackets with numbers on their pockets, dark trousers or skirts, and identical ties.

Pulsating, mechanical-sounding music introduced and ended the show.

My Client Curley   by Norman Corwin

A radio script, adapted for Readers Theatre by Melvin R. White, and presented at Brooklyn College, California State University, Hayward, and Bancroft Junior High School, San Leandro, California.

Mr. Corwin's satire about a caterpillar that becomes a celebrity tosses delightful fun at faddism in America, deftly directing barbed, albeit kindly, attention to the near-hysteria with which many greet each new celebrity idol.

A cast of eight may double in roles, or up to twenty-five readers may participate. The three main characters are the Agent (Narrator), a live-wire type and effective storyteller; Stinky, a rather small, thin boy; and Fatso, a somewhat overweight boy. The other five readers suggest such widely diverse characters as lepidopterists, secretaries, reporters, Walt Disney, waiters, and shippers. When a large cast was decided upon, many of the readers were placed in the audience, scattered near the front and at the sides. It proved more effective to have the interpreters who sat in the audience memorize their lines, thus not calling attention in advance to the fact that they were in the show.

If a longer reading hour is desired, a tap dancer and a singer may be inserted for variety. Music, harmonica or otherwise, may be employed for transition purposes, as was done in the original Corwin script. Sound effects may also be used.

In this production, seven chairs and one stool were placed on the stage, and some readers were seated in the audience. Houselights were kept on throughout the reading. Onstage focus and much movement proved to be the most effective approach to this radio script. The Agent told his story to the audience, and various newsmen and speakers talked directly with the audience also. The rest of the scenes were played Chamber Theatre style, with memorized dialogue and onstage focus. No special costuming was arranged; the boys wore sweaters, the agent a somewhat flashy "Hollywood-agent" sport jacket, and others were dressed in suits and dresses appropriate to the humorous theme of the script and to the characters involved.

Since radio scripts are written for the ear and are provocative to the imaginations of the listeners, very few changes were necessary in adapting "My Client Curley" for Readers Theatre.

No Sense of Decency

A Readers Theatre script based on the Army-McCarthy hearings, devised and directed by Phillis Rienstra, and presented at the University of Texas at Austin. Beverly Whitaker provided the following information on this production.

A one-hour documentary Readers Theatre production, "No Sense of Decency" was an attempt to demonstrate the clash of ideologies and the repressive atmosphere that characterized the McCarthy era. While the Special Senate Investigation transcript of the Army-McCarthy hearings provided the nucleus for the drama, the script derived its unity from the rearrangement of episodes in the investigation, as well as from biographies and autobiographies of McCarthy and his contemporaries, news coverage of the period, historical documents, and *Point of Order,* an educational film of the hearings.

In addition to the four principal characters, Stuart Symington, Joseph Welch, Joseph McCarthy, and Roy Cohn, five minor characters, James Juliana, Miles Reber, Robert Stevens, Karl Mundt, and G. David Schine, contributed to the script's thematic probability. An objective reporter (the Voice) and a Narrator, both positioned in the audience, speaking from microphones, related events precipitating the hearings and made transitional editorial comments. An introduction to McCarthy with period epithets (the Voice), a review of the charges and countercharges in the dispute (Narrator), and self-descriptive character introductions provided the necessary background for the reenactment of the hearings. With Symington's summary of the charges and countercharges the principals assumed their original stage positions while the minor characters moved to the first row of house seats.

Forty groups of visuals (four two-inch-by-two-inch slides per group) rear-projected on ten-feet-by-ten-feet screens on either side of the stage served to support or extend the dialogue. Two conference tables, one raised platform, and three woodtone cardboard constructions were designed to suggest the original caucus room.

The structural components of "No Sense of Decency" included a prologue, followed by six episodes, which culminated in Welch's denunciation of McCarthy. The episodes were arranged to reveal progressively more harmful personal characteristics of McCarthy, as each episode encompassed progressively more destructive acts. Fear of impairing the spontaneity of dialogue precluded the use of scripts in the production.

Nobody Loves a Drunken Indian   by Clair Huffaker

A novel adapted for Readers Theatre by Pearl H. Galloway, and presented at the University of Arkansas, Fayetteville, with setting and lights by Preston Magruder. The following notes on the production were provided by Pearl Galloway.

This contemporary novel lends itself admirably to the Readers Theatre medium because it has much dialogue and the dramatic thread of an Indian revolt running throughout. This builds logically and excitingly to the final step, the march on Phoenix. Though it ends tragically, the viewer is amused throughout by the unusual schemes of the Indians to gain recognition. Because it is told in first person, the Narrator fits easily into the scenes and neatly furnishes all the transitions.

The basic set was a relatively simple one which remained fixed throughout the performance. Two benches and several stools were used at various intervals in different areas of the stage to provide different settings. A simple set unit with a hanging rug of Indian design was placed R and was consistently the local meeting place of the Indians. C was a three-foot long platform with step units before and behind it. Two benches sat parallel to the sides of the platform and were used as seating units in the courtroom scene, the mountain scene, and the scene set in the home of one of the characters. The steps and center platform served as the courtroom, as a pickup truck bouncing across the desert, and as the steps of the Phoenix County Court House. Characters moved in and out of scenes as necessary, and no delays resulted from scene changing.

Lighting was generally basic, with a few blackouts and some use of "night" light and special spots. Music was an integral part of the production, with authentic Indian chants and songs furnishing appropriate mood. Costuming was minimal, with a "flapping eagle" armband used to denote Flap's band of revolting Indians. Construction workers wore hard hats, the mayor a top hat, and the city lawyer a suit. But the main emphasis was on the nondescript attire of a group of very poor Indians. Only the Indian who capitulated to the white man wore an Indian costume and feathers.

The cast was large and demanded a few readers with great skill, but the results were amply rewarding for both the cast and the director.

A series of eleven scenes in Nobody Loves a Drunken Indian *utilized a simple step unit stage R and a platform and step unit stage C. Area lighting served to focus attention and enhance mood.*

Nothing Gold Can Stay[5]

A Readers Theatre production, adapted and directed by Betty Dayoub under the supervision of Leslie Irene Coger, and presented at Southwest Missouri State University at the Ozark Spring Interpretation Festival.

This full-length Readers Theatre production was based on a novel by Susan Hinton, *The Outsiders,* which is included on many high school reading lists. It is *West Side Story* type literature, dealing with juvenile gang warfare in the cities. The production was chosen for demonstration purposes to introduce high school students and their teachers, English and speech, to this medium of vitalized literary study.

The story, told in first person by the young lad Pony Boy, was framed in this production by the boy sitting at his desk, writing a personal-experience theme for his English teacher. As narrator, Pony walked in and out of the scenes as he related the conflicts between the "Greasers" and the "Socs." When the story was completed, Pony Boy was at his desk again.

The stage was bare except for three stools, one used by Pony Boy as his desk, and two others which were moved unobtrusively from place to place as needed. Sufficient stools were lined across the back, out of the lighted area, for the entire cast to sit on when not participating in a scene. (See picture on p. 84.)

The Odyssey: A Modern Sequel   by Nikos Kazantzakis. Translation by Kimon Friar

Books I through IV were presented at the University of Michigan, Trueblood Theatre, under the direction of Claribel Baird. The following notes on the production were furnished by Professor Baird.

A text was prepared using 1572 of the more than 5000 lines in the first four "books" or rhapsodes of Kazantzakis' *Odyssey.* No alteration was made in Friar's lines or language. Kazantzakis' *Odyssey* begins where Homer's leaves off, with Odysseus' return to Ithaca. The excerpt presented ends with his abduction of Helen from the court of Menelaus.

A group of eight—five men and three women—spoke twenty-six roles, including those of two narrators. All were graduate students vocally adequate for the poetry and for the great variety of vocal characterizations required.

---

[5] For complete information, pictures, and the script, see Betty Dayoub's MA production thesis on "Nothing Gold Can Stay," Library, Southwest Missouri State University, Springfield, Mo.

Of the eight performers only the one taking the part of Odysseus spoke a single role. Costumes, therefore, were not designed around a single character, but were uniform in design, with variety achieved through color. Men wore corduroy pants with girdled overblouses of brown, red-brown, gold, or green; the women's long, simple dresses were designed for freedom of movement, with only a slight nod in the direction of Grecian style. Long stoles permitted a variety of drapings for the numerous characters.

Platforms of three levels with steps allowed changes of position which, with lighting changes, enabled the focus to be altered and accentuated at given times. DC a triangular unit jutted out toward the audience. This could suggest, by turns, the prow of Odysseus' ship or Menelaus' chariot. It also provided a DC focus for Odysseus to deliver his reflective cicada speech. Slides projected from the back of a scrim cyclorama helped suggest change of locale, while color abstractions served to accentuate mood. Music composed by Morton Achter provided transitions, supported mood changes, and augmented crowd noises.

The performers entered as a group and remained on platform throughout the performance. They spoke from memory directly to the audience in expository passages; in direct dialogue each speaker visualized the character to whom he spoke only slightly in the direction of his colleague, but never with the actor's eye-to-eye address or lateral interaction. The text demanded this kind of presentation since often the speaker began in third person and shifted, even within a single line, to first person. This recurrent exposition enabled the speaker to sustain his presentational communication with the audience.

This production photo of The Odyssey: A Modern Sequel *emphasizes the use of offstage focus—the "visualization-forward technique," as well as special lighting for focus purposes.*

Movement was designed with three goals: first, and most important, to control the audience's focus of attention; second, to provide appropriate movement of a character into a scene, again to focus attention, but also to accentuate motivation of character; third, to achieve variety and effectiveness in pictorial groupings that would heighten the script's dramatic values. In intimate scenes, such as Odysseus' meeting with his son, Telemachus, and his scenes with Helen, performers were brought close together. Freedom from books enabled them to employ interrelated gesture, although they of course never touched one another since eye contact was suggested by visualization forward. Such interpretation demanded the closest concentration on the part of the speakers, and exactness of motivated timing which was achieved only by dedicated work over an eight-week period. The reward lay in the audience's concentrated attention simultaneously to the action of the narrative and to its poetry.

Purists of Readers Theatre might argue the validity of this presentation which may not have adhered to all "the rules." The goal here was to find the best possible way of engaging audience interest in a great poem and at the same time retaining focus on its dynamic theme of man's freedom. These were felt to be the demands of this particular script.

One Flew over the Cuckoo's Nest by Ken Kesey

Adapted and directed by Judith Ten Eyck, under the supervision of Leslie Irene Coger, for presentation at Southwest Missouri State University.

The story takes place in a mental institution and is seen through the eyes of the Chief, a patient (Narrator). He tells of the fun-loving ruffian McMurphy, who feigns insanity in order to get out of work on a penal pea farm.

The majority of the action occurs in a mental ward, where the patients are observed through a glass cage above them by the cruel eyes of the Big Nurse. Simplicity and mobility of scenery allowed the show to move effortlessly from scene to scene. The Nurse sat on a three-foot platform behind the patients, who were seated on low swivel stools which were moved to various positions to establish different scenes. Throughout the production the presence of the Nurse was felt, as she sat above the inmates even when she did not participate in a scene.

A staircase unit was located R. The Narrator (Chief) remained in this area for most of his scenes since he was a chronic patient and the other patients were acutes. This device showed his alienation from the others.

The bulk of the two-act production took place on the large stage apron; however, following the intermission the apron was cleared and the main curtain opened for a scene on stage, in which the patients traveled to the sea for a boat trip. Several large stacked boxes served as both car and boat. Following the boat trip scene, the readers returned to the apron for the remainder of the presentation.

The adaptation employed offstage focus except for one climactic scene, the one which highlights the beginning of the Chief's recovery and of the overthrow of the domineering Big Nurse.

Lighting helped establish mood and accomplish smooth scene changes. As the Narrator moved out of a scene the lights dimmed. The color of the lights established the mood or character type in a scene. For instance, red was employed for the confusion or anger of a patient, blue for the coldness of the Nurse or loneliness of the patients, and warm lights for the fun-loving McMurphy and times of happiness among the patients. During one scene thoughts of the Big Nurse were tormenting the Chief who was in the disturbed ward receiving shock treatment. To heighten the narration of this treatment a red spotlight was flashed on and off as it streamed over the Chief's body. As he twisted and turned in his torment, the lights created a psychedelic effect and underscored his response to the electric shocks.

Through simplicity of scenery and reinforcement of mood by lighting, the story came alive for the audience.

A Singular Man   by J. P. Donleavy

A novel adapted and directed for Chamber Theatre by Elbert R. Bowen at Central Michigan University. The following notes were provided by Dr. Bowen.

We believe that the primary strength of all forms of Readers Theatre is the opportunity to work upon the imaginations of the audience. In spite of this premise which we hold dear, we set out to give Donleavy's boisterous novel its due action on the stage. Our restraining guide was: No one must question that we are doing "Readers" Theatre. Our most perceptive compliment upon our work from an observer was: How did you ever have so much action on stage and yet not take away our right to imagine for ourselves?

We began by putting one reading stand onto a bare platform. The single manuscript rested there when not used by the major character. This stand remained DR, a constant reminder of the source of the action. The actor of George Smith referred to it at the start of each of the thirteen scenes and at any other time he needed it, but it was the *actor,* not the character, who used it.

Then we put our five actors on this bare stage. Those not in the action needed a place to go. They sat on straight chairs upstage, facing the action and the audience. So that they would not distract, they remained pokerfaced; the audience soon learned that there was nothing to watch there, and yet they were aware of their presence, as actors off-duty. Now onstage we placed the very minimum needed for our performance, a single chair. If two characters needed to sit, we pulled down another chair from the rear. Everything else was imagined: desk, typewriter, telephone, table, food, eating utensils, doors, walls, articles of clothing, and all. We made one exception: in one scene George Smith wore blue-tinted eyeglasses. We could have done without them, but it was desirable not to see his eyes; therefore, we used them along with the chairs. But we had action, lots of action! It was overdrawn, for there was farce in this black comedy.

Characterizations were assumed and dropped instantaneously as performers stepped from their chairs into the action and back again. Caricature was used freely. Three actors were associated with only one character. Another played a bit part in addition to her major role, and one man played all male roles other than the lead. The performers were frankly presentational. The actors obviously knew the audience was present, but only the two male actors acknowledged it. George Smith delivered part of his narration to the audience and muttered part of it openly for the audience to hear if it wished to. The little man who played nine roles was around so much being helpful that he, too, was a direct pipeline to the audience.

Smith's unique narration, written in third person and in Donleavy's characteristic style, helped make it an interesting show. It was a "different" kind of production with lots to see and hear and yet with much left to the imagination.

In A Singular Man *the audience is able to picture two characters viewing—with different reactions—an object in a store window.*

Skin of Our Teeth   by Thornton Wilder

> *A three-act stage play, adapted by Melvin R. White for presentation at the University of Hawaii, Brooklyn College, Banff School of Fine Arts, University of Alberta, and Surfside Theatre, Canal Zone.*

Many of the conventions and devices used by Thornton Wilder in his plays are the same as or similar to those employed in Readers Theatre; for this reason, his plays easily lend themselves to group-reading interpretation. As presented on the conventional stage, *Skin of Our Teeth* is often extremely theatrical, with trick sets, animal characters, and elaborate costumes. This theatricalism has sometimes confused an audience not acquainted with the play, for they tend to watch the fascinating creatures and stage effects rather than concentrate on the dialogue and its meaning. Readers Theatre, by its very nature, tends to trim away the trappings, and perhaps this is one reason why this story of man's ability to escape destruction "by the skin of his teeth" has proved so successful and appealing in its Readers Theatre presentations in the United States and Canada.

In the various productions, the focus (with few exceptions) was onstage, with the characters relating directly to each other. The exceptions were at those places in the original acting edition where Wilder specifically called for performer contact with the audience. Some readers, such as various mob-scene characters, came up onto the stage from the audience.

In the Hawaiian production, no special lighting was possible because of technical limitations; in Canada, no special lighting was used because the presentation was given in a sun-filled music-rehearsal room; in Brooklyn, special lighting was used to establish place and evoke mood. Also in the Brooklyn production, special sound effects of storm and wind were provided for the flood scene, whereas in the other presentations the audience had to use its imagination. Only a suggestion of costuming was ever used: Mrs. Antrobus dressed a bit matronly; Mr. Antrobus, somewhat somberly; the Fortune Teller, with a small shawl; Sabina, in a tight-fitting red dress; and the children, in clothing appropriate for the young. Henry, for example, wore a shirt and trousers in Act I, adding his coat later when he was a man returning from the war.

The cast for this play is large, but even so it was possible to keep most of the readers onstage in two rows of chairs. There were a few exceptions, of course, including those who made their entrances from the audience and the Fortune Teller, who was not needed until the second act. In Hawaii, the two rows of chairs faced the audience; in Brooklyn, they faced the rear of the stage, an arrangement which is much easier for the readers because they need not sit quite so sedately and motionless for lengthy intervals. In Banff, the platform was very long and narrow, not deep enough to accommodate the two rows of chairs and still have a playing area in front of them. Therefore, the double row of chairs was divided in the middle, and the center of the platform became the playing area for those scenes requiring special movement or enactment. As a result of this space limitation, more readers remained in the audience or returned to their seats in the auditorium once the episode in which they had been participating was completed.

At Surfside Theatre, Canal Zone, for the Army Recreation Program, *Skin of Our Teeth* was staged arena style (or in-the-round), with the audience elevated on four sides. The actors' entrances and exits were made from the four corners. Entrances of the actors from the front door were made through Entrance I; from upstairs, Entrance II; from the backyard and kitchen, Entrance III; and from the side yard, Entrance IV. Imaginary windows were established as indicated in Figure 13. Two long benches and a center "pedestal-fireplace" constituted the scenery, but elaborate area and mood lighting and extensive sound effects served to enhance the theatricalism of the production. All lines were memorized, and action was completely blocked, as in a regular theatre presentation. The audience's imagination, however, supplied costumes and scenery. The success of this Readers Theatre production prompted the Army to send the show on a tour of other base theatres in the area after the Surfside Theatre run ended, vouching for the possibilities of arena-style productions of Readers Theatre.

This adaptation of Thornton Wilder's Skin of Our Teeth *involved few scenic elements and little costuming. Reality was achieved principally through lighting effects and the imaginative capacities of a participating, rather than a passive, audience.*

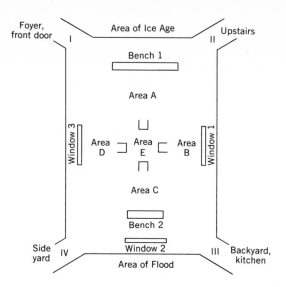

FIGURE 13. Floor plan for *Skin of Our Teeth*, Surfside Theatre, Canal Zone

The Sound of the Sixties

A multimedia-framed Chamber Theatre production, adapted and directed by Nancy Fox under the supervision of Leslie Irene Coger, and presented at the Ozark Spring Interpretation Festival at Southwest Missouri State University.

A desire to explore the sixties inspired this program. It was determined that alienation and withdrawal were two major characteristics of the human condition in this period, which was marked by poverty, violence, demonstration, immolation, and assassination. To frame (or introduce and conclude) the production, a montage of slides and movies were flashed on screens immediately above a three-tiered platform consisting of ramps, oblong cubes, and levels. Pictures from various publications of the period of mob violence, police action, hungry children, burning bodies, grieving relatives, the assassinations of John Kennedy, Robert Kennedy, and Martin Luther King, Jr., were often superimposed as well as juxtaposed in contextual patterns of terrifying comment.

Toward the end of the projected sequence the Narrator's voice was heard describing the major response of the general populace as one of alienation and withdrawal. Then, revealed by light, the Narrator led the audience into the story of one man's nineteen-year withdrawal from the active world. At the end of his nineteen years, as told in Peter Beagle's novel *A Fine and Private Place,* the man is persuaded to return to the active world of hope, and a movie is shown of green fields, flowers, children at play, and a colored balloon ascending into a blue sky, thus completing the multimedia framework.

Grey-textured oblongs and cubes represented gravestones and mausoleums, since the story occurred in a cemetery. The dead girl wore a wraithlike, flowing, filmy, greyish-lavendar gown; the dead man, a grey suit; the Raven, a black dinner jacket. Area lighting assisted in designating varying locales. Non-distracting simplicity was the keynote of the staging.

In Readers Theatre the interpreter takes advantage of his entire physical aspect to convey his emotions. In this scene from The Sound of the Sixties, *note how both the narrator, with his book in hand, and the characters convey the prevailing attitude of the material.*

Tell Me That You Love Me, Junie Moon   by Marjorie Kellogg

A novel adapted and directed in Chamber Theatre form by Elbert R. Bowen at Central Michigan University. Dr. Bowen supplied the following information about the production.

The most significant thing about the production was the aesthetic justification for a *pretended* public reading of a shortened version of the novel. Imagine yourself entering a large lecture hall and seeing on the bare platform only chairs, one of them a wheelchair, and a small table. Presently some young people carrying manuscripts enter from the rear and mount the platform, standing about and talking for a time. Eventually a young woman enters, and judging from the attentive behavior of the others, she is an authority. She asks them to be seated. The audience becomes quiet as it is obvious something is about to begin. She explains to the people on the platform that they are there to participate in a reading of portions of *Tell Me That You Love Me, Junie Moon* for an audience composed of persons who will be connected with the production of a new motion picture of the novel and who wish to assess the dramatic potentialities of the story. The readers, we discover, are actors who have been cast for the picture roles. They are told to sit or stand or move about at will while reading. In order to help Warren get the feeling for his paraplegic role, a wheelchair is being provided. Although the novelist herself is writing the scenario for the film, the script for this reading is an abridged version of the novel, including important narration which probes character motivation.

The Director seats the leading characters (Junie Moon, Arthur, and Warren) on two ordinary chairs and the wheelchair C. Then she begins to read the opening narration herself. The house lights go down, stage lights come up, and the story begins to unfold. The Director reads narration to the actors. Eventually the actors take over those portions of the narration about their own characters, particularly subjective narration. They read to the director as if to verify their interpretation of the characters. Sometimes they read into space as they digest the story or character motivations. Actors sharing scenes often read dialogue to each other. They sometimes read directly to the audience. Everyone in the room, including the viewers, is analyzing this book, its characters and events. Junie Moon stares into an imaginary mirror directly toward the audience as she examines the image of her terribly scarred face for the first time. Then, without emotion, the actress turns to the Director and speaks the next line of narration as if it were her analysis of the situation: "It was worse than she had thought." The Director nods in agreement. Arthur pantomimes a trial spastic movement. Beach Boy opens his shirt to display his manly chest, for the actor playing Beach Boy is proud of his own chest and practices a bit of exhibitionism just like that of the character he will play. The Director's assistant, picking up the narration about the dog in the book, gets his chance to perform. During one long passage, he even lifts his leg in an actor's response to a line—a crude action at which the other male actors laugh aloud. The production has become the drama of actors reading to each other, all from manuscript. Everything is worked out logically. Even the Director reads two different characters who are sympathetic to the major trio of characters. Never, however, is the audience aware of any theatrical gimmicks, any artificiality or contrivances. Except for the opening statement by the Director, only her short statements at half time ("Let's take a five-minute break.") and at the close ("That's fine. We'll call you when the scripts arrive.") do not appear in the novel itself. Aesthetic distance and alienation are provided by constant reminders that this is only a reading of the novel, yet nothing is permitted to destroy the moods of the book. When you leave the room after this performance, you too have "read" the book. You have attended the theatre more to read for yourself than to see a "show."

Thidwick: The Big-Hearted Moose   by Theodor Seuss Geisel (Dr. Seuss)

A children's story, adapted and directed by Ronnie Moskowitz under the supervision of Melvin R. White for presentation at Brooklyn College.

As previously explained, children's stories lend themselves admirably to presentation in this medium; and children's audiences, accustomed to using their imaginations, accept its conventions even more readily than do more sophisticated audiences. The setting for *Thidwick* consisted of nine low stools, four revolving stools, one lectern, and a series of stage steps which became—in the imaginations of the children—Thidwick's antlers. These physical elements were arranged as shown in Figure 14.

FIGURE 14.   *Thidwick, the Big-Hearted Moose* floor plan

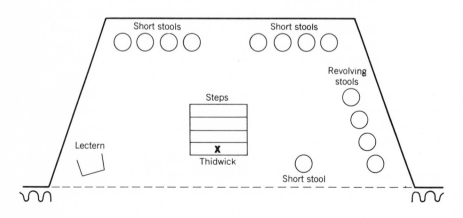

The storyteller stood at the lectern. Thidwick and four other moose entered DR from backstage. Thidwick sat down wearily on the bottom step at C, while the other four lumbered and ate their way to the revolving stools at L and DL, eventually turning their backs to the audience and sitting motionless until they were again needed near the end of the presentation. As each subsequent bird and animal entered, he left one of the nine short stools and climbed onto Thidwick's antlers—the steps above Thidwick. Each reader was provided with some suggestion of a costume. For example, the large, heavy students who played the moose were dressed in cumbersome, thick, winter attire: coats, winter caps with earmuffs, and galoshes or heavy boots. The birds had feather boas around their necks and feathers in their hats, and the mouse had big ears—just big enough to tickle the children's imaginations.

The only changes in the dialogue of the story were in those lines about Thidwick's running from the hunters. In order to maintain the illusion that the steps were his antlers, Thidwick obviously could not leave his place on the bottom step; instead, struggling valiantly in that position, he pantomimed ducking the bullets. The sound effects of gunshots added to the excitement; and the "inhabitants" of his antlers struggled in unison with him, ducking as he ducked. So the line "took to his heels" became "tried to get up," and the four lines which described Thidwick's running way from the hunters were omitted.

To Kill a Mockingbird   by Harper Lee

A novel, adapted for Readers Theatre and presented by Robert Wilhoit at Drury College.

Mr. Wilhoit's program notes for this production read:

Readers Theatre is our medium . . . it is not new . . . it is not really "theatre" as we have come to expect it. It is a reader who shares with you the first thrill of discovery . . . who brings to you vocally the sounds and sights and emotions of a fine piece of literature. An actor says: "Look at me . . . I am this person." A reader says: "Look . . . here is this person, this experience. Let us share it together." And so, here is *To Kill a Mockingbird*.

This sharing was the guiding principle in the Drury College presentation of Harper Lee's popular novel. According to additional information provided by Mr. Wilhoit, two approaches seemed possible: (1) The script could be presented as if the author were looking back at incidents in her life, or (2) Scout, one of the central characters, could narrate the events as they happened to her, day by day. The latter approach was chosen. The content of

Many theatrical enhancements—costuming, makeup, and suggested set pieces placed on multiple levels against black drapes—were employed in this production of Harper Lee's To Kill a Mockingbird. *Scout, as narrator, talked directly to the audience; but in all other scenes, the readers used onstage focus.*

the script was restricted to the dialogue scenes already in the novel; these were linked by Scout's narration and commentary. The readers carried their scripts in their hands at all times to impress upon themselves and the audience that this was a reading and not a conventional play.

The adaptation emphasized the mystery of Boo Radley, the death of Mrs. Dubose, and the trial of Tom Robinson. This required a rather large cast of nineteen. The stage space was divided into six playing areas, some of them raised above stage level to facilitate swift and easy transition from one unit of the story line to the next. Each area served only temporarily as a designated place. To aid in the identification of the various readers, a suggestion of costuming and a number of character makeups were employed.

In adapting *To Kill a Mockingbird* for a summer-session Readers Theatre workshop at the University of Arkansas, the director had one reader serve as both Scout the grown narrator and Scout the little girl. Her "present" location was at a lectern DR, although she did not always return to it when she "returned" to the present. At the lectern she used the script; but as a scene from the past began to unfold, she left the stand to "join her childhood memories" and played the scene in the character of the little girl she once had been. All of these "remembered" scenes were completely memorized by the readers and enacted on the stage without manuscripts. These episodes were given area lighting to fade them in and out as the narrator "remembered" them. The readers in these onstage scenes were dressed in character-suggesting costumes.

To the Lighthouse   by Virginia Woolf

A novel adapted for Readers Theatre by Harold Hancock and presented at the University of Arizona. Mr. Hancock provided the following information on this adaptation.

The largest problem in doing *To the Lighthouse* for Readers Theatre was creating a script true to the aesthetic design of the novel. Virginia Woolf develops her story principally by revealing the moment-by-moment subjective experiences of about twenty-five characters as they go through the ordinary activities of two days which are separated in time by ten years. The completed novel becomes a carefully patterned mosaic of individual moments of consciousness whose emotive power and symbolic significance are greatly enhanced by their relationship to the whole. In the final section of the novel a simple trip across the bay to the lighthouse becomes within the context of the novel a mystical journey of homage to the dead and of personal discovery.

The script tried to capture the major patterns of the mosaic by concentrating on ten characters and a Narrator, with one performer cast in each role. The characters of Mr. and Mrs. Ramsay, Cam and James Ramsay, and Lilly Briscoe were developed as fully as possible. (The final production ran for two hours and forty minutes.) William Bankes and Charles Tansley received less development. Three characters, Prue and Andrew Ramsay and Mrs. McNab, appeared as individualized roles only in the short middle section. Every word spoken on stage came directly from the novel.

In the book it is often impossible to separate the experience of the Narrator from the experience of the characters. Indeed, it is often impossible to determine in the language where the experience of one character stops and the experience of another begins. In this production the words which might stem from more than one sensibility were spoken by an actor who was also a college student. The production tried, in its costuming and staging, to parallel Woolf's use of simultaneous sensibility in the novel. The performers wore no obvious makeup. Their clothes identified them as college students. The production tried to say to the audience that the performers were only college students who because of training and skill as actors could share with the audience an illusion that characters in an imaginary world were being created.

The production was presented on a bare stage with general lighting except for one short night sequence. Five stools were placed in varying relationships depending upon the action of the moment. When a scene change demanded a new relationship for the stools, the performers moved the stools themselves, sometimes in character, sometimes simply as actors. One large wooden reading stand was placed DL between the audience and the playing area. The Narrator began at this stand and returned to it for occasional highly general commentary. Most of the time the Narrator hovered around the immediate action relating both to the action on stage and to the audience. The characters generally used offstage focus, but were free to relate directly to each other and to the narrator when this helped establish the sense of a scene. Each performer carried a script which was used sometimes as a book containing his lines, sometimes as a prop, or sometimes simply as an extension of his gesturing hand.

The Waking

A compiled script for Readers Theatre based on the poetry of Theodore Roethke, arranged and directed by Karen Connell Hold, and presented as part of the Festival of the Arts at Syracuse University. This description of the presentation was furnished by Karen Connell Hold.

The Waking was an hour-long program designed to reflect the humanity of the contemporary poet Theodore Roethke, through readings from his poetry, with connecting commentary taken from critical sources and from Allan Seager's biography, *The Glass House.*

The theme poem, "The Waking," unified the production. In that poem Roethke stated, "I learn by going where I have to go." Since the script traced both his human and his poetic growth, the audience was brought to a knowledge of the man and his works. The poems were arranged in three different groupings: Roethke's beginnings, his greenhouse imagery, and the early poems; Roethke's childhood and his poems for children; and the mature Roethke, his philosophy, and the later poems.

Two men and three women read; each was assigned poetry revealing a particular tone of the poet. One male reader was responsible for the "childhood" poems, while the other handled the more mature selections. Within the connecting commentary the latter reader was responsible for all direct quotations from Roethke, so he took on a stable characterization. The other readers were more varied. One of the women read basically narrative material; one read lyric; and the third, mature in tone, was primarily employed in reading a lengthy cutting of "Meditations of an Old Woman." All were involved in the commentary, which was delivered from memory, thereby providing a contrast to the reading of the poetry. This technique also fostered an intimacy between readers and audience.

Music was composed specifically for the production. One reader played the flute and another the guitar. This music eased transitions and set themes. In two instances, "Interlude" and "The Monotony Song," poems were sung.

The set, which was designed to suggest a corner of a greenhouse, was left "unfinished" at one end to permit an extension of the location in the minds of the audience (see Figure 15). A variety of levels was used to enhance the stage picture. Geometric shapes, a cylinder and a triangle, allowed for varied and symbolic use. In one instance the cylinder (at C) represented a greenhouse. For "Child on Top of a Greenhouse" the reader leapt to a standing position on it. At other times it was the place from which readers revealed the character of Roethke by reciting excerpts from his unpublished notebooks. A good deal of movement was planned. For instance, the entire section based on Roethke's poems for children was choreographed with a heavy use of pantomime, and became a very entertaining romp.

Both onstage and offstage focus were employed to aid the audience in visualizing the selections. In the love poetry, for ir,tance, cross-focus between a male and female reader provided a poignant effect. Throughout, dialogue was used substantially within the poems. Choral reading, too, played an integral part, varying the voicing in "Big Wind" and one of the poems for children, "The Serpent."

Costuming was simple and suggested greenhouse attire. All readers wore jeans, turtleneck sweaters, and smocks dyed in a variety of green and gold shades.

The collage of conventions and techniques employed in this production was tightly unified and highly disciplined, which gave a sense of control throughout. One observer remarked, "What a painless way to get to know a poet!"

The setting for The Waking, *suggesting a corner of a greenhouse, provided a variety of levels and geometric shapes which, combined with extensive lighting, were used to enhance composition in stage pictures.*

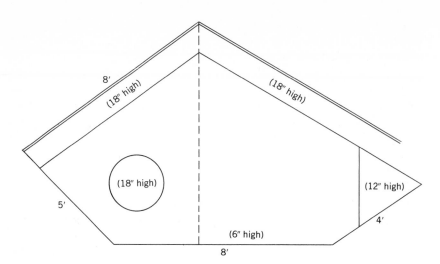

FIGURE 15.   Floor plan for *The Waking*

What Color Is Black?

A compiled script, arranged and directed by Bernard Goldman, and presented at Los Angeles Trade-Technological College. Subsequently it was performed at the Awards Assembly at the 1970 national tournament of Phi Rho Pi, held at the University of Michigan, as well as in over forty performances in Southern California.

An edited collage of poetry, prose, music, conversation, and humor, *What Color Is Black?* expressed in a bright, witty, sometimes sad, but always prideful and optimistic way what it means to be black in America today. Drawing upon the words and ideas of Langston Hughes, Paul Lawrence Dunbar, Carl Sandburg, Martin Luther King, Jr., Stymean Karlen, the Watts Writers' Workshop, and many others, this production utilized six interpreters who read and sang solo and in chorus about the dilemma of blacks in a white world. The simple staging provided for four seated interpreters in the front row and two behind them, with a minimum of individual action in place to suggest rhythm and movement.

   In structure, the program's calculated orchestration of serious intent, lyricism, and faith in humanity—counterpointed by adroitly placed moments of humor and satire—resulted in a vehicle that had a strong emotional impact on the consciousness and feelings of self-identity of both black and white audiences. Margaret Harford wrote in her Los Angeles *Times* review of the production, " 'What Color Is Black?' never whines and never loses faith in the humanity of all people or the strength of the

The six readers in What Color Is Black? *are photographed following one of their award-winning performances.*

individual to survive the sting of racial bias."[6] In the program's conclusion, the six readers affirmed that "there is but one color of people; each is a different shade of the same color."

The list of successful Readers Theatre productions could, of course, go on and on. The amount of experimentation and production in classes and elsewhere at all levels—elementary school, secondary school, college and university, as well as presentations in community theatres and by professional groups—is increasing rapidly as interest in Readers Theatre grows. The Production Lists Project of the American Theatre Association makes an annual report on play selection in four-year collegiate institutions which present dramatic productions, and for the past several years it has included statistics on the number of Readers Theatre productions being done. The Interpretation Division of the Speech Communication Association has a Readers Theatre Bibliography Committee which each year collects pertinent information not only on materials written *about* Readers Theatre, but on materials annually *presented* in this art form. Students of this subject

6 " 'Black' on College Circuit," Los Angeles *Times,* June 23, 1970, IV, p. 8.

are encouraged to familiarize themselves with these sources and materials and to report their own activities in this medium to the current chairman of the Readers Theatre Bibliography Committee. (See Selected and Annotated Bibliography, pp. 293–302.)

PART THREE

Sample Scripts
for Readers Theatre

BY JOHN UPDIKE

Amor Vincit Omnia ad Nauseam

A modernized nursery rhyme arranged for Readers Theatre by Melvin R. White

A parenthetical subtitle is printed under the title of this charming short story from the *New Yorker: After Awaking from "Bruno's Dream" by Iris Murdoch, and Falling into the Nursery.* A highly imaginative and humorous tale, the characters are all those found in the old nursery rhyme "The Cat and the Fiddle." It affords the readers splendid opportunities to suggest caricatures of them all—the cat, the fiddle, the little dog, the cow, and the moon. But it is not a child's story; rather, it is highly sophisticated, and probably will require some use of the dictionary, and many rehearsals.

CAST OF CHARACTERS

Two Men, Three Women, and a Narrator—either a Man or a Woman

NARRATOR. *An enthusiastic storyteller with a mature, pleasing voice*

CAT. *A sophisticatedly "feline" girl, quite sexy of physique and voice*

FIDDLE. *The leading man—tall, dark, and handsome*

COW. *Bovine in physique, voice, and personality—perhaps even a bit stupid-sounding*

MOON. *A serene and calm lady, probably with a smooth, contralto voice*

DOG. *A cheerful little pixie of a dog, quick of speech and manner*

APPAREL

No special dress is necessary, but the characters might be attired in animal costumes and makeup, if desired. This was not done in the first production. Rather, the cat wore a too-tight and somewhat revealing dress, the fiddle wore a tannish-brown suit (sort of the color of some violins), the moon was frilly and feminine in an ethereal pale blue, all suggesting the personalities of the characters rather than the physical appearance.

PHYSICAL ARRANGEMENT OF THE SCENE

As always, the platform arrangement can be as elaborate or as simple as desired. In the first production, the NARRATOR read from a lectern DR; DOG, CAT, and FIDDLE sat on three short stools; the COW, slightly upstage, had a tall stool a bit DL of C; and the MOON sat serenely atop a tall stepladder, DL adjacent to the COW.

The characters did not move from their stools, lectern, or stepladder, but they did vary their positions as the lines suggested. The focus was offstage, in the realm of the audience.

(*Brief introductory violin music may introduce the program, perhaps "Tales of the Vienna Woods."*)

NARRATOR. Hey diddle, diddle . . .
CAT. The cat and . . .
FIDDLE. The fiddle . . .
COW. The cow . . .

FIGURE 16. Stage arrangement for *Amor Vincit Omnia ad Nauseam*

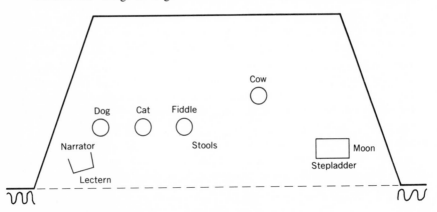

NARRATOR. Jumped over . . .

MOON. The moon . . .

DOG. The little dog . . .

NARRATOR. Laughed . . .

DOG. (*Laughs.*)

NARRATOR. To see such sport . . .

FIDDLE. Hey diddle . . . ?

CAT. Diddle.

FIDDLE. You're thinking about God again.

CAT. I was thinking about *you.*

NARRATOR. It was true. She had been. The cat had been thinking about the fiddle. She had been looking at him. He had a long thin stringy neck and a plump brown resinous hollow body. His voice had vibrato.

CAT. (*Narrating.*) Yes. I've been his mistress for four years. It has been ecstatic, but not extremely. You see, I was attracted by his voice.

NARRATOR. They had met, the cat and the fiddle, at a benefit performance given for church mice. A bow had scraped him and he had sung.

(*A short violin solo may be inserted here if desired, perhaps "Tales of the Vienna Woods."*)

NARRATOR. The cat had gone up afterwards and had rubbed herself against him, and in her whiskers, so decisively parallel, he had recognized something kindred. So he sang to her, and she related to him tales of her previous lovers.

CAT. (*Narrating.*) Oh yes, there had been a succession of toms behind the gasworks. They all had terrible voices. They clawed me. They bit me. And slowly I formed an image of a tom who was hairless and toothless, a fragile and lean lover. He would have resonance, yes—but he would be powerless to pounce. I told the fiddle all this.

FIDDLE. (*Narrating.*) It pleased and flattered me. I sang to her. She rubbed against me, and told me of her countless lovers. I did not mind, for now she had chosen me.

NARRATOR. That had been in those days. These were these days. All day the cat took a small abrasive pleasure in licking the calico fur of her chest while the fiddle failed to sing but instead leaned in the corner and almost hummed. She looked at him, his shape, his texture, his state of tension.

CAT. (*Narrating.*) One of my toms had been made into a tennis racket. Perhaps that had been the attraction. But I needed a larger fate, warmer, kinder, yet more perilous in its dimensions, coarsely infinite yet mottled like me.

NARRATOR. Her vertically slit eyes, hoarding depths of amber, dilated at a shadow memory from her barnyard days as a kitten in the straw. Something large had been often above her. Something smelling of milk. It had mooed.

cow. (*Narrating.*) I am only a cow, but I am so in love with the moon. Throughout the first three quarters I wept solidly, streams and streams. Then the moon became full. Tears poured down my muzzle in an invincible tide. The full moon spoke to me.

moon. You are seeking to purify yourself by giving rein to impossibility.

cow. (*Weeping.*) Oh God . . . I can't . . . I don't . . .

moon. Go on.

cow. (*Very emotional.*) When I first saw you, you were new—a sort of weak bent splinter of a sort of nibbled thing. How loathesome, I thought. I think even then I was protecting myself from the truth. I believe even then I deeply knew you were cheese. You began to grow. Mare Serenitatis showed, and one bluish blind mad eye, and the side of your lopsided leprous smile. At first I loved you in spite of your leprosity. Then I loved it because it was part of *you*. Then I loved the leprosity itself, and you because you were the vehicle whereby it was boldly imposed upon the cold night sky. I have never known pain so ungainsayable. I beg you, what . . . ?

moon. Jump.

cow. Jump?

moon. *Jump.*

cow. *Jump?*

moon. JUMP!

narrator. A little dog had been eavesdropping and gave the cow advice.

dog. Imagine the moon as only slightly higher than the Albert Memorial. Or consider the Albert Hall. It is round and deep and vast and many-entranced like a woman's love. Oppositely, the Memorial is phallic and gaudy. Between them there is only the Kensington Road.

narrator. The cow was jumping. Splendidly. Galaxies upon diamantine sphere chimed the diatonic music that mesmerized Jerusalem the Golden. Time and space were fooled at their own game. *Ab ovo,* lacto-galactic.

cow. Moon, you are near! You, ashy, awful, barren, lunar, luminous. You! Oh, I touched you, dear Moon—just a hint of a ghost of a breath of a touch. But I am now descending, reentering earth's orbit . . .

narrator. (*Building toward climax.*) The atmosphere sizzled. The cat's sensitive amber eyes dilated as the shadow from above gathered. She felt the ponderous loved thing smelling of milk close and warm above her again.

cat. Is it to be . . . ?

cow. Can't stop. Gravity.

cat. Oh . . . how *right!*

narrator. Black ecstasy flattened the cat. Her ego was, if not eliminated, expanded beyond the bounds of dissatisfaction. She was ever so utterly content. The little dog laughed to see such sport.

dog. (*Laughs heartily.*)

FIDDLE. (*Clearing his throat.*) Er . . . er . . . when you laughed like that, I . . . er . . . *twanged.* Strange to say, I love you insanely.

DOG. Too bad, I love the cow. This fact was asleep in me until I saw her jump. What an august uncanny leap that was!

NARRATOR. He was a beagleish dog. A history of bitches had lengthened his ears and bloodied his eyes. His forepaws, however, had an engaging outward twist. He yapped amorously at the cow.

DOG. (*Yaps at* COW.)

NARRATOR. Startled, she stepped back into the fiddle. Her glossy hoof fragmented the ruddy wood.

FIDDLE. (*Sobbing.*) Thank you . . . thank you.

NARRATOR. He had been excessively pampered heretofore. It was bliss to be hurt. And nothing arouses gratitude like an eruption of violence.

FIDDLE. Oh Cow, I love you . . . of course I love *you!*

NARRATOR. The cow became haughty. Her high hot sides made a mist like fog off the Greenwich Reach.

COW. I am sorry, but I have dedicated myself to the memory of the cat. The cat has become the angel of death whose abiding iron presence is the destiny of all life to worship. What else is love? Nothing else.

DOG. (*Yowling.*) I discover I was confused. It is the moon I adore, for having permitted itself to be so splendidly jumped. (*Yowls and yowls at the* MOON.)

MOON. (*Beaming.*) I love everyone. I shine on just and unjust alike. I give to all the gift of madness. That is my charm. That is my *truth.*

NARRATOR. The fiddle lived with his wound for a fortnight, as one would live with the shifting shades and fluorescent evanescences of an unduly prolonged sunset. Then . . . he found he could sing. He had once sung! He was again singing!

FIDDLE. (*Singing.*) "*A questo seno, deh! vieni, idolo mio,*
*Quanti timori, quante lacrime . . . *"

NARRATOR. Hey diddle, diddle . . .

CAT. The cat . . . and . . .

FIDDLE. The fiddle . . .

COW. The cow . . .

NARRATOR. Jumped over . . .

MOON. The moon.

DOG. The little dog . . .

NARRATOR. Laughed . . .

DOG. (*Laughs.*)

NARRATOR. To see such sport . . .

ALL. And the dish ran away with the spoon.

Clever Gretel

Arranged for Chamber Theatre by Margaret Brown and Leslie Irene Coger

Many of Grimm's fairy tales have been performed successfully, not only in schools for children, but professionally for adults. The characters are sharply but simply drawn. Each of the stories makes some point about the human condition. *Clever Gretel* deals with the laughable confusion which can result from misunderstanding.

This adaptation is arranged for Chamber Theatre, with movement and pantomime accompanying the text.

CAST OF CHARACTERS

Two Men, One Woman, and a Narrator, Man or Woman

NARRATOR. *An effective storyteller, man or woman*

GRETEL. *A cheerful young cook*

HER MASTER. *A middle-aged man*

GUEST. *His friend*

PHYSICAL ARRANGEMENTS

A platform is placed C with steps leading to it from DC and two ramps, one from the front and one from the back of the platform. Only one stool is required. Or an empty stage may be used, as in the picture on page 103, with the readers moving from one area to another. The action in this version is to be pantomimed.

Notice: This adaptation may be presented without payment of a royalty fee.

(Gay music is heard, something like the tune to a light Old English ballad. The NARRATOR *and* GRETEL *enter from R, the* NARRATOR *acting as an escort. He leads her to the step unit, and as she proceeds up to the center of the platform, he faces the audience and begins his story on the first step.)*

NARRATOR. There was once a cook named Gretel, who wore shoes with red heels, and when she walked out with them on *(Emphasizes walking by making a slight jump to the next step.)* she turned herself this way and that and was quite happy.

GRETEL. You certainly are a pretty girl! *(Coming down downstage ramp.)* And when she came home, she drank, in her gladness of heart, a draught of wine.

NARRATOR. *(Stepping onto the platform.)* And as wine excites a desire to eat, she tasted the best of whatever she was cooking until she was satisfied. (GRETEL *pantomimes.)*

GRETEL. The cook must know what the food is like.

NARRATOR. It came to pass that the master one day said to her (MASTER *enters from upstage ramp,* GRETEL *is DC, the* NARRATOR *is on the right side of the platform, the* MASTER *remains on the left side of the platform.)*,

MASTER. Gretel, there is a guest coming this evening; prepare me two fowls very daintily.

GRETEL. I will see to it, Master.

NARRATOR. She killed two fowls, scalded them, plucked them, put them on the spit, and towards evening set them before the fire, that they might roast. (GRETEL *pantomimes this as the* MASTER *watches.)* The fowls began to turn brown, and were nearly ready, but the guest had not yet arrived.

GRETEL. *(Almost distraught.)* Master, if the guest does not come, I must take the fowls away from the fire, but it will be a sin and a shame if they are not eaten the moment they are at their juiciest.

MASTER. *(Comes down to look at the chickens as* GRETEL *turns the spit.)* I will run myself and fetch the guest. *(Runs offstage, but looks back every so often at chickens.)*

NARRATOR. *(Comes down steps on lines and heads towards* GRETEL, *but always telling the story to the audience.* GRETEL *looks slyly after the* MASTER.) When the master had turned his back, Gretel laid the spit with the fowls on one side, and thought—

GRETEL. Standing so long by the fire there makes one sweaty and thirsty. Who knows when they will come? *(Resolutely.)* Meanwhile, I will run into the cellar and take a drink.

NARRATOR. She ran down and got a jug. (NARRATOR *and* GRETEL *do a counter cross as she moves about three or four steps quickly R, and pantomimes the action.)*

GRETEL. God bless it for you, Gretel. (*Raising her glass high.*)

NARRATOR. She took a good drink, and thought that wine should flow on, and should not be interrupted, and took yet another hearty draught.

GRETEL. God bless it for you, Gretel.

NARRATOR. Then she went and put the fowls down again to the fire, basted them and drove the spit merrily around. But as the roast meat smelled so good, Gretel thought—

GRETEL. Something might be wrong, it ought to be tasted! (*She touches it with her finger.*) Ah! How good fowls are! It certainly is a sin and a shame that they are not eaten at the right time!

NARRATOR. She ran to the window to see if the master was not coming with his guest, but she saw no one and went back to the fowls. (GRETEL *goes upstage to stand in front of the ramp and looks off R; she comes back to the spit, turns it once or twice, and discovers that one of the wings is getting very brown.*)

GRETEL. One of the wings is burning! I had better take it off and eat it.

NARRATOR. So she cut it off, ate it . . .

GRETEL. And enjoyed it.

NARRATOR. But when she had finished, she thought—

GRETEL. The other must go down too, or else Master will observe that something is missing. (*She delightedly laughs and gobbles the wing.*)

NARRATOR. When the first two wings were eaten she went and looked for her master, and did not see him. (*She goes to the window again, starts line at the window.*)

GRETEL. Who knows? They are perhaps not coming at all, and have turned in somewhere. (*As she stands in front of the fowls she taps her foot on the floor; then, as if she has thrown all fear to the wind, says.*) Well, Gretel, enjoy yourself, one fowl has been cut into. Take another drink and eat it up entirely; when it is eaten you will have some peace. Why should God's gifts be spoiled?

NARRATOR. So she ran into the cellar again, took an enormous drink . . .

GRETEL. God bless it for you, Gretel.

NARRATOR. And ate up the one chicken in great glee. When one of the chickens was swallowed down, and still her master did not come, Gretel looked at the other . . .

GRETEL. (*She is beginning to feel just the slightest bit of elation from the wine. She looks around, and then giggles.*) Where one is, the other should be likewise, the two go together! What's right for the one is right for the other. I think if I were to take another draught it would do me no harm. (*She goes again to the keg.*)

NARRATOR. So she took another hearty drink.

GRETEL. (*The wine is making her exultant.*) God bless it for you, Gretel!

NARRATOR. And the second chicken followed the first. (GRETEL *sits down, drinks her wine, eats her chicken, and hums happily.*) While she was making the most of it, her master came and cried . . .

MASTER. (*Entering right, he goes up the steps.*) Hurry up, Gretel, the guest is coming directly after me!

GRETEL. (*Getting up, she returns to the empty spit.*) Yes, sir, I will soon serve up.

MASTER. Meanwhile, the master looked to see that the table was properly laid, and took the great knife with which he was going to carve the chickens, and sharpened it on the steps.

NARRATOR. Presently, the guest came and knocked politely and courteously at the house door. Gretel ran and looked to see who was there, and when she saw the guest, said—

GRETEL. (*She runs to the door, opens it, and, as* GUEST *starts to come in, pushes him back out, putting a finger to her lips.*) Hush, hush! Go away as quickly as you can. If my master catches you it will be the worse for you. He certainly did ask you to supper, but his intention is to cut off your two ears. Just listen how he is sharpening the knife for it!

GUEST. Oh, my! Thank you, thank you! (GUEST *hurries away.*)

NARRATOR. The guest heard the sharpening and hurried away as fast as he could. (*He exits L.*) Gretel ran screaming to her master. (*First,* GRETEL *lets out an ear-shattering scream, then she runs up the ramp to where the master has gotten up after hearing the scream.*)

GRETEL. You have invited a fine guest! (*Crying.*)

MASTER. Why, Gretel, what do you mean by that?

GRETEL. A fine guest! (*Crying.*) He has taken the chickens which I was just going to serve up and has run away with them!

MASTER. (*Enraged.*) That's a nice trick. (*Lamenting.*) Oh, my chickens, if he had but left me one, so that something remained for me to eat. (MASTER *runs down the steps and off L as he speaks the line.* GRETEL *looks very pleased and begins to laugh, running down the ramp to the cellar for more wine.* MASTER *continues to yell.*) Stop! Stop!

NARRATOR. The guest pretended not to hear. The master ran after him with the knife in his hand.

MASTER. Just one! Just one!

NARRATOR. Meaning that the guest should leave him one chicken and not take both.

GUEST. The guest, however, thought otherwise, that he was to give up one of his ears, and ran as if fire were burning under him, in order to take them both home with him. (GUEST *runs down ramp, around downstage to steps, runs upstairs, around on platform, and down the upstage ramp offstage, followed by the* MASTER, *who continues to yell.*)

MASTER. Stop! Let me have just one. I only want one. (*Ad lib.*)

GUEST. Leave me alone! Go home! You can't have any. (*Ad lib.*)

NARRATOR. (*Over the above.*) Gretel danced into the cellar and poured an enormous draught.

GRETEL. God bless it for you, Gretel!

Dandelion Wine

by **Ray Bradbury**

Adapted for Readers Theatre
by **Duane Hunt** and **Leslie Irene Coger**

Presented by
Southwest Missouri State College
for
The Speech Association of America
December 29, 1960

Reader One: Dr. Harry J. Siceluff

Reader Two: Gwen Theis

Reader Three: Joe Bowman

Reader Four: Dean Compton

Reader Five: Duane Hunt

Reader Six: Dr. Leslie Irene Coger

THE AWAKENING: The Joys of Summer

The First Ritual
Narrator .... Reader One
Douglas Spaulding .... Reader Three

The First Harvest
Narrator .... Reader One
Douglas Spaulding .... Reader Three
Tom Spaulding .... Reader Five
Grandpa .... Reader Four
Mom .... Reader Two
Voices ..... Readers Two, Three, Four, Five, Six

Wings of Summer
Narrator .... Reader One
Douglas .... Reader Three
John Huff .... Reader Four
Dad .... Reader Five
Mr. Sanderson of
   Sanderson's Shoe Emporium ..... Reader Five

The Time Machine
Tom .... Reader Five
Douglas .... Reader Three
Narrator .... Reader One
Lucy Cavins, a friend of Douglas.... Reader Two
John Huff, a friend of Douglas..... Reader Four
Colonel Freeleigh .... Reader Five
Pawnee Bill .... Reader One

THE REALIZATION: The Sorrows of Summer

A Game of Statues
Douglas .... Reader Three
John Huff .... Reader Four
Voices .... Readers Two, Five, Six
Narrator .... Reader One

The Closing Window
Voices .... Readers Two, Three, Four, Five, Six
Narrator .... Reader One
Colonel Freeleigh .... Reader Five
Telephone Operator .... Reader Two
Miguel .... Reader Four
Nurse .... Reader Six

A Sum in Arithmetic
Great-Grandma .... Reader Six
Douglas........................... Reader Three
Grandpa .... Reader Four

The Fever Dream
Douglas........................... Reader Three
Tom .... Reader Five
Voices .... Readers One, Two, Four
Mother .... Reader Two

The Last Ritual
Voices .... Readers One, Two, Four, Five, Six
Tom .... Reader Five
Douglas........................... Reader Three
Narrator .... Reader One

BY RAY BRADBURY

Dandelion Wine

A novel adapted for Readers Theatre by Leslie Irene Coger and Duane Hunt

Mr. Bradbury's novel abounds in those special qualities which characterize ideal literary material for Readers Theatre: impelling imagery, fluid phrasing, evocative power, unique characters with whom an audience can readily empathize, skillfully wrought moods ranging from comedy to deep sadness, and an overall sense of authentic beauty emerging from the universal experiences of mankind. The following script provides a definitive and useful example of one way in which a novel can be cut to a workable time limit. The approach and procedures used in preparing this adaptation are discussed in detail in Chapter 3 of Part One, "Selecting and Adapting Materials for Readers Theatre," pages 54–57. (See photos on p. 58.)

CAST OF CHARACTERS

Nine Men, Five Women, and a Narrator, who may be played by either a Man or a Woman. This adaptation may also be read by Four Men and Two Women, with lines assigned as follows: READER #1: *the Narrator, Pawnee Bill, and a Voice;* READER #2: *Mom, a Voice, Lucy Cavins, and the Telephone Operator;* READER #3: *Douglas and a Voice;* READER #4: *Grandpa, a Voice, John Huff, and Miguel;* READER #5: *Tom, a Voice, Dad, Mr. Sanderson, and Colonel Freeleigh;* READER #6: *Great-Grandma, a Voice, and the Nurse.*

NARRATOR. *Effective storyteller, man or woman*

DOUGLAS SPAULDING. *A young boy of twelve*

TOM SPAULDING. *His brother; a little older*

GRANDPA. *A lively old man*

MOM. *Doug's mother*

JOHN. *Doug's young friend*

DAD. *Doug's father*

MR. SANDERSON. *Owner of a shoe store*

LUCY CAVINS. *Another one of Doug's friends*

COLONEL FREELEIGH. *An old man with a wonderful memory*

PAWNEE BILL. *A man of the Wild West*

TELEPHONE OPERATOR.

MIGUEL. *Colonel Freeleigh's friend in Mexico City*

NURSE.

GREAT-GRANDMA. *Doug's wise great-grandmother*

CHORUS OF VOICES. *Composed of all the Readers*

THE PHYSICAL ARRANGEMENT OF THE SCENE

Six stools and six lecterns are provided for the readers, all of whom are sitting as the program begins.

I. THE AWAKENING: THE JOYS OF SUMMER

The First Ritual

NARRATOR [R1].[1] It is a quiet morning, the town covered over with darkness and at ease in bed. Summer gathers in the weather; the wind has

---

[1] The designation [R1] following a character's name and occurring at the beginning of a scene, segment, or episode indicates that this particular role may be read by Reader #1. Later in the script, [R1] may also read the roles of Pawnee Bill and a Voice, [R2] may be assigned the roles of Mom, a Voice, Lucy Cavins, and the Telephone Operator, and so on. These assignments are optional, however, and will vary with the director's preferences and the interpretive abilities of the respective readers.

the proper touch; the breathing of the world is long and warm and slow. To the nostrils of earth comes a sweet scent, the smell of freedom and of living. This, indeed, is the first morning of summer.

Douglas Spaulding, age twelve, freshly awakened, lets summer idle him on its early morning stream. Lying in his third-story cupola bedroom, the tall power comes to him, lifts him high in the June wind.

DOUG [R3]. (*Stands.*) A whole summer ahead to cross off the calendar, day by single, wonderful day . . . pluck sour apples, peaches, midnight plums. I will be clothed in trees, in bushes, and in rivers. I will freeze, and gladly, in the hoarfrost of the ice house and each day at dusk sadly cross that number from the page of numbers.

NARRATOR. But now, Douglas Spaulding, a familiar task awaits you. Move slowly, Douglas, through your sorcerer's tower . . . third-story cupola bedroom of Grandma's home . . . dark, secret tower, alive with thunders and visions; move to the portal of glass through which the stars are fading. Lift slowly your finger and perform your ritual magic.

DOUG. (*Steps forward.*) There! Lights on!

VOICE TWO. Lights on!

DOUG. And there! Lights . . . on!

VOICE FOUR. Lights on!

DOUG. Now over here:

VOICE FIVE. Lights on!

DOUG. And now here:

VOICE SIX. Lights on!

DOUG. Windows, up; morning, flow in. Everyone, yawn. Everyone, up! Gran'pa, get your teeth from the water glass. Gran'ma and Mom, fry hot cakes. Street-where-old-people-live, wake up! Cough, get up, move around. Come back, come back to this world of summer. Street-of-children-playing, awake. John Huff, Lucy Cavins, ready? Ready to baseballs lying deep in wet grass. Ready to rope swings hanging unused in gnarled trees. Mom, Dad, Tom, everyone—wake up now!

NARRATOR. Bleak mansions across town open baleful, dragon eyes. Little white cottages lift sleepy blinds to the warm sun. Clock alarms tinkle faintly. Courthouse clock booms. Birds flit from trees, singing sweetly in the morning breeze. Douglas, conduct your orchestra of sight, sound, and smell; point to the east. The sun warms the avenues of wet sidewalks and sleeping dogs and cool milk bottles on back porches.

DOUG. One . . . two . . . three . . . Overture, begin! Everyone, jump. Everyone, run. It's going to be a whale of a fine season. (*Sits.*)

NARRATOR. Give the town a last snap of your fingers, Doug. Doors, slam open; people, step out. Douglas and Tom, out of the house—filled, stuffed, and dressed for the day on Gran'ma's special pancakes—Grandfather ahead of them standing on the wide front porch like a captain surveying the vast, unmotioned calms of a season dead ahead. Summer 1928, begin! (*There is a pause.*)

The First Harvest

TOM [R5]. (*Rises.*) Are the dandelions ready now, Gran'pa?

DOUG [R3]. (*Rises.*) They've got to be ready now, please.

GRANDPA [R4]. (*Rises.*) Five hundred, a thousand, two thousand easy. Yep, a good supply. Pick 'em easy, boys, but pick 'em all. A dime for every sack delivered to the press!

DOUG. Hey! Come on, Tom. I'll pick more than you today!

NARRATOR [R1]. Mom opens the front screen door, steps out to stand beside her titan father. (MOM *rises.*) She places a strong, loving hand on the old man's frail shoulder.

MOM [R2]. Dad, are they ready so early?

GRANDPA. Yep. I guess so, Daughter. Besides, you think I could hold off those Injuns for another day?

MOM. Boys, boys! Don't work so hard. Leave a few for tomorrow, you know.

TOM. Can't, Mom. There'll never be another day like today.

NARRATOR. And there never is, Doug and Tom. Bend your backs, smiling. Pick the golden flowers, the flowers that flood the world, drip off lawns onto brick streets, tap softly at crystal cellar windows, and agitate themselves so that on all sides lie the dazzle and glitter of molten sun.

MOM. Dandelion . . . it's summer on the tongue.

GRANDPA. Yep, every year they run amuck. I let 'em. A pride of lions in the yard. Stare, and they burn a hole in your eye. Common flower, weed no one sees—but for me, for us, a noble thing, the dandelion. Careful, boys . . . pick 'em easy!

NARRATOR. So plucked carefully, in sacks, the dandelions are carried below. The cellar dark glows with their arrival. Wine press stands open, cold.

GRANDPA. Keep them comin', Injuns. Got the ketchup bottles ready, Daughter?

MOM. They're all cleaned and waiting, Dad.

GRANDPA. Here she comes!

NARRATOR. The golden liquid runs, then gushes from the spout of the press. The essence of the fine, fair month of June flows down, to be crocked, skimmed of ferment, boiled in clean ketchup shakers, then ranked in sparkling rows in the cellar gloom.

DOUG. And labeled! Don't forget we have to label them.

TOM. Label them? What for, Doug?

DOUG. Tom, this is going to be a summer of unguessed wonders. I want it all labeled, so that any time I want to, I can tiptoe down and hold summer in my hand.

NARRATOR. Label the bottles, then, Tom! Put the date of each sparkling day on the cool glass; label, so Douglas Spaulding can peer through the mystery on a winter day and recall June sunshine glowing through a skim of January dust. Label, so Douglas can remember what happened on every day of this summer, forever.

MOM. Summer will be over before it begins, Doug.

NARRATOR. Your words go unheeded, Mom. Tom and Doug are lost in magic!

TOM. Boy, what a swell way to save June, July, and August! Real practical, Doug.

GRANDPA. Better than puttin' things in an old attic you never use again. This way, you get to live summer over for a minute or two here and there, along the way through winter. When the bottles are empty, the summer's gone for good and no regrets and no sentimental trash lying around for you to stumble over forty years from now.

TOM. Clean . . .

MOM. Smokeless . . .

DOUG. Eff—efficient . . .

GRANDPA. (*Chuckling.*) That's dandelion wine! (GRANDPA, TOM, MOM, *and* DOUG *sit.*)

NARRATOR. That's dandelion wine, a bit of summer captured. Even Gran'ma—when snow is falling fast, blinding windows, stealing breath from gasping mouths—will vanish to the cellar for a moment.

Above . . . coughing, sneezing, groans . . . stealthy microbes everywhere. Then, rising from the cellar like a June goddess, Gran'ma with a balm of sun and idle August afternoons. The sounds of ice cream wagons passing on brick avenues . . .

VOICE THREE. The "woosh" of silver skyrockets.

VOICE FOUR. The fountaining of lawn mowers roaming through the July grass.

VOICE TWO. All this in a glass from the cellar.

NARRATOR. A cellar of winter for a June adventure. Mom, Dad, Gran'pa, Gran'ma, or one of the boarders standing in secret conclave with his own spirit and soul . . . communing with the last touch of a calendar long departed and repeating the golden words for every winter in time . . .

VOICE SIX. Dandelion wine . . . (*The other voices echo with a chorus-like effect.*)

VOICE TWO. Dandelion wine . . .

VOICE THREE. Dandelion wine . . .

VOICE FOUR. Dandelion wine . . .

VOICE FIVE. Dandelion wine . . .

NARRATOR. And so the first harvest of golden wine is complete. Pressed, bottled . . .

DOUG. (*Stands.*) And labeled!

NARRATOR. Uh . . . yes . . . labeled and stacked in rows upon the shelves. Stand there—in the cellar gloom, Douglas—you and Tom—and shiver a bit. The early June evenings are cool. Or is it altogether the coolness, Doug?

DOUG. (*Steps forward.*) It's the magic—the magic in the bottles . . .

TOM. (*Rises and steps forward.*) What'd you say, Doug?

DOUG. It's magic, Tom! . . . Tom . . . I'm alive!

TOM. Heck! That's not new.

DOUG. But thinking about it, down here . . . noticing it . . . that's new. Tom, I walked past old Miss Fern's house yesterday. Do you know there's colored glass in two of her windows?

TOM. Never noticed.

DOUG. I never did either . . . before. But I did yesterday. My gosh, Tom, what else have I never seen before . . . I mean *really* seen?

TOM. I dunno.

DOUG. Well, at least, every time we bottle dandelion wine, we got a whole chunk of 1928 put away, safe. See?

TOM. Nope.

DOUG. Oh, well, gee! See, next winter we come down here, and we look at each bottle—and then we can relive that particular day! We'll remember just what happened; but now we gotta look and *really* see what happens. Each bottle is one whole day of our lives, Tom; and come Labor Day, we'll total up the summer and see what we got. O.K.?

TOM. Yeah—sure, Doug! Sure!

(TOM *and* DOUG *step back and sit. There is a pause while all of the* READERS *change positions to mark a transition in time.*)

Wings of Summer

NARRATOR [R1]. You do not hear them coming. You hardly hear them go. The grass bends down, springs up again. They pass like cloud shadows downhill . . . the boys of summer, running.

DOUG [R3]. (*Rises and steps forward.*) Hey! John Huff! Charlie Woodman! Wait for me.

JOHN [R4]. (*Stands.*) Doug—come on! Doug!

NARRATOR. It's no use. . . . They're gone. The second rite of summer, the dandelion picking, the starting of the wine . . . over. Now the third rite awaits Douglas to make the motions, but he stands very still.

JOHN. Doug! Come on, Doug! (JOHN *sits.*)

NARRATOR. The running boys fade.

DOUG. (*Still standing.*) I'm alive. But what's the use? They're more alive than me. How come? How come?

NARRATOR. You know the answer, Douglas Spaulding. Standing alone there, you know. Look down, Doug. Stare down at your motionless feet . . .

DOUG. It's these shoes . . .

NARRATOR. Late that night, Douglas Spaulding, going home from the two-reeler with your mother and father and brother Tom, you see the *tennis shoes* in the bright store window. Your ankles are seized, feet suspended. The earth spins. Mom and Dad and brother walk quietly forward. You, Douglas, trudge backward, watching the shoes in the midnight window.

DOUG. Dad . . . back there in the window, those creamy-sponge Para Litefoot shoes . . .

DAD [R5]. (*Rises.*) Suppose you tell me why you need a pair of sneakers. Can you do that?

DOUG. Well . . .

NARRATOR. Tell him, Doug. Tell him how they feel like running through summer grass without any shoes on. Like sticking your feet out of hot covers to let cool breezes slip soothingly across them. Tell him how tennis shoes feel like it always feels the first time each year, wading in the slow waters of the clear creek.

DOUG. Dad—it's kind—kind of hard to explain.

DAD. But what's wrong with last year's shoes? Dig *them* out of the closet.

NARRATOR. The people that make tennis shoes seem to know what boys need and want. They must have watched a lot of winds blow the trees and a lot of rivers going down to lakes. Whatever it is, it is in the shoes, and it is summer. Douglas, try to say all this in your words.

DOUG. Don't you see, Dad? I just can't use last year's pair . . .

NARRATOR. They were great last year. But now . . . why, Mr. Spaulding, now they're all dead inside!

DAD. Well . . . we'll see, Doug. (*Meaning "no."*) We'll see. (DAD *sits.*)

DOUG. I just gotta, Dad. I just gotta. Why, with those shoes I could do anything . . . anything at all! (DOUG *sits.*)

NARRATOR. The next morning, old Mr. Sanderson moves through his shoe store as the proprietor of a pet shop must move through his shop where are kenneled animals from every place in the world, touching each one on his way. Brush the shoes in the window . . . some dogs, some cats . . . touch each pair with concern, adjusting laces, fixing tongues . . .

There is the sound of thunder! One moment the door to Sanderson's shoe emporium, empty. Next, Douglas Spaulding standing clumsily in the opening. The thunder had stopped when his shoes stopped. (DOUG *stands.* MR. SANDERSON *rises and remains at left of lectern.*)

SANDERSON [R5]. Don't say a word, Douglas.

NARRATOR. Douglas freezes. All the night before—before he had gone to bed—dreaming of cream-sponge Para Litefoot tennis shoes, he had carefully stacked the nickels, dimes, and quarters of his piggy-bank. He had said to himself . . .

DOUG. Whatever you want, you got to make your own way.

NARRATOR. Now he stands frozen in the doorway, in the bright sunlight of the shoe emporium—frozen, staring down at his leather shoes as if these heavy things could not be pulled up out of the cement.

SANDERSON. (*Moving forward.*) First, I know just what you want to buy.

NARRATOR. Mr. Sanderson's voice reaches Douglas' ears . . . but he cannot respond. He cannot move.

SANDERSON. Secondly, I see you every afternoon at my window. You think I *don't see?* You're wrong. Third, to give it its full name, you want the *Royal Crown cream-sponge Para Litefoot tennis shoes:* "Like menthol on your feet!" Fourth, you want credit!

DOUG. (*Moves forward.*) No! I got something better than credit to offer! Before I tell, Mr. Sanderson, you got to do me one small favor. Can you remember when was the last time you yourself wore a pair of Litefoot sneakers?

SANDERSON. Oh, ten, twenty, say thirty years ago. Why?

DOUG. Oh? . . . Well . . . don't you think you owe it to your customers to at least *try* the tennis shoes you sell, so you'd know how they feel?

SANDERSON. You may not have noticed, but I'm wearing shoes.

DOUG. But not sneakers, sir. How can you rave about them if you haven't worn them for thirty years?

SANDERSON. Well, now I . . .

DOUG. Mr. Sanderson, you sell me something, and I'll sell you something just as valuable.

SANDERSON. Is it absolutely necessary to the sale that I put on a pair of the sneakers, boy?

DOUG. I sure wish you would, sir.

SANDERSON. Well . . . (*He sighs and shrugs resignedly.*)

NARRATOR. A minute later, seated, panting quietly, he laces the tennis shoes to his long narrow feet. They look detached and alive down there next to the dark cuffs of his business suit.

DOUG. How do they feel?

SANDERSON. "How do they feel?" he asks. They . . . they feel just fine.

DOUG. Oh sir! Please don't sit down; kinda rock back and forth, sponge around while I tell you the rest.

NARRATOR. Better sit back, Mr. Sanderson. Sink deep into your shoes, flex your toes. You can't stop this flow of words. A dike has burst. Limber your arches. All the flood will come out in one gigantic inundation of words. So sit back, test your ankles . . . feel the softness on your feet.

DOUG. Mr. Sanderson, I'll give you my money; you give me the shoes. I still will owe you a dollar. But, Mr. Sanderson—soon as I get those shoes on, you know what *happens?*

SANDERSON. What?

DOUG. Bang! I deliver your packages, pick up packages, bring you coffee, burn trash, run to the post office, library . . . you'll see twelve of me in and out every minute. Feel those shoes . . . see how fast they'd take me? Feel all that running inside? You stay in the nice cool store while I'm jumping all over town! But it's not me, really; it's the shoes. They go like mad down alleys, cutting corners . . . there they go! Whoooooooooosh! . . .

NARRATOR. Feel those shoes, Mr. Sanderson. Douglas is right. Feel how they hush themselves deep into the carpet, sink as in jungle grass, in loam and resilient clay. You should look in a mirror, Mr. Sanderson. How many years has it been since *that* light shown in your face, in your eyes?

SANDERSON. Boy! In five years, how'd you like a job selling shoes in this emporium?

DOUG. Gee, thanks, sir! I don't know what I'm going to be, yet.

SANDERSON. Anything you want to be, son—you'll be it. No one will ever stop you. Find your size and lace 'em up. There's a dozen things you have to do for me today. Finish them, we're even-steven, and you're fired.

DOUG. Thanks, Mr. Sanderson, I'm on my way!

SANDERSON. Stop! . . . How do they feel, boy?

NARRATOR. The boy looks down at his feet in deep rivers, in fields of wheat in the wind, already rushing him out of town. He looks up at the old man; his eyes flame; his mouth moves . . . but no sound comes out.

SANDERSON. Antelopes, son? Gazelles?

NARRATOR. Douglas hesitates, nods a quick yes and vanishes. (DOUG *sits*.) With a whisper he spins around and is gone. The door stands empty. The sound of tennis shoes drifts away on the jungle air. From a long time ago a memory comes to old Mr. Sanderson.

SANDERSON. I remember when I was a boy . . . I remember the sound. Beautiful creatures leaping under the sky, gone through brush, under trees, away. Only the soft echo of their running left behind. Antelopes. Gazelles.

NARRATOR. Mr. Sanderson stoops to pick up the boy's abandoned winter shoes, heavy with forgotten rains and long melted snows. (MR. SANDERSON *sits*.) And across town, out of the blazing sun, Grandpa places another shiny new bottle of dandelion wine on the shelf in the cellar.

(*There is a short pause, during which the* READERS *shift their positions to denote time passage.*)

The Time Machine

TOM [R5]. (*Rises, moves forward.*) What'cha doin', Doug?

DOUG [R3]. (*Rises, moves forward.*) I'm writin'.

TOM. Yeah, Doug, sure. I can see that. (*After a pause.*) What'cha writin'?

DOUG. Boy! Brothers can sure be ex—exas—be a bother! (*After another pause.*) Tom, you know summer is rituals, and each one's got its own time and place.

TOM. Like what?

DOUG. Like . . . like the ritual of lemonade or iced-tea making, the ritual of the wine making, shoes or no shoes.

TOM. Oh!

DOUG. What have you got to report, Tom: A new first, a fancy ceremony of some sort—like creek-crab catching or water-strider-spider grabbing?

TOM. Ain't nobody ever grabbed a water-strider-spider in his life. You ever know anyone that did? Go ahead, think, Doug.

DOUG. I'm thinking.

TOM. Well?

DOUG. You're right. Nobody ever did. They're just too fast.

TOM. It ain't that they're fast. They just don't exist. (*After still another pause.*) That's right! They just never did exist at all. Well, that's all.

DOUG. What's that mean?

TOM. Water-strider-spiders don't exist, because you can't catch them. And only the things you can hold and touch . . . and look onto . . . exist.

DOUG. I don't believe you.

NARRATOR [R1]. Can you tell him, Doug? Can you tell him what is just a nucleus of thought in your youthful mind? Can you tell him of the endlessness of time? Of the great circle in which those things that were, and those things that are to be, and those things that never were . . . except in the minds of young boys . . . are all together and a part of . . . and forever are one with time. Can you tell him, Doug?

TOM. Nothing exists except what you can hold and touch.

DOUG. Phoooiii!

(DOUG *and* TOM *return to their stools and sit. There is a slight pause but no shifting of the* READERS' *positions.*)

NARRATOR. The lazy days of July are long and full. The bright warm days are filled to the very brim of being with warm sweet odors of dandelions; and in the cellar of Grandma's house the shelves are filling, day by wonderful day, with ketchup bottles transformed into crystal vessels of dandelion wine. Each day a new, shiny bottle . . . labeled and filled with the events of that day. There's the first harvest . . . and there's the day of the time machine . . .

DOUG [R3]. (*Rises.*) Now, John Huff, what are you feeding me? A time machine?

JOHN [R4]. (*Rises.*) A time machine. Mother's scout's honest Injun's honor!

LUCY [R2]. (*Rises.*) An' it travels in the past and future, too?

JOHN. No, Lucy. Only in the past. But you can't have everything. Here we are.

DOUG. Heck, this is just old Colonel Freeleigh's place.

LUCY. Can't be no time machine in there. He's no inventor.

JOHN. Okay! Be knuckleheads. Sure, Colonel Freeleigh didn't invent it, but he's got prop . . . prop . . . prop—pri-e-tary interest in it. An' it's been here all the time. Come on. (JOHN *and* LUCY *step to the side of their lecterns.*)

NARRATOR. John escorts Lucy in past the screen door. (DOUG *steps out from behind his lectern.*) It does not slam. Douglas catches it and follows Lucy and John into Colonel Freeleigh's house. They peer down a long dark hall toward a room that is like an undersea grotto . . . soft green, dim, and watery.

JOHN. Colonel Freeleigh? (*After a pause.*) He don't hear so good. Colonel!

NARRATOR. No answer . . . only the dust, sifting down and around the spiral stairwell from above. Then a faint stir in that undersea chamber at the far end of the hall. Move carefully, children . . . peer into the room. You will see two pieces of furniture—an old man and a chair. They resemble each other, both so thin you can see how they are put together. The rest of the room . . . naked ceiling and walls and vast quantities of air . . . silent and still.

DOUG. He . . . he looks dead.

JOHN. Naw, he's just dreaming of places to travel. Colonel?

NARRATOR. One of the pieces of brown furniture moves. It's the Colonel— blinking, focusing, smiling a wild and toothless smile.

COLONEL [R5]. (*Rises and steps forward.*) Eh? Oh, Johnny! Why . . . why, come in, boy! Come in!

JOHN. Colonel, Doug and Lucy are here, too . . .

COLONEL. Eh? Oh, oh, yes! Well, all of you, come in. Come on, now.

LUCY. But where's the . . .

JOHN. Sssssh!

COLONEL. Where's what?

JOHN. Uh . . . she means . . . but where's the . . . uh . . . point in *us* talking? . . . I . . . uh . . . *you* talk, Colonel. Huh?

COLONEL. (*Laughing.*) Beware, Johnny Huff! Old men lie in wait for people to ask them to talk. Then they rattle on like a rusty elevator wheezing up a shaft.

JOHN. Tell us about Pawnee Bill!

COLONEL. Eh? What?

JOHN. Pawnee Bill . . . the way west!

COLONEL. Ah . . . yes . . . the way west . . . me and Pawnee Bill. (DOUG, JOHN, *and* LUCY *return to their stools and sit.*)

NARRATOR. The Colonel's voice murmurs; it drifts away on serene lake waters.

COLONEL. This is how it was over fifty years ago . . . 1875! People asleep in the small towns of the East . . . or not yet asleep in their beds, and hearing sounds of horses in the night and the creak of the Conestoga ready to go . . . the brooding of oxen under the trees . . . and the small crying of children, old before their time. Sound of arrivals and departures, blacksmiths in red hells through midnight. . . . The smell of bacon and hams ready for travel . . . heavy feel of wagons, ships floundering with goods. . . . Dogs running out to the edge of the wilderness ahead and, fearful, running back with a look of empty space in their eyes. . . . This is how it was, going west so long ago . . . out on the rim of the precipice, on the edge of the cliff of stars . . .

That's how it was in 1875 . . . an' me an' Bill out there, somewhere in that wilderness, on a little rise in the middle of the prairie, waitin'. Bill, he leans over to me—

PAWNEE BILL [R1]. (*Stands.*) Colonel?

COLONEL. Huh? What is . . . ?

PAWNEE BILL. Listen.

COLONEL. The prairie's like a big stage all set for the storm to come. Thunder! Softness in the gloom. Thunder again!

PAWNEE BILL. Out there, Colonel. Look at the size o' that cloud! Yellow —fer az th' eye kin see. Full o' black lightnin' sunk down to earth. Fifty miles wide, twice't as long, an' a mile high.

COLONEL. Lord . . .

PAWNEE BILL. Yellow cloud, Colonel—inch off'n th' groun'—hit's a comin'.

COLONEL. Lord . . . Lord A'mighty, Bill!

PAWNEE BILL. Look at hit, Colonel!

COLONEL. The earth pounding like a heart gone mad. Children . . . a heart gone to panic. Our bones shaking fit to break. The very earth, quivering and shaking, and rumbling.

PAWNEE BILL. That's 'em, Colonel!

COLONEL. Let's git 'em, Bill! (PAWNEE BILL *sits.*) And I shouted again. The veil of dust lifted, and I saw 'em! I swear to God, I saw 'em! The grand army of the prairie: the bison, the buffalo!

NARRATOR. (*After a pause.*) There is thunder and lightning in the Colonel's room. The air is unbreathable with dust; a roar drowns out all sight, all sound.

COLONEL. Heads like giant fists, bodies like locomotives. Twenty, fifty, two hundred thousand iron missiles shooting out of that yellow cloud, flailing cinders from their hooves, eyes a-glowin' with the heat of hell! Six hours . . . six hours it took them to pass away over the horizon toward less kind men than me. I couldn't shoot them. I tried to, but I couldn't do it. Bill was gone. I stood alone on the prairie. But I saw 'em—the great herds of American buffalo. I saw, but couldn't shoot. Six hours it took to pass on over to eternity. I hear them still, roaring like a great wind. I wish you children could have heard—could have seen—the roaring . . . the hot breaths searing the grass. Wish you could have . . . could have . . .

DOUG. (*Stands.*) Is—is he asleep?

JOHN. (*Stands.*) No . . . he's just recharging the batteries.

LUCY. (*Stands.*) But where's the time—?

JOHN. My gosh, Lucy. You're sure dumb. (LUCY *sits.*)

COLONEL. Antietam . . . Bull Run . . . Shiloh . . .

DOUG. Gee! Does he know about the Civil War, too? (*In the background, a voice softly sings "The Battle Hymn of the Republic."*)

JOHN. Do you remember the Civil War, sir? (JOHN *sits.*)

COLONEL. Do I remember the—? Oh, yes . . . I do, I do! Everything! Except . . . which side I fought on . . .

DOUG. The color of your uniform. (DOUG *sits. The singing stops, but a humming begins.*)

COLONEL. Colors begin to run on you. It's gotten hazy. I see soldiers with me, but a long time ago I stopped seeing color in their coats or caps. (*Humming stops.*) Born in Illinois . . . raised in Virginia . . . married in New York . . . built a house in Tennessee, an' now—very late —here I am, good Lord, back in Greentown. . . . The *soldiers* are there, but the colors run an' blend.

NARRATOR. The light is dimming in the western sky, children. The time machine is running down. Hurry! Ask him about Bull Run! Ask him about Shiloh! John Huff, ask the time machine which side of the hills he fought on!

JOHN. Did the sun rise on your left or right? Did you march toward Canada or Mexico?

COLONEL. Seems some mornings the sun rose on my good right hand, some mornings over my left shoulder. . . . Son, we marched *all* directions. It's almost seventy years since—

NARRATOR. Seventy years since Chattanooga and Lookout Mountain, since Gettysburg. You forget suns and mornings and directions *that* long past. But a battle, Colonel—a battle won somewhere?

A VOICE. (*Singing softly.*) "Oh, I wish I was in the land of cotton! Old times there are not forgotten . . ." (*The singing stops, but a humming begins.*)

COLONEL. No. I don't remember anyone winning . . . anywhere . . . any time. (*Humming stops.*) War's just not a winning thing. You lose— all the time—and the ones who lose last asks for terms. All I remember is a lot of losing and sadness and nothing good at the end of it all. Ah! The end of it. *That* was a winning . . . but a winning all to itself and had nothing to do with the guns. But that ain't a winning you want me to talk about, is it, young'uns?

LUCY. (*Rises.*) What about Antietam?

COLONEL. I was there.

DOUG. (*Rises.*) Bull Run!

COLONEL. I was there.

JOHN. (*Rises.*) Shiloh? Were you at Shiloh, Colonel?

COLONEL. A beautiful name, Shiloh. What a shame to see it only on battle records!

JOHN. Shiloh, then? Fort Sumter? (LUCY, DOUG, *and* JOHN *sit again.*)

COLONEL. I saw the first puffs of powder smoke. So many things come back . . . oh, so many things . . . soldiers lying peacefully near the Potomac . . . dreaming. Tents in the clear autumn moon. Watchfires gleaming . . . no sound save the rush of the river . . . and the dew falls softly on the faces of the dead . . . the picket's off duty forever! . . . After the surrender . . . there stands Mr. Lincoln on the White House balcony. What's that he's sayin'? . . . Did he say, "Will the band play 'Dixie' "? (*A voice hums "Dixie," continuing through the* COLONEL'*s speech.*) Late at night I feel my mouth move . . . singing the songs back in another time . . . the songs . . . I remember the songs . . . singing! (*The humming stops, and various voices sing snatches of Civil War songs.*)

VOICE TWO. "Look away, look away, look away, Dixie Land . . ."

VOICE ONE. "Mine eyes have seen the glory of the coming of the Lord."

VOICE FOUR. "He is trampling out the vintage where the grapes of wrath are stored."

VOICE TWO. (*To the tune of "The Yellow Rose of Texas."*) "Ye cavaliers of Dixie, who guard the southern shores . . ."

VOICE ONE. "When the boys come home in triumph, with the laurels they shall gain . . ."

COLONEL. So many songs, sung on both sides, blowing north, blowing south on the high winds . . .

VOICE ONE. "We are coming, Father Abraham, three hundred thousand more . . ."

VOICE FOUR. "Tenting tonight, tenting tonight, tenting on the old camp ground . . ."

VOICE TWO. "Hurrah, hurrah, we bring the Jubilee. . . . Hurrah, hurrah, the flag that makes us free."

COLONEL. (*Singing.*) "Hurrah, hurrah, we bring the Jubilee . . ."

(*There is a long pause. The* COLONEL *steps back to his stool but does not sit.* JOHN *rises and steps to the side of his lectern.*)

JOHN. Well! Is he or isn't he? (LUCY *and* DOUG *rise and step to the side of their lecterns.*)

LUCY. He sure is!

COLONEL. Huh? I sure am *what?*

DOUG. A time machine, a time machine.

COLONEL. Is that what you call me?

JOHN. Yes . . . yes, sir, Colonel.

DOUG. Well, I guess we'd better go . . .

LUCY. Yes—uh—thank you, Colonel.

COLONEL. What? Oh . . . oh, so long, children.

NARRATOR. Quietly . . . ever so quietly the children tiptoe out of the room and down the long hall. (LUCY, JOHN, *and* DOUG *step back from their lecterns but remain standing.*) Colonel Freeleigh does not see them go. In the street they are startled as someone shouts from a first-floor window above.

COLONEL. (*With a step forward.*) Hey!

JOHN. Yes, sir, Colonel?

COLONEL. You're right! Why didn't I think of that? A time machine, by God. I *am* a time machine.

LUCY. Yes, sir.

DOUG. (*At the same time.*) You sure are, sir.

COLONEL. So long children . . . and . . . and come aboard any time. (*He steps back to his lectern and sits.*)

LUCY, JOHN, DOUG. (*All together.*) Yes, sir! We will! Good-bye!

NARRATOR. And you will go aboard many times this summer, Douglas and Johnny and Lucy. You're riding a very special train.

DOUG. The Colonel . . . well, he's been down the track before, and he knows. And now here we come, you and me, along the same track, but further on. . . . We need old Colonel Freeleigh to shove us and say "Look alive" so we remember every second! So when kids come around when *we* are old, we can do for them what the Colonel once did for us. That's the way it is. We all got to go visit him a lot and listen . . . we got to go far-traveling with him as often as we can!

JOHN. Far-traveling?

LUCY. Far-traveling. You make that up, Doug?

DOUG. Maybe . . . maybe no.

LUCY. Far-traveling . . .

DOUG. Yes, one thing I am sure of . . . (*His voice hollow, fading out—and into an echo effect.*) . . . far-traveling—it sure sounds lonely.

(LUCY, DOUG, *and* JOHN *sit. There is a long pause, during which all of the* READERS *shift their positions slightly to mark the passage of time. Then* DOUG *rises and steps forward.*)

II. THE REALIZATION: THE SORROWS OF SUMMER

A Game of Statues

DOUG [R3]. People shouldn't be in such a hurry. People are always running. I put that down in my nickel tablet. "People shouldn't run." Because if you run, time runs. You yell and scream and race and roll and tumble, and all of a sudden the sun is gone and the whistle is blowing.

JOHN [R4]. (*Rises, steps forward.*) I'm leaving you, Douglas Spaulding. Going away.

DOUG. John! Say that again.

JOHN. You heard me the first time, Doug.

DOUG. Did you say you were—going away?

JOHN. Got my train ticket here in my pocket. Whoo-whoo-clang! Sush-sush-sush . . . whoooooooooo . . . going tonight.

DOUG. Tonight! But, my gosh! Tonight we're playing "Red-Light–Green-Light." And "Statues"! How come all of a sudden?

JOHN. It's my father. He's got a job in Milwaukee.

DOUG. Going away—gee! Summer sure is changing.

JOHN. Changing?

DOUG. Why, John, I just realized this summer I was alive. And now things are happening too fast. I—I—I—thought everything would go on forever: the perfection, the sound of a good friend whistling like an oriole . . .

VOICE ONE. Pegging the softball . . .

VOICE FIVE. Key-jingling the dusty path . . .

VOICE SIX. All of it complete . . .

VOICE TWO. Everything can be touched.

VOICE SIX. Things stay near . . .

VOICE ONE. Things are at hand and will remain.

DOUG. (*After a pause.*) People shouldn't run. The only way to keep things slow is to watch everything and do nothing! You can maybe stretch a day—a night—into three days, three nights. Sure . . . just by watching! And everything stays as it is forever!

JOHN. Doug?

DOUG. Yes?

JOHN. I got time, time for maybe one game of "Statues," then I got to go home. The train leaves at eight. Who's going to be "it"?

DOUG. Me! I'm "it"! Start running!

VOICE ONE. Boys scatter, yelling . . .

VOICE SIX. John backs away, then turns . . .

VOICE TWO. Begins to lope.

VOICE SIX. Douglas counts slowly.

VOICE FIVE. Let them run far . . .

VOICE ONE. Spread out . . . separate . . . each to his own small world.

VOICE TWO. Momentum up!

VOICE FIVE. Almost out of sight! . . .

DOUG. Statues! Everyone, freeze!

NARRATOR [R1]. Very quietly, Douglas moves across the lawn to where John Huff stands like an iron deer in the twilight.

DOUG. John, now—don't you move so much as an eyelash. I absolutely command you to stay here and not move at all for the next—*three hours!*

JOHN. Doug . . .

DOUG. (*Commandingly.*) Freeze!

JOHN. (*In a small whisper.*) I've got to go.

DOUG. Not a muscle. It's the game.

JOHN. I've got to go home now.

VOICE SIX. Now the statue moves . . .

VOICE TWO. Takes its hands down out of the air . . .

VOICE FIVE. Moves its head to look at Douglas.

NARRATOR. The two boys stand looking at each other.

JOHN. We'll play one more round. But this time, I'll be "it." Run!

VOICE SIX. The boys run.

JOHN. Freeze!

VOICE TWO. The boys freeze, Douglas with them.

JOHN. Not a muscle . . . not a hair! Doug, this is the only way to do it.

DOUG. John . . .

VOICE FIVE. Douglas feels John walking around him . . .

VOICE ONE. Even as he had walked around John a moment before.

VOICE SIX. He feels John sock him on the arm once—not too hard.

JOHN. So long, Doug. (JOHN *moves back to his stool and sits.*)

VOICE ONE. Then there is a rushing sound . . .

VOICE TWO. The sound of boys running in summer.

VOICE FIVE. He knows there is nobody behind him. (*There is a pause, and* VOICE FOUR *vocalizes the sound of a faraway train whistle.*)

VOICE FOUR. Whoo-whoo-oooo . . .

DOUG. (*After another pause.*) So long, John Huff, so . . . long.

VOICE ONE. Statues are best.

VOICE TWO. They are the only things you can keep on your lawn.

VOICE FIVE. Don't ever let them move.

VOICE SIX. Once you do, you can't do a thing with them.

DOUG. John? John! John, you're my enemy, you hear? You're no friend of mine. Don't come back now, ever! Get away! Enemy! You hear me? That's what you are. It's all off! Now you're dirt . . . (*crying*) . . . John, you hear me? *John?*

VOICE ONE. Doug stands on the porch.

VOICE TWO. The sky darkens like a wick down a notch.

VOICE SIX. He looks at his fist pointed down the street . . .

VOICE TWO. He looks at his fist . . .

VOICE FIVE. And it dissolves . . .

VOICE ONE. The world dissolves beyond it.

DOUG. I'm mad, I'm angry, I hate him, I'm mad, I'm angry, I hate him, I'm mad, I'm angry, I hate him! Hate—hate—hate . . .

(DOUG *returns to his stool and sits. There is a long pause as the* READERS *change positions to mark the transition.*)

Dandelion Wine 221

The Closing Window

(*As successive* READERS *speak the following lines, each rises and moves to a position in front of his lectern.*)

VOICE SIX. There's the day of the new tennis shoes . . .

VOICE TWO. There's the day of the first dandelion harvest . . .

VOICE FOUR. And the day a god left Greentown, and the world dissolved.

VOICE ONE. And then there comes the day when, all around, you hear the dropping of apples . . .

VOICE FIVE. One . . . by one . . . from the trees.

NARRATOR [R1]. Falling like horses' hoofs in the soft, darkening grass . . .

VOICE THREE. And *you* are the last apple on the tree.

NARRATOR. You wait. Wait for the wind to work you slowly from the tree —from your hold upon the sky . . .

VOICE TWO. To drop you down . . .

VOICE THREE. Down . . . to fall into darkness . . .

VOICE SIX. From the light of perpetual day . . .

NARRATOR. To the coldness and blackness of eternal night. (READERS THREE, FOUR, *and* SIX *return to their stools and sit.*)

COLONEL [R5]. (*Steps forward.*) No! No, not like that! Please, God—not like that.

TELEPHONE OPERATOR [R2]. Colonel Freeleigh? Colonel Freeleigh, here is your call. Mexico City, Erickson 3-8-9-9.

NARRATOR. Now far away but infinitely clear . . . (MIGUEL *rises and steps to the right side of his lectern.*)

MIGUEL [R4]. Bueno.

COLONEL. Miguel?

MIGUEL. Señor Freeleigh! Again? Thees cost you much money.

COLONEL. Let it cost! You know what to do, Miguel?

MIGUEL. Sí, señor. The window?

COLONEL. Yes, Miguel . . . and hurry. Hurry!

MIGUEL. Sí. Un minuto, señor.

NARRATOR. Thousands of miles away, in a southern climate, the sounds of footsteps move away from a telephone receiver. Then can be heard the grate of a window opening.

COLONEL. Ahhh. Yes—yes. I can hear . . . all the sounds.

VOICE SIX. The sounds of Mexico City on a hot, yellow noon . . .

VOICE TWO. Sounds rising through an open window into a waiting phone . . .

VOICE ONE. A man named Miguel holding the mouthpiece out into the bright day.

MIGUEL. Señor? (MIGUEL *sits.*)

COLONEL. No! No, please . . . let me listen.

NARRATOR. Listen to hooting metal horns . . .

VOICE SIX. Squealing brakes . . .

VOICE TWO. The call of vendors selling red-purple bananas and jungle oranges . . .

VOICE FOUR. Tires ripping on hot pavements . . .

VOICE SIX. Eyes shut tight, and the vision of meat hanging in great slabs . . .

VOICE TWO. The smell of stone alleys, wet with the morning rain.

VOICE SIX. The clean feeling of a hot sun burning on brown straight shoulders.

VOICE FIVE. Young—twenty-five—no more wheelchair, no more failing heart . . . but twenty-five, and walking . . . alert . . . looking, seeing . . .

VOICE SIX. Drinking all colors and all smells.

NARRATOR. A rap on the door. The old man quickly hides the phone under his lap robe.

VOICE TWO. The nurse enters. (*The* NURSE *rises and stands at the right of her lectern.*)

NURSE [R6]. Hello. Have you been good?

COLONEL. Yes.

NARRATOR. It is an effort . . . mechanical. He can hardly see. The shock of a simple rap on a door is such that part of him is still in another city far removed. He waits for his mind to rush home—it must be there to answer questions, act sane, be polite.

NURSE. I've come to check your pulse.

COLONEL. Not *now!*

NURSE. You're not going anywhere, are you?

NARRATOR. He looks steadily at the nurse.

COLONEL. I haven't been anywhere for ten years.

NURSE. Give me your wrist.

VOICE TWO. Fingers, hard and precise, search like a pair of calipers for the sickness in his pulse.

NURSE. What have you been doing to excite yourself?

COLONEL. Nothing!

VOICE TWO. Her gaze shifts and stops on the empty phone table.

NURSE. Why do you do this? You promised you wouldn't. That's how you hurt yourself in the first place—getting excited, talking too much, those children in here jumping around . . .

COLONEL. They sat quietly and listened, and I told them things they'd never heard before. The buffalo, I told them. It was worth it. I was in a pure fever. I was alive. It doesn't matter if being alive kills a man. Now give me the phone. I can at least talk to someone outside this room!

NURSE. I'm sorry, Colonel. Your grandson will have to know about this. I prevented his having the phone taken out last week. Now it looks like I'll have to let him have his head.

COLONEL. This is my house, my phone! I pay your salary!

NURSE. To make you well. Not to allow you to get yourself excited. To bed with you now, young man.

NARRATOR. From the bed he looks back at the phone and *keeps* looking at it.

NURSE. I'm going to the store for a few minutes. And just to be sure you don't use the phone again, I'm hiding your wheelchair in the hall. (*The NURSE sits.*)

VOICE TWO. She wheels the empty chair out the door.

NARRATOR. He hears her pause in the downstairs entry and dial the extension phone.

COLONEL. Mexico City? She wouldn't dare!

VOICE TWO. The front door shuts.

NARRATOR. He thinks of the last week here, alone, in his room . . . of the secret, narcotic calls across the continents, an isthmus, whole jungle countries of rain forests, blue orchid plateaus, lakes, hills . . .

COLONEL. Talking . . . talking . . . to Buenos Aires . . . and Lima . . . Rio de Janeiro.

NARRATOR. He lifts himself in the cool bed. Tomorrow . . . the phone gone.

COLONEL. What a greedy fool I've been!

NARRATOR. He slips his brittle ivory legs down from the bed, marveling at their desiccation.

COLONEL. They seem to be things that were fastened to my body one night when I slept—my younger legs taken off and destroyed in the cellar furnace.

NARRATOR. Over the years, they had destroyed all of him, removing hands, arms, and legs.

COLONEL. Leaving me with substitutes as delicate and useless as chess pieces.

NARRATOR. And now they are tampering with something more intangible —the memory.

COLONEL. They're trying to cut wires leading back into another year!

NARRATOR. He crosses the room in a stumbling run. Grasping the phone, he takes it with him as he slides down the wall to sit upon the floor.

COLONEL. Must get the long-distance operator.

NARRATOR. Heart pounding—exploding within—faster and faster—a blackness in the eyes.

COLONEL. Hurry, hurry!

MIGUEL [R4]. (*After a pause, rising.*) Bueno?

COLONEL. Miguel, we were . . . cut off.

MIGUEL. We must not phone again, señor. Your nurse called me. She says you are very ill. I must hang up.

COLONEL. No, Miguel! Please. One last time, listen to me. They're taking the phone out tomorrow. I can never call again. (*After a short, tense pause.*) For the love of God, Miguel! For friendship . . . the old days. I haven't moved in ten years.

NARRATOR. He drops the phone and has trouble picking it up, his chest thick with pain.

COLONEL. Miguel, you *are* still there, aren't you?

MIGUEL. Thees weel be the last time?

COLONEL. I promise.

NARRATOR. The phone is laid on a desk thousands of miles away. Once more, the footsteps, the pause, and—at last—the raising of a window.

VOICE TWO. From somewhere drifts across the silent air flamenco music.

COLONEL. Listen!

NARRATOR. And he hears a thousand people in another sunlight—

VOICE SIX. The faint tinkling music of a guitar . . .

VOICE FOUR. The people in the city of early siesta . . .

VOICE ONE. Shops closing . . . little boys crying, "*Lotería, nacional para hoy!*"

VOICE FOUR. "*Lotería, nacional . . . !*" (*The voice becoming an echo.*) "*Lotería, nacional para hoy!*"

NARRATOR. And at last, the clearest, most improbable sound of all . . .

COLONEL. The sound of a . . . a green trolley car going around a corner . . .

VOICE ONE. A trolley burdened with a brown, alien, and beautiful people.

VOICE SIX. And the sound of other people running and calling out with triumph as they swing aboard . . .

VOICE TWO. Vanishing around a corner on shrieking rails and borne away in a sun-blazed distance.

COLONEL. Hurry . . . hurry! The people . . . places . . . are falling . . . falling away . . . (*The* COLONEL *sits.*)

NARRATOR. Long before you hit the grass, you will have forgotten there ever was a tree, or other apples, or a summer, or dandelion wine, or green grass below. You fall into a darkness.

VOICE TWO. (*After a pause.*) And above the static of two thousand miles, a strange sound. From two thousand miles away, the closing of a window.

(*There is a longer pause during which all of the* READERS *shift positions slightly to mark the passage of time.*)

NARRATOR. Tom sits on the Civil War cannon in the courthouse square.

TOM [R5]. (*Rises and steps forward.*) Boom! Boom! Boom!

VOICE ONE. Douglas, in front of the cannon, clutches his heart and falls down on the grass. But he doesn't get up; he just lies there, his face thoughtful.

DOUG [R3]. (*Rises and steps forward.*) Tom, it just hit me!

TOM. What?

DOUG. Yesterday the Civil War ended right here in this town forever! Yesterday Mr. Lincoln died right here, and so did General Lee and Grant and a hundred thousand others facing north and south. And yesterday afternoon, at Colonel Freeleigh's house, a herd of buffalo as big as all Greentown, Illinois, went off a cliff into nothing at all. Tom, it's awful! Yesterday a whole lot of dust settled for good. I never dreamed so many people could die so fast.

TOM. They sure did, though. They sure did . . . when Colonel Freeleigh died.

DOUG. You know, Tom, I'm worried.

TOM. 'Bout what?

DOUG. 'Bout the way God runs the world.

TOM. He's all right, Doug. He tries!

(TOM *and* DOUG *step back and sit. There is a pause; all of the* READERS *change their positions slightly to denote a transition in time and place.*)

A Sum in Arithmetic

NARRATOR [R1]. She was a woman with a broom or a dustpan or a mixing bowl in her hand, Great-Grandma was.

GREAT-GRANDMA [R6]. (*Rises.*) In a few hours I shall be dead.

NARRATOR. She strolled but twice in any garden, and flowers bloomed in the warm air.

GREAT-GRANDMA. I'm not afraid.

NARRATOR. And walking, she touched people like pictures, setting the frames a little straighter.

GREAT-GRANDMA. (*Steps forward.*) When you have lived as long as I have, you put away the fear. I never liked lobster in my life, and mainly because I never tried it. On my eightieth birthday, I tried it. Can't say as I am greatly excited over it; but still, I have no doubt as to its taste.

NARRATOR. Death will be a lobster, too.

GREAT-GRANDMA. And I can come to terms with it.

DOUG [R3]. (*Rises.*) Gran'ma . . . Great-Gran'ma . . .

NARRATOR. Now the huge sum in arithmetic is almost completed.

GREAT-GRANDMA. I've stuffed turkeys, chickens, men, and boys. I've washed ceilings, walls, invalids, and children . . .

NARRATOR. Look back now, Sara Spaulding . . . look back on thirty billion things started, carried, and finished and done. It all sums up, totals out. The last decimal placed, the final zero is swinging into place on the line.

GREAT-GRANDMA. I've drawn shades, pinched candles, turned switches . . . and grown old.

NARRATOR. You finished the arithmetic, Sara Spaulding. Now stand back from life a silent hour before reaching for the eraser.

DOUG. Great-Gran'ma . . . ?

GREAT-GRANDMA. (*Very weak.*) Let me see now. Let me see . . .

MOTHER [R2]. (*Choking.*) Great-Gran'ma . . .

GREAT-GRANDMA. Here now, here! All of you here? Well, just let me lie. I'm sleepy . . . so sleepy. I'm ninety-two years old . . . and I'm tired . . .

GRANDPA [R4]. (*Rises.*) Mother, now you listen to me. What you're doin' is no better than breakin' a lease. This house will fall down without you. You gotta give us a year's notice! (GRANDPA *sits.*)

GREAT-GRANDMA. No, son. I can't wait so long, I'm afraid. . . . Is Doug here?

DOUG. Yes, Gran'ma.

GREAT-GRANDMA. I'm so like you sometimes, Doug . . . sittin' through Saturday matinees until your father has to come down after you.

DOUG. I'm sorry . . . I . . .

GREAT-GRANDMA. No, no, child. . . . Doug, when the time comes that the same cowboys are shootin' the same Indians on the same hill, then it's time to fold back the seat and head for home, with no regrets . . . so I'm just leavin' while I'm still happy and still entertained. (DOUG *cries.*) Doug . . . ? Doug, are you cryin' . . . ?

DOUG. Y—yes . . .

GREAT-GRANDMA. What are you cryin' for, child?

DOUG. Be—because you won't be here tomorrow.

GREAT-GRANDMA. Why, honey, I'm not *dying* today. Look in the mirror with me, Doug. Tomorrow morning, I'll get up at seven and wash behind my ears; I'll go to church with Charlie Woodruff; I'll picnic at Electric Park; I'll swim, run barefoot, fall out of trees, chew spearmint gum. . . . Douglas . . . Douglas, for shame! You cut your fingernails, don't you, Douglas?

DOUG. (*Sniffs.*) Yes'm.

GREAT-GRANDMA. And you don't yell when your body makes itself over every seven years or so . . . old cells dead and new ones added to your fingers and your heart. You don't mind that, do you?

DOUG. No'm.

GREAT-GRANDMA. Well, consider then, boy. Any man saves fingernail clippings is a fool. You ever see a snake bother to keep his peeled skin?

DOUG. No . . .

GREAT-GRANDMA. That's about all you got here today in this bed. Fingernails and snake skin. One good breath would send me up in flakes. (*After a pause.*) Important thing is not the me that's lying here, but the me that's downstairs gettin' supper or outside in the backyard tinkerin' with the old car . . . or in the parlor readin'. Why, Douglas, bless you, child! I'm not dying today. No person ever did die that has a family. I'll be around a long time. (*After another pause.*) The world's goin' on . . . and since the part of me which is called—for convenience—Great-Gran'ma won't be here to step it along, all the *other* parts of me—the parts called Uncle Bert and Tom, Mother and Pa, and Douglas and all the other names . . . they'll have to take over, each to his own.

DOUG. Yes, Gran'ma.

GREAT-GRANDMA. So . . . now don't you all worry over me. All of you go . . . go and let me get my work *all* finished . . . (*There is a pause.* DOUGLAS *steps back to his stool but does not sit.*)

NARRATOR. They're all gone now, Sara Spaulding.

GREAT-GRANDMA. Well, that's better. Alone.

A GIRL'S VOICE [R2]. (*Singing.*) "Yes, we'll gather at the river, the beautiful, the beautiful river . . ."

VOICE ONE. No regrets, Sara Spaulding . . .

A GIRL'S VOICE. (*Continuing to sing.*) "Yes, we'll gather at the river . . ."

GREAT-GRANDMA. (*Breaking in on the song.*) No. No regrets. Death's fitting and proper. Like everything else in life, it's fitting.

A GIRL'S VOICE. (*Finishing her song.*) "That flows by the throne of God!"

(GREAT-GRANDMA *sits. There is a pause, the* READERS *shift their positions, and again there is a transition in time and locale.*)

The Fever Dream

DOUG [R3]. Here it is, all written down in my nickel tablet: "You can't depend on things, because . . .

VOICE ONE. Like machines . . . they fall apart or rust or run down.

VOICE TWO. Like tennis shoes, you can run so far, so fast, and then the earth's got you again.

VOICE FIVE. Like wine presses. Presses, big as they are, always run out of dandelions, and squeeze, and squeeze to a halt."

DOUG. "You can't depend on people, because . . .

VOICE FOUR. They go away . . .

VOICE TWO. Strangers die . . .

VOICE FIVE. People you know die . . .

VOICE ONE. Friends die . . .

VOICE SIX. Your own folks can die."

DOUG. So . . . (*With a big breath.*) . . . so . . .

VOICE ONE. So if wine presses and friends and near-friends can go away for awhile or go away forever,

VOICE TWO. Or rust,

VOICE SIX. Or fall apart,

VOICE FIVE. Or die,

DOUG. And if . . . if someone like Great-Gran'ma . . .

VOICE FOUR. Who was going to live forever . . . can die . . .

DOUG. Then . . .

VOICE TWO. Then you, Douglas Spaulding, someday must . . .

DOUG. Then I, Douglas Spaulding, someday must . . . no!

VOICE ONE. Colonel Freeleigh . . .

VOICE FIVE. Dead!

VOICE ONE. Great-Gran'ma . . .

VOICE SIX. Dead!

DOUG. Me! No, they can't kill me!

VOICE FOUR. Yes.

VOICE TWO. Yes.

VOICE SIX. Yes!

VOICE FIVE. Yes, anytime they want to . . .

VOICE ONE. No matter how you kick or scream . . .

VOICE TWO. They just put a big hand over you,

VOICE FIVE. And you're still.

DOUG. I don't want to die!

VOICE SIX. You'll have to, anyway.

VOICE ONE. You'll have to, anyway.

VOICE SIX. Write it in your notebook, Douglas:

VOICE FOUR. I, Douglas Spaulding—someday—must . . .

DOUG. "I . . . Douglas Spaulding . . . someday . . . must . . . must . . . (*very small*) . . . die." (DOUG *sits. There is a short pause.*)

TOM [R5]. (*Stands.*) Mom! Mom! Mom!

MOM [R2]. (*Stands.*) Tom, yes, Tom? What's the matter, boy?

TOM. It's Doug, Mom! He's sick. Terribly sick! He's gonna die, Mom! He's gonna die! (TOM and MOM *slowly reseat themselves.*)

VOICE ONE. Noon:

VOICE FOUR. Sun smashing Doug to the ground. Doctor arrives . . .

VOICE ONE. One o'clock:

VOICE SIX. Doctor exits house, shaking head. He doesn't know . . .

VOICE ONE. Two o'clock:

VOICE TWO. Mother and Tom carry ice packs to Doug's face and body . . .

VOICE ONE. Inside redness, inside blackness . . . Doug, listen to the dim piston of your heart, the muddy ebb and flow of the blood in your arms and legs.

VOICE FIVE. (*Slowly and heavily.*) Thoughts . . . heavy and barely ticking . . .

VOICE SIX. Like seed pellets falling in an hourglass . . .

VOICE FOUR. Slow . . . one by falling one.

VOICE ONE. *Tick* . . .

VOICE FOUR. Chug-a-chug-ding! Woo-wooooooo! (*The "Woo-wooooooo!" is echoed; the scene begins to build, to pick up speed.*)

VOICE TWO. Boy on rooftop—a boy locomoted, pulling an invisible whistle string . . .

VOICE SIX. Then freezing into a statue.

DOUG. John! John Huff—you! Hate you . . . John! John, we're pals, we're pals! Don't hate you, no . . . (*The pace slows down momentarily.*)

VOICE ONE. *Tick* . . .

VOICE FOUR. John falls down an elm-tree corridor . . .

VOICE TWO. Down an endless summer well . . . dwindling away.

VOICE ONE. *Tick . . .*

DOUG. John Huff . . .

VOICE ONE. *Tick . . .*

VOICE FOUR. Sand pellet dropping . . .

VOICE ONE. *Tick . . .*

DOUG. (*Stands.*) John . . .

VOICE ONE. *Tick! Tick . . .*

VOICE FIVE. (*Stands.*) Colonel Freeleigh leans out of the face of a clock . . .

VOICE FOUR. (*Stands.*) Buffalo dust springs down the street . . .

VOICE ONE. *Tick! Tick! Tick . . .*

VOICE FIVE. And buffalo dust clears, whirls, forms shapes . . .

VOICE ONE. *Tick!*

VOICE SIX. (*Stands.*) Fingernails and a heart—a flake upon a white bed . . . (READER TWO *stands and sings in a voice that becomes increasingly wild and off-key.*)

VOICE TWO. "Shall we gather at the river . . . river? Shall we gather at the river . . . river . . . river . . . ?"

DOUG. Gran'ma! Great-Gran'ma!

VOICE TWO, VOICE FOUR, VOICE FIVE. (*Climactically.*) "River . . . river . . . !"

VOICE SIX. Soft . . . soft . . .

VOICE TWO. (*Fading out.*) River . . . (*All of the* READERS *sit.*)

VOICE ONE. (*Slowly; in a low pitch.*) Five o'clock in the afternoon:

VOICE FOUR. Flies dead on the pavement . . .

VOICE SIX. Dogs wet mops in their kennels . . .

VOICE ONE. Six o'clock in the afternoon:

VOICE FIVE. Shadows herded under the trees . . .

VOICE SIX. Downtown stores shut up and locked.

VOICE ONE. Seven o'clock:

VOICE TWO. Greentown resembles a vast hearth . . .

VOICE FIVE. Shudderings of heat move again and again from the west.

VOICE ONE. Seven-thirty: (*The tempo of the scene accelerates again as it builds anew.*)

VOICE SIX. A slight breeze from the east . . .

VOICE ONE. Seven forty-five:

DOUG. Burning . . . burning up . . . an ash . . . a cinder . . . water . . . please . . . Tom? . . . water . . . Mom?

VOICE ONE. Eight o'clock:

VOICE TWO. Far away, barely audible . . .

VOICE FIVE. Thunder.

DOUG. Someday, I, Douglas Spaulding, must die!

VOICE FIVE. Thunder . . .

VOICE TWO. Closer now . . .

VOICE FIVE. Thunder!

VOICE SIX. (*The climax.*) Summer rain—begins light—(*hope begins now*) —increases—and falls heavily!

VOICE TWO. A scent of cool night and cool water . . . and cool white snow . . .

VOICE SIX. And cool green moss and cool silver pebbles lying at the bottom of a quiet river . . .

VOICE ONE. And Douglas—inside like a fall of snow in his bed—turns and opens his eyes to the freshly falling sky . . .

DOUG. Someday *I*, Douglas Spaulding, must die . . . and . . . (*rises*) . . . and someday . . . someday I will.

TOM [R5]. (*Also rises.*) Mom! Mom! It's Doug. He's all right! He's all right! He's not going to die, Mom! Mom! He's alive!

(DOUG *and* TOM *sit. There is a pause. The* READERS *vary their positions slightly, effecting another transition.*)

The Last Ritual

VOICE ONE. Then, quite suddenly, summer is over.

VOICE TWO. Doug knows it first when walking downtown.

VOICE SIX. Tom grabs his arm and points, gasping, at the dime-store window.

TOM [R5]. (*Rises and steps forward.*) Pencils, Doug—ten thousand pencils!

DOUG [R3]. (*Also rises and steps forward.*) Oh, my gosh!

VOICE ONE. Nickel tablets, dime tablets . . .

VOICE FOUR. Notebooks, erasers . . .

VOICE SIX. Water colors, rulers, compasses . . .

DOUG. A hundred thousand of them!

TOM. Don't look. Maybe it's a mirage.

DOUG. No. It's school! School—straight on ahead.

TOM. They've ruined what's left of vacation. Why did they go and do that?

DOUG. Don't know. Didn't make the world. (*After a pause.*) Though sometimes I feel like I did . . . like I got every bit of it right here inside me, Tom.

TOM. You and two zillion other people, I bet.

DOUG. Come on . . . race you home. Bet Gran'pa's in the cellar puttin' up the last of the dandelion wine.

TOM. Come on! (DOUG *and* TOM *quickly return to their stools and sit.*)

VOICE ONE. Down in the cellar, they all look at the summer they have shelved there in glimmering, motionless streams, the bottles of dandelion wine. Numbered from one to ninety-odd, there in ketchup bottles, most of them full now, burning in the cellar twilight—one for every living summer day.

DOUG. (*Rises.*) There's the first day of summer.

VOICE TWO. (*Rises.*) The new-tennis-shoes day . . .

DOUG. There's the day I found out I was alive. Why isn't it a bit brighter?

VOICE FOUR. (*Rises.*) There's the day John Huff fell off the edge of the world.

VOICE SIX. (*Rises.*) The day the part of us called Great-Grandmother quit working.

VOICE FIVE. (*Rises.*) There's the day Colonel Freeleigh fell six feet into the earth.

VOICE FOUR. Seems like it ought to be different—just a speck, mebbe, of buffalo dust or something. But it's just like all the others.

VOICE ONE. As he climbs the stairs from the golden cellar to the real world upstairs, Douglas breaks a spider's web with his face. A single invisible line on the air touches his brow and snaps without a sound.

DOUG. I'm alive. (*In a whisper.*) I am *alive.*

VOICE ONE. (*After a pause.*) Move slowly, Douglas, to your sorcerer's tower . . . dark, secret tower . . . alive with the distant thunders and visions. Move to the portal of glass through which the stars are blinking. Lift slowly your finger and perform the last magic ritual.

DOUG. (*Steps forward.*) Everyone, clothes off! (*After a pause.*) Brush teeth. (*After another pause.*) Climb into bed. (*After a final pause.*) Now, out with the lights.

VOICE SIX. And the town winks out its lights, sleepily, here and there.

DOUG. (*Steps back, still standing.*) The last ones now . . . there . . . there.

VOICE ONE. (*After a long pause.*) He lies in his bed now . . . the town dark . . . and around him his family, his friends, the old people and the young.

VOICE FIVE. And the people . . .

VOICE FOUR. And the world . . .

VOICE SIX. And all of time are in you—*are* you, Douglas Spaulding . . .

VOICE TWO. Never to fade away—never to die . . .

VOICE FIVE. But to go on, as Colonel Freeleigh goes on.

VOICE FOUR. As John Huff . . .

VOICE SIX. As Great-Grandma goes on . . .

DOUG. (*Triumphantly.*) Never to die—but to go on forever.

VOICE ONE. And so thinking, Douglas, sleep; and sleeping, put an end to summer, 1928.

BY MARK TWAIN

The Diaries of Adam and Eve

Adapted for Readers Theatre by Leslie Irene Coger

Excerpts from the private and intimate journals of the world's first man
and woman are amusingly juxtaposed and movingly meshed in such a way
as to lay bare their innermost yearnings, to contrast their shrewd and often
conflicting estimations of each other's foibles and frustrations, their fragil-
ities and fortitudes as the pair come to live—and eventually to love—in
that Never-to-Be-Rediscovered Garden . . . and later . . . after the Fall.

CAST OF CHARACTERS

One Man and One Woman

ADAM. *The first man*

EVE. *The first woman*

THE PHYSICAL ARRANGEMENT OF THE SCENE

In the Beginning, we are told, was a void . . . and probably a darkness
all about. Let there be light, however, upon the face of Eternally Feminine EVE and on the somewhat worried countenance of ADAM, the Man
in Her Life and the Fellow Who Started It All. As it is nearing the end
of the week—Saturday, to be exact—it is appropriate that these two mor-
tals have a place to rest: two simple stools, with or without lecterns, in
the center of the stage. And since both are writing entries in their respective diaries, it is also appropriate that they make known the day of the
week on which the entry is being made.

EVE. *Saturday:* I am almost a whole day old now. I arrived yesterday. That is as it seems to me. And it must be so for if there was a day-before-yesterday, I was not there when it happened, or I should remember it. I feel like an experiment. I feel exactly like an experiment.

ADAM. *Monday:* The new creature with the long hair is a good deal in the way. It is always hanging around and following me about. I don't like this; I am not used to company. I wish it would stay with the other animals. . . . Cloudy today, wind in the east; think we shall have rain. . . . *We?* Where did I get that word? . . . I remember now—the new creature uses it.

EVE. *Tuesday:* I followed the other Experiment around yesterday afternoon, at a distance, to see what it might be for—if I could. But I was not able to make out. I think it is a man. I had never seen a man, but it looked like one, and I feel sure that that is what it is. I realize that I feel more curiosity about it than about any of the other reptiles. It has no hips; it tapers like a carrot; when it stands, it spreads itself apart like a derrick; maybe it is architecture.

I was afraid of it at first, and started to run every time it turned around, for I thought it was going to chase me; but by-and-by I found it was only trying to get away, so after that I was not timid any more, but tracked it along, several hours, about twenty yards behind, which made it nervous and unhappy. At last it was a good deal worried and climbed a tree. I waited a while, then gave it up and went home.

ADAM. *Sunday:* Pulled through. This day is getting to be more and more trying. It was selected and set apart last November as a day of rest. I already had six of them per week, before. This morning found the new creature trying to clod apples out of that forbidden tree.

EVE. *Tuesday:* It is up in the tree again. Resting, apparently. It looks to me like a creature that is more interested in resting than in anything else.

ADAM. *Sunday:* Pulled through.

EVE. *Wednesday:* It has low tastes . . . and is not kind. When I went there earlier this evening in the gloaming, it had crept down from the tree and was trying to catch the little speckled fishes that play in the pool, and I had to clod it to make it go up the tree again and let them alone. One of the clods took it back of the ear, and it used language. It gave me a thrill, for it was the first time I had ever heard speech, except my own. I did not understand the words, but they seemed expressive.

When I found it could talk, I felt a new interest in it, for I love to talk; I talk all day, and in my sleep, too.

ADAM. *Wednesday:* I wish it would not talk; it is always talking right at my shoulder, right at my ear, and I am used only to sounds that are more or less distant from me.

EVE. *Next Sunday:* All week I tagged around after him and tried to get acquainted. I had to do the talking, because he was shy, but I didn't mind it. He seemed pleased to have me around, and I used the sociable *we* a good deal, because it seemed to flatter him to be included.

ADAM. *Thursday:* She told me she was made out of a rib taken from my body. This is at least doubtful, if not more than that. I have not missed any rib. . . .

EVE. *Monday:* This morning I told him my name, hoping it would interest him. But he did not care for it. It is strange. If he should tell me his name, I would care. I think it would be pleasanter in my ears than any other sound.

ADAM. *Monday:* The new creature says its name is Eve. That is all right. I have no objections. Says it is to call it by when I want it to come. I said it was superfluous, then. This word evidently raised me in its respect; and indeed it is a large, good word and will bear repetition. It says it is not an It; it is a She. This is probably doubtful; yet it is all one to me; what she is were nothing to me if she would but go by herself and not talk.

EVE. *Tuesday:* No, he took no interest in my name. I tried to hide my disappointment, but I suppose I did not succeed. I went away and sat on the mossbank with my feet in the water. It is where I go when I hunger for companionship, someone to look at, someone to talk to. It is not enough—that lovely white body painted there in the pool—but it is something, and something is better than utter loneliness.

ADAM. *Sunday:* Pulled through.

EVE. *Wednesday:* We are getting along very well indeed now, and getting better and better acquainted. He does not try to avoid me any more, which is a good sign, and shows that he likes to have me with him.

ADAM. *Friday:* She has taken to beseeching me to stop going over the Falls. What harm does it do? Says it makes her shudder. I wonder why.

I went over the Falls in a barrel—not satisfactory to her. Went over in a tub—still not satisfactory. Swam the Whirlpool and the Rapids in a fig-leaf suit. It got much damaged. Hence, tedious complaints about my extravagance. I am too much hampered here. What I need is a change of scene.

EVE. *Wednesday:* During the last day or two I have taken all the work of naming things off his hands, and this has been a great relief to him, for he has no gift in that line, and is evidently very grateful. He can't think of a rational name to save him, but I do not let him see that I am aware of his defect. Whenever a new creature comes along, I name it before he has time to expose himself by an awkward silence. The minute I set eyes on an animal, I know what it is.

When the dodo came along, he thought it was a wildcat—I saw it in his eye. But I saved him. I just spoke up in a quite natural way with pleased surprise—not as if I was dreaming of conveying information—and said, "Well, I do declare if there isn't the dodo!"

ADAM. *Wednesday:* I get no chance to name anything myself. The new creature names everything that comes along, before I can get in a protest. And always that same pretext is offered—it *looks* like the thing. There is the dodo, for instance. Says the moment one looks at it, one sees at a glance that it "looks like a dodo." Dodo! It looks no more like a dodo than I do.

EVE. *Friday:* My first sorrow. Yesterday he avoided me and seemed to wish I would not talk to him. I could not believe it, and thought there was some mistake, for I loved to be with him and loved to hear him talk, and how could it be that he could feel unkind toward me when I had not done anything? But at last it seemed true, so I went away and sat lonely in the place where I first saw him the morning that we were made and I did not know what he was and was indifferent about him; but now it was a mournful place, and every little thing spoke of him, and my heart was very sore. I did not know why very clearly, for it was a new feeling; I had not experienced it before, and it was all a mystery, and I could not make it out.

But when night came, I could not bear the lonesomeness and went to the new shelter which he has built, to ask him what I had done that was wrong and how I could mend it and get back his kindness again; but he put me out in the rain, and it was my first sorrow.

ADAM. *Friday:* Built me a shelter against the rain, but could not have it to myself in peace. The new creature intruded. When I tried to put it out, it shed water out of the holes it looks with, wiped it away with the back of its paws, and made a noise such as some of the other animals make when they are in distress.

She has taken up with a snake now. The other animals are glad, for she was always experimenting with them and bothering them; and I am glad, because the snake talks, and this enables me to get a rest.

EVE. *Sunday:* It is pleasant again, now, and I am happy; but those were heavy days; I do not think of them when I can help it. I tried to get him some of those apples, but I cannot learn to throw straight. I failed, but I think the good intention pleased him. They are forbidden, and he says I shall come to harm; but so I come to harm through pleasing him, why shall I care for that harm?

ADAM. *Wednesday:* About an hour after sunup, as I was riding through a flowery plain where thousands of animals were grazing, slumbering, or playing with each other, according to their wont, all of a sudden they broke into a tempest of frightful noises, and in one moment the plain was in a frantic commotion, and every beast was destroying its neighbor. I knew what it meant—Eve had eaten that fruit, and death was come into the world. . . . I looked up, and there was Eve. I was not sorry she came, for there are but meagre pickings here, and she had brought me some of those apples. I was obliged to eat them, I was so hungry. It was against my principles, but I find that principles have no real force except when one is well fed. . . . She came curtained in boughs and bunches of leaves; and when I asked her what she meant by such nonsense, and snatched them away and threw them down, she tittered and blushed. I had never seen a person titter and blush before, and to me it seemed unbecoming and idiotic. She said I myself would soon know why it was thus. This was correct. Hungry as I was, I laid down the apple, half-eaten—certainly the best one I ever saw, considering the lateness of the season—and arrayed myself in the discarded boughs and branches, and then spoke to her with some severity and ordered her to go and get some more and not make such a spectacle of herself. She did it. And afterward, we crept down to where the wild-beast battle had been, and collected some skins; and I made her patch together a couple of suits proper for public occasions. They are uncomfortable, it is true, but stylish; and that is the main point about clothes. . . . I find she is a good deal of a companion. I see I should be lonesome and depressed without her. Another thing, she says it is ordered that we work for our living hereafter. She will be useful. I will superintend.

EVE. *Friday:* I tried once more to persuade him to stop going over the Falls. That was because the fire which I had discovered had revealed to me a new passion—quite new, and distinctly different from love, grief, and those others which I had already discovered—fear. And it is horrible!

ADAM. *Friday:* Perhaps I ought to remember that she is very young, a mere girl, and make allowances. She is all interest, eagerness, vivacity, the world is to her a charm, a wonder, a mystery, a joy; she cannot speak for delight when she finds a new flower; she must pet it and caress it and smell it and talk to it, and pour out endearing names upon it. And she is color-mad: brown rocks, yellow sand, gray moss, green foliage, blue sky, the pearl of the dawn—none of them is of any practical value, so far as I can see; but because they have color and majesty, that is enough for her, and she loses her mind over them. If she could but quiet down and keep still a couple of minutes at a time, it would be a reposeful spectacle. In that case, I think I could enjoy looking at her; indeed, I am sure I could; for I am coming to realize that she is a quite remarkably comely creature—lithe, slender, trim, rounded, shapely, nimble, graceful; and once when she was standing marble-white and sun-drenched on a boulder, with her young head tilted back and her hand shading her eyes, watching the flight of a bird in the sky, I recognized that she was beautiful.

EVE. *After the fall:* When I look back, the Garden is a dream to me. It was beautiful, surpassingly beautiful, enchantingly beautiful; and now it is lost, and I shall not see it any more.

The Garden is lost, but I have found *him,* and am content. He loves me as well as he can; I love him with all the strength of my passionate nature, and this, I think, is proper to my youth and sex. If I ask myself why I love him, I find I do not know. I love certain birds because of their song; but I do not love Adam on account of his singing—no, it is not that; the more he sings, the more I do not get reconciled to it! Yet I ask him to sing, because I wish to learn to like everything he is interested in. His singing sours the milk, but it doesn't matter. I can get used to that kind of milk.

It is not on account of his gracious and considerate ways and his delicacy that I love him. No, he has lacks in these regards, but he is well enough just so, and is improving.

It is not on account of his chivalry that I love him—no, it is not that. He told on me, but I do not blame him; it is a peculiarity of sex, I think, and he did not make his sex. Of course, I would not have told on him; I would have perished first; but that is a peculiarity of sex, too; and I do not take credit for it, for I did not make my sex.

Then why is it that I love him? *Merely because he is masculine,* I think.

At bottom he is good, and I love him for that, but I could love him without it. If he should beat me and abuse me, I should go on loving him. I know it. It is a matter of sex, I think.

He is strong and handsome, and I love him for that, and I admire him for that, and I am proud of him, but I could love him without those qualities. If he were plain, I should love him; and I would work for him, and slave over him, and pray for him, and watch by his bedside until I died.

Yes, I think I love him merely because he is *mine* and is *masculine.* There is no other reason, I suppose. This kind of love is not a product of reasonings and statistics. It just *comes*—none knows whence—and cannot explain itself. And doesn't need to.

It is what I think. But I am only a girl, and the first that has examined this matter, and it may turn out that in my ignorance and inexperience I have not got it right.

ADAM. *Ten years later:* After all these years, I see that I was mistaken about Eve in the beginning; it is better to live outside the Garden with her than inside it without her. At first I thought she talked too much, but now I should be sorry to have that voice fall silent and pass out of my life. Blessed be the goodness of her heart and the sweetness of her spirit!

EVE. *Forty years later:* It is my prayer, it is my longing, that we may pass from this life together—a longing which shall never perish from the earth, but shall have a place in the heart of every wife that loves, until the end of time; and it shall be called by my name.

But if one of us must go first, it is my prayer that it shall be I; for he is strong, I am weak, I am not so necessary to him as he is to me—life without him would not be life; how could I endure it? This prayer is also immortal, and will not cease from being offered up while my race continues. I am the first wife, and in the last wife I shall be repeated.

ADAM. *At Eve's grave:* Wheresoever she was, *there* was Eden.

BY RUDYARD KIPLING

The Elephant's Child

A children's story adapted for Readers Theatre by Melvin R. White

Kipling's *Just So Stories* lend themselves to Readers Theatre, especially those with talking animals. Such characters intrigue children. This script is arranged and production suggestions made so that only one character, the Elephant's Child, moves. The presentation which used this arrangement was performed with one elementary school teacher serving as the mobile elephant and another teacher as the narrator. These two divided the major performing responsibility. The children played the other characters, not burdened by long speeches or movement. Later a college cast performed it for second- and third-graders, again keeping the production vital through characterization, but with only the Elephant's Child mobile. No sets, lights, or costumes were used in either production. Children have vivid imaginations.

CAST OF CHARACTERS

Six Men, Two Women, and a Narrator, Man or Woman

NARRATOR. *Effective storyteller, warm, friendly, and intimate with the audience*

ELEPHANT'S CHILD. *A large boy with a juvenile, "different" voice. The "shining halo" type; innocent but curious*

AUNT OSTRICH. *A screeching soprano, possibly tall and thin*

UNCLE GIRAFFE. *A tall man; the timid soul, Edward Everett Horton type*

AUNT HIPPOPOTAMUS. *Resembles the fat woman in the circus; has gruff voice, but is ladylike; the Hattie McDaniel type*

UNCLE BABOON. *An older man, solemn and dignified; has a whiskered voice*

MR. KOLOKOLO BIRD. *An obliging and charming man*

MR. BI-COLORED-PYTHON-ROCK-SNAKE. *Literal and precise, with excessive sibilance*

MR. CROCODILE. *The villain or "heavy"; deep-voiced, with superb diction*

PHYSICAL ARRANGEMENT OF THE STAGE

All of the characters in this adaptation are stationary except the Elephant's Child, who moves about the platform as he talks to the various members of the cast. Seven chairs, or stools of various heights, are arranged across the stage.

"Spanking" music is provided by either a guitarist or a violinist, who also produces "stretching" and "pulling" music.

(There may be guitar background music if desired.)

STORYTELLER. In the high and far-off times, there was once an Elephant, a new Elephant, an Elephant's Child, who was full of 'satiable curiosity —that means he asked ever so many questions. He lived in Africa, and he filled all Africa with his 'satiable curiosity. He asked his tall aunt, the Ostrich: *(Music is out by now.)*

FIGURE 17.   Platform arrangement for *The Elephant's Child*

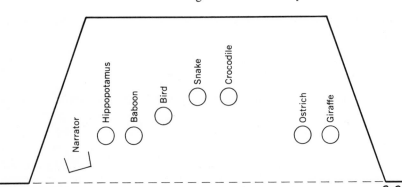

ELEPHANT. (*Lumbers over to her.*) Aunt Ostrich, why do your tail-feathers grow just so?

OSTRICH. Naughty Elephant's Child, you ask too many questions. Come here!

STORYTELLER. And his tall aunt, the Ostrich, spanked him (*Spanking music.* OSTRICH *may pantomime spanking in time to the music, with* ELEPHANT *reacting to each pantomimed blow physically and vocally.*) with her hard, hard claw. Then he asked his tall uncle, the Giraffe:

ELEPHANT. (*Lumbers over to him.*) Uncle Giraffe, what makes your skin so spotty?

GIRAFFE. Naughty Elephant's Child, you are too inquisitive. Come here!

STORYTELLER. And his tall uncle, the Giraffe, spanked him (*Spanking music.*) with his hard, hard hoof. (*Pantomime and reactions as above.*) And still he was full of 'satiable curiosity! He inquired of his broad aunt, the Hippopotamus:

ELEPHANT. (*Lumbers over to her.*) Aunt Hippopotamus, why are your eyes so red?

HIPPO. Naughty Elephant's Child, you talk too much. Come here!

STORYTELLER. And his broad aunt, the Hippopotamus, spanked him, too (*Spanking music. Pantomime and reactions as before.*), with her broad, broad hoof. Next he asked his hairy uncle, the Baboon:

ELEPHANT. (*Lumbers over to him.*) Uncle Baboon, what makes your hair grow just so?

BABOON. Naughty Elephant's Child, you are never quiet. Come here!

STORYTELLER. And naturally, his hairy uncle, the Baboon, spanked him (*Spanking music. Pantomime and reactions as before.*) with his hairy, hairy paw. And still he was full of 'satiable curiosity! He asked questions about everything he saw:

ELEPHANT. (*Lumbers from one character to another on the following sequence of questions.*) How can birds fly?

STORYTELLER. Or heard.

ELEPHANT. Why do lions roar?

STORYTELLER. Or felt.

ELEPHANT. What makes the rain feel wet?

STORYTELLER. Or smelled.

ELEPHANT. Why do bananas smell so good?

STORYTELLER. Or touched.

ELEPHANT. What's this?

STORYTELLER. And all his uncles and his aunts spanked him. (*Spanking music. Pantomime and reactions as before.*) And still he was full of 'satiable curiosity! (*Several climactic chords of music for transition purposes.*) One fine morning in the middle of a big parade, this 'satiable Elephant's Child asked a new question that he had never asked before:

ELEPHANT. (*Speaking to all his relatives.*) What does the Crocodile have for dinner?

OSTRICH. Hush, Child!

GIRAFFE. Be quiet, inquisitive one!

HIPPO. Shhh, someone might hear, naughty Elephant's Child!

BABOON. What a question to ask, talkative one!

STORYTELLER. Then everybody said:

ALL. Hush!

STORYTELLER. In a loud and dreadful tone, and they spanked him (*Spanking music. Pantomime and reactions as before, with all of the relatives participating.*) immediately and without stopping, for a long time. (*Repeat spanking music, pantomime, and reactions.*) By and by, when that was finished, the Elephant's Child decided to take a walk, and came upon a Kolokolo Bird sitting in the middle of a thornbush, and he said:

ELEPHANT. (*Lumbers over to him.*) My father has spanked me (*One chord of spanking music.*), and my mother has spanked me (*Two chords of spanking music.*), and all my aunts and uncles have spanked me (*Chords build to finish.*) for my 'satiable curiosity, and *still* I want to know what the Crocodile has for dinner! Can you tell me, Mr. Kolokolo Bird?

KOLOKOLO BIRD. Go to the banks of the great grey-green, greasy Limpopo River, all set about with fever-trees, and find out.

STORYTELLER. The very next morning, this 'satiable Elephant's Child prepared for his journey:

ELEPHANT. Let's see . . . I'll take a hundred pounds of bananas . . .

STORYTELLER. The little short red kind.

ELEPHANT. And a hundred pounds of sugarcane . . .

STORYTELLER. The long purple kind.

ELEPHANT. And seventeen melons.

STORYTELLER. The green-crackly kind.

ELEPHANT. (*Speaking to all his relatives.*) Goodbye, all my dear families. I am going to the great grey-green, greasy Limpopo River, all set about with fever-trees, to find out what the Crocodile has for dinner.

STORYTELLER. And they all spanked him once more for luck (*Spanking music. Pantomime and reactions as before.*), though he asked them most politely:

ELEPHANT. Please stop!

STORYTELLER. Then he went away, a little warm but not at all astonished. He went from Grahams' Town to Kimberley, and from Kimberley to Khama's County, and from Khama's County he went east by north, till at last he came to the banks of the great grey-green, greasy Limpopo River, all set about with fever-trees.

ELEPHANT. (*Looking around.*) Why, this is precisely as Kolokolo Bird told me.

STORYTELLER. Now you must know and understand that till that very week, and day, and hour, and minute, this 'satiable Elephant's Child had never seen a Crocodile, and didn't know what one was like. It was all his 'satiable curiosity. The first thing that he found was a Bi-Colored-Python-Rock-Snake curled around a rock. Said the Elephant's Child most politely:

ELEPHANT. (*Lumbers over to him.*) 'Scuse me, but have you seen such a thing as a Crocodile in these parts?

SNAKE. (*Speaking with excessive sibilance.*) Have I seen a Crocodile? What will you ask me next?

ELEPHANT. 'Scuse me, but could you kindly tell me what he has for dinner?

STORYTELLER. Then the Bi-Colored-Python-Rock-Snake uncoiled himself very quickly from the rock, and spanked the Elephant's Child with his scalesome, flailsome tail. (*Spanking music. Pantomime and reactions as before.*)

ELEPHANT. This is odd, because my father and my mother, and my uncle and my aunt, not to mention my other aunt, the Hippopotamus, and my other uncle, the Baboon, have all spanked me for my 'satiable curiosity —and I suppose this is the same thing.

STORYTELLER. So he said good-bye very politely to the Bi-Colored-Python-Rock-Snake, and went on, a little warm, but not at all astonished, till he trod on what he thought was a log of wood at the very edge of the great grey-green, greasy Limpopo River, all set about with fever-trees. But it was really the Crocodile, and the Crocodile winked one eye, like this. (*Sound of something heavy closing.*)

ELEPHANT. (*Stumbling as he approaches* CROCODILE.) 'Scuse me, but do you happen to have seen a Crocodile in these parts?

STORYTELLER. Then the Crocodile winked the other eye. (*Sound of something heavy closing.*) And he lifted his tail out of the mud; and the Elephant's Child stepped back most politely, because he did not wish to be spanked again.

CROCODILE. (*Speaking ingratiatingly in his deep bass voice.*) Come hither, Little One. Why do you ask such things?

ELEPHANT. 'Scuse me, but my father has spanked me (*One spanking chord.*), my mother has spanked me (*Two spanking chords.*), not to mention my tall aunt, the Ostrich, and my tall uncle, the Giraffe, who can kick ever so hard, as well as my broad aunt, the Hippopotamus, and my hairy uncle, the Baboon, and the Bi-Colored-Python-Rock-Snake, with the scalesome, flailsome tail, just up the bank, who spanks harder than any of them. (*Spanking chords to climactic finish.*) *So,* if it's all the same to you, I don't want to be spanked any more.

CROCODILE. Come hither, Little One, for I am the Crocodile.

STORYTELLER. And he wept crocodile-tears to show it was quite true. Then the Elephant's Child grew all breathless, and panted, and leaned over the bank and said:

ELEPHANT. You're the very person I've been looking for all these long days. Will you please tell me what you have for dinner?

CROCODILE. Come hither, Little One, and I'll whisper.

STORYTELLER. And the Elephant's Child put his head down close to the Crocodile's musky, tusky mouth, and the Crocodile caught him by his little nose, which up to that very week, day, hour, and minute, had been no bigger than a boot, though much more useful. Then the Crocodile said—and he said it between his teeth, like this:

CROCODILE. (*Speaking with his teeth and jaws tightly closed.*) I think today I will begin with the Elephant's Child!

STORYTELLER. At this, the Elephant's Child was much annoyed, and he said, speaking through his nose, like this:

ELEPHANT. (*Speaking through his nose, and pantomiming pulling away from the* CROCODILE.) Let go! You're hurting me!!

STORYTELLER. Then the Bi-Colored-Python-Rock-Snake scuffled down from the bank and said:

SNAKE. (*May scuffle over to the* ELEPHANT'S CHILD.) My young friend, if you do not now, immediately and instantly, pull as hard as ever you can, it is my opinion that your acquaintance in the large-pattern leather ulster . . .

STORYTELLER. And by this he meant the Crocodile.

SNAKE. . . . will jerk you into yonder limpid stream before you can say Jack Robinson.

STORYTELLER. This is the way Bi-Colored-Python-Rock-Snakes always talk. Then the Elephant's Child sat back on his little haunch, and pulled (*One sustained chord of pulling music.*), and pulled (*Two chords.*), and pulled (*Three chords, music accompanied by pulling activity by the* ELEPHANT'S CHILD.), and his nose began to stretch. (*Short chord.*) The Crocodile floundered into the water, making it all creamy with great sweeps of his tail, and *he* pulled, and pulled, and pulled. (*Again, music of pulling and stretching.*) And the Elephant's Child's nose kept on stretching (*Chords.*); and the Elephant's Child spread all his little four legs and pulled (*One Chord.*), and pulled (*Two chords.*), and pulled (*Three chords.*), and his nose kept on stretching (*Stretching music.*); and the Crocodile threshed his tail like an oar, and *he* pulled (*One chord.*), and pulled (*Two chords.*), and pulled. (*Three chords.*) And at each pull the Elephant's Child's nose grew longer and longer (*Stretching music.*) and it hurt him hijjus! Then the Elephant's Child felt his legs slipping, and he said through his nose, which was now nearly five feet long:

ELEPHANT. (*Speaking through nose.*) This is too much for me!

STORYTELLER. Then the Bi-Colored-Python-Rock-Snake knotted himself in a double-clove-hitch round the Elephant's Child's hind legs, and he said:

SNAKE. (*Throughout the following,* SNAKE *and* ELEPHANT'S CHILD *pantomime as the narration suggests.*) Rash and inexperienced traveler, we'll now seriously devote ourselves to a little high tension, because if we do not, it is my impression that yonder self-propelling man-of-war with the armor-plated upper deck . . .

STORYTELLER. And by this he meant the Crocodile.

SNAKE. . . . will permanently vitiate your future career.

STORYTELLER. This is the way all Bi-Colored-Python-Rock-Snakes always talk. So he pulled (*One chord of pulling music.*), and the Elephant's Child pulled (*Higher chord of pulling music.*), and the Bi-Colored-Python-Rock-Snake pulled (*Another chord higher.*); and at last the Crocodile let go of the Elephant's Child's nose with a plop that you could hear all up and down the Limpopo. (*Plop chord.*) Then the Elephant's Child sat down most hard and sudden; but first he was careful to say to the Bi-Colored-Python-Rock-Snake:

ELEPHANT. Thank you!

STORYTELLER. And next he was kind to his poor pulled nose, and wrapped it all up in cool banana leaves, and hung it in the great grey-green, greasy Limpopo to cool. The Bi-Colored-Python-Rock-Snake asked:

SNAKE. What are you doing that for?

ELEPHANT. 'Scuse me, but my nose is badly out of shape, and I am waiting for it to shrink.

SNAKE. Then you will have to wait a long time. Some people do not know what is good for them.

STORYTELLER. The Elephant's Child sat there for three days waiting for his nose to shrink. But it never grew any shorter, and besides, it made him squint. For you will see and understand that the Crocodile had pulled it out into a really truly trunk same as all elephants have today. (*Transition chords.*) At the end of the third day a fly came and stung him on the shoulder, and before he knew what he was doing he lifted up his trunk and hit that fly dead with the end of it. (*Pantomime hitting the fly.*) Cried the Bi-Colored-Python-Rock-Snake:

SNAKE. 'Vantage number one! You couldn't have done that with a mere-smere nose. Try to eat a little now.

STORYTELLER. Before he thought what he was doing the Elephant's Child put out his trunk (*Pantomime throughout.*) and plucked a large bundle of grass, dusted it clean against his forelegs, and stuffed it into his own mouth. Exclaimed the Bi-Colored-Python-Rock-Snake:

SNAKE. 'Vantage number two! You couldn't have done that with a mere-smere nose. Don't you think the sun is very hot here?

ELEPHANT. It is.

STORYTELLER. And before he thought what he was doing, he schlooped up a schloop of mud from the banks of the great grey-green, greasy Limpopo, and slapped it on his head, where it made a cool schloopy-sloshy mudcap all trickly behind his ears. (*With pantomime, as always.*) Said the Bi-Colored-Python-Rock-Snake:

SNAKE. 'Vantage number three! You couldn't have done that with a mere-smere nose. Now how do you feel about being spanked again?

ELEPHANT. 'Scuse me, but I should not like it at all.

SNAKE. How would you like to spank somebody?

ELEPHANT. I should like it very much indeed.

SNAKE. Well, you'll find that new nose of yours very useful with which to spank people.

ELEPHANT. Thank you, I'll remember that; and now I think I'll go home to all my dear families and try.

STORYTELLER. (*Throughout the following narration,* ELEPHANT'S CHILD *pantomimes all business as is suggested.*) So the Elephant's Child went home across Africa frisking and whisking his trunk. When he wanted fruit to eat he pulled fruit down from a tree . . .

ELEPHANT. I'm hungry. I'll have some fruit. (*Reaches up in tree and takes it.*)

STORYTELLER. . . . instead of waiting for it to fall as he used to do. When he wanted grass he plucked grass up from the ground, instead of going on his knees as he used to do.

ELEPHANT. I'm still hungry. I think I'll have some of that grass. (*Fly bites him.*) Ouch, that fly bit me. (*Pantomime breaking off a branch from a tree and hitting flies from his shoulders with it.*)

STORYTELLER. When the flies bit him he broke off the branch of a tree and used it as a fly-whisk; and he made himself a new, cool, slushy-squishy mudcap whenever the sun was hot. When he felt lonely walking through Africa he sang to himself down his trunk. (ELEPHANT *sings very loudly.*) The noise of his singing was louder than several brass bands. He went especially out of his way to find a broad Hippopotamus (she was no relative of his), and he spanked her very hard, just to make sure that the Bi-Colored-Python-Rock-Snake had spoken the truth. (*Transition chords.*) One dark evening he came back to all his dear families, and he coiled up his trunk and said:

ELEPHANT. (*Speaking to all his relatives.*) How do you do?

STORYTELLER. They were very glad to see him, and immediately said:

OSTRICH. Elephant's Child . . .

GIRAFFE. Come here . . .

HIPPO. And be spanked . . .

BABOON. For your 'satiable curiosity.

ELEPHANT. Pooh! I don't think you people know anything about spanking; but I do, and I'll show you.

STORYTELLER. Then he uncurled his trunk and knocked two of his dear relations (*Crashing sound.*) head over heels. They said, quite amazed:

BABOON. O, bananas! Where did you learn that trick?

OSTRICH. What have you done to your nose?

ELEPHANT. I got a new one from the Crocodile on the banks of the great grey-green, greasy Limpopo River. I asked him what he had for dinner, and he gave me this to keep.

BABOON. It looks very ugly.

ELEPHANT. It does, Uncle Baboon, but it's very useful. Let me show you.

STORYTELLER. He picked up his hairy uncle, the Baboon, by one hairy leg, and threw him into a hornet's nest. (*Pantomime.*) Then that bad Elephant's Child spanked all his dear families for a long time (*Spanking chords.*), till they were very warm and greatly astonished. He pulled out his tall Ostrich aunt's tail-feathers. (*Pantomime.*)

OSTRICH. (*Reacts to pain of losing feathers, and screams.*) My feathers!

STORYTELLER. And he caught his tall uncle, the Giraffe, by the hind leg, and dragged him through a thornbush. (*Pantomime.*)

GIRAFFE. Owww! The thorns!

STORYTELLER. And he shouted at his broad aunt, the Hippopotamus, and blew bubbles (*Pantomime.*) into her ear when she was sleeping in the water after meals.

HIPPO. Don't blow bubbles!

STORYTELLER. But he never let anyone touch Kolokolo Bird. At last, things grew so exciting that his dear families went off one by one in a hurry to the banks of the great grey-green, greasy Limpopo River, all set about with fever-trees, to borrow new noses from the Crocodile. (*One by one the relatives may leave the platform, if desired, during the narration.*) When they came back nobody spanked anybody any more. (*If background music was used under the opening narration, it may be employed here also.*) And ever since that day, all the elephants you will ever see, besides all those that you won't, have trunks precisely like the trunk of the 'satiable Elephant's Child.

(*Music up to climax and out.*)

BY BEVERLY CLEARY

Henry and Ribsy

A chapter from a children's novel arranged for Readers Theatre by Leslie Irene Coger

This script is adapted from the first chapter of the children's book *Henry Huggins*. In it we see the boy Henry being adopted by the dog, eventually named Ribsy because his ribs stick out. The story takes place on a street corner, in a drugstore, on a city bus, in a police car, and on the porch of Henry's home. Bus drivers, a former schoolteacher, a fat man, policemen, and numerous others become involved in Henry's attempt to take a dog home on the bus.

CAST OF CHARACTERS

Six Men, Three Women, and a Narrator—either Man or Woman, playing thirteen roles. Or a cast of fourteen may read: a Narrator—either Man or Woman—Nine Men, and Four Women.

NARRATOR. *An effective storyteller with a mature, pleasing voice*

HENRY. *A small boy*

RIBSY. *A mongrel dog*

MOTHER. *An understanding woman*

BUS DRIVER I. *A pleasant bus driver*

CLERK. *A young woman who can't understand boys*

BUS DRIVER II. *A gruff driver*

SCOOTER. *Henry's loud-mouthed, curious friend*

Adapted from *Henry Huggins* by Beverly Cleary. Reprinted by permission of William Morrow & Company, Inc. Copyright 1950 by William Morrow & Company, Inc. **Important Notice:** Permission to present or perform this adaptation publicly will not be granted.

LADY. *A middle-aged former teacher*

FAT MAN. *A genial passenger*

WOMAN. *A passenger with arms laden*

POLICEMAN I. *A man who sympathizes with boys*

POLICEMAN II. *Always agrees with his partner*

FATHER. *A middle-aged, good-natured man*

THE PHYSICAL ARRANGEMENT OF THE SCENE

Six tall stools and two short ones are needed if a cast of nine readers interprets the script. If it is decided to have one reader in each role, thirteen
are necessary. With the nine-reader cast, the two low stools are placed
slightly DC for HENRY and RIBSY. The NARRATOR stands behind them.
Three of the taller stools are placed on either side of the center ones and
slightly back of them for the other characters. In Figure 18, Stool 2 was
assigned to the woman who read MOTHER and the SCHOOLTEACHER; Stool
4 to RIBSY, Stool 5 to HENRY, and Stool 6 to SCOOTER. Readers on Stools
1, 3, 7, and 8 portrayed the various other characters. (See photos on pp. 51
and 133.)

*(As the presentation begins, the readers take their positions on the stools.
Then the NARRATOR walks to the area behind and between the low stools
4 and 5, C, and speaks directly to the audience.)*

NARRATOR. Henry Huggins (HENRY *raises head.*) was in the third grade.
His hair looked like a scrubbing brush and most of his grown-up front
teeth were in. He lived with his mother and father in a square white

FIGURE 18. *Henry and Ribsy* floor plan

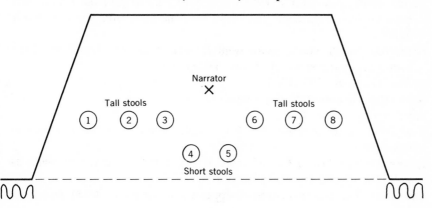

house on Klickitat Street. Except for having his tonsils out when he was six and breaking his arm falling out of a cherry tree when he was seven, nothing much happened to Henry.

HENRY. I wish something exciting would happen.

NARRATOR. But nothing very interesting ever happened to Henry, at least not until one Wednesday afternoon in March. Every Wednesday after school, Henry rode downtown on the bus to go swimming at the Y.M.C.A. After he swam for an hour, he got on the bus again and rode home just in time for dinner.

HENRY. It was fun but not really exciting.

NARRATOR. When Henry left the Y.M.C.A. on this particular Wednesday, he stopped to watch a man tear down a circus poster. Then, with three nickels and one dime in his pocket, he went to the corner drugstore to buy a chocolate ice-cream cone.

HENRY. He thought he would eat the ice-cream cone, get on the bus, drop his dime in the slot, and ride home.

NARRATOR. That is not what happened. He bought the ice-cream cone and paid for it with one of his nickels. On his way out of the drugstore he stopped to look at funny books.

HENRY. It was a free look because he had only two nickels and one dime left. He stood there licking his chocolate ice-cream cone and reading one of the funny books when he heard . . . (RIBSY *raises head.*)

RIBSY. (*Thump, thump, thump.*)

NARRATOR. Henry turned and there behind him was a dog. The dog was scratching himself. He wasn't any special kind of dog. He was too small to be a big dog, but on the other hand, he was much too big to be a little dog. He wasn't a white dog, because parts of him were brown and other parts were black and in between there were yellowish patches. His ears stood up and his tail was long and thin.

RIBSY. (*Looks hungry, head tilted.*)

NARRATOR. When Henry licked (HENRY *licks.*) the dog licked (RIBSY *licks.*). When Henry swallowed the dog swallowed.

HENRY. Hello, you old dog. (RIBSY *barks and tries to get cone.*) You can't have my ice-cream cone. (*He jerks his cone back from the dog;* RIBSY *barks.*)

NARRATOR. Swish, swish, swish went the tail. "Just one bite," the dog's brown eyes seemed to say. (RIBSY *whines.*)

HENRY. Go away. (*Weakly.*)

NARRATOR. He patted the dog's head.

RIBSY. (*Wags harder.*)

NARRATOR. Henry took one last lick. (HENRY *does so;* RIBSY *also tries to lick cone.*)

HENRY. (HENRY *licks.*) Oh, all right. If you're that hungry, you might as well have it. (*He gives it to* RIBSY.)

NARRATOR. The ice-cream cone disappeared in one gulp. (RIBSY *gulps.*)

HENRY. Now go away. I have to catch a bus for home.

NARRATOR. He started for the door. The dog started, too. (RIBSY *barks.*)

HENRY. Go away, you skinny old dog. Go on home.

NARRATOR. The dog sat down at Henry's feet. Henry looked at the dog and the dog looked at Henry. (RIBSY *tilts head toward* HENRY *and* HENRY *tilts head toward* RIBSY.)

HENRY. I don't think you've got a home. You're awful thin. Your ribs show right through your skin.

RIBSY. (*Whines.*)

HENRY. And you haven't got a collar.

NARRATOR. He began to think.

HENRY. If only he could keep the dog! He had always wanted a dog of his very own and now he had found a dog that wanted him. He couldn't go home and leave a hungry dog on the street corner. If only he knew what his mother and father would say! He fingered the two nickels in his pocket. That was it! He would use one of the two nickels in his pocket to phone his mother. Come on, Ribsy. Come on, Ribs, old boy. I'm going to call you Ribsy because you're so thin. (RIBSY *barks.*)

NARRATOR. The dog trotted after the boy to the telephone booth in the corner of the drugstore. Henry shoved Ribsy into the booth and shut the door. (HENRY *pantomimes shove,* RIBSY *responds to the shove.*) He had never used a pay telephone before. He had to put the telephone book on the floor and stand on tiptoe on it to reach the mouthpiece. He gave the operator his number and dropped his nickel into the coin box. (MOTHER *stands.*)

HENRY. Hello—Mom!

MOTHER. Why, Henry! (*Surprised.*) Where are you?

HENRY. At the drugstore near the Y.

RIBSY. (*Thump, thump, thump.*)

NARRATOR. Inside the telephone booth the thumps sounded loud and hollow.

MOTHER. For goodness' sake, Henry, what's that noise?

RIBSY. (*Whimpers, howls.*)

MOTHER. Henry, are you all right?

HENRY. (*Shouting.*) Yes, I'm all right.

NARRATOR. He never could understand why his mother always thought something had happened to him when nothing ever did.

HENRY. That's just Ribsy.

MOTHER. Ribsy? Henry, will you please tell me what is going on?

HENRY. I'm trying to.

RIBSY. (*Howls.*)

NARRATOR. People were gathering around the phone booth to see what was going on. (*All come in scene.*)

HENRY. Mother, I've found a dog. I sure wish I could keep him. He's a good dog, and I'd feed him and wash him and everything. Please, Mom.

MOTHER. I don't know, dear. You'll have to ask your father.

HENRY. Mom! That's what you always say!

NARRATOR. Henry was tired of standing on tiptoe and the phone booth was getting warm.

RIBSY. (*Whines and whimpers.*)

HENRY. Mom, please say yes and I'll never ask for another thing as long as I live.

MOTHER. Well, all right, Henry. I guess there isn't any reason why you shouldn't have a dog. But you'll have to bring him home on the bus. Your father has the car today and I can't come after you. Can you manage?

HENRY. Sure! Easy.

MOTHER. And Henry, please don't be late. It looks as if it might rain.

HENRY. All right, Mom.

RIBSY. (*Thump, thump, thump.*)

MOTHER. Henry, what's that thumping noise?

HENRY. It's my dog, Ribsy. He's scratching a flea.

RIBSY. (*Scratching.*)

MOTHER. Oh, Henry, couldn't you have found a dog without fleas?

NARRATOR. Henry thought that was a good time to hang up. (MOTHER *sits.*)

HENRY. Come on, Ribs. We're going home on the bus.

RIBSY. (*Barks happily.*)

NARRATOR. When the big green bus stopped in front of the drugstore (DRIVER I *raises head.*), Henry picked up his dog. (HENRY *pantomimes this.*) Ribsy was heavier than he expected. He had a hard time getting him into the bus and was wondering how he would get a dime out of his pocket when—

DRIVER I. Say, sonny, you can't take that dog on the bus.

RIBSY. (*Whines.*)

HENRY. Why not?

DRIVER I. It's a company rule, sonny. No dogs on buses.

HENRY. Golly, Mister, how'm I going to get him home? I just have to get him home.

DRIVER I. Sorry, sonny. I didn't make the rule. No animal can ride on a bus unless it's inside a box.

HENRY. Well, thanks anyway.

NARRATOR. Henry lifted Ribsy off the bus. (*Pantomimes lifting* RIBSY *off bus and setting him down.*)

RIBSY. (*Barks.*)

HENRY. Well, I guess we'll have to get a box. I'll get you onto the next bus somehow.

NARRATOR. He went back into the drugstore (CLERK *stands.*), followed closely by Ribsy.

HENRY. Have you got a big box I could have, please?

NARRATOR. He asked the clerk at the toothpaste counter.

HENRY. I need one big enough for my dog. (RIBSY *barks.*)

NARRATOR. The clerk leaned over the counter to look at Ribsy.

CLERK. A cardboard box?

HENRY. Yes, please.

NARRATOR. The clerk pulled a box out from under the counter.

CLERK. This hair tonic carton is the only one I have. I guess it's big enough, but why anyone would want to put a dog in a cardboard box I can't understand.

NARRATOR. The box was about two feet square and six inches deep. On one end was printed, "Don't Let Them Call You Baldy," and on the other, "Try Our Large Economy Size."

HENRY. Thank you. (CLERK *sits.*)

NARRATOR. Then he carried the box out to the bus stop, and put it on the sidewalk. Ribsy understood. He stepped into the box and sat down just as the bus came around the corner.

RIBSY. (*Barks.*)

NARRATOR. Henry had to kneel to pick up the box. It was not a very strong box and he had to put his arms under it. He staggered as he lifted it, feeling like the strong man who lifted weights at the circus. (*Pantomimes this action.*) Ribsy lovingly licked Henry's face with his wet pink tongue. (RIBSY *pantomimes this.*)

HENRY. Hey, cut that out! You better be good if you're going to ride on the bus with me.

NARRATOR. The bus stopped at the curb when it was Henry's turn to get on. (DRIVER II *raises head.*)

HENRY. He had trouble finding the step because he couldn't see his feet. He had to try several times before he hit it. Then he discovered he had forgotten to take his dime out of his pocket. He was afraid to put the box down for fear Ribsy might escape.

NARRATOR. He turned sideways to the driver and asked politely,

HENRY. Will you please take the dime out of my pocket for me? My hands are full.

DRIVER II. Full! I should say they *are* full! And just where do you think you're going with that animal?

RIBSY. (*Whimpers.*)

HENRY. Home.

NARRATOR. (*All come into the scene.*) The passengers were staring and most of them were smiling. The box was getting heavier every minute.

DRIVER II. Not on this bus, you're not!

HENRY. But the man on the last bus said I could take the dog on the bus in a box.

NARRATOR. Henry was afraid he couldn't hold Ribsy much longer.

DRIVER II. He meant a big box tied shut. A box with holes punched in it for the dog to breathe through.

RIBSY. (*Growls.*)

NARRATOR. Henry was horrified to hear Ribsy growl.

HENRY. Shut up.

NARRATOR. Ribsy began to scratch his right ear with his right hind foot. The box began to tear. Ribsy jumped out of the box and off the bus. Henry jumped after him. The bus pulled away with a puff of exhaust. (*Watches bus from right to left.*)

HENRY. Now see what you've done! You've spoiled everything.

RIBSY. (*Whimpers.*)

HENRY. If I can't get you home, how can I keep you? (RIBSY *whines.*)

NARRATOR. Henry sat down on the curb to think. It was so late and the clouds were so dark that he didn't want to waste time looking for a big box. His mother was probably beginning to worry about him. People were stopping on the corner to wait for the next bus. Among them Henry noticed an elderly lady carrying a large paper shopping bag full of apples. The shopping bag gave him an idea.

HENRY. Jumping up, he snapped his fingers at Ribsy (RIBSY *barks.*) and ran back into the drugstore. (CLERK *rises.*)

CLERK. You back again? What do you want this time? String and paper to wrap your dog in?

HENRY. No, ma'am. I want one of those big nickel shopping bags.

NARRATOR. He laid his last nickel on the counter.

CLERK. Well, I'll be darned.

NARRATOR. The clerk handed him the bag and Henry set it up on the floor. Henry picked up Ribsy and shoved him, hind feet first, into the bag. (RIBSY *barks.*) Then he pushed his front feet in. (RIBSY *barks.*) A lot of Ribsy was left over.

NARRATOR. (RIBSY *barks.*) The clerk was leaning over the counter watching.

HENRY. I guess I'll have to have some string and paper, too, if I can have some free.

CLERK. Well! Now I've seen everything.

NARRATOR. The clerk shook her head as she handed a piece of string and a big sheet of paper across the counter. (*She pantomimes this, then sits.*)

RIBSY. (*Whimpers.*)

NARRATOR. (HENRY *pantomimes this action.*) Ribsy held still while Henry wrapped the paper loosely around his head and shoulders and tied it with the string. The dog made a lumpy package. But by taking one handle of the bag in each hand, Henry was able to carry it to the bus stop. He didn't think the bus driver would notice him. It was getting dark and a crowd of people, most of them with packages, were waiting on the corner. A few spatters of rain hit the pavement.

HENRY. This time Henry remembered his dime. Both hands were full, so he held the dime in his teeth (HENRY *does so.*) and stood behind the lady, quickly set the bag down (*Pantomimes.*), dropped his dime in the slot, picked up the bag, and squirmed through the crowd to a seat behind a fat man near the back of the bus. (*All passengers indicate riding by a slight bounce.*) Whew! The driver was the same one he had met on the first bus! But Ribs was on the bus at last. Now if he could only keep him quiet for fifteen minutes they would be home and Ribsy would be his for keeps.

NARRATOR. The next time the bus stopped (*All stop motion.*) Henry saw Scooter McCarthy, a fifth-grader at school, get on and make his way through the crowd to the back of the bus. (SCOOTER *raises head.*)

HENRY. (*All indicate motion of bus.*) Just my luck. I'll bet he wants to know what's in my bag.

SCOOTER. Hi.

HENRY. Hi.

SCOOTER. Watcha got in the bag?

HENRY. None of your beeswax.

NARRATOR. Scooter looked at Henry, Henry looked at Scooter. Crackle, crackle, crackle went the bag. Henry tried to hold it more tightly between his knees.

SCOOTER. There's something alive in that bag!

HENRY. Shut up, Scooter!

SCOOTER. (*Loudly.*) Aw, shut up yourself! You've got something alive in that bag!

NARRATOR. By this time the passengers at the back of the bus were staring at Henry, and his package. Crackle, crackle, crackle. Henry tried to pat Ribsy again through the paper. The bag cracked even louder.

RIBSY. (*Wiggles.*)

FAT MAN. Come on, tell us what's in the bag.

HENRY. N-n-nothing. Just something I found.

LADY. Maybe it's a rabbit.

RIBSY. (*Kicking.*)

FAT MAN. No, it's too big for a rabbit.

SCOOTER. I'll bet it's a baby. I'll bet you kidnaped a baby!

HENRY. I did not!

NARRATOR. Ribsy began to whimper (RIBSY *whimpers.*) and then to howl. (RIBSY *howls.*) Crackle, crackle, crackle. Thump, thump, thump, Ribsy scratched his way out of the bag.

FAT MAN. Well, I'll be doggoned! I'll be doggoned! (*Laughing, others laughing also.*)

SCOOTER. It's just a skinny old dog.

HENRY. He is not. He's a good dog.

NARRATOR. Henry tried to keep Ribsy between his knees. The bus lurched (*Lurch to the right.*) around a corner and started to go uphill. Henry was thrown against the fat man. (*Passengers lean back.*) The frightened dog wiggled away from him, squirmed between the passengers, and started for the front of the bus.

HENRY. Here Ribsy, old boy! Come back here.

NARRATOR. Henry started after him.

LADY. E-e-eek! A dog!

NARRATOR. Squealed the lady with the bag of apples.

LADY. Go away, doggie, go away!

NARRATOR. Ribsy was scared. He tried to run and crashed into the lady's bag of apples. The bag tipped toward the back of the bus, which was grinding up a steep hill. (*All lean back.*) The apples rolled around the feet of the people who were standing.

WOMAN I. Passengers began to slip and slide.

LADY. They dropped their packages and grabbed one another.

FAT MAN. Crash!

NARRATOR. A high school girl dropped an armload of books.

LADY. Rattle!

WOMAN I. Bang!

FAT MAN. Crash!

LADY. Clatter!

WOMAN I. Clang!

NARRATOR. A lady dropped a big paper bag. The bag broke open and pots and pans rolled out.

ALL. Clatter, clang, bang!!! Plop!

NARRATOR. A man dropped a coil of garden hose. The hose unrolled and the passengers found it wound around their legs.

LADY. People were sitting on the floor.

FAT MAN. They were sitting on books and apples.

WOMAN I. They were even sitting on other people's laps.

LADY. Some of them had their hats over their faces and their feet in the air.

(*During the above,* HENRY *is trying to catch* RIBSY *and* RIBSY *is running. This is pantomimed from their stools.*)

ALL. Skree-e-etch!

NARRATOR. The driver threw on the brakes (*All jerk forward.*) and turned around in his seat just as Henry made his way through the apples and books and pans and hose to catch Ribsy. (*Action stops with characters in positions of disarray.*)

DRIVER I. The driver pushed his cap back on his head. O.K., sonny. Now you know why dogs aren't allowed on buses! (RIBSY *whines.*)

HENRY. Yes, sir, I'm sorry. (*Weakly.*)

DRIVER I. You're sorry! A lot of good that does. Look at those people!

HENRY. I didn't mean to make any trouble. My mother said I could keep the dog if I could bring him home on the bus.

NARRATOR. The fat man began to snicker. Then he chuckled. Then he laughed, and then he roared. He laughed until tears streamed down his cheeks. (*Laughing.*) Other passengers were laughing, too (FAT LADY *snickers.*), even the man with the hose and the lady with the apples. The driver didn't laugh.

DRIVER I. Take that dog and get off the bus!

RIBSY. (*Tucks tail between legs and whimpers.*)

NARRATOR. The fat man stopped laughing.

FAT MAN. See here, driver, you can't put that boy and his dog off in the rain.

RIBSY. (*Whimpers.*)

DRIVER I. Well, he can't stay on the bus.

HENRY. Henry didn't know what he was going to do. He guessed he'd have to walk the rest of the way home. He wasn't sure he knew the way in the dark.

NARRATOR. Just then a siren screamed. (*Siren sounds.*) It grew louder and louder until it stopped (*Sound stops.*), right alongside the bus. A policeman appeared in the entrance.

POLICEMAN I. (*Stands.*) Is there a boy called Henry Huggins on this bus? (RIBSY *growls.*)

SCOOTER. Oh boy, you're going to be arrested for having a dog on the bus! I'll bet you have to go to jail!

RIBSY. (*Whines.*)

HENRY. I'm him. (*Weakly.*)

LADY. I am he.

NARRATOR. Corrected the lady with the apples, who had been a schoolteacher.

LADY. And couldn't help correcting boys.

POLICEMAN I. You'd better come along with us.

SCOOTER. Boy, you're sure going to get it!

LADY. Surely going to get it.

NARRATOR. Henry and Ribsy followed the policeman off the bus and into the squad car, where Henry and the dog sat in the back seat.

HENRY. (*Timidly.*) Are you going to arrest me?

POLICEMAN I. Well, I don't know. Do you think you ought to be arrested?

HENRY. No, sir.

NARRATOR. He thought the policeman was joking, but he wasn't sure. It was hard to tell about grown-ups sometimes.

HENRY. I didn't mean to do anything. I just had to get Ribsy home. My mother said I could keep him if I could bring him home on the bus.

POLICEMAN I. Well now, let's see. What do you think we should do?

NARRATOR. The officer asked his partner, who was driving the squad car.

POLICEMAN II. We-e-ll, I think we might let him off this time.

POLICEMAN I. His mother must be pretty worried about him if she called the police, and I don't think she'd want him to go to jail.

POLICEMAN II. Yes, he's late for his dinner already. Let's see how fast we can get him home. (POLICEMEN *sit.*)

NARRATOR. The driver pushed a button and the siren (*Siren shrieks.*) began to shriek. Ribsy raised his head and howled. (RIBSY *howls.*) The tires sucked at the wet pavement, and the windshield wipers slip-slopped.

HENRY. Henry began to enjoy himself. Wouldn't this be something to tell the kids at school! Automobiles pulled over to the curb as the police car went faster and faster. Even the bus Henry had been on had to pull over and stop. Henry waved to the passengers. (HENRY *waves.*) They waved back. (*Passengers wave.*)

NARRATOR. Up the hill (*Leans back.*) the police car sped and around the corner (*Leans to the right.*) until they came to Klickitat Street and then to Henry's block and then pulled up (*Jerks forward.*) in front of his house. (MOTHER *and* FATHER *rise.*) Henry's mother and father were standing on the porch waiting for him. The neighbors were looking out of their windows. After the policemen had gone, Henry's father said:

FATHER. Well, it's about time you came home. So this is Ribsy!

RIBSY. (*Barks.*)

MOTHER. I've heard about you, fellow, (*She looks at* RIBSY *who looks back and whines.*) and there's a big bone and a can of Feeley's Flea Flakes waiting for you. (RIBSY *barks happily.*) Henry, what *will* you do next?

HENRY. Golly, Mom, I didn't do anything. I just brought my dog home on the bus like you said.

NARRATOR. Ribsy sat down and began to scratch.

RIBSY. (*Scratches and barks happily. All laugh at the dog.*)

BY JAMES THURBER

The Last Clock

A short story adapted for Readers Theatre by Leslie Irene Coger and Donna Drewes

In this humorous tale, Thurber satirizes man's modern concern over waste of time, as well as specialization, by offering differing opinions from many characters. He lampoons specialists and court procedures, along with man's dependence on the clock. In one production an almost mechanical regularity was employed at times, suggesting the clock and its ever present ticking.

CAST OF CHARACTERS

Four Men, One Woman, and a Narrator, Man or Woman; or a cast of seventeen is possible, each reader portraying only one character.

NARRATOR. *A good storyteller*

OGRE. *An old man who cannot speak plainly*

OGRESS. *A bossy woman*

DOCTOR. *A haughty, middle-aged man*

CLOGMAN. *A quick-speaking young man*

GENERAL PRACTITIONER. *A sophisticated, proud man*

INSPIRATIONALIST. *A double-talker*

PSYCHRONOLOGIST. *A slow-spoken, methodical man*

CLOCKONOMIST. *Very sure of himself*

LORD MAYOR. *A severe ruler*

CHIEF DIAGNOSTICIAN. *A matter-of-fact man*

SUPREME MAGISTRATE. *A bored man*

SUPREME PROSECUTOR. *An eager young attorney*

HOUSEWIFE. *A practical woman*

LEADER OF THE OPPOSITION. *A wily politician*

MAN IN THE STREET. *Tries to be helpful*

BAILIFF. *A full-voiced man, proud of his profession*

SPECIALIST. *An eager collector*

SCIENTIST. *Definite, scientific*

DIGGER. *An uneducated fellow*

VOICES.

These characters may be played by six readers. The NARRATOR is always the NARRATOR. Reader #2 plays the OGRE and a VOICE; Reader #3, the OGRESS, a HOUSEWIFE, and a VOICE; Reader #4, the DOCTOR, INSPIRATIONALIST, CLOCKONOMIST, MAGISTRATE, and a VOICE; Reader #5, the CLOGMAN, PSYCHRONOLOGIST, CHIEF DIAGNOSTICIAN, PROSECUTOR, DIGGER, and a VOICE; Reader #6, the GENERAL PRACTITIONER, LORD MAYOR, LEADER OF THE OPPOSITION, MAN IN THE STREET, BAILIFF, SPECIALIST, SCIENTIST, and a VOICE.

PHYSICAL ARRANGEMENT

The Last Clock may be performed simply with six stools. Or a scrim may be hung back of the readers, with five cardboard clocks of different colors hung at different levels in front of the scrim. Colored boxes for the readers to sit on may be used instead of stools.

NARRATOR. In a country the other side of tomorrow, an Ogre who had eaten a clock and had fallen into the habit of eating clocks was eating a clock in the clockroom of his castle when his Ogress and their ilk knocked down the locked door and shook their hairy heads at him.

OGRE. (*Gurgling.*) Wulsa malla?

NARRATOR. Too much clock oil had turned all his 'ts' to 'ls.'

OGRESS. (*Exclaiming.*) Just look at this room!

NARRATOR. And they all looked at the room, the Ogre with eyes as fogged as the headlights of an ancient limousine. The stone floor of the room was littered with fragments of dials, oily coils and springs, broken clock hands, and pieces of pendulums.

OGRESS. I've brought a Doctor to look at you.

DOCTOR. (*Haughtily.*) The Doctor wore a black beard, carried a black bag, and gave the Ogre a black look. This case is clearly not in my area!

NARRATOR. The Ogre struck three and the Doctor flushed.

DOCTOR. This is a case for a Clockman, for the problem is not what clocks have done to the Ogre, but what the Ogre has done to clocks.

OGRE. (*Gurgling.*) Wulsa malla?

OGRESS. Eating clocks has turned all his 'ts' to 'ls.' That's what clocks have done to him.

DOCTOR. Then your Clockman may have to call in consultation a semanticist or a dictionist or an etymologist or a syntaxman.

NARRATOR. And the non-clock Doctor bowed stiffly and left the room. (*All shift positions to denote passage of time.*) The next morning, the Ogress brought into the clockroom a beardless man with a box of tools under his arm.

OGRESS. I've brought a Clockman to see you.

CLOGMAN. No, no, no, I'm not a Clockman. I thought you said Clogman. I'm a Clogman. I cannot ethically depart from my area, which is clogged drains and gutters. I get mice out of pipes, and bugs out of tubes, and moles out of tiles, and there my area ends.

NARRATOR. And the Clogman bowed and left the room.

OGRE. Wuld wuzzle?

NARRATOR. He hiccupped (OGRE *hiccups.*) and something went *spong!*

OGRESS. That was an area man, but the wrong area. I'll get a General Practitioner.

NARRATOR. And she went away and came back with a General Practitioner.

GENERAL PRACTITIONER. This is a waste of time. As a General Practitioner, modern style, I treat only generals. This patient is not even a private. He sounds to me like a public place—a clock tower, perhaps, or a belfry.

OGRESS. What should I do? Send for a tower man, or a belfry man?

GENERAL PRACTITIONER. I shall not venture an opinion. I am a specialist in generals, one of whom has just lost command of his army and of all his faculties, and doesn't know what time it is. Good day.

NARRATOR. And the General Practitioner went away. The Ogre cracked a small clock, as if it were a large walnut, and began eating it.

OGRE. Wulsy wul?

NARRATOR. The Ogress, who could now talk clocktalk fluently, even oilily, but wouldn't, left the room to look up specialists in an enormous volume entitled *Who's Who in Areas*. She soon became lost in a list of titles:

OGRESS. Clockmaker, clocksmith, clockwright, clockmonger, clockician, clockometrist, clockologist, and a hundred others dealing with clockness, clockism, clockship, clockdom, clockation, clockition, and clockhood.

NARRATOR. The Ogress decided to call on an old Inspirationalist who had once advised her father not to worry about a giant he was worrying about. The Inspirationalist had said to the Ogress's father:

INSPIRATIONALIST. Don't pay any attention to it, and it will go away.

NARRATOR. The Ogress's father had paid no attention to it, and it had gone away, taking him with it, and this had pleased the Ogress. The Inspirationalist was now a very old man whose inspirationalism had become a jumble of mumble.

INSPIRATIONALIST. (*Mumbling.*) The final experience should not be mummum.

OGRESS. But what is mummum?

INSPIRATIONALIST. Mummum is what the final experience should not be.

NARRATOR. And he mumbled over to a couch, lay down upon it, and fell asleep. . . . As the days went on, the Ogre ate all the clocks in town . . .

VOICE FIVE. Mantle clocks,

VOICE SIX. Grandfather clocks,

VOICE FOUR. Traveling clocks,

VOICE FIVE. Stationary clocks,

VOICE SIX. Alarm clocks,

VOICE FOUR. Eight-day clocks,

VOICE THREE. Steeple clocks,

OGRE. And tower clocks! (*Self-satisfied gluttony.*)

NARRATOR. Sprinkling them with watches, as if the watches were salt and pepper, until there were no more watches . . .

VOICE SIX. People overslept, and failed to go to work, or to church, or any place else where they had to be on time.

VOICE THREE. Factories closed down,

VOICE FOUR. Shopkeepers shut up their shops,

VOICE SIX. Schools did not open,

VOICE FIVE. Trains no longer ran,

ALL. And people stayed at home.

NARRATOR. The town council held an emergency meeting and its members arrived at all hours, and some did not show up at all. A Psychronologist was first called to the witness stand when the meeting finally began to testify as to what should be done.

PSYCHRONOLOGIST. This would appear to be a clear case of clock eating, but we should not jump so easily to conclusions. We have no scientific data whatever on clock eating, and hence no controlled observations. All things, as we know, are impossible in this most impossible of all impossible worlds. That being the case, no such thing as we think has happened could have happened. Thus the situation does not fall within the frame of my discipline. Good day, gentlemen.

NARRATOR. The Psychronologist glanced at where his wristwatch should have been and, not finding it there, was disturbed.

PSYCHRONOLOGIST. I have less than no time at all, which means that I am late for my next appointment!

NARRATOR. And he hurriedly left the council room. The Lord Mayor of the town, arriving late to preside over the meeting, called a clockonomist to the stand. The Clockonomist began:

CLOCKONOMIST. What we have here appears on the surface to be a clockonomic crisis. It is the direct opposite of what is known, in my field, as a glut of clocks. That is, instead of there being more clocks than the consumer needs, so that the price of clocks would decrease, the consumer has consumed all the clocks. This should send up the price of clocks sharply, but we are faced with the unique fact that there are no clocks. Now, as a Clockonomist, my concern is the economy of clocks, but where there are no clocks there can be no such economy. The area, in short, has disappeared.

LORD MAYOR. What do you suggest then?

CLOCKONOMIST. I suggest that it is high time I go into some other line of endeavor, or transfer my clockonomy to a town which has clocks. Good day, gentlemen.

NARRATOR. And the Clockonomist left the council room. The clockmakers of the town, who had been subpoenaed, were then enjoined, in a body, from making more clocks.

LORD MAYOR. You have been supplying the Ogre with clocks, whether intentionally or willy-nilly is irrelevant. (*Severely.*) You have been working hand in glove, or clock in hand, with the Ogre.

NARRATOR. The Lord Mayor frowned threateningly and the clockmakers left to look for other work. Then the Lord Mayor spoke again:

LORD MAYOR. I should like to solve this case by deporting the Ogre, but, as a container of clocks, he would have to be exported, not deported. Unfortunately, the law is clear on this point: clocks may not be exported in any save regulation containers, and the human body falls outside the legal definition.

(*All heads down except the* NARRATOR'*s.*)

NARRATOR. Three weeks to the day after the Ogre had eaten the last clock, he fell ill and took to his bed. The Ogress sent for the Chief Diagnostician of the Medical Academy, a diagnostician familiar with so many areas that totality itself had become to him only a part of wholeness. He explained to the Ogress:

CHIEF. The trouble is we don't know what the trouble is. Nobody has ever eaten all the clocks before, so it is impossible to tell whether the patient has clockitis, clockosis, clockoma, or clocktheria. We are also faced with the possibility that there may be no such diseases. The patient may have one of the minor clock ailments, if there are any, such as clockets, clockles, clocking cough, ticking pox, or clumps. We shall have to develop area men who will find out about such areas, if such areas exist, which, until we find out that they do, we must assume do not.

OGRESS. (*Eagerly.*) What if he dies?

CHIEF. Then we shall bury him.

NARRATOR. And the Chief Diagnostician left the Ogre's room and the castle. . . . The case of the town's clocklessness was carried to the Supreme Council, presided over by the Supreme Magistrate.

MAGISTRATE. Who is prosecuting whom?

NARRATOR. The Supreme Prosecutor stood up.

PROSECUTOR. Let somebody say something and I will object. We have to start somewhere.

NARRATOR. A Housewife took the witness stand.

HOUSEWIFE. Without a clock, I cannot even boil a three-minute egg.

PROSECUTOR. Objection. One does not *have* to boil a three-minute egg. A three-minute egg, by definition, has already been boiled for three minutes, or it wouldn't be a three-minute egg.

MAGISTRATE. (*Droning.*) Objection sustained.

NARRATOR. The Leader of the Opposition then took the stand.

LEADER. The party in power has caused the mess in the Ogre's Castle.

PROSECUTOR. Objection. There isn't any party in power. The Ogre was the party in power, but he no longer has any power. Furthermore, the mess caused by the party cleaning up the mess caused by the party in power, which is no longer in power, would be worse than the mess left by the party that was in power.

MAGISTRATE. (*Droning.*) Objection sustained.

NARRATOR. The Man in the Street now took the stand.

MAN IN THE STREET. Why don't we use sundials?

PROSECUTOR. Sundials work only when the sun is shining, and nobody cares what time it is when the sun is shining.

(*Sound cue: Ticking of a clock.*)

NARRATOR. The Man in the Street left the witness chair, but nobody noticed his going because they were listening. What everybody in the Council Room heard was the slow tick-tock of a clock, a wall clock, the clock on the wall behind the Supreme Magistrate's bench.

VOICES FOUR AND FIVE. The officials,

VOICES THREE AND SIX. And the witnesses,

VOICES THREE, FOUR, FIVE, AND SIX. And the spectators,

NARRATOR. . . . had grown so used to not hearing clocks it wasn't until the clock struck the hour that they realized there was a clock on the wall. The Supreme Magistrate was the first to speak:

(*Sound cue: The clock fades to a barely audible sound.*)

MAGISTRATE. Unless I am mightily mistaken, and I usually am, we have here the solution to all our problems, namely, a clock. Unless there is an objection and I sustain the objection, which I do not think I shall, we will place this clock in the clock tower of the town, where it can be seen by one and all. Then we shall once again know what time it is. The situation will be cleared up, and the case dismissed.

(*Sound cue: Clock stops.*)

PROSECUTOR. One minute. What is to prevent the Ogre from eating the clock in the clock tower?

MAGISTRATE. If you are asking me, I do not know, but I do not have to confess my ignorance, since affirmations of this sort do not fall within my jurisdiction.

NARRATOR. Just then a Bailiff stepped to the bench and handed the Supreme Magistrate a note. Then he announced:

BAILIFF. The Ogre is dead.

PROSECUTOR. Objection!

MAGISTRATE. Objection overruled, if you are objecting to the fact of the Ogre's death.

PROSECUTOR. I accept the Ogre's death as a fact, but we are moving too fast, and I should like to call a Specialist to the stand.

NARRATOR. And he called a Specialist to the stand.

SPECIALIST. I am a collector. The clock on the wall is the only clock there is. This makes it not, in fact, a clock but a collector's item, or museum piece. As such, it must be placed in the town museum. One does not spend the coins in a museum. The wineglasses in a museum do not hold wine. The suits of armor in a museum do not contain knights. The clocks in a museum do not tell time. This clock, the last clock there is, must therefore be allowed to run down, and then placed in the museum, with proper ceremonies, addresses, and the like.

PROSECUTOR. I move that this be done.

MAGISTRATE. I should like to continue to know, as much as everybody else, what time it is. Under the circumstances, however, there is but one thing to do in conformity with the rule which establishes the inalienable fact that the last clock is a collector's item, or museum piece. I therefore decree that the last clock, the clock here on the wall, be allowed to run down, and then placed in the town museum, with proper ceremonies, addresses, and the like.

NARRATOR. The next day, at nine minutes of twelve o'clock noon, the last clock ran down and stopped. It was then placed in the town museum as a collector's item, or museum piece, with proper ceremonies, addresses, and the like.

(*All but the* NARRATOR *get up, take two steps, and form a straight line.*) The officials who spoke all chose the same subjects, without verbs or predicates, and the subjects were:

VOICE TWO. Glorious past . . .

(*All heads turn to the right. As each says his line, all heads turn toward him. The effect should be like a typewriter carriage, using precise head movement.*)

VOICE THREE. Challenging future . . .
VOICE FOUR. Dedication . . .
VOICE FIVE. Inspired leadership . . .
VOICE SIX. Enlightened followership . . .
VOICE TWO. Rededication . . .
VOICE THREE. Spiritual values . . .
VOICE FOUR. Outer space . . .
VOICES FIVE. Inner man . . .
VOICE SIX. Higher ideals . . .
VOICE TWO. Lower taxes . . .
VOICE THREE. Unswerving devotion . . .
VOICE FOUR. Coordinated efforts . . .
VOICE FIVE. Dedicated rededication . . .
VOICE SIX. And rededicated dedication.

(*All but the* NARRATOR *bow and step back to the stools.*)

NARRATOR. After that, nobody in the town ever knew what time it was.
VOICE FOUR. Factories and schools remained closed.
VOICE SIX. Church bells no longer rang, because the bell ringers no longer knew when to ring them.
VOICE FIVE. Dates and engagements were no longer made because nobody knew when to keep them.
VOICE THREE. Trains no longer ran, so nobody left town and no strangers arrived in town to tell the people what time it was.
NARRATOR. Eventually, the sands of a nearby desert moved slowly and inexorably toward the timeless town, and in the end it was buried.
(*All but the* NARRATOR *put their heads down and crumple.*) Eras, epochs, and aeons passed before a party of explorers from another planet began digging in the sands above the buried town.

(*All heads up except the* INSPIRATIONALIST.)

SCIENTIST. They were descendants of people from Earth who had reached Venus a thousand years before and intermarried with Venusians.
NARRATOR. Among them were a young woman and a young man, and it was their fortune to be the first to come upon the ancient library of the old Inspirationalist. Among some papers still preserved upon his desk was the last bit of verse he had written:
INSPIRATIONALIST. (*As old* INSPIRATIONALIST.) We can make our lives sublime, and, departing, leave behind us, mummum in the sands of time.
SCIENTIST. What is mummum?
DIGGER. I don't know, but something tells me we shall find a lot of it.
NARRATOR. They went on digging, and, in the end, came upon the last

clock in the town museum, so clogged with sand they could not tell what it had once been used for, and so they marked it:

SCIENTIST. (*In a very scientific tone.*) Antique mechanism. Function uncertain. Possibly known to the ancients as mummum.

NARRATOR. And they took it back to Venus, in a cargo rocket ship, with other mysterious relics of the Time of Man on Earth.

(*Heads down.*)

BY MAX SHULMAN

Love Is a Fallacy

A short story adapted for Readers Theatre by Melvin R. White

Max Shulman's satire of the "collegiate rah-rah" side of campus life adapts readily to group reading with a cast of three. The Narrator tells the story and plays the role of "I," a rather sharp lad, contrasting with Petey, his roommate, a young man in college for the fun he can get out of it. Polly, the girl, is a cute little flirt, not as dumb as she appears to be.

CAST OF CHARACTERS

Two Men, One Woman

I (NARRATOR). *A sharp, intellectual collegian*

PETEY BELLOWS. *A rah-rah playboy-type collegian*

POLLY ESPEY. *A devastatingly cute co-ed, not as dumb as she appears*

PRODUCTION NOTES

The stage arrangement is a simple one of three chairs (or one chair and one piano bench) and one lectern (or one high stool in place of the lectern).

In some ten different productions of this story, the most effective ones have been those in which some stage action and onstage focus were used. In fact, in the most effective, all dialogue was memorized; only I (the NARRATOR) held his book—and he, too, was free from the script on all dialogue.

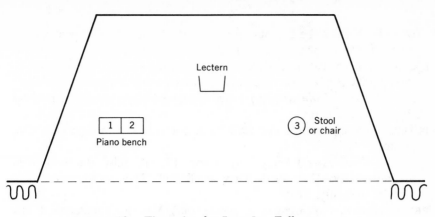

FIGURE 19.   Floor plan for *Love Is a Fallacy*

As the reading begins, the NARRATOR is at the lectern C; PETEY, in chair #3 to the left of the lectern; POLLY, in chair #1 at the right—or she may enter later. If desired, introductory music adds to the fun, an ideal selection being an old record such as "Collegiate."

I. (*Narrating at lectern.*) Keen, calculating, acute, and astute—I was all of these. My brain was as powerful as a dynamo, as precise as a chemist's scales, as penetrating as a scalpel. And—think of it!—I was only eighteen. It is not often that one so young has such a giant intellect. Take, for example, Petey Bellows, my roommate at the university. Same age, same background, but dumb as an ox. A nice enough fellow, you understand, but nothing upstairs. Emotional type. Unstable. Impressionable. Worst of all, a faddist. Fads, I submit, are the very negation of reason. To be swept up in every new craze that comes along, to surrender yourself to idiocy just because everybody else is doing it—this, to me, is the acme of mindlessness. Not, however, to Petey. (*Moves toward chair #3 at L where* PETEY *is sitting.*) One afternoon I found Petey lying on his bed with an expression of such distress on his face that I immediately diagnosed appendicitis. (*To* PETEY.) Don't move. Don't take a laxative. I'll get a doctor.

PETEY. (*Mumbles thickly.*) Raccoon.

I. Raccoon?

PETEY. (*Wailing.*) I want a raccoon coat!

I. (*Narrating.*) I perceived that his trouble was not physical but mental. (*To* PETEY.) Why do you want a raccoon coat?

PETEY. (*Crying out.*) I should have known it. I should have known they'd come back when the Charleston came back. Like a fool I spent all my money for textbooks, and now I can't get a raccoon coat.

I. Can you mean that people are actually wearing raccoon coats again?

PETEY. All the Big Men on Campus are wearing them. Where've you been?

I. In the library, (*To audience.*) I said, naming a place not frequented by Big Men on Campus.

PETEY. (*Stands, paces DL and back.*) I've got to have a raccoon coat. I've got to.

I. (*May follow* PETEY.) Petey, why? Look at it rationally. Raccoon coats are unsanitary. They shed. They smell bad. They weigh too much. They're unsightly. They . . .

PETEY. (*Interrupting. Crosses to* NARRATOR.) You don't understand. It's the thing to do. Don't you want to be in the swim?

I. No.

PETEY. Well, I do. I'd give anything for a raccoon coat. Anything! (*Returns to chair #3 and plunks into it with determination.*)

I. (*Narrating.*) My brain, that precision instrument, slipped into high gear. I asked, (*To* PETEY.) Anything?

PETEY. (*In ringing tones.*) Anything. (PETEY *freezes.*)

I. (*Returning to lectern.*) I stroked my chin thoughtfully. It so happened that I knew where to get my hands on a raccoon coat. My father had had one in his undergraduate days; it now lay in a trunk in the attic back home. It also happened that Petey had something I wanted. He didn't *have* it exactly, but at least he had first rights on it. I refer to his girl, Polly Espey. I had long coveted Polly Espey. Let me emphasize that my desire for this young woman was not emotional in nature. She was, to be sure, a girl who excited the emotions, but I was not one to let my heart rule my head. I wanted Polly for a shrewdly calculated, entirely cerebral reason. I was a freshman in law school. In a few years I would be out in practice. I was well aware of the importance of the right kind of wife in furthering a lawyer's career. The successful lawyers I had observed were, almost without exception, married to beautiful, gracious, intelligent women. With one omission, Polly fitted these specifications perfectly. Beautiful she was. Gracious she was. Intelligent she was not. In fact, she veered in the opposite direction. But I believed that under my guidance she would smarten up. At any rate, it was worth a try. It is, after all, easier to make a beautiful dumb girl smart than to make an ugly smart girl beautiful. (*Leaves lectern, crosses to* PETEY, *who comes alive. To* PETEY.) Petey, are you in love with Polly Espey?

PETEY. I think she's a keen kid, but I don't know if you'd call it love. Why?

I. Do you have any kind of formal arrangement with her? I mean, are you going steady or anything like that?

PETEY. No. We see each other quite a bit, but we both have other dates. Why?

I. Is there any other man for whom she has a particular fondness?

PETEY. Not that I know of. Why?

I. In other words, if you were out of the picture, the field would be open. Is that right?

PETEY. I guess so. What're you getting at?

I. Nothing, nothing. Well, better dig my suitcase out of the closet.

PETEY. Where are you going?

I. Home for the weekend.

PETEY. (*Coming to life.*) Listen, while you're home, you couldn't get some money from your old man, could you, and lend it to me so I can buy a raccoon coat?

I. I may do better than that. Well, so long. See you next week. (*Crosses DR to talk with audience, returning to lectern in time to point to raccoon coat on "Look." To audience.*) When I got back Monday morning, I threw open the suitcase and revealed the huge, hairy, gamy object my father had worn in 1925, and said to Petey, "Look!"

PETEY. (*Comes to L of lectern, and gazes reverently at the imaginary raccoon coat.*) Holy Toledo! Holy Toledo!!

I. Would you like it?

PETEY. Oh yes! (*Canny look appears in eyes.*) What do you want for it?

I. Your girl.

PETEY. (*Unbelievingly.*) Polly? You want Polly?

I. That's right.

PETEY. (*Turning resolutely away from the lectern and crossing DL.*) Never!

I. (*Crossing R toward chair.*) Okay. If you don't want to be in the swim, I guess it's your business. (*Sits DR in chair #2. To audience.*) I sat down in a chair and pretended to read a book, but out of the corner of my eye I kept watching Petey. He was a torn man. (PETEY *crosses back to lectern.*) First he looked at the coat with the expression of a waif at a bakery window. (PETEY *turns away resolutely.*) Then he turned away and set his jaw resolutely. (PETEY *looks back at lectern over his shoulder.*) Then he looked back at the coat, with even more longing in his face. (PETEY *turns away.*) Then he turned away, but with not so much resolution this time. (PETEY *suits action to the words.*) Back and forth his head swiveled, desire waxing, resolution waning. (PETEY *crosses back to lectern.*) Finally he didn't turn away at all; he just stood and stared with mad lust at the coat.

PETEY. (*Crossing to* NARRATOR *at R.*) It isn't as though I were in love with Polly. Or going steady or anything like that. (*Returning to R of lectern.*)

I. (*Still sitting calmly.*) That's right.

PETEY. (*Crossing UR.*) What's Polly to me, or me to Polly?

I. Not a thing.

PETEY. (*Crossing DR.*) It's just been a casual kick—just a few laughs, that's all.

I. (*Crossing to lectern.*) Try on the coat. (*Pantomimes picking up the coat and helping* PETEY, *who comes over, into it, then stands back to inspect. To audience.*) The coat bunched high over his ears and dropped all the way down to his shoe tops. He looked like a mound of dead raccoons. But he said happily . . .

PETEY. Fits fine.

I. (*Crossing to* PETEY.) Is it a deal?

PETEY. (*Swallowing.*) It's a deal. (*They shake hands, and* PETEY *leaves. As* NARRATOR *returns to lectern,* POLLY *enters R and sits in chair #2.*) I had my first date with Polly the following evening. This was in the nature of a survey; I wanted to find out just how much work I had to do to get her mind up to the standard I required. I took her first to dinner.

POLLY. (*Comes alive, looks up at* NARRATOR, *and gushes.*) Gee, that was a delish dinner.

I. (*To audience.*) . . . she said as we left the restaurant. Then I took her to a movie.

POLLY. Gee, that was a marvy movie.

I. (*To audience.*) . . . she said as we left the theatre. And then I took her home.

POLLY. Gee, I had a sensaysh time.

I. (*To audience.*) . . . she said as she said goodnight. I went back to my room with a heavy heart. I had gravely underestimated the size of my task. This girl's lack of information was terrifying. Nor would it be enough merely to supply her with information. First she had to be taught to *think*. This loomed as a project of no small dimensions, and at first I was tempted to give her back to Petey. But then I got to thinking about her abundant physical charms, and about the way she entered a room and the way she handled a knife and fork, and I decided to make an effort. (*Transition.*) I went about it, as in all things, systematically. I gave her a course in logic. It happened that I, as a law student, was taking a course in logic myself, so I had all the facts at my fingertips. When I picked her up on our next date (*Crossing to* POLLY *at R.*) I said to her: Polly, tonight we are going over to the Knoll and talk.

POLLY. Oo, terrif!

I. (*To audience.*) One thing I will say for this girl: you would go far to find another so agreeable. (*Strolls across stage and sits in chair #2.*) We went to the Knoll, the campus trysting place, and we sat down under an old oak, and she looked at me expectantly.

POLLY. What are we going to talk about?

I. Logic.

POLLY. Magnif!

I. Logic is the science of thinking. Before we can think correctly we must first learn to recognize the common fallacies of logic. These we will take up tonight.

POLLY. (*Clapping hands delightedly.*) Wow-dow!

I. (*To audience.*) I winced, but went bravely on. (*To* POLLY.) First let us examine the fallacy called Dicto Simpliciter.

POLLY. (*Eagerly.*) By all means.

I. Dicto Simpliciter means an argument based on an unqualified generalization. For example: Exercise is good. Therefore everybody should exercise.

POLLY. I agree. I mean exercise is wonderful. I mean it builds the body and everything.

I. Polly, the argument is a fallacy. *Exercise is good* is an unqualified generalization. For instance, if you have heart disease, exercise is bad, not good. Many people are ordered by their doctors *not* to exercise. You must *qualify* the generalization. You must say exercise is *usually* good, or exercise is good *for most people*. Otherwise you have committed a Dicto Simpliciter. Do you see?

POLLY. No. But this is marvy. Do more! Do more!! (*Tugs at his sleeve.*)

I. It will be better if you stop tugging at my sleeve. Next we take up a fallacy called Hasty Generalization. Listen carefully: You can't speak French. I can't speak French. Petey Bellows can't speak French. I must therefore conclude that nobody at the university can speak French.

POLLY. Really? *Nobody?*

I. Polly, it's a fallacy. The generalization is reached too hastily. There are too few instances to support such a conclusion.

POLLY. Know any more fallacies? This is better than dancing even.

I. (*To audience.*) I fought off a wave of despair. I was getting nowhere with this girl, absolutely nowhere. Still, I am nothing if not persistent. I continued. (*To* POLLY.) Next comes Post Hoc. Listen to this: (*Stands, crosses behind* POLLY *to CR.*) Let's not take Bill on our picnic. Every time we take him out with us, it rains.

POLLY. (*Gets up, crosses to* NARRATOR.) I know somebody just like that, a girl back home—Eula Becker, her name is. It never fails. Every single time we take her on a picnic . . .

I. (*Interrupting.*) Polly, it's a fallacy. Eula Becker doesn't *cause* the rain. She has no connection with the rain. You are guilty of Post Hoc if you blame Eula Becker.

POLLY. I'll never do it again. (*Cuddles up to him a bit.*) Are you mad at me?

I. No, Polly, I'm not mad.

POLLY. Then tell me some more fallacies.

I. (*Escorts* POLLY *back to seat.*) All right. Let's try Contradictory Premises.

POLLY. Yes, let's. (*Blinking eyes happily.*)

I. Here's an example of Contradictory Premises: If God can do anything, can He make a stone so heavy that He won't be able to lift it?

POLLY. Of course.

I. But if He can do anything, He can lift the stone.

POLLY. Yeah. Well, then I guess He can't make the stone.

I. But He can do anything.

POLLY. I'm all confused.

I. Of course you are. Because when the premises of an argument contradict each other, there can be no argument. If there is an irresistible force, there can be no immovable object. If there is an immovable object, there can be no irresistible force. Get it?

POLLY. (*Eagerly.*) Tell me some more of this keen stuff!

I. (*Almost patronizingly.*) Polly, I think we'd better call it a night. I'll take you home now, and you go over all the things you've learned. We'll have another session tomorrow night. (POLLY *freezes as* NARRATOR *returns to lectern at C. To audience.*) I deposited her at the girls' dormitory, where she assured me that she had had a perfectly "terrif" evening, and I went glumly home to my room. Petey lay snoring in his bed, the raccoon coat huddled like a great hairy beast at his feet. For a moment I considered waking him and telling him that he could have his girl back. It seemed clear that my project was doomed to failure. The girl simply had a logic-proof head. But then I reconsidered. I had wasted one evening; I might as well waste another. Who knew? Maybe somewhere in the extinct crater of her mind a few embers still smoldered. Maybe somehow I could fan them into flame. Admittedly it was not a prospect fraught with hope, but I decided to give it one more try. (NARRATOR *crosses to chair #1 and sits next to* POLLY.) Seated under the oak next evening I said: (*To* POLLY.) Our first fallacy tonight is called Ad Misericordiam. (*To audience.*) She quivered with delight. (*To* POLLY.) Listen closely. A man applies for a job. When the boss asks him what his qualifications are, he replies that he has a wife and six children at home, the wife is a helpless cripple, the children have nothing to eat, no clothes to wear, no shoes on their feet, there are no beds in the house, no coal in the cellar, and winter is coming.

POLLY. (*Tearfully.*) Oh, this is awful, awful.

I. Yes, it's awful, but it's no argument. The man never answered the boss's question about his qualifications. Instead he appealed to the boss's sympathy. He committed the fallacy of Ad Misericordiam. Do you understand?

POLLY. (*Sobbing.*) Have you got a handkerchief?

I. (*To audience.*) I handed her a handkerchief and tried to keep from screaming while she wiped her eyes. Then I said in a carefully controlled tone: (*To* POLLY.) Next we will discuss False Analogy. Here is an example: Students should be allowed to look at their textbooks during examinations. After all, surgeons have X rays to guide them during an operation, lawyers have briefs to guide them during a trial, carpenters have blueprints to guide them when they are building a house. Why, then, shouldn't students be allowed to look at their textbooks during an examination?

POLLY. There, now, is the most marvy idea I've heard in years!

I. Polly, the argument is all wrong. Doctors, lawyers, and carpenters aren't taking a test to see how much they have learned, but students are. The situations are altogether different, and you can't make an analogy between them.

POLLY. I still think it's a good idea.

I. (*Mumbles to self.*) Nuts. (*To* POLLY.) Next we'll try Hypothesis Contrary to Fact.

POLLY. Sounds yummy.

I. Listen: If Madame Curie had not happened to leave a photographic plate in a drawer with a chunk of pitchblende, the world would not know about radium.

POLLY. (*Nodding her head in agreement.*) True, true! Did you see the movie? Oh, it just knocked me out. That Walter Pidgeon is so dreamy. I mean he fractures me.

I. If you can forget Mr. Pidgeon for a moment, I would like to point out that the statement is a fallacy. Maybe Madame Curie would have discovered radium at some later date. Maybe somebody else would have discovered it. Maybe any number of things would have happened. You can't start with a hypothesis that is not true and then draw any supportable conclusions from it.

POLLY. They ought to put Walter Pidgeon in more pictures; I hardly ever see him any more.

I. (*To audience.*) One more chance, I decided. But just one more. There is a limit to what flesh and blood can bear. (*To* POLLY.) The next fallacy is called Poisoning the Well.

POLLY. (*Gurgling.*) How cute!

I. Two men are having a debate. The first one gets up and says, "My opponent is a notorious liar. You can't believe a word that he is going to say." Now, Polly, think. Think hard. What's wrong? (*To audience.*) I watched her closely as she knit her creamy brow in concentration. Suddenly a glimmer of intelligence—the first I had seen—came into her eyes.

POLLY. It's not fair. It's not a bit fair. What chance has the second man got if the first man calls him a liar when he hasn't even begun talking?

I. Right! One hundred percent right. It's not fair. The first man has *poisoned the well* before anybody could drink from it. He has hamstrung his opponent before he could even start. . . . Polly, I'm proud of you!

POLLY. (*Murmurs, blushing with pleasure.*) Pshaw.

I. You see, my dear, these things aren't so hard. All you have to do is concentrate. Think . . . examine . . . evaluate. Come now, let's review everything we have learned.

POLLY. (*Airily.*) Fire away. (POLLY *remains in seat and freezes;* NARRATOR *returns to the lectern.*)

I. (*To audience.*) Heartened by the knowledge that Polly was not altogether a cretin, I began a long, patient review of all I had told her. Over and over and over again I cited instances, pointed out flaws, kept hammering away without letup. Five grueling nights this took, but it was worth it. I had made a logician out of Polly; I had taught her to think. My job was done. She was worthy of me at last. She was a fit wife for me, a proper hostess for my many mansions, a suitable mother for my well-heeled children. (*Transition.*) It must not be thought that I was not without love for this girl. Quite the contrary. Just as Pygmalion loved the perfect woman he had fashioned, so I loved mine. I decided to acquaint her with my feelings at our very next meeting. The time had come to change our relationship from academic to romantic. So when next we sat beneath our oak, I said: (*To* POLLY.) Polly, tonight we will not discuss fallacies.

POLLY. Aw, gee . . .

I. (*Crosses to her R.*) My dear, we have now spent five evenings together. We have gotten along splendidly. It is clear that we are well matched.

POLLY. (*Brightly.*) Hasty Generalization.

I. (*Taken aback.*) I beg your pardon.

POLLY. Hasty Generalization. How can you say that we are well matched on the basis of only five dates?

I. (*Chuckles with amusement.*) My dear, five dates is plenty. After all, you don't have to eat a whole cake to know that it's good.

POLLY. False Analogy. I'm not a cake. I'm a girl.

I. (*Crosses to C. To audience.*) I chuckled with somewhat less amusement. The dear child had learned her lessons perhaps too well. I decided to change tactics. Obviously the best approach was a simple, strong, direct declaration of love. I paused for a moment while my massive brain chose the right words. Then I began (*Crosses to* POLLY, *sits beside her.*) Polly, I love you. You are the whole world to me, and the moon and the stars and the constellations of outer space. Please, my darling, say that you will go steady with me, for if you will not, life will be meaningless. I will languish. I will refuse my meals. I will wander the face of the earth, a shambling, hollow-eyed hulk.

POLLY. Ad Misericordiam.

I. (*To audience.*) I ground my teeth. I was not Pygmalion; I was Frankenstein, and my monster had me by the throat. Frantically I fought back the tide of panic surging through me. At all costs I had to keep cool. Forcing a smile, I said: (*To* POLLY.) Well, Polly, you certainly have learned your fallacies.

POLLY. You're darned right.

I. And who taught them to you, Polly?

POLLY. You did.

I. That's right. So you do owe me something, don't you, my dear? If I hadn't come along you never would have learned about fallacies.

POLLY. Hypothesis Contrary to Fact.

I. (*A bit desperately.*) Polly, you mustn't take all these things so literally. I mean this is just classroom stuff. You know that the things you learn in school don't have anything to do with life!

POLLY. (*Wagging her finger playfully.*) Dicto Simpliciter.

I. (*Leaps to feet, bellowing like a bull.*) Will you or will you not go steady with me?

POLLY. (*Stands, crosses toward DC.*) I will not.

I. (*Still yelling.*) Why not?

POLLY. Because this afternoon I promised Petey Bellows that I would go steady with him.

I. (*Reeling back, overcome with the infamy of it, shouting, uncontrolled.*) The rat! You can't go with him, Polly. He made a deal. He shook my hand. He's a liar! He's a cheat! He's a rat!

POLLY. Poisoning the Well. And stop shouting. I think shouting must be a fallacy too.

I. (*Forcing himself to modulate his temper—and his voice.*) All right. You're a logician. Let's look at this thing logically. How could you choose Petey Bellows over me? Look at me—a brilliant student, a tremendous intellectual, a man with an assured future. Look at Petey—a knothead, a jitterbug, a guy who'll never know where his next meal is coming from. Can you give me one logical reason why you should go steady with Petey Bellows?

POLLY. I certainly can. He's got a raccoon coat. (*She flounces out.* NAR-RATOR, *stunned, bewildered, beats his head, throws up his hands in despair or sinks into his chair, head in hands—or exits in the opposite direction—depending on whether there is a curtain to be drawn or not.*)

BY JEAN KERR

The Ten Worst Things About a Man

A humorous essay adapted for Readers Theatre by Leslie Irene Coger

In its original form, a chapter from Mrs. Kerr's book *The Snake Has All the Lines,* the material was expressed entirely by one person—a woman. In this adapted version, a second character—a man—has been added in order to provide an element of contrast and a degree of good-natured conflict to spark the dialogue, thereby converting what was essentially a monologue into a sketch for two people.

CAST OF CHARACTERS

One Woman and One Man

SHE. *A typical young wife*

HE. *A typical young husband*

THE PHYSICAL ARRANGEMENT OF THE SCENE

Two stools are provided at or near the center of the stage for the readers, and lecterns may be added if desired; or the stools may be dispensed with, and the two interpreters may remain standing behind their lecterns. Off-stage focus is used throughout. SHE is wearing a uniquely feminine afternoon dress, HE a solidly masculine business suit; or, if something more glamorous seems in order, SHE may be sheathed in a svelte evening gown and HE in a tuxedo. In the beginning there might be a bit of appropriate music; but, if so, it quickly becomes indistinct and fades out altogether as SHE begins to speak.

SHE. Actually, I feel a bit of a fraud to be picking on men when I always pretend to be so crazy about them. And, deep down inside, I am crazy about them. They are sweet, you know, and so helpful. At parties, men you've barely met will go back to the buffet to get you a muffin, and they will leap to their feet to tell you that you've got the wrong end of the cigarette in your mouth. Notice that when you are trying to squeeze into a tight parking space, there will always be some nice man driving by who will stick his head out the window and shout:

HE. (*Bawling loudly.*) Lady, you've got a whole mile back there! (SHE *shrugs as a response to his words.*)

SHE. But, charming as men are, we can't honestly pretend they're perfect. It wouldn't be good for them, and it wouldn't be true. Marrying a man is like buying something you've been admiring for a long time in a shop window. You may love it when you get it home, but it doesn't always go with the other things in the house. One reason for this is that most men insist on behaving as though this were an orderly, sensible universe, which naturally makes them hard to live with. The other reason they're hard to live with—and I know this sounds illogical—is that they're so good. Perhaps I can clarify that last statement by allowing one of them to enumerate a few of their more intolerable virtues:

HE. A man will not meddle in what he considers his wife's affairs.

SHE. He may interfere at the office, driving secretaries to drink and premature marriage by snooping into file drawers and tinkering with the mimeograph machine. Back home in the nest, he is the very model of patience. He will stare at you across the dining-room table—as you simultaneously carve the lamb and feed the baby—and announce in tones so piteous as to suggest that all his dreams have become ashes:

HE. (*Piteously.*) Honey, there's no salt in this shaker! (*Her expression says, "What can a wife do with a man like that?"*)

SHE. What a wife objects to in this situation is not just the notion that Daddy has lived in this house for thirteen years without discovering where the salt is kept. It's more the implication that only she has the necessary fortitude, stamina, and simple animal cunning to pour the salt into the little hole in the back of the shaker.

HE. (*With impressive self-importance.*) A man remembers important things.

SHE. It really is remarkable the fund of information he keeps at his fingertips:

HE. Why, I can give you the date of the Battle of Hastings, the name of the man who invented the printing press, the formula for water, the Preamble of the Constitution, and every lyric Larry Hart ever wrote.

SHE. (*Smiling indulgently.*) It is obviously unreasonable to expect one so weighted down with relevant data to remember a simple fact like what size shirt he takes, or what grade Gilbert is in, or even that you told him fifteen times that the Bentleys are coming to dinner. A woman just has to go through life remembering for two. As an example of this, I was recently told about a wife who, from time to time, pinned a tag on her husband's coat. The tag read:

HE. (*As if reading from a card.*) "Please don't give me a ride home from the station; I have my own car today."

SHE. However, this technique wouldn't work with *my* husband because he usually forgets and leaves his coat on the train.

HE. (*Changing the subject.*) A man will try to improve his wife's mind.

SHE. Working on the suspicion that women read nothing in the newspapers except bulletins from Macy's and Dorothy Kilgallen, the average man takes considerable pains to keep his scatterbrained wife *au courant* with the contemporary political situation. And we get the following bit of profound dialogue across the dinner table:

HE. Did you read Walter Lippman today on the shake-up in the Defense Department?

SHE. No, what did he have to say?

HE. (*Laconically.*) You should have read it. It was a damn good piece.

SHE. Well, what was the gist of it?

HE. Where's the paper? It should be around here someplace.

SHE. (*Very firmly.*) It's not around here someplace. It went out with the garbage.

HE. That's too bad, because it would have clarified the whole situation for you.

SHE. I'm sure. But what was he saying?

HE. Oh, he was talking about the shake-up in the Defense Department.

SHE. (*Pushing for a definite answer.*) I know that, but what did he *say?*

HE. (*Simply.*) He was against it. (SHE *registers her "What can you do?" response.*)

SHE. A man allows you to make the important decisions because he has such respect for your superior wisdom and technical know-how. He is constantly asking questions:

HE. Does this kid need a sweater?

SHE. Or:

HE. (*Ugh!*) Is this baby wet?

SHE. Personally, I am willing to go down through life being the court of last appeals on such crucial issues as bedtime . . .

HE. Bedtime! (*Surprised.*) Is it?

SHE. Cookies . . .

HE. (*Meaning "Let's be indulgent!"*) Can they have another?

SHE. Rubbers . . .

HE. Do they have to wear them?

SHE. And baths . . .

HE. (*In shocked disbelief.*) Tonight? But they just took one last night! (SHE *responds silently but expressively to this unbelievable man of hers.*)

SHE. But just between us, I have no confidence in a man who wanders into the kitchen, peers into the icebox, and asks plaintively:

HE. (*Plaintively and uncertainly.*) Do I want a sandwich?

SHE. A man will give you an honest answer. If you say, "Honey, do you think this dress is too tight for me to wear?" he'll say:

HE. (*Quickly and definitely.*) Yes! (SHE *reacts facially to his lack of tact, but she loves him.*)

SHE. A man takes pride in his personal possessions. A woman will go all her days in the wistful belief that her husband would give her the shirt off his back. Thus, she is in no way prepared for the cries of outrage that will go up should she ever be rash enough to *take* the shirt off his back. It doesn't matter that the shirt in question has a torn pocket, a frayed collar, and has—in any case—been at the bottom of the clothes hamper for three years. It's his, and you wear it at your own risk. My husband will say to me:

HE. (*Incredulously.*) What are you doing in that shirt, for heaven's sake?

SHE. (*Quickly.*) Now he doesn't really want to know what I'm doing. (*Very deliberately.*) He can see what I'm doing. I'm painting the garage doors. He just wants me to know that that shirt was near and dear to him, and now—as a result of my vandalism—it's totally ruined. There are two possible solutions to this problem. You can hire a painter to paint the garage doors, or you can dye the shirt purple so he won't be able to recognize it.

HE. (*Thinking he's changing the subject.*) A man believes in sharing.

SHE. Men are all advocates of togetherness . . . up to a point. They will agree that it is our house, our mortgage, and of course our song. It is interesting, however, to observe the circumstances under which items that once were under joint concern suddenly become your exclusive possession. For instance, a man will return from a stroll in your back yard to tell you:

HE. (*Half-plaintively, half-accusingly.*) Honey, I think your daffodils are getting clump-bound.

SHE. Or on other occasions:

HE. (*As though he has made a discovery.*) I see that the hinge is off your medicine chest.

SHE. In my opinion, this policy of disassociating from anything that is temporarily out of order reaches its ultimate confusion with statements like:

HE. Hey, your man is here to fix the chimney!

SHE. (*Incredulous at his obtuseness.*) My man? I never saw him before in my life!

HE. (*Indulgently.*) A man doesn't want his little woman to worry.

SHE. Since he supposes—and quite correctly—that you worry a great deal about his health, he will go to any lengths to spare you the least alarm about his physical condition. He will say, as though it were the most casual thing in the world:

HE. (*Casually.*) Well, I almost keeled over in Grand Central today.

SHE. Good heavens, what happened?

HE. Nothing, nothing. I leaned against a pillar and didn't actually fall down.

SHE. (*Pressing for information.*) But, honey, what happened? Did you feel faint? You didn't have a terribly sharp pain in your chest, did you?

HE. (*Offhandedly.*) Oh, no . . . no, nothing like that.

SHE. Well, what do you mean—you almost keeled over?

HE. (*Indifferently.*) I almost keeled over, that's all.

SHE. But there must have been some reason.

HE. (*Matter-of-factly.*) Oh, I guess it's that foot again.

SHE. (*Very excitedly.*) What foot again? Which foot?

HE. Oh, I told you about my foot.

SHE. (*Almost beside herself with worry.*) You most certainly did *not* tell me anything about your foot.

HE. The one that's been numb since last summer.

SHE. (*Incredulously; nearly frantic.*) Your foot has been numb since last summer?

HE. Now it's more like the whole leg.

SHE. Good Heavens, let's call a doctor! Let's call this minute!

HE. Why?

SHE. Why? Are you out of your mind? Because there's something the matter with your leg, that's why.

HE. There you go flying off again. I'm sorry I mentioned it. And there's nothing the matter with my leg. Nothing.

SHE. A man idealizes his wife. This is another way of saying that he hasn't really looked at her in fourteen years. To get me the housecoat for my birthday, my husband will make the unthinkable sacrifice of entering Lord and Taylor's, and even penetrate the awesome portals of the lingerie department. There, as I reconstruct the scene later, he selects the slimmest, trimmest little salesgirl on the floor and announces: (HE *thinks it through and sizes up the saleslady.*)

HE. She's about your size.

SHE. Naturally I have to take the thing back and get one four sizes larger. On second thought, I shouldn't complain about that. If you stop and think . . . (*and she does*) . . . it's really rather charming of him. (SHE *turns to her partner and winks.*)

BY ART BUCHWALD

What Is It, Mrs. Perkins?

A newspaper column adapted for Readers Theatre by Leslie Irene Coger and Melvin R. White

Although the characters and the situation in this adaptation are fictive and satiric, the arrangement is basically that of a news documentary.

CAST OF CHARACTERS

One Man, One Woman, and a Narrator, who may be played by either a Man or a Woman

NARRATOR. *An effective storyteller*

MR. MAHONEY. *Whose nerves of steel get somewhat frayed*

MRS. LILA PERKINS. *A housewife astronaut*

THE PHYSICAL ARRANGEMENT OF THE SCENE

The NARRATOR stands at a lectern near UC. MR. MAHONEY and MRS. PERKINS are seated on two stools—or in two chairs—on opposite sides of the platform area, one DR and one DL, their backs to the audience.

NARRATOR. I read in the newspaper recently that woman's lib is very upset because there are no women astronauts. What nobody knows is that there *was* a woman astronaut, but the people in charge of the program have kept it all a deep dark secret. . . . Through a source that must remain secret, I was able to get a transcript of America's first attempt to launch a woman astronaut into space. It took place some six months ago, and the would-be astronaut's name was Mrs. Lila Perkins, a housewife who had volunteered for the program. Mrs. Perkins was placed in the capsule at six o'clock one morning. Here, an exact record of what transpired. (NARRATOR *may be seated in a chair behind the lectern.* MR. MAHONEY *and* MRS. PERKINS *turn around on their stools.*)

MR. MAHONEY. (*Facing front.*) This is tower control. Okay, Mrs. Perkins. We're all set to go.

MRS. PERKINS. Thank you, Mr. Mahoney.

MR. MAHONEY. We're starting the countdown. Ten . . . nine . . . eight . . . seven . . .

MRS. PERKINS. Just a second, Mr. Mahoney.

MR. MAHONEY. (*Patiently.*) What is it, Mrs. Perkins?

MRS. PERKINS. I don't think I'm zipped up. Oh, dear.

MR. MAHONEY. (*With forbearance, but sardonically.*) Launch control, go up there and zip up Mrs. Perkins.

MRS. PERKINS. Mr. Mahoney.

MR. MAHONEY. Yes, Mrs. Perkins?

MRS. PERKINS. Do you think I'm doing the right thing, wearing a silver spacesuit with a green oxygen mask?

MR. MAHONEY. (*With a sigh of resignation.*) Mrs. Perkins, you've changed your spacesuit three times this morning. We can't wait any longer.

MRS. PERKINS. I think a more neutral color would have been better, particularly since I'll be going around day and night.

MR. MAHONEY. You look beautiful, Mrs. Perkins, just as you are. Is she all zipped, launch control? Okay, let's go. Ten . . . nine . . . eight . . . seven . . . six . . .

MRS. PERKINS. (*Suddenly.*) Mr. Mahoney?

MR. MAHONEY. (*With the patience of an angel, but a note of "Now what?" in his voice.*) What is it, Mrs. Perkins?

MRS. PERKINS. I forgot to tell my husband something.

MR. MAHONEY. (*A bit of desperation in his voice.*) Please, Mrs. Perkins, we're trying to get you launched on time.

MRS. PERKINS. (*Adamant.*) Well, it's important.

MR. MAHONEY. (*In resignation.*) Launch control, plug in the phone to her home.

MRS. PERKINS. (*Pick up imaginary phone.*) Hello, dear. Did you find your breakfast in the icebox? . . . Now don't get angry—you said I could work part-time . . . . Well, it's the only job I could find. Are the *Life* photographers there to catch the anguished look on your face as I go into space? . . . Well, don't let them photograph the bedroom; I didn't have time to make the beds this morning. Good-bye, dear. I'll be home in about three hours. (*Put down the phone.*)

MR. MAHONEY. (*Pleadingly.*) Please, Mrs. Perkins. This is tower control. We have to get started.

MRS. PERKINS. You're such a fuss-budget, Mr. Mahoney. All right, I'm ready.

MR. MAHONEY. Ten . . . nine . . . eight . . . seven . . . six . . .

MRS. PERKINS. Mr. Mahoney?

MR. MAHONEY. (*With an "Oh Lord" expression in his voice.*) Yes, Mrs. Perkins.

MRS. PERKINS. What am I supposed to do over Australia?

MR. MAHONEY. (*I've-told-you-a-thousand-times-already quality.*) You're supposed to look for the lights of Perth.

MRS. PERKINS. (*Brightly.*) That's right. Now I remember.

MR. MAHONEY. Are there any other questions?

MRS. PERKINS. Do I push the black button with the green lights to reenter, or the white button with the blue lights?

MR. MAHONEY. (*Losing his temper.*) You push the red button with the yellow lights! How many times do I have to tell you?!

MRS. PERKINS. (*Injured.*) Well, you don't have to get so upset. I can't remember everything.

MR. MAHONEY. (*At the end of his patience.*) Mrs. Perkins, we've repainted the interior of the capsule three times in three different colors, at your suggestion. We've changed the instrument panels around four times, to suit your decorative tastes. We've installed a mirror and a dressing table at your insistence, so you could look your best when you got out of the capsule. But NOW WE'VE GOT TO GET YOU OFF THE LAUNCHING PAD!!

MRS. PERKINS. (*Patiently, almost as if talking to a child.*) All right, Mr. Mahoney. If you feel so strongly about it.

MR. MAHONEY. I'm starting the countdown. Ten . . . nine . . . eight . . . seven . . . six . . .

MRS. PERKINS. Mr. Mahoney . . .

MR. MAHONEY. Five . . .

MRS. PERKINS. (*A bit desperate.*) Mr. Mahoney, I'm calling you.

MR. MAHONEY. Four . . .

MRS. PERKINS. (*More desperate.*) Mr. Mahoney, can you hear me?

MR. MAHONEY. Three . . .

MRS. MAHONEY. (*Desperate.*) Mr. Mahoney!

MR. MAHONEY. Two . . .

MRS. PERKINS. (*Screaming in desperation.*) Mr. Mahoney!!

MR. MAHONEY. What is it, Mrs. Perkins?

MRS. PERKINS. (*Plaintively.*) I've got a run in my stocking! (*Turns her back to the audience.*)

NARRATOR. (*Returns to the lectern.*) That is the end of the transcript. No one knows if Mrs. Perkins made it or not. The only one who could shed any light on the mystery is Mr. Mahoney—but he's living in a mental institution now, and all he does all day is sit there and keep muttering:

MR. MAHONEY. Ten . . . nine . . . eight . . . seven . . . six . . . five . . . four . . . three . . . two . . . (*Yelling, sobbing, out of control.*) WHAT IS IT, MRS. PERKINS?

BY JOHN CIARDI

A Year-End Dialogue
with Outer Space

A compiled script from two poems, "A Year-End Dialogue with Outer Space" and "Nine Beeps for Year's End," arranged for Readers Theatre by Melvin R. White

The content and basic structure of the two poems, as originally written by the poet, are unchanged, and lend themselves admirably to the oral interpretive medium. Combined, they provide a powerful and highly evocative comment on the national and international scene. The author stipulated in giving permission to use his material that " 'Nine Beeps' must be produced in entirety since they are an effort to satirize *all* sacred cows and are saved from bigotry only by the fact that they satirize equally on all fronts."

CAST OF CHARACTERS

Two Men

READER ONE. *Man skilled in character suggestion*

READER TWO. *Man skilled in character suggestion*

THE PHYSICAL ARRANGEMENT OF THE SCENE

In a test production of this script, two lecterns were placed DC, side by side. Later the script was performed successfully on a bare stage. However, if desired, two stools can be provided, or a piano bench, or two tall stools on which the men can sit behind two lecterns. Focus can be either onstage, offstage, or a combination of the two. The latter proved most satisfactory to the readers in a 1970 performance, and this shift from offstage

---

First published in *Saturday Review*. Reprinted by permission of the author. **Notice:** This adaptation may not be presented or performed without the written consent of Mr. John Ciardi.

to onstage focus is indicated in this version. When the poems refer to the General and the President, and other officials, real names of current gentlemen in these positions should be inserted.

(As the reading starts, the two readers take their positions side by side on stage, either behind two lecterns, on two stools, on a bench, or simply standing without furniture side by side.)

READER TWO. (*As* NARRATOR, *speaks to audience.*) A year-end dialogue with outer space.

READER ONE. (*Offstage focus throughout until script indicates otherwise.*) Do you?

READER TWO. (*Also offstage focus.*) Yes.

READER ONE. Do you what?

READER TWO. Whatever—to the unqualified question the unqualified answer: I do.

READER ONE. Everything?

READER TWO. Yes.

READER ONE. *Every*thing?

READER TWO. I do:
in the fact or in the thought of it—everything:
what is done in fact and without much thought,
what is done in fact in place of thought,
what is done premeditatively and thoughtfully in fact,
what is done in thought only—to escape fact,
or to make it bearable, or to confirm it—everything.

READER ONE. And do you now confess?

READER TWO. To myself, everything.
To the world in practical fact what is in practical fact
convenient, except that in an anger like an assault
of honesty, I do now and then not care, and do openly
admit being and having been and meaning to be everything,
and to relive it.

READER ONE. You have lied?

READER TWO. I recall that life.

READER ONE. Cheated?

READER TWO. And that one.

READER ONE. Stolen?

READER TWO. Negligently.
What has there been that would have been worth the time
it would have taken to steal it?

READER ONE. But you *have?* sometimes there *was* something?

READER TWO. At times, a trifle, and that always instantly not worth keeping.

READER ONE. You have killed?

READER TWO. Always, alas, for the worst reasons.

READER ONE. For what reasons?

READER TWO. For duty. For my captain's approval.

READER ONE. Not for survival?

READER TWO. Survival lay with my captain, the controls his.
I killed because I could.

READER ONE. You were proud?

READER TWO. For no reason I have not survived.

READER ONE. Envious?

READER TWO. At times. But I have admired many.

READER ONE. Wrathful?

READER TWO. In bursts from the sperm center. A screeing
of sensation, like a Morse code I could not read
that was in any case drowned in a cosmic whine.

READER ONE. Slothful?

READER TWO. Yawningly, when that was my mood's pleasure.

READER ONE. Avaricious?

READER TWO. No.

READER ONE. Gluttonous?

READER TWO. Hungry.

READER ONE. Lustful?

READER TWO. Gladly.

READER ONE. What then do you believe should be done with your soul?

READER TWO. Erase its name and make room for another experience.

READER ONE. Why?

READER TWO. First, because this one is completed and time is not.

READER ONE. And second?

READER TWO. Because it will in any case be erased.

READER ONE. And third?

READER TWO. Because, though it does not matter, eternity
would be the one experience beyond mercy.

READER ONE. And you claim mercy?

READER TWO. I do.

READER ONE. Why?

READER TWO. Because I was born.

READER ONE. (*As* NARRATOR, *after a transition pause, speaks to the audience.*) Thus spake John Ciardi on December 24th, Christmas Eve, in the year of our Lord 1966. (*Pause. Then makes "Beep-Beep" sounds, followed by the announcement:*) Nine Beeps for Year's End.
Beep One. (*Sound: one beep, made vocally or recorded.*)

READER TWO. "Stop war," he said.

READER ONE. "Fine," I said. "How?"

READER TWO. "You," he shrieked, "are the ENEMY!"

READER ONE. (*Sound: two beeps.*)

READER TWO. (*As black panelist.*) "I am your equal in every way,"
said the educated, moderate-militant
black panelist maintaining a balance
on the *Let's Find a Subject* show.

READER ONE. "Probably," I suggested,
"I am better than you
at remembering limericks, and you
better than I at, say, math,
volleyball, and the first names
of the eternal verities, though ethno-
genetico-politically, yes,
how should we not be equal?"

READER TWO. (*As black panelist.*) "So," he said. "You admit my superi-
ority!" (*Slight pause. Then three beeps.*)

READER ONE. (*As Catholic layman.*) "Ecumenically moved to *caritas*
toward even the unwashed,"
said the genial Catholic intellectual
layman of new dispensations,
"I am ready to meet with you,
to listen, and to pretend
you are an admissable entity.

"I am even willing to think of you
as a decent bit of misguidance.

"Shucks, I am willing to pretend
you could, given a miracle,
make it to heaven without
benefit of the True Road Map.
Though, of course, we both know better."
(*Sound of four beeps.*)

READER TWO. (*As kosher urbanist.*) "Yes, of course, the Arabs
have a right to live,"
said the kosher urbanist smiling,
"but only the Jews are the chosen,
and how can there be room for two choices
when the right one has made the desert bloom?"

READER ONE. (*Makes sound of five beeps. On this, the Beep V section, the
two readers break their offstage focus, leave their scripts, turn, and talk
directly to each other.*)

READER TWO. "I love you."

READER ONE. "I adore you."

READER TWO. "I love you more."

READER ONE. "More than what?"

READER TWO. "Than you love me."

READER ONE. (*Irritably.*) "Impossible."

READER TWO. (*Sharply.*) "Don't argue."

READER ONE. "I was only . . ."

READER TWO. (*In anger.*) "Shut up!"

READER ONE. (*Sound of six beeps. Return to offstage focus.*)
"We need 50,000 more men,"
said the General in springtime,
"and that will end it."

READER TWO. "It's a lot," said the President,
"but all right, if you're sure."

READER ONE. "I'm sure," said the General. (*Pauses, then continues.*)
"We need 100,000 more men
and tanks, copters, planes,
and everything by the billion and *that*
will end it," said the General in winter.
"And, yes, I'm sure as shooting."

READER TWO. "It's a lot," said the President.
"Explain it to the Pentagon, please."

READER ONE. "I need 150,000 men
and tanks, copters, planes,
and some more billions and that
will *really* end it," said the General
back at the spring offensive.

READER TWO. "I've spoken to the staff," said the Pentagon,
"and you'll have to settle for
148,000 and only 98
percent of everything else.
Can you end it with that?"

READER ONE. "Hm," said the General,
"can you promise me
a million men this summer?" (*Makes sound of seven beeps.*)

READER TWO. (*As Nasser.*) "I don't want to be affiliated
with your rotten capitalist
imperialist degeneracy," said Nasser.
"All I want is a market
for the oil, cash on the barrelhead,
plus some tourist dollars. And that
only until these Russian credits turn edible."

READER ONE. (*Makes sound of eight beeps.*)

READER TWO. (*As undergraduate.*) "Bloodsucker," said the undergraduate
to his uncle, the customer's man,
"Don't you know we're in a war economy
and that only a vulture
would try to turn a profit in it?"

READER ONE. (*As the uncle.*) "So you have nothing to invest,"
said his uncle. "Maybe someday you will."

READER TWO. (*As associate professor.*) "Hi, Unk," said the associate professor
someday. "Janie just inherited
four thousand. Is that enough
to start a fund for the kids' tuition?"

READER ONE. (*Makes nine beep sounds.* Turns to other reader, and uses onstage focus.*) "You don't rhyme."

READER TWO. "What does? It's the world I'm writing about."

READER ONE. (*To audience.*) Thus spake John Ciardi on December 24th, Christmas Eve, in the year of our Lord 1967. (*Makes two loud beep sounds, if desired.*)

---

* In performance, it was found that making the beeps with the human voice was more effective than recorded sounds. Also, in some performances the readers used only a double beep ("Beep-Beep"), rather than adding an extra beep for each of the nine sections.

SELECTED, ANNOTATED BIBLIOGRAPHY

The articles, essays, and textbooks listed contain information useful to the Readers Theatre practitioner. A number are included more for their historical significance than for their present-day usefulness.

ABERNATHY, ELTON. *Directing Speech Activities.* Wolfe City, Texas: The University Press, 1971. Chapter V, "Readers Theatre," pp. 51–66; and Chapter IX, "Duet Acting," pp. 143–62.
Chapter V defines Readers Theatre and its values, and discusses materials for group reading, casting, rehearsals, physical adjuncts (costumes, makeup, scenery, properties, lighting, sound effects, and music), summarizing the basic, standard approaches. The chapter on duet acting should be of value to the beginning reader in preparing characterizations.

AGGERTT, OTIS J., and ELBERT R. BOWEN. *Communicative Reading.* New York: The Macmillan Company, 1972. 3rd ed. Chapter 16, "Suggestions on the Forms of Multiple Reading," pp. 469–87.
An extensive and thorough chapter on the subject which defines and illustrates several forms of multiple reading, with particular emphasis on Readers Theatre and Chamber Theatre. The natures of these forms are explained in detail, and descriptions of specific productions illustrate various modes of presentation. The manner of handling narration in Chamber Theatre is concretely exemplified by analyses of quotations from various literary scripts.

BACON, WALLACE A. *The Art of Interpretation.* New York: Holt, Rinehart & Winston, Inc., 1972. 2nd ed. Chapter 13, "Group Interpretation: Choric Interpretation, Choreographed Interpretation, Readers Theatre, Chamber Theatre, Mixed Media," pp. 399–448.
A useful resume of these various forms of group interpretation. Bacon

distinguishes between Readers Theatre and Chamber Theatre, defining the latter as a hybrid form, a method of staging narrative prose fiction by retaining the text of the story or novel, but locating the scenes onstage. With Readers Theatre, the author contends, the locus is usually kept offstage. The problems of locus are discussed effectively on pp. 409–11. Bacon analyzes in detail "The Beast in the Jungle," by Henry James, and "Morning in Nagrebcan," by Manuel E. Arguilla.

BAKER, VIRGIL. "Reading-in-Action Production of New Plays." *Players Magazine,* 35, no. 5 (February 1959), 102–3. Also in Coger and White, *Studies in Readers' Theatre,* pp. 14–16.
Recommends reading-in-action productions of new plays to encourage new playwrights.

BENNETT, GORDON C. *Readers Theatre Comes to Church.* Richmond, Va.: John Knox Press, 1972.
An excellent manual of current practices in Readers Theatre, emphasizing its use by pastors and directors of Christian education. Includes eleven sample scripts.

BENSON, ALAN W. "The Dramatic Director and Readers' Theatre: Blessing or Curse?" *The Speech Teacher,* 17, no. 4 (November 1968), 328–30. Develops the point that Readers Theatre must be approached as a separate and distinct form that shares some of its techniques with both theatre and oral interpretation, and should not be considered a substitute for "real theatrical experience."

BREEN, ROBERT S. "A Chamber Theatre Production of *Jealousy." IIG Newsletter,* March 1966, pp. 4–6.
Study of an imaginative Chamber Theatre production of Alain Robbe-Grillet's *Jealousy.*

BREEN, ROBERT S. "Chamber Theatre." In *A Course Guide in the Theatre Arts at the Secondary School Level.* Washington, D.C.: American Theatre Association, Inc., 1968. Rev. ed. Supplement VII, pp. 107–10.
An excellent source of information on Chamber Theatre, written by the man who chose to call his techniques of preparing and presenting prose fiction by that name. Explains the choice of the name and the history of Breen's work with Chamber Theatre, and offers suggestions on methodology.

BREEN, ROBERT S. "Chamber Theatre." *Illinois Speech and Theatre Journal/ Illinois Speech Association,* 26 (Fall 1972), 20–23.
Describes Chamber Theatre and how it works, contrasting it with conventional theatre.

BROOKS, KEITH. "Readers Theatre: Some Questions and Answers." *Dramatics,* 24, no. 3 (December 1962), 14, 27. Also in Coger and White,

Studies in Readers' Theatre, pp. 12–13.

Discusses a definition of Readers Theatre, suggested methodology for the preparation and presentation of programs, and a philosophy of Readers Theatre as a communication-oriented art form.

BROOKS, KEITH, and JOHN E. BIELENBERG. "Readers' Theatre as Defined by New York Critics." *Southern Speech Journal,* 29, no. 4 (Summer 1964), 288–302.

A scholarly consideration of fourteen New York Readers Theatre productions prior to the 1963–1964 season, as reviewed by the critics. Summarizes what was done, and how effective the productions were.

BROOKS, KEITH, EUGENE BAHN, and L. LAMONT OKEY. *The Communicative Art of Oral Interpretation.* Boston: Allyn & Bacon, Inc., 1967. Chapter XIII, "Readers' Theatre," pp. 384–97.

An effective summary of Readers Theatre, past and present. After a brief discussion of conflicts in philosophy, the authors make practical suggestions on sound effects and music, costuming, the arrangement of the readers, exits and entrances, and choice of literature for group interpretation.

BROOKS, KEITH, ROBERT C. HENDERHAN, and ALAN BILLINGS. "A Philosophy on Readers Theatre." *The Speech Teacher,* 12, no. 3 (September 1963), 229–32. Also in Coger and White, *Studies in Readers' Theatre,* pp. 6–8, and *Readers Theatre Handbook,* 1st ed., pp. 225–29.

In this essay, Readers Theatre is defined in terms of audience response, and approaches to staging are suggested.

CHAPMAN, MICHAEL C. "Mezza Theatre: A New Venture." *Dramatics,* 41 (February 1970), 11–13, 18.

Provides information on staging techniques for Readers Theatre and Chamber Theatre at Florida State University and Morehead State University, Kentucky, describing the approach as "a combination of reading and acting on stage."

COGER, LESLIE IRENE. "Let's Have a Readers' Theatre." *Oral Interpretation.* Cincinnati: The National Thespian Society, 1957–1958. Pp. 25–27.

Emphasizes methods and values of Readers Theatre in secondary schools, with invaluable recommendations on suitable literature.

COGER, LESLIE IRENE. "Interpreters Theatre: Theatre of the Mind." *Quarterly Journal of Speech,* 49, no. 2 (April 1963), 157–64. Also in Coger and White, *Studies in Readers' Theatre,* pp. 1–5.

A definition of Readers Theatre, a summation of its background and history, and extensive analyses of various productions.

COGER, LESLIE IRENE. "Theatre for Oral Interpreters." *The Speech Teacher,* 12, no. 4 (November 1963), 304–7. Also in Coger and White, *Studies in Readers' Theatre,* pp. 29–34.

Focuses on the values of Interpreters Theatre in education, the preparation of a script, and its presentation to an audience.

COGER, LESLIE IRENE. "Let It Be a Challenge: A Production of *Up the Down Staircase.*" *Dramatics,* 40, no. 5 (February 1969), 11–14.
A detailed study of adapting the book *Up the Down Staircase* into a two-hour script for Readers Theatre, with extensive notes on staging, lighting, and directing a cast of twenty-four readers.

COGER, LESLIE IRENE. "Staging Literature with Minimal Props for Maximal Meaning." *Scholastic Teacher,* October 11, 1971, pp. 24–25.
A practical introduction to Readers Theatre for high school students, which points out its growth in both educational and professional theatre, and its usefulness to the classroom teacher of English, speech, and dramatics, and includes suggestions on choosing and adapting materials and staging productions.

COGER, LESLIE IRENE. "Put Drama in Your Life—Try Readers Theatre." *Scholastic Voice,* 51, no. 4 (October 11, 1971), 2–3.
A special issue devoted to Readers Theatre for high schools. Purposeful information on writing and presenting scripts and setting the scene; an adaptation of "What Men Live By"; a short story, "The Warning in the Fortune Cookies," to adapt; and a quiz over the various materials.

COGER, LESLIE IRENE. "Interpreters Theatre in the Secondary Curriculum." *Illinois Speech and Theatre Journal/Illinois Speech and Theatre Association,* 26 (Fall 1972), 17–19.
Defines Interpreters Theatre and focuses on its uses and values in the teaching of nonspeech classes, with suggestions for useful materials.

COGER, LESLIE IRENE, and MELVIN R. WHITE. *Studies in Readers' Theatre.* Piedmont, Calif.: S & F Press, 1963.
Reprints of eleven provocative articles on Readers Theatre published before 1963, and a selected bibliography.

COGER, LESLIE IRENE, and MELVIN R. WHITE. *Readers Theatre Handbook: A Dramatic Approach to Literature.* Glenview, Ill.: Scott, Foresman and Company, 1967. 1st ed. Part III, "Sample Scripts for Readers Theatre," pp. 156–221.
The First Edition of *Readers Theatre Handbook* contains the following scripts not included in this, the Second Edition: *Behind the Beyond,* Stephen Leacock; *The Reluctant Dragon,* Kenneth Grahame; *Observer: The Person at Bay,* Russell Baker; *The Song Caruso Sang,* George P. McCallum; and *The Day That Was That Day,* Amy Lowell.

DALAN, NONNA CHILDRESS. "Audience Response to Use of Offstage Focus and Onstage Focus in Readers Theatre." *Speech Monographs,* 38, no. 1 (March 1971), 74–77.

Report on an investigation at Evangel College, Springfield, Missouri, of the claim that onstage focus increases audience comprehension and aesthetic response to the meaning of the selection, using Raymond G. Smith's semantic differential for theatre concepts. It was concluded that the choice of scene location should be guided by the demands of the literature and genre of the literary subject.

FRANDSEN, KENNETH D., JAMES R. ROCKEY, and MARION KLEINAU. "Changes in the Factorial Composition of a Semantic Differential as a Function of Differences in Readers' Theatre Productions." *Speech Monographs,* 32, no. 2 (June 1965), 112–18.
Study of the possibility of measuring response to Readers Theatre productions by means of a general semantic differential. The five dimensions resulting from this procedure were labeled evaluation (general), potency, activity, content evaluation, and interest evaluation.

GARDNER, DONALD P. "Do Your Own Thing." *Playbill,* Alpha Psi Omega, 1970, pp. 13–14.
Brief report on twenty-two recent Readers Theatre productions by chapters of Alpha Psi Omega.

HADLEY, DOROTHY S. "A Readers' Theatre Performance." *Dramatics,* 36, no. 7 (April 1965), pp. 13, 29.
Details of a production of Edgar Lee Masters' *Spoon River Anthology.*

HOLLAND, DONALD. "Script-in-Hand Performances." *Players Magazine,* May 1951, p. 175. Also in Coger and White, *Studies in Readers' Theatre,* pp. 19–20.
Discusses weekly Readers Theatre-style productions of plays at Five O'Clock Theatre at Pennsylvania State College in the early 1950s.

KAFKA, FRANCIS I. "What's All This About Readers Theatre?" *Encore,* 4, no. 2 (March–April 1965), 5.
Interesting summary of Readers Theatre activity at Eastern Montana College.

KING, JUDY YORDAN. "Chamber Theatre by Any Other Name . . . ?" *The Speech Teacher,* 21, no. 3 (September 1972), 193–96.
Explains the differences between conventional Readers Theatre and Chamber Theatre and stresses the need to feature the text in performance.

KLEINAU, MARION L., and MARVIN D. KLEINAU. "Scene Location in Readers Theatre: Static or Dynamic?" *The Speech Teacher,* 14, no. 3 (September 1965), 193–99. Also in Coger and White, *Readers Theatre Handbook,* 1st ed., pp. 238–46.
A thorough scrutiny of the theory of locus, or scene location, in Readers Theatre, and the perception theory underlying it. Discusses the significance of perception theory in scene location, the relationship of aural and visual cues, and focus as a technique for control of scene location.

KLYN, MARK S. "A Note on Farce in Readers Theatre." *IIG Newsletter,* November 1966, p. 5.
Argues that farce can be presented effectively Readers Theatre style, citing the successful production of three of Chekhov's short farces at the University of Washington.

KUYKENDALL, RADFORD B. "Oral Interpretation and Readers' Theatre." *The Bulletin of the National Association of Secondary School Principals,* 54, no. 350 (December 1970), 86–93.
Discusses Readers Theatre—its definition, customs, purposes, and advantages—with emphasis on its growth in high schools. Of special interest are comments on its uses in classes other than speech: literature, history, social science, drama, and core or pontoon-scheduled courses. Multimedia possibilities are pointed out, as well as the special advantages of Readers Theatre for the "fringe student."

LEE, CHARLOTTE I. *Oral Interpretation.* Boston: Houghton Mifflin Company, 1971. 4th ed. "Chamber Theatre," pp. 229–31; "Readers Theatre," pp. 343–45.
Introduces Chamber Theatre, reflecting Breen's ideas. Practical, albeit brief, remarks on Readers Theatre, but the material used is limited almost entirely to drama, and to one role per reader.

MacARTHUR, DAVID E. "Readers' Theatre: Variations on a Theme." *The Speech Teacher,* 13, no. 1 (January 1964), 47–51.
Interesting remarks on some of the variations of and experiences with Readers Theatre at Milwaukee-Downer College, with numerous ideas on programming.

MACLAY, JOANNA HAWKINS. *Readers Theatre: Toward a Grammar of Practice.* New York: Random House, Inc., 1971.
Emphasizes Readers Theatre as a valuable critical tool in the study of literature. Brief chapters make practical suggestions on selecting literature for performance, casting, directing, designing, and performing.

MARLOR, CLARK S., ed. "Readers' Theatre Bibliography: 1959–1961." *Central States Speech Journal,* 12, no. 2 (Winter 1961), 134–37.
A compilation of the 1959, 1960, and 1961 lists of Readers Theatre productions issued by the Readers Theatre Bibliography Committee of the Interpretation Interest Group of the Speech Association of America (now the Interpretation Division of the Speech Communication Association).

MARLOR, CLARK S., ed. "Readers' Theatre Bibliography: 1960–1964." *Central States Speech Journal,* 17, no. 1 (February 1966), 33–39.
As above, a bibliography of the plays, poems, and other literary materials presented in group readings between 1960 and 1964.

MATTINGLY, ALETHEA SMITH, and WILMA H. GRIMES. *Interpretation: Writer, Reader, Audience.* Belmont, Calif.: Wadsworth Publishing Company, Inc., 1970. 2nd. ed. "Readers Theatre," pp. 315–23.
Brief summary of the history of group reading. Suggestions on selection of literature and techniques of production. Emphasizes that the demands of the literature should be given primacy in Readers Theatre.

MCCOARD, WILLIAM B. "Report on the Reading of *Hiroshima.*" *Quarterly Journal of Speech,* 34, no. 2 (April 1948), 174–76. Also in Coger and White, *Studies in Readers' Theatre,* pp. 24–25.
Provocative study of the preparation for, and audience and reader reaction to, a group reading of John Hershey's *Hiroshima.*

MCCOARD, WILLIAM B. "An Interpretation of the Times: A Report on the Oral Interpretation of W. H. Auden's *Age of Anxiety.*" *Quarterly Journal of Speech,* 35, no. 4 (December 1949), 489–95.
A highly useful, purposeful, and provocative discussion of one of the first widely performed university Readers Theatre productions.

MONROE, E. ANNETTE. "The Group Reading: Expression for Drama of Mental Action." *Central States Speech Journal,* 15, no. 3 (August 1964), 170–76. Also in Coger and White, *Readers Theatre Handbook,* 1st ed., pp. 230–37.
An analytical summary of Dr. Mazzaferri's doctoral dissertation, emphasizing the suitability for Readers Theatre of dramas in which the playwright develops covert rather than overt action. A basic source article.

NICHOLS, JOSEPHINE. "Readers' Theatre on Tour." *Drama Critique,* 6, no. 3 (Fall 1963), 132–35.
Concerns the growth and activity of Readers Theatre at Adelphi University from 1949 to 1963, including information on the literature performed, and some performance suggestions.

NIELSEN, MARGARET A. "Have You Tried Readers' Theatre?" *Secondary School Theatre Conference News,* 1, no. 1 (Winter 1962), 10–12. Also in Coger and White, *Studies in Readers' Theatre,* pp. 9–11, and *Readers Theatre Handbook,* 1st ed., pp. 247–51.
Reviews the purposes and methods of Readers Theatre in secondary schools.

NIELSEN, MARGARET A. "Readers Theatre." In *A Course Guide in the Theatre Arts at the Secondary School Level.* Washington, D.C.: American Theatre Association, Inc., 1968. Rev. ed. Supplement VI, pp. 103–6.
Discusses secondary school Readers Theatre: its objectives, classroom uses, materials, script preparation, production and presentation mechanics, and rehearsal procedures.

OMMANNEY, KATHERINE ANNE, and HARRY H. SCHANKER. *The Stage and School.* New York: Webster Division, McGraw-Hill Book Company, 1972. 4th ed. Chapter 9, "Readers Theatre," pp. 273–91.
Defines Readers Theatre as "glorified group playreading," and stresses basic techniques and approaches for high school students, emphasizing especially the importance of the director and the narrator.

PARK, LEA. "A Chamber Theatre Production of *The Centaur.*" *IIG Newsletter,* May 1967, pp. 4–5.
Detailed description of a successful Chamber Theatre production of John Updike's novel, with provocative material on the setting for the performance.

PARRET, MARGARET. "Teaching Oral Interpretation to Children Through Readers Theatre." *Illinois Speech and Theater Journal,* 26 (Fall 1972), 5–8.
Extolls the values of Readers Theatre for the lower grades as well as for the middle and upper grades. Lists materials that have proved effective.

RANG, JACK. "The Play's the Thing." *Playbill,* Alpha Psi Omega, 1970, pp. 12–13.
Develops the concept that the text is to be featured, and points out the dangers in multimedia techniques.

RICKERT, ALFRED E. "Production Notes for a Staged Reading of *Othello.*" *Oral English,* 1, no. 1 (Winter 1972), 9–13.
Offers ideas on preparing the text for performance, determining the style of production, and handling the problems of production of a staged reading. Useful suggestions for cutting a Shakespearean play.

ROBERTSON, RODERICK. "Producing Playreadings." *Educational Theatre Journal,* 12, no. 1 (March 1960), 20–23. Also in Coger and White, *Studies in Readers' Theatre,* pp. 21–23.
Offers reasons for public reading performances of works written for the stage, and methods for staging playreadings.

ROBINSON, KARL F., and CHARLOTTE LEE. *Speech in Action.* Glenview, Illinois: Scott, Foresman and Company, 1965. Chapter 12, "Readers Theatre," pp. 466–79.
A purposeful, practical chapter on Readers Theatre in secondary schools which limits its use to the production of plays.

ROLOFF, LELAND H. *The Perception and Evocation of Literature.* Glenview, Illinois: Scott, Foresman and Company, 1973. Encourages students to transform their perceptions about literature into a presentational act. Each chapter has exercises and a performance evaluation form.

SANDIFER, CHARLES M. "From Print to Rehearsal: A Study of Principles for Adapting Literature to Readers Theatre." *The Speech Teacher,* 20, no. 2 (March 1971), 115–20.
A thorough report on the responses to a questionnaire concerning the adaptation of literature to Readers Theatre, attempting to formulate principles and techniques for adaptations.

SANDOE, JAMES. "A Note or Two About Playreadings." *Western Speech,* 17, no. 4 (October 1953), 225–29. Also in Coger and White, *Studies in Readers' Theatre,* pp. 26–28.
An early article which concerns itself with group readings of plays, emphasizing that they may be used as entertainment, as a means of training the actor's voice, of trying out new plays, and of "letting us hear older plays that discourage fuller productions," and as an accompaniment to the classroom lecture on drama.

SCHNEIDER, RAY. "Readers' Theatre: Experiment in Intimate Literature." *IIG Newsletter,* March 1968, pp. 5–7.
Inspirational notes on a compiled script on human alienation from non-fictional sources, and on the special sets and lightings which enhanced the production at Eastern Illinois University.

SIMPSON, VERA L. "A Readers Theatre Production of *The Comedy of Errors." IIG Newsletter,* November 1967, pp. 5–6.
Reports on the cutting, staging, costuming, and performing with little visible action of Shakespeare's farce at Texas Technological College.

STUURMAN, KAY ARTHUR. "Staged Readings of Plays." *Players Magazine,* 18, no. 1 (October 1941), 18–19. Also in Coger and White, *Studies in Readers' Theatre,* pp. 17–18.
An interesting early account, anticipating the later development and growth of various types of group play readings into today's Readers Theatre techniques.

SUSAN, SISTER MARY. "Chamber Theatre." *Catholic Theatre,* 18, no. 8 (May 1960).
Explains "verbatim presentation" of prose fiction on stage with conventional theatre techniques of music, lighting, costume, decor, and movement, reflecting Breen's precepts.

VEILLEUX, JERE. "The Concept of Action in Oral Interpretation." *Quarterly Journal of Speech,* 53, no. 3 (October 1967), 281–84.
An excellent elaboration of action in oral interpretation, of the characters of literature, and of the problems of focus in ensemble interpretations.

VEILLEUX, JERE S. "Approaches to Oral Interpretation: A Symposium," IV, "Convention and Style in Interpretation." *The Speech Teacher,* 18,

no. 3 (September 1969), 197–99.
Notes on the two productions, "Don Juan in Hell" and "Under Milk Wood," that marked the advent of modern Readers Theatre, and the conventions of stool, stand, and script used therein.

WHITE, MELVIN R. *The Mikado for Readers Theatre and Stage.* Piedmont, Calif.: S & F Press, 1964.
A Readers Theatre adaptation of Gilbert and Sullivan's operetta, with detailed suggestions for staging and directing.

WHITE, MELVIN R. *From the Printed Page (Interpretation Assignment Handbook).* Piedmont, Calif.: S & F Press, 1964. "Multiple Readings of Dialogue-Type Poetry," pp. 13–17.
Provides a group project to introduce beginning students to concepts of analysis of literature, suggestion of character, and various approaches to, and techniques of, Readers Theatre.

WHITE, MELVIN R. "The Current Scene and Readers Theatre." *Today's Speech,* 15, no. 1 (February 1967), 22–23.
Points out the dramatic possibilities of the news column, and demonstrates these with a Russell Baker *New York Times* essay.

WHITE, MELVIN R. "Story—Readers Theatre." *Dramatics,* 42, no. 4 (January 1971), 12–13, 24.
Background and resources of the Readers Theatre movement, with a brief report which places Paul Sills' Story Theatre in the context of the history of Readers Theatre, and provides a list of the resources available in this field of theatre interpretation.

WITT, DANIEL M. "Audience Response to Acting, Readers' Theatre, and Silent Reading of Realistic and Anti-Realistic Drama." *Western Speech,* 30, no. 2 (Spring 1966), 123–29.
Conclusions of an experiment to determine differences in audience response to acting, Readers Theatre, and silent reading of realistic (*The Zoo Story*) and anti-realistic (*The American Dream*) drama.

WORRELL, ELIZABETH. "Readers Theatre and the Short Story." In *Oral Interpretation and the Teaching of English,* ed. Thomas L. Fernandez. Champaign, Illinois: National Council of Teachers of English, 1969. Pp. 45–52.
Provides a strong case for Readers Theatre classroom performances of short stories, and offers numerous suggestions on how the secondary school teacher and student should approach such an activity.

YOUNG, JERRY D. "Evaluating a Readers Theatre Production." *The Speech Teacher,* 19, no. 1 (January 1970), 37–42.
Suggestions on criticism and evaluation of Readers Theatre, with three judgment blanks for use by critics.

Kipling, Rudyard, 124, 135, 239–247
Kleinau, Marion L., 79
Kleinau, Marvin D., 79
Kop, Bernard, 147–148

L

Ladies Lib, 98
Lament for a Matador, 59, 100
Lampell, Millard, 59
Lanier, Sidney, 59
Last Clock, The, 110–111, 127, 259–267
Last Summer, The, 64, 157–159
Lawrence, Jerome, 28
Lazarus Laughed, 159–160
Leacock, Stephen, 57
Lee, Charlotte, 118
Lee, Harper, 185–186
Lee, Robert E., 28
Lighting, 90–97
Lisa and David, 161
Little Foxes, The, 40
Little Red Riding Hood, 127
Locomotive, The, 64
Locus, 4, 76. *See also* focus
Lonesome Train, The, 59
Lorca, Federico Garcia, 59, 100
Lord of the Rings, 88
Lost in the Stars, 45, 162–163
Love Is a Fallacy, 268–277
Lowell, Amy, 59
Lowrey, Sara, 112

M

Macbeth, 69, 116–117
McCallum, George P., 64, 157–158
McCloskey, Robert, 100
McCoard, William, 26
McCullers, Carson, 57
McCurdy, Francis, 164–165, 168–169
McDonnell, William E., 144–146
McGinley, Phyllis, 57, 59, 128
Maclay, Joanna Hawkins, 4–5
MacLeish, Archibald, 48
Magee, John Gillespie, Jr., 12, 71
Magruder, Preston, 172–173
Major Barbara, 40
Man for All Seasons, A, 28
Marat/Sade, 7
Mary and the Fairy, 48
Mary Poppins, 164–165
Massey, Raymond, 19
Mazzaferri, E. Annette, 156–157
Me Nobody Knows, The, 63
Medea, 45, 72
Melville, Herman, 168–169
Memorization, 101–102
Menze, William, 29
Merchant of Venice, The, 38, 45, 48
Mikado, The, 45, 93, 165–168
Millay, Edna St. Vincent, 95

Milne, A. A., 128
Milton, John, 59
Moby Dick: Rehearsed, 168–169
Modern Melee, 170
Mood, 11, 70. *See also* attitude
Moskowitz, Ronnie, 184–185
Mother to Son, 112
Movement, 81–86
Multimedia, 99–101
Murder of Lidice, The, 95–96
My Client Curley, 32, 48, 170–171

N

Narration, 30, 46, 49–53, 72–73, 109
Nicoll, Allardyce, 31
Night Thoreau Spent in Jail, The, 28
No Sense of Decency, 171–172
Nobody Loves a Drunken Indian, 172–173
Nonprofessional Readers Theatre, 26–27
Not at Home, 59
Nothing Gold Can Stay, 84, 174

O

O'Casey, Sean, 20–21, 90, 93
Odyssey: A Modern Sequel, The, 174–176
Oedipus Rex, 18, 69
Offstage focus. *See* focus
Okey, L. LaMont, 4, 146–147
Old Christmas Morning, 59
One Flew over the Cuckoo's Nest, 95, 176–177
O'Neill, Eugene, 159–160
Onstage focus. *See* focus
Origin. *See* history
Original scripts, writing of, 64–65
Othello, 80–81
Our Town, 28
Outsiders, The, 102, 174

P

Paraphrasing, 115–116
Passionella, 119
Performances, 120–121
Personal development, 12
Phantom Toll Booth, The, 127
Physical arrangements, 86–103: costuming, 97–98; lighting, 90–96; multimedia, 99–101; properties, 98–99; settings, 86–90
Pictures in the Hallway, 20, 93
Plays, selection criteria for, 40
Polish Laboratory Theatre, 28
Portrait of the Artist as a Young Man, 49
Post, Robert M., 136
Preparing the typed script, 65–66
Prideaux, Tom, 25
Private Eye, The, 35

73